FERRIES 2009

BRITISH ISLES AND NORTHERN EUROPE EDITION

ISBN 978 1 871947 96 0
Ferry Publications, PO Box 33,
Ramsey, Isle of Man IM99 4LP
Tel: +44 (0) 1624 898446
Email: ferrypubs@manx.net   Website: www.ferrypubs.co.uk

europe's **leading** guide to the ferry industry

contents...

Above: **Pride of Rotterdam** (*Mike Louagie*)
Title Page: **Ulysses** (*Gordon Hislip*)
Front Cover: **Oscar Wilde** (*Gordon Hislip*)

europe's **leading** guide to the ferry industry

introduction...

This is the twenty-first edition of this book, which first appeared in 1983 as the 24-page 'home published' *'Car Ferries from Great Britain and Ireland'*. The book aims to list every passenger/vehicle ferry in Great Britain and Ireland, ro-ro freight vessels which operate regular services between Great Britain and Ireland and to nearby Continental destinations and major passenger/vehicle ferries in other parts of Northern Europe. The coverage of Northern Europe is not fully comprehensive (to make it so would probably triple the size of the book) and does not include freight-only operations and vessels - although freight-only vessels have been included where the operators also run passenger services. Also, ro-ro vessels engaged in 'deep sea' trade and those operated solely for the carriage of trade cars or paper are not included.

Each operator is listed alphabetically within sections - international and Northern Ireland routes, domestic services, freight-only operations, chain, cable and float ferries, passenger-only ferries, other North European passenger operators and vehicle/passenger vessels owned by companies not currently engaged in operating services. After details relating to each company's management, address, telephone numbers, email, website and services, there is a fleet list with technical data and then a potted history of each vessel with previous names and dates. Please note I have changed some of the national two-digit country codes to bring them into line with those used on Internet URLs.

The ferry industry faced another difficult year in 2007 as fuel costs continued to rise. However, there were signs that the public's love affair with air travel was waning, faced with more and more stringent security checks, luggage restrictions and delays and many areas showed growth. Freight continued to be buoyant, although the forthcoming 'credit crunch' led recession will inevitably lead to decline in some areas. The collapse of Ferryways in June demonstrates that running ferries is no licence to print money. The grounding of the *Riverdance* in January 2008, following the development of a severe list, once again highlights the problem of cargo (over whose loading the ship operators have no control) shifting within trailers and bursting through the flimsy curtain sides most of them have, creating a domino effect. Some operators already specify stabilisers on their freight vessels and it is clear that such fittings can be seen, not so much as a luxury to keep the crew comfortable but as a vital safety requirement.

Nick Widdows
Whitstable, Kent
June 2008

europe's **leading** guide to the ferry industry
foreword...

It is my pleasure to write the foreward for this annual publication, especially in these challenging times. Whilst the Ferry industry seems to have new challenges every year, and 2008 is no exception, I think that we should focus on the positives in our sector and the opportunities which the current turmoil offers.

As an industry, we need to present and communicate our Green credentials (relative to the airline sector) as the 'carbon footprint' is evolving into a more significant factor in influencing how our customers choose to travel. Apart from our better carbon footprint per passenger, there is the very valid argument that, as we need ferries for facilitating our exports and imports, there are no additional carbon emissions attributable to passengers travelling by sea compared to those travelling by air.

Eamonn Rothwell

The second opportunity we have as an industry is to present ferry travel as hassle free compared with travel by air. There is increasing customer frustration with airline add on charges for seat allocation, priority boarding, bag check in, airport check in, etc. In Irish Ferries we have developed our marketing campaigns in recent years by positioning ourselves directly against air travel rather than our ferry competitors. I believe if the industry shared in this initiative the whole ferry sector would benefit.

Finally, the current extraordinary high level of fuel costs creates an opportunity for the ferry sector to compete with the airline sector, whose relative cost exposure to fuel is at a much higher level. Whilst airlines traditionally have some fuel hedges in place these are running out and current oil price levels will see a lot of airlines struggle financially. Not only will new orders be put on hold but some aircraft will be grounded in the coming months. As an industry, we too have to look closely at our fast craft capacity in the light of current oil prices. A slowdown in point to point regional airline capacity and a reduction in our industry's fast craft capacity will help us to weather the current economic slowdown.

I am sure you will find Ferries 2009 to be very useful for keeping abreast of many of the changes which have taken place within the ferry business and I wish you well in the coming year.

Eamonn Rothwell
CEO
Irish Ferries

Oscar Wilde *(Miles Cowsill)*

a **guide** to using
this book

Sections Listing is in seven sections. *Section 1* - Services from Great Britain and Ireland to the Continent and between Great Britain and Ireland (including services to/from the Isle of Man and Channel Islands), *Section 2* - Domestic services within Great Britain and Ireland, *Section 3* - Freight-only services from Great Britain and Ireland and domestic routes, *Section 4* - Minor vehicle ferries in Great Britain and Ireland (chain and cable ferries etc), *Section 5* - Major passenger-only operators, *Section 6* - Major car ferry operators in Northern Europe, *Section 7* - Companies not operating regular services possessing vehicle ferries which may be chartered or sold to other operators.

Order The company order within each section is alphabetical. Note that the definite article and words meaning 'company' or 'shipping company' (eg. 'AG', 'Reederei') do not count. However, where this is part of a ship's name it does count. Sorting is by normal English convention eg. 'Å' is treated the same as 'A' and comes at the start, not as a separate character which comes at the end of the alphabet as is the Scandinavian convention. Where ships are numbered, order is by number whether the number is expressed in Arabic or Latin digits or words (eg. SUPERSEACAT THREE comes before SUPERSEACAT FOUR).

IMO Number All ships of 100t or greater (except vessels solely engaged in fishing, ships without mechanical means of propulsion (eg. chain ferries), pleasure yachts, ships engaged on special service (eg. lightships), hopper barges, hydrofoils, air cushion vehicles, floating docks and structures classified in a similar manner, warships and troopships, wooden ships) are required to be registered by the International Maritime Organisation (IMO), an agency of the United Nations. The number is retained by the ship throughout her life, however much the vessel is rebuilt. This number is now required to be displayed on the ship externally and on top so that it can be read from the air. The scheme is administered by Lloyd's Registry-Fairplay, who maintain a database of all ships in excess of 100t (with some exceptions), not just those classified through them.

Company information This section gives general information regarding the status of the company ie nationality, whether it is public or private sector and whether it is part of a larger group.

Management The Managing Director and Marketing Director or Manager of each company are listed. Where these posts do not exist, other equivalent people are listed. Where only initials are given, that person is, as far as is known, male.

Address This is the address of the company's administrative headquarters. In the case of some international companies, British and overseas addresses are given.

Telephone and Fax Numbers are expressed as follows: + [*number*] (this is the international dialling code which is dialled in combination with the number dialled for international calls (00 in the UK, Ireland and most other European countries; it is not used for calling within the country), ([*number*]) (this is the number which precedes area codes when making long-distance domestic calls - it is not dialled when calling from another country or making local calls (not all countries have this)), [*number*] (this is the rest of the number including, where appropriate, the area dialling code). UK '08' numbers are sometimes not available from overseas and the full number must be dialled in all circumstances.

Internet Email addresses and **Website** URLs are given where these are available; the language(s) used is shown. In a few cases **Email** facility is only available through the **Website**. To avoid confusion, there is no other punctuation on the Internet line. All these addresses can be accessed from homepages.enterprise.net/nickw00000 and this will be updated at regular intervals. It should be noted that some sites are not always up-to-date and it is disappointing that few operators use this facility for 'real time' data showing day-by-day service changes. However, the standard is generally much higher than a few years ago and many operators now allow on-line booking, often at a discount over other methods. It is also often possible to find up-to-date times for freight-only sailings.

Routes operated After each route there are, in brackets, details of **1** normal journey time, **2** regular vessel(s) used on the route (number as in list of vessels) and **3** frequencies (where a number per day is given, this relates to return sailings). In the case of freight-only sailings which operate to a regular schedule, departure times are given where they have been supplied. Please note that times are subject to quite frequent change and cancellation.

Winter and Summer In this book, Winter generally means the period between October and Easter while Summer means Easter to October. The peak Summer period is generally June, July and August. In Scandinavia, the Summer peak ends in mid-August whilst in the UK it starts rather later and generally stretches into the first or second week of September. Dates vary according to operator.

Spelling The convention is used in respect of town and country names is that English names are used for towns and areas of countries where such names exist (eg. Gothenburg rather than Göteborg) and English names for countries (eg. Germany rather than Deutschland). Otherwise local names are used, accented as appropriate. In a few cases, English names have slipped out of common usage and the local name is more commonly used in Britain, ie Dunkerque not Dunkirk, Helsingør not Elsinore and Vlissingen not Flushing. Many towns in Finland have both Finnish and Swedish names; we have used the Finnish name except in the case of Åland which is a Swedish-speaking area. In the case of Danish towns, the alternative use of 'å' or 'aa' follows local convention. The following towns, islands and territories are expressed using their English names - the local name is shown following: Antwerp - Antwerpen/Anvers, Fyn - Funen, Genoa - Génova, Ghent - Gent, Gothenburg - Göteborg, Hook of Holland - Hoek van Holland, Jutland - Jylland, Copenhagen - København, Ostend - Oostende, Oporto - Porto, Seville - Sevilla, Sealand - Sjælland and Venice - Venezia.

Terms The following words mean *'shipping company'* in various languages: Redereja (Latvian), Rederi (Danish, Norwegian, Swedish), Rederij (Dutch), Reederei (German) and Żegluga (Polish). The following words mean *'limited company'*: AB - Aktiebolaget (Swedish) (Finnish companies who use both the Finnish and Swedish terms sometimes express it as Ab), AG - Aktiengesellschaft (German), AS - Aksjeselskap (Norwegian), A/S - Aktie Selskabet (Danish), BV - Besloten Vennootschap (Dutch), GmbH - Gesellschaft mit beschränkter Haftung (German), NV - Naamloze Vennootschap (Dutch), Oy - (Finnish), Oyj - (Finnish (plc)) and SA - Société Anonyme (French).

Types of Ferry

These distinctions are necessarily general and many ships will have features of more than one category.

Car Ferry Up until about 1970, most vehicle ferries were primarily designed for the conveyance of cars and their passengers and foot passengers. Little regard was paid to the conveyance of lorries and trailers, since this sort of traffic had not begun to develop. Few vessels of this type are still in service.

Multi-purpose Ferry From about 1970 onwards vehicle ferries began to make more provision for freight traffic, sharing the same ship with passengers and cars. Features usually include higher vehicle decks, often with retractable mezzanine decks, enabling two levels of cars or one level of freight and coaches, and separate facilities (including cabins on quite short crossings) for freight drivers.

Cruise Ferry In the 1980s the idea of travelling on a ferry, not just to get from A to B but for the pleasure of the travel experience, became more and more popular and ferries were built with increasingly luxurious and varied passenger accommodation. Such vessels also convey cars and freight but the emphasis is on passenger accommodation with a high level of berths (sometimes providing berths for all passengers).

Ro-pax Ferry A vessel designed primarily for the carriage of freight traffic but which also carries a limited number of ordinary passengers. Features generally include a moderate passenger capacity - up to about 500 passengers - and a partly open upper vehicle deck. Modern ro-pax vessels are becoming increasingly luxurious with facilities approaching those of a cruise ferry.

Ro-ro Ferry A vessel designed for the conveyance of road freight, unaccompanied trailers and containers on low trailers (known as 'Mafis' although often made by other manufacturers). Some such vessels have no passenger accommodation but the majority can accommodate up to 12 passengers - the maximum allowed without a passenger certificate. On routes where there is a low level of driver-accompanied traffic (mainly the longer ones), ordinary passengers, with or without cars, can sometimes be conveyed. On routes with a high level of driver-accompanied traffic, passenger capacity will sometimes be higher but facilities tend to be geared to the needs of freight drivers eg. lounge with video, high level of cabins on routes of three hours or more. Technically such vessels are passenger ferries (having a passenger certificate) but are included in the freight section when exclusively or mainly conveying freight drivers.

Con-Ro Many ro-ro vessels are capable of having ISO (International Standards Organisation) containers crane-loaded on the upper 'weather' deck. In this book the term con-ro applies only to vessels whose upper deck can only take containers and has no vehicle access.

Fast Ferry Streamlined vessel of catamaran or monohull construction, speed in excess of 30 knots, water jet propulsion, generally aluminium-built but some have steel hulls, little or no freight capacity and no cabins.

Timescale Although the book goes to press in April 2008, I have sought to reflect the situation as it will exist in early Summer 2008 with regard to the introduction of new ships or other known changes. Vessels due to enter service from June 2008 are shown as '**Under Construction**'. The book is updated at all stages of the production process where this is feasible, although major changes once the text has been paginated are not possible; there is also a 'Late News' section on page xxx for changes which cannot be incorporated into the text.

List of vessels

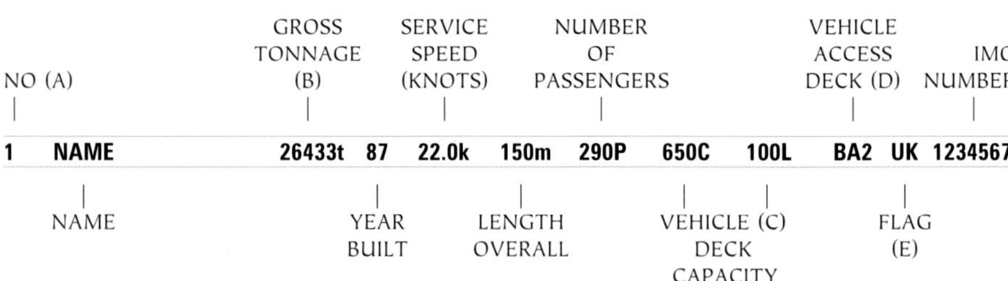

	GROSS TONNAGE		SERVICE SPEED		NUMBER OF				VEHICLE ACCESS		IMO
NO (A)	(B)		(KNOTS)		PASSENGERS				DECK (D)		NUMBER
1 NAME	**26433t**	**87**	**22.0k**	**150m**	**290P**		**650C**	**100L**	**BA2**	**UK**	**1234567**
	NAME		YEAR BUILT	LENGTH OVERALL			VEHICLE (C) DECK CAPACITY			FLAG (E)	

(A) > > = fast ferry, • = vessel laid up, F = freight-only vessel, p = passenger-only vessel

(B) '‡' = not measured in accordance with the 1969 Tonnage Convention; c = approximate.

(C) C = Cars, L = Lorries (**15m**), T = Trailers (**13.5m**), r = can also take rail wagons, - = No figure quoted.

(D) B = Bow, A = Aft, S = Side, Q = Quarterdeck, R = Slewing ramp, 2 = Two decks can be loaded at the same time, C = Vehicles must be crane-loaded aboard, t = turntable ferry.

(E) The following abbreviations are used:

AG = Antigua and Barbuda	ES = Spain	LB = Liberia	RU = Russia
	FO = Faroes	LT = Lithuania	SG = Singapore
AX = Åland Islands	FI = Finland	LV = Latvia	SW = Sweden
BB = Barbados	FR = France	LX = Luxembourg	UA = Ukraine
BM = Bermuda	GI = Gibraltar	MT = Malta	UK = United Kingdom
BS = Bahamas	GR = Greece	NL = Netherlands	
BZ = Belize	IM = Isle of Man	NO = Norway	VI = British Virgin Islands
CY = Cyprus	IT = Italy	PA = Panama	
DE = Germany	IR = Irish Republic	PT = Portugal	VC = St Vincent and the Grenadines
DK = Denmark	JM = Jamaica	PL = Poland	
EE = Estonia	KZ = Kyrgyzstan	RO = Romania	

In the notes ships are in CAPITAL LETTERS, shipping lines and other institutions are in *italics*.

Capacity In this book, capacities shown are the maxima. Sometimes vessels operate at less than their maximum passenger capacity due to reduced crewing or to operating on a route on which they are not permitted to operate above a certain level. Car and lorry/trailer capacities are the maximum for either type. The two figures are not directly comparable; some parts of a vessel may allow cars on two levels to occupy the space that a trailer or lorry occupies on one level, some may not. Also some parts of a vessel with low headroom may only be accessible to cars. All figures have to be fairly approximate.

Ownership The ownership of many vessels is very complicated. Some are actually owned by finance companies and banks, some by subsidiary companies of the shipping lines, some by subsidiary companies of a holding company of which the shipping company is also a subsidiary and some by companies which are jointly owned by the shipping company and other interests like a bank, set up specifically to own one ship or a group of ships. In all these cases the vessel is technically chartered to the shipping company. However, in this book, only those vessels chartered from one shipping company to another or from a ship-owning company unconnected with the shipping line are recorded as being on charter. Vessels are listed under the current operator rather than the owner. Charter is 'bareboat' (ie without crew) unless otherwise stated. If chartered with crew, vessels are 'time-chartered'.

Gross Tonnage This is a measure of enclosed capacity rather than weight, based on a formula of one gross ton = 100 cubic feet. Even small alterations can alter the gross tonnage. Under old measurement systems, the capacity of enclosed car decks was not included but, under the 1969 Convention, all vessels laid down after 1982 have been measured by a new system which includes enclosed vehicle decks as enclosed space, thereby considerably increasing the tonnage of vehicle ferries. Under this Convention, from 1st January 1995 all vessels were due to be re-measured under this system. Tonnages quoted here are, where possible, those given by the shipping companies themselves.

The following people are gratefully thanked for their assistance with this publication, many of them in ferry companies in the UK and abroad: Tony Kelly (Irish Ferries), Gary Andrews, Cees de Bijl, Dick Clague, Andrew Cooke, Matthew Davies, Ian Hall, Erik B Jonsen, William Mayes, Willie Mackay, Barry Mitchell, David Parsons, Jack Phelan, Pekka Ruponen, Michael Speckenbach (FERRYinformation), Henk van der Lugt, Ian Smith (The Camrose Organisation), and Gomer Press.

Whilst every effort has been made to ensure that the facts contained here are correct, neither the publishers nor the writer can accept any responsibility for errors contained herein. We would, however, appreciate comments from readers, which we will endeavour to reflect in the next edition which we plan to publish in Spring 2009.

IRISH FERRIES – THE STORY SO FAR

The Irish Continental Group story goes back to 17th May 1968 when the first direct Rosslare-Le Havre car ferry sailing took place. This first venture, of one round trip sailing per week using the *Dragon* and *Leopard*, was a joint Anglo-French operation provided by Normandy Ferries, part of the P&O group, in partnership with French shipping line SAGA, owned by the Rothschild family. In its first season, the new service carried 31,000 passengers.

The following year sailings were increased to two per week between mid-June and mid-August. Public reaction was enthusiastic with the result that 1969 passenger carryings more than doubled to 68,000, and the *Dragon* and *Leopard* continued to operate during the 1970 and 1971 seasons with two sailings per week during the summer peak. Just as the service was maturing, it came to an abrupt end. In planning their 1972 schedules, Normandy Ferries found that they required both the vessels exclusively on their English Channel services in order to retain their competitive position. Given the short notice, it was impossible to charter suitable replacement ships for the route with the result there was no Ireland-France service.

Behind the scenes, frantic efforts were being made to re-establish the service on a sounder footing, one that would have its commercial roots in Ireland. Consequently, in 1972, the then Government requested B&I Line and Irish Shipping to consider the possibility of re-opening the service; the request was answered by Irish Shipping.

Irish Shipping had a fascinating history in its own right. In 1940, the first full year of World War II, the Irish Government led by Taoiseach Eamonn De Valera was experiencing difficulty chartering ships to bring essential supplies to Ireland. A decision was taken to establish Irish Shipping as the national shipping line. Operations began in March 1941 and by the end of that year they had performed heroic service transporting essential supplies into Ireland, utilising ships that had been chartered for this purpose. After the War in 1945, the company began to return its chartered vessels and, by 1948, had begun to acquire its own, newly-built fleet. By 1972, when the decision was made to restart the Rosslare-Le Havre service, Irish Shipping was a substantial shipping company with 31 years' service.

IRISH CONTINENTAL LINE FORMED

In order to implement their plan, Irish Shipping established a new company, Irish Continental Line, in partnership with other Irish and Scandinavian interests. Irish Shipping held a 30% shareholding, Lion Ferry of Sweden and the Norwegian shipping company Fearnley & Egar held 25% each while Aerlod Teo, a subsidiary of Corus Iompair Eireann (CIE), held the remaining 20%. A ferry with 547 berths and space for 210 cars which was then under construction for Lion Ferry was duly purchased for the Rosslare-Le Havre service and on 17th January 1972 the *Saint Patrick* was launched at the shipyard of Schichau Unterweser in Bremerhaven, Germany.

On 31st May 1973 the *Saint Patrick* arrived at Rosslare for the first time, flying the Irish flag. Immediately, she began regular scheduled sailings to France, beginning with three round trips per week increasing to every second day in each direction during July and August. The new service operated until the end of December 1973. Thereafter, it became an all-year-round operation.

Three years after the new service was started, the Scandinavian involvement in Irish Continental Line was to draw to a close. In 1977 Irish Shipping bought out the Lion Ferry and Fearnley & Egar shareholdings to become 80% owners of the company while CIE continued to hold the balance. In the same year Irish control was further consolidated when ownership of the *Saint Patrick* transferred from Irish Shipping to Irish Continental Line. This was a far-sighted move that was to prove itself during the liquidation of Irish Shipping in the mid-1980s.

SAINT KILLIAN ENTERS SERVICE

After the transfer of the *Saint Patrick* to Irish Continental Line ownership, a decision was made to purchase a second vessel for the link; built in 1973 in Yugoslavia for Stena Line, she was purchased and came into service between Ireland and France in 1978 as the *Saint Killian*. She offered a substantial increase in capacity on the route with over 1,400 berths and 490 car spaces. Now, for the first time, Irish Continental Line could offer during the summer of 1978 a daily service between Rosslare and France.

Saint Killian II (*Miles Cowsill*)

Isle of Innisfree (*Miles Cowsill*)

Isle of Inishmore *(Miles Cowsill)*

Saint Patrick II *(Miles Cowsill)*

The *Saint Killian* also enabled the company to open a second route from Rosslare to Cherbourg with a sailing time of 17 hours, four hours shorter than the run to Le Havre. This service was aimed at holidaymakers heading for Brittany and Western France. Despite the successes, it was not always plain sailing and, by the winter of 1978, Irish Continental Line had suffered a decline in trade due to the state of the international economy. Traffic fell and costs rose. In the early days of the route, facilities at Rosslare were not as finely developed as they are today; ships had to be refuelled in France where prices rose by 20%, amounting to a £10,000 a day fuel bill for the two ships, increases which then proved a heavy burden for the company.

BELFAST-LIVERPOOL SERVICE

Once the company surmounted the difficulties of the late 1970s, it was able to plan ahead. Two fundamental decisions were made: to start a Belfast-Liverpool car ferry service and to 'jumboize' the *Saint Killian*.

The Belfast-Liverpool service had been in operation for over 100 years. After the withdrawal of P&O from the service, Irish Continental Line decided to take over the route, restarting it as Belfast Car Ferries on 1st May 1982. The *Saint Patrick*, which started the Rosslare-Le Havre run in 1973, was transferred to the Belfast-Liverpool service and renamed *Saint Colum I*. In the early years, the outlook for the Belfast-Liverpool service was promising. In 1984, for instance, the *Saint Colum I* made 350 voyages, carried 208,000 passengers, 46,056 cars and 7,108 freight units with a total of 19,000 trade cars also being carried, a quarter of all the trade cars imported into Northern Ireland that year, but gradually the economics of the service became worse. In the face of competition from other routes, and with no hope of improvement, the service was finally closed down in October 1990 and the ship sold to Greek owners.

SAINT KILLIAN JUMBOISED

A Dutch shipyard was appointed to 'jumboize' the *Saint Killian* by cutting her in two and adding a new 32-metre mid-section at a cost of £7.5 million. The contract, which took just three months to complete, added enormously to the overall carrying capacity of the vessel. Berths were increased from 800 to 1,400 and car spaces from 200 to 300. Following this work she was renamed the *Saint Killian II* and returned to the Ireland-France services.

To replace the *Saint Patrick* on the Ireland-France route, Irish Continental Line purchased the Viking Line vessel *Aurella* at a cost of 16.5 million. She was refitted in Amsterdam and renamed *Saint Patrick II* prior to joining *Saint Killian II* on the Ireland-France service.

In 1983, a third summer service came into operation from Ireland to France on the Cork-Le Havre route, with sailings from the end of June to the end of August. This new route proved popular with Irish holidaymakers and with French and other Continental visitors wishing to arrive closer to their holiday destinations in Counties Cork and Kerry.

While Irish Continental Line was growing the market year-on-year with improvements in traffic, the other part of the Group was not doing so well. In 1979 and 1980 a series of charter deals for Irish Shipping vessels was arranged in Hong Kong, commitments that were considered financially ruinous for the company. Irish Shipping was trading against a dismal world economic background which made freight carrying an unprofitable proposition. When the then Government decided to place Irish Shipping into liquidation towards the end of 1984, there was a public outcry with calls that Ireland was being deprived of a strategically important deep sea fleet, one that had proved its worth for over 40 years in conditions of war and peace. Despite these calls, the Government proceeded with the liquidation of Irish Shipping that became effective in November 1984.

This immediately placed Irish Continental Line management in a quandary: their company had enjoyed a successful, profitable trading record, but it was largely owned by Irish shipping and had now become part of the liquidation process. Despite this, the company continued to trade as a going concern with the Irish Shipping liquidation having little practical effect. For two-and-a-half years, Irish Continental Line carried on in a state of uncertainty in an interregnum between ownership.

Finding a buyer for what was a financially sound operation proved slow and frustrating with legalities over title and other matters having to be resolved. It was not until Christmas 1985 that advertisements appeared in the national press inviting purchase offers. The scramble to settle the ownership of the company was only just beginning.

In January 1986 B&I Line placed a valuation of £7 million on Irish Continental Line and led the bidding. In all, 24 potential bidders emerged, including a consortium of freight companies. During the course of 1986 two bids materialized from groups within the management of Irish Continental Line itself.

Complex taxation matters concerning the ownership of the two vessels used on the Rosslare-France routes were another complication that had to be resolved. In November 1986 sole ownership of the two Irish Continental Line vessels was acquired, a move which cleared the way for the completion of the sale which took place in March 1987 when a consortium of institutional investors was successful in its bid for the company.

For the Irish Continental Group, as the new holding company was now known, 1987 was to be one of the most exciting in the 19-year history of the Ireland-France ferry service. Under new ownership, a big revamp began. Irish Ferries and Belfast Ferries (then in operation) were the new operating divisions. The Board of Directors was restructured, a new Managing Director was recruited and steps were taken to revitalise the company. APEX fares and other incentives were introduced to give customers the benefit of discounts for early bookings. Freight customers were given a new, more competitive tariff structure. New quality standards were introduced throughout the company and the ships were refurbished to become 'floating hotels'. Much organisational change took place internally and outwardly there came a change of image. A new corporate identity and logotype were introduced with strong new colour themes and a shamrock motif which featured prominently. This new design style was carried through in all the company's promotional literature and advertising.

The Group enjoyed slightly belated success with its Stock Exchange debut. Originally it had been planned to launch the company's shares on the Smaller Companies' Market of the Stock Exchange in Autumn 1987 but the timing was hardly propitious. On 19th October 1987, world stock markets plummeted, in what became known as 'Black Monday'. The Irish Continental Group share launch was deferred until 9th February 1988 when a total of IR£2.7 million was raised. The first day of dealings was 6th April 1988. About 80% of the company's staff subscribed to the issue with the result that the employees now hold a significant proportion of the Group's shares.

Trading improved with 1988 turnover up to IR£34 million and pre-tax profits at IR£823,000. With the new structure in place, the Line was moving in the right direction. Two shore-based changes reflected this direction. The sales headquarters of the company was moved to Merrion Row in Dublin while reservations procedures were fully computerised with on-line connections to travel agents and sales offices abroad.

Within a short period, the fruits of re-organisation were being felt. For the year to 31st October 1989, its first as a publicly-quoted company, Irish Continental Group reported a turnover of IR£35.63 million and a pre-tax profit of IR£1.5 million, a 31% increase on the previous year.

A NEW DECADE OF GROWTH BEGINS

During 1990, Irish Continental Group recorded turnover up 12% to just over £40 million, with pre-tax profits up 60% to £2.4 million. Passenger numbers also increased by 13% over the previous year, from 285,000 to 324,000 with the strongest growth coming from mainland Europe where traffic increased by 22%.

From November to March each year, freight is the important source of revenue with 90% of loads accounted for by roll-on/roll-off freight vehicles, the remaining 10% coming from trade car imports from France and other mainland European countries. To ensure that hauliers received a year-round freight service, a freight-only vessel was chartered during the summer to support the passenger fleet.

In early 1991, Irish Continental Group reached conditional heads of agreement to purchase the share capital of the B&I Line and in early 1992 a major milestone was passed when it was formally announced that the Irish Continental Group had acquired outright ownership of B&I Line, following almost two years of talks with the Irish Government. The acquisition immediately enhanced the status of the Irish Continental Group and positioned the company as Ireland's leading passenger car ferry and freight shipping enterprise with an extensive range of services to France, the United Kingdom, Belgium and Holland. A new Managing Director joined Irish Continental Group and a new management structure was set in place at B&I Line.

During 1992, following the acquisition of B&I Line, the enlarged Irish Continental Group was re-structured into three divisions: Ferry Services, European Container Service and Dublin Ferryport Terminals. Frank Carey was appointed as Group Marketing Director, Alex Mullin as Group Operations Director and along with Managing Director Eamonn Rothwell and Finance Director Gearoid O'Dea they formed the senior management team.

Major investment was made by acquiring the *Isle of Innisfree* to replace the *Munster* on B&I Line's Rosslare - Pembroke Dock route, while a winter charter was secured for the Irish Ferries vessel *Saint Patrick II* sailing in the Baltic between Finland and Estonia. In 1992, B&I Line joined with Dublin Port to mount a campaign arguing the merits of having a new multi-user ferry terminal sited in Dublin Port.

In 1993, the Irish Continental Group continued on the investment trail, first by acquiring a 25% shareholding in Bell Lines and later by purchasing the ferry vessel *Pride of Bilbao* – the fifth largest night ferry in the world. At the time of her purchase, the *Pride of Bilbao* was under charter to P&O operating between the UK and Spain.

NEW SHIP FOR DUBLIN-HOLYHEAD LINK

In April 1994 a £46 million order was placed with Dutch shipbuilders Van der Giessen-de Noord for the construction of a new 23,000 gross tons ro-pax vessel for the Dublin-Holyhead route. The new vessel would enter service in June 1995 replacing the existing chartered vessel the *Isle of Innisfree*.

Meanwhile, in August 1994, Irish Ferries announced their intention to establish a service between Ireland and the Brittany port of Brest. However, because of the failure of the French Government to give their approval for the construction of the necessary linkspan at Brest, the company were forced to shelve their plan to sail there in 1995. The failure by the French Government was the subject of a complaint by Irish Ferries under European Union (EU) competition laws. As an alternative measure, agreement was reached with the port of Roscoff for the introduction of a 1995 summer service between Rosslare, Cork and Roscoff. Similarly, local opposition in the Roscoff region against the introduction of the Irish Ferries service to Roscoff also gave rise to a complaint by Irish Ferries to the EU.

On 27th January 1995 the new *Isle of Innisfree* was launched at the Rotterdam yard of Van der Giessen-de Noord. The new ferry was at the time the largest capacity multi-purpose passenger/ro-ro ferry operating between Ireland and the UK with capacity for 600 passenger cars, 108 accompanied freight trucks (or 142 trailers/coaches) and a passenger/crew complement of 1,760. In size, the new vessel has an overall length of 600 feet (181.6 m), a beam of 80 feet (23.4 m) and a distance of 124 feet (37.8 m) from keel to mast head. Mrs Clodagh Rothwell, wife of Irish Continental Group Managing Director Eamonn Rothwell, performed the naming ceremony.

1995 marked the beginning of a new era on the Irish Sea when the name and identity of Ireland - UK ferry operators B&I Line changed to that of its sister company Irish Ferries, operators of the Ireland-France ferry services. The name change to Irish Ferries saw B&I Line adopt the familiar Irish Ferries green/blue flag motif and white shamrock with vessels being repainted in white with the name Irish Ferries and a new colourful design on each hull.

The *Isle of Innisfree* made her maiden voyage on 23rd May on the Dublin - Holyhead route, signalling a new era in passenger ferry travel on the Irish Sea. The following year a contract for the design and construction of a second new superferry at a cost of approximately IR£60 million was placed with Dutch shipbuilders Van der Giessen-de Noord. When introduced in January 1997 the new 33,000 ton ferry would be the largest car-carrying ferry operating in North Western Europe with a passenger / freight capacity substantially larger than either of Irish Ferries' existing Irish Sea vessels.

In 1996, due to falling summer revenues on the French services brought about by various competitive factors, it was decided to discontinue loss-making winter services to France. Having operated year-round since 1973, services ended in September to be recommenced in March 1997. Meanwhile, the *Saint Patrick II* was offered for sale.

The new IR£60million *Isle of Inishmore* was launched in Rotterdam in October 1996. The ceremony was performed by Mrs. Sandra Carey, wife of Irish Continental Group Marketing Director Frank Carey. With space for 2,200 passengers, a car capacity of 855 units and truck capacity of 122 units, the *Isle of Inishmore* arrived at Dublin from Rotterdam on 17th February 1997, entering service on the Dublin-Holyhead route on 2nd March following sea trials and crew training. With the arrival of the *Isle of*

Isle of Inishmore (*Gordon Hislip*)

Jonathan Swift (*Gordon Hislip*)

Inishmore , the *Isle of Innisfree* was released from the Dublin-Holyhead route and transferred to the Rosslare-Pembroke Dock route.

The *Saint Killian II* was withdrawn from service after fourteen years sailing under the Irish flag, making her final departure from Ringaskiddy, Cork to Le Havre on 27th September 1997. During 1998 the vessel was sold to Cap Enterprises (Marintas) of Piraeus and re-named *Medina Star* before entering service on a new Black Sea rail/ferry route between Poti in Georgia and Odessa in the Ukraine.

In April 1997 the chartered Swedish-owned *Normandy* entered service on the Ireland - France routes. Meanwhile the *Saint Patrick II* was chartered for four-and- a-half years to Hellenic Mediterranean Lines of Greece. Under the charter agreement, Hellenic would obtain title to the vessel on completion of the charter.

FASTEST AND BIGGEST FERRIES

In June 1998, agreement was reached with Austal Ships of Australia for the construction of a new £29 million high-speed ferry to be introduced on to the Dublin - Holyhead route in Summer 1999. The twin-hulled aluminum-built vessel with a capacity for 800 passengers and 200 cars would complete the voyage from Dublin to Holyhead in just 110 minutes. She would operate up to four return sailings daily and though named *Jonathan Swift* would be marketed under the name 'Dublin Swift'. The fast craft would operate alongside the *Isle of Inishmore* providing a total of six return sailings daily.

Meanwhile, in July 1999, Irish Continental Group contracted with Aker Finnyards, Finland to build a 50,000 gross ton vessel – the world's largest car ferry ever – at a cost of 100 million Euro. The new vessel would be large enough to double Irish Ferries' freight-carrying capacity on their premier Dublin-Holyhead route when in service by Spring 2001. In January 2000 the giant keel section of the *Ulysses* was laid at a ceremony at Aker Finnyards.

The following January the *Normandy* was sent for a IR£4 million refit. Two months later the *Ulysses* arrived at Dublin Port on Sunday 4th March after her four-day voyage from Finland. Swimmer Mairead Berry – Ireland's 25-year-old Paralympic Games gold medallist – was named the 'golden godmother' to *Ulysses* at a special naming ceremony held in Dublin and attended by the Taoiseach, Bertie Aherne TD, some two weeks later in advance of her maiden voyage to Holyhead on Sunday 25th March 2001.

In 2005 the *Normandy* was transferred to the Bahamas flag and the bulk of her Irish staff replaced with staff from the new EU countries. This was followed in 2006 by the decision to switch the rest of the fleet to Cypriot registry, with mainly eastern European crews. This provoked a lengthy strike by both officers and crew which, once eventually settled, then allowed the company to introduce its new manning arrangements in an effort to save costs and to allow them to meet the now increased competition from the airlines. The new crews soon established themselves with a reputation for excellent customer service.

The next priority was the replacement of the now ageing *Normandy*. Whilst a new build could still not be justified, the Color Line vessel *Kronprins Harald* was due to become available in 2007 and was eagerly snapped up by Irish Ferries at an overall cost of some 60 million Euro. She was sent for an extensive refit prior to entering full commercial service early in 2008 between Ireland and France. The former Norwegian vessel was renamed the *Oscar Wilde*, continuing the literary theme of the Group.

With three modern vessels and one fast craft, Irish Ferries have placed themselves in a strong position on the Irish Sea, not only to compete with their shipping rivals but also with the cheap airlines between Ireland and the UK. Already passengers are showing signs of returning to Irish Ferries, with their competitive fares and luxurious and reliable ships. Passengers are now re-discovering the ease of ferry travel compared with airline travel and all that this style of travel entails today.

Miles Cowsill

THE OSCAR WILDE -
IRISH FERRIES' NEW LUXURY LINK TO FRANCE

Following completing her career with Color Line, the *Kronprins Harald* was sent to Denmark for refit and modifications to meet the requirements of Irish Ferries. The company were extremely impressed with the maintenance of the hull and public areas of the 20-year-old vessel by her previous owners and in this light the only major improvements to the ferry have been centred around the re-branding of the ship's outlets and conversion of the restaurants to suit the Irish/French market. The mechanical improvements included an additional bow thruster for the 312 nautical mile crossing, which at certain times of the year can be extremely difficult, especially in port. The vessel today boasts three restaurants, the first of which is the former Smorgasbord restaurant now re-modelled as the Left Bank Brasserie, which operates as the principal dining area for the ship with seating for 350 passengers. The other two restaurants also situated on Deck 7, include the Berneval waiter restaurant and the new and now very popular Steakhouse. The waiter restaurant with 120 covers offers a pleasant ambience and realistically-priced three-course dinner from 35 Euro. She boasts three bar areas, the Gaiety Lounge with live entertainment, the Oscar Piano Bar, which offers a quiet environment to have a drink, and the Merrion Lounge which is located forward giving panoramic sea views. Also on Deck 7 is the children's play area plus extensive seating for passengers running along the portside of the vessel in typical Scandinavian style.

On Deck 5 the *Oscar Wilde* boasts a large retail shop, a hairdressers / beauty salon, and reception area. Five decks above she has two cinemas and an extensive reclining seating area. She has four decks of cabins with 1,370 beds overall, ranging from 15 luxury cabins to a variety of two and three berth cabins, all of which are very spacious.

Irish Ferries have introduced a nice touch on board with a series of plaques around the ship covering the life and literature of Oscar Wilde.

The *Oscar Wilde* in line with other ships in the fleet of Irish Ferries is manned principally by crews from the Baltic states of Latvia and Estonia. Many of the key positions on the ship are covered by British and Irish staff. The Baltic crews work some two months on and then one month off, which offers a good structure for the running of the ship. The British and Irish officers normally work a shift around their Baltic counterparts of two weeks on and two weeks off. The *Oscar Wilde* operates normally with a crew of 130. From a relatively easy life of working between Oslo and Kiel for nearly

Kronprins Harald (*Mike Louagie*)

Oscar Wilde (*Gordon Hislip*)

Merrion Lounge (*Irish Ferries*)

The Gaiety Lounge (*Irish Ferries*)

Left Bank Brasserie (*Irish Ferries*)

5 Star Double Bed Suite *(Irish Ferries)*

The Berneval Restaurant *(Irish Ferries)*

20 years, the *Oscar Wilde* has now a fairly tight schedule to maintain on the Irish Sea all the year round. During the winter period (October to mid-May) she is employed on the 19-hour Rosslare-Cherbourg route with a lay-over on Mondays at the French port. During the peak season the schedule is more intense with the shorter route of Rosslare-Roscoff included. During the winter period the Cherbourg service is an important freight operation and with the re-scheduling of its operations for 2007/2008 with a 23.00 hour departure from Rosslare, this has proved an overwhelming success for the company in bringing new freight business for the route. The Oscar Wilde has two freight decks, one of which is on a lower deck, for 16 lorries. Access to this lower hold is via a lift, which can be a little frustrating for the crews when tight turnarounds are demanded. The main car deck can be loaded and discharged simultaneously once the freight has been cleared from Deck 3 on the portside.

The *Oscar Wilde* takes on stores at Rosslare every other day. She has a container-style loading system for stores which normally offers an efficient method at Rosslare. However, when she is forced to use Berth 2 all supplies have to be loaded via the car deck.

With the introduction of the *Oscar Wilde* the writer was somewhat surprised by the lack of improvements to Rosslare since his last visit to the port some five years ago. The railway station has now at last been moved to ensure free and easy movement of traffic in the port but the infrastructure itself is in need of modernisation, compared to other European terminals. When Rosslare terminal was built it offered some of the most modern facilities. If Rosslare is to live up to its name as the Europort of Ireland, radical improvements to the dowdy terminal and its infrastructure are required. The berth facilities for Irish Ferries and their counterparts are in need of upgrading to more double-deck loading for efficient and quick turnarounds; it is understood that a new berth will be built at the port during late 2009.

The *Oscar Wilde* heralds a new era for the company with greatly-improved passenger facilities, cabins and capacity on their links between Ireland and France. With their new vessel Irish Ferries are able compete with the rival operations out of Cork, something they were less able to do with the Normandy, which the Oscar Wilde replaced last year. The introduction of the former Norwegian vessel has already paid dividends for Irish Ferries with increased bookings and more freight loadings.

Miles Cowsill

The Berneval Restaurant (*Irish Ferries*)

ROUND BRITISH ISLES REVIEW
EAST COAST

Nexus, the maritime arm of the Tyne and Wear Passenger Transport Executive, introduced a new ship to operate the ferry between North and South Shields and Tyne cruises. The Portsmouth-built *Spirit of the Tyne* replaced the 1976-built *Shieldsman*.

In May the *Queen of Scandinavia* and the *Princess of Norway* swapped routes, with the 'Queen' taking over the Newcastle - Stavanger - Bergen route which DFDS Seaways had adopted from Fjord Line. The argument was that the 'Queen' had better facilities for the longer journey and there would be advantages in having two sisters on the Newcastle - IJmuiden service. The 'Princess' had been having difficulty keeping to time, a problem which continued on the Dutch route as it was apparent that, despite the *King of Scandinavia* being a twin sister, her engines were in much better condition. The 'Queen' meanwhile had a reputation as sometimes displaying poor sea-keeping qualities on the North Sea and there were some lively trips on her on the even more exposed waters between the UK and Norway during the year.

The increasingly busy port of Killingholme saw two brand-new ferries during the year with the *Yasmine* of Cobelfret Ferries joining her 2006-built sister *Pauline* on the Zeebrugge service and the *Stena Traveller* joining the *Stena Trader* on the service to Hook of Holland. The latter vessel was away for the first part of the year covering for the major rebuilding of the two Harwich - Hook of Holland vessels. Orders from the Russian yard which built the hulls of the *Stena Trader* and *Stena Traveller* for two similar vessels but with an additional vehicle deck were cancelled and orders were placed with Samsung Heavy Industries of South Korea. When delivered in 2011, it seems likely that they will replace the current vessels on the Hook - Killingholme service and the 'Trader' and 'Traveller' will replace the three 'Stena SeaRunner' class vessels on the Rotterdam - Harwich service.

The Immingham/Killingholme - Ostend service was suspended for a few weeks in June following the liquidation of Ferryways and, when resumed by Cobelfret Ferries, it was, not unexpectedly, to Killingholme only (Cobelfret Ferries owning the port) and operated by the *Phocine* and *Cervine*, two former Dart Line vessels. The service was actually branded as a Dart Line service by Cobelfret.

Sea-Cargo, who operate from Immingham to various ports in western Norway, replaced the *SC Norrland* with the *Nordia*, previously used by Attica Enterprises in the Baltic. A new service was started to Esbjerg, initially using the *Lygra* and later the *Amber*. There was no sign of any of their new ships, being built at Mumbai in India. The first of these con-ro vessels was originally due in 2006!

Over at Hull, P&O Ferries introduced a second ro-ro freighter on the Rotterdam and Zeebrugge routes in the form, initially, of the ex-Ferryways *Calibur* and later Cobelfret's *Ursine*. Finnlines continued to operate a mixture of their modern Chinese-built craft and the ex-Transfennica *Birka Trader* on their services to and from Finland.

Ipswich ceased to be a ferry port in June with the sudden demise of Ferryways. It was initially announced that Ferryways had been taken over by Cobelfret Ferries but that it would be 'business as usual'. However, a few days later they stated that there were discrepancies in the company's accounts and that it would be placed into liquidation. The charters of the above-mentioned *Calibur* and the Clarkson-owned *CFF Seine* were immediately terminated and the rest of the fleet laid up in and just outside Ostend harbour. After a few weeks Cobelfret Ferries re-launched the company's routes but to Harwich rather than Ipswich and to Dartford (initially Purfleet) rather than Tilbury. All the former Ferryways 'Way' ships eventually re-entered service on these routes, which were branded as Roroco and Dart Line.

Harwich saw the end of the HSS service operated by the *Stena Discovery* in January and the lengthening of the two ro-pax vessels *Stena Britannica* and *Stena Hollandica* at Lloyd Werft, Bremerhaven. During the period this was happening, the *Stena Trader* covered the route, the Rotterdam-based *Stena Transfer* being moved to the Hook - Killingholme service and the former Cobelfret ro-ro freighter *Amanda* being chartered for Harwich - Rotterdam. Orders were placed at Aker Yards for two 62,000 ton giants to be delivered in 2010 to take over the Harwich - Hook of Holland service from the existing ships, which will be moved to the Karlskrona - Gdynia route.

Cobelfret Ferries' new Ostend - Harwich service started in July, initially as a single-ship service with the

roll-on, roll-off in Oostende, it's fast, it's easy

The port of Oostende in Belgium offers you a long-established know-how in handling ro-ro freight. Its up-to-date infrastructure includes versatile berthing facilities and well-situated parking areas. Major terminus of European highways, inland waterways, railroads and an international airport make Oostende a true global cargo hub.

AG PORT OOSTENDE-BELGIUM
Slijkensesteenweg 2 – B-8400 Oostende
Tel. +32(0)59 34 07 11 – Fax +32(0)59 34 07 10
website: www.portofoostende.be – e-mail: info@portofoostende.be

Anglian Way, then joined by the *Flanders Way* in August; it reverted to a single-ship operation a couple of months later.

Somewhat outside the scope of this book, the Essex port saw a new ro-ro service in the spring in the form of a new Antwerp - Harwich - Lagos (Nigeria) service operated by Dutch shipping agents AMR Shipping. The Cobelfret Ferries vessel *Vulpine* was chartered for this route and a second vessel - initially the *Victoria VI* and then the ex-Ferryways *Humber Way* - was introduced in the summer. The service now operates every 14 days and has been extended to Monrovia in Liberia.

THAMES AND MEDWAY

Cobelfret Ferries terminated their Dartford - Vlissingen service at the end of April. The two vessels used - the *Equine* and *Ursine* - were redeployed. The upper berth at Dartford did not remain unoccupied for long as, following the demise of Ferryways, a new Ostend - Purfleet service thrice daily was established in early July. To make space for these new arrivals, the Rotterdam - Purfleet service was switched to Dartford - although the ships often had to pay a visit to Purfleet during their lay-over to unload trade cars. After a few weeks, the two services swapped over and the Ostend service became a two-ship operation, with two daily services. Cobelfret Ferries closed the Dart Line Dartford - Zeebrugge service just before Christmas and from the New Year, the Rotterdam service switched to Dartford once again.

In July, P&O Ferries started a Tilbury - Zeebrugge service, using the same berth as Ferryways' abruptly terminated Tilbury - Ostend route. Initially operated by the *Calibur*, she was joined by the chartered *Hoburgen* in September; the *Calibur* was replaced by the larger *Global Carrier* in November but returned to the route in January 2008 when the latter's charter ended.

The weekly one-way RoRo2London Bremerhaven - Sheerness service introduced in 2006 proved rather short-lived as, in the spring, Mann Lines took over the northbound capacity of the two Wagenborg ships *Balticborg* and *Bothniaborg* operated for the Smurfit Kappa Group (paper and card manufacturers). The northbound Södertälje (Sweden) call was replaced by one at Paldiski in Estonia and the Terneuzen - Södertälje RoRo2Stockholm service was also scrapped. Whilst the ships continued to call at Bremerhaven and Sheerness, the capacity was no longer marketed.

Thames Clippers took delivery of no less than four new craft in 2007 - *Typhoon Clipper*, *Tornado Clipper*, *Cyclone Clipper* and *Monsoon Clipper* - with two more - *Aurora Clipper* and *Meteor Clipper* - delivered in 2008 for their expanding Thames river-bus service. The twin-hulled craft were slightly smaller versions of the *Hurricane Clipper* delivered in 2002. They were designed by AIMTEK and built by Brisbane Ship Constructions in Australia. In November they increased the frequency of their sailings to every 15 minutes between The O2 (the former Millennium Dome) and Waterloo (with service extended to Woolwich during the early morning and evening).

EASTERN CHANNEL

Dover had a quiet year with few changes. The most interesting visitor was probably the Pentland Ferries vessel *Pentalina B* (formerly the *Iona* of Caledonian MacBrayne) which was chartered for the controversial livestock trade to Dunkerque. As she is fitted with stabilisers the animals probably had a more comfortable trip than with the ro-ro freighter *Lygra* with which the route was shared. The service was suspended in September following the outbreak of foot and mouth disease and did not resume until January 2008. This proved fortunate for Pentland Ferries, as their other passenger vessel, the *Claymore*, was out of service for over seven weeks for dry-docking and survey work from mid-November and *Pentalina B* was sent north to operate a 12-passenger/cargo service on the St Margaret's Hope - Gills Bay route until January 2008.

SeaFrance continued to operate five passenger ships but generally with the *SeaFrance Cézanne* and *SeaFrance Renoir* sharing a single roster and the *SeaFrance Manet* operating in freight-only mode. In December it was announced that the company had purchased the *Jean Nicoli*, the former *Superfast X*, and she would enter service, replacing the *SeaFrance Manet* and *SeaFrance Renoir*, in Summer 2008.

P&O Ferries operated in a similar way to previous years and, although there were rumours of new ships being ordered to replace the *Pride of Calais* and *Pride of Dover*, no orders were placed.

SpeedFerries moved their operation from the Eastern Docks to the old Hoverport, using the old SeaCat berth. Although some office space was brought back into use, most of the passenger terminal remained unused. The old hovercraft engine maintenance building was converted into a café for passengers who had already checked in.

A company called Euroferries spent most of 2006 and the early part of 2007 claiming that it was about to start a new fast ferry service between Dover and Calais, using the Austal fast ferry *Spirit of Ontario* which had operated an unsuccessful service on the lake of that name between the USA and Canada. Eventually, the failure of the company to come up with the money after almost a year caused her somewhat frustrated American owners to sell the vessel to German company FRS. Euroferries then faded away.

LD Lines took over the operation of Transmanche Ferries under contract to the company's owners. The new management quickly made their mark through the introduction of a summer season Newhaven - Le Havre service. This service was generally operated by the *Seven Sisters*. On a less happy note, they reduced Dieppe services to only two a day during the off-peak (the first of the day leaving Newhaven at 17.30), precluding any sort of day trip from the UK, but this decision was reversed in early 2008 and the morning departure became all-year.

WESTERN CHANNEL AND SOLENT

Acciona Trasmediterranea suspended their Bilbao - Portsmouth service in January, claiming that the vessel, the *Fortuny*, was needed elsewhere but that the service would resume in April. In the event it did not resume and it seems doubtful the company had any intention that it should do so. It seems likely that the decision of P&O Ferries to renew the charter of the *Pride of Bilbao*, which operates on the same route, until 2010 was a major influence on their decision.

Brittany Ferries introduced their new ro-pax vessel the *Cotentin* (which normally carries only freight) in December, including a new weekend trip to Santander in Spain. The older *Coutances* switched to a new roster which included Portsmouth - Caen services during the week, Poole - Cherbourg at weekends and a couple of 'in service' positioning trips between Portsmouth and Cherbourg (although this ceased in May 2008). Brittany Ferries' passenger services remained much as before. The fast ferry *Normandie Express*, previously chartered each summer, was purchased by the company as was the *Pont L'Abbé*, previously on charter from DFDS.

Plans for Celtic Link Ferries to establish a new service between Portsmouth and Cherbourg came to nothing. They planned to charter the former LISCO ro-pax train ferry, the *Klaìpeda*, which had been acquired by Jay Ship Management of Greece in 2006. After a somewhat protracted refit in Greece she sailed, as the *Celtic Mist*, to Portsmouth, where she was promptly banned from operating by inspectors from the Maritime & Coastguard Agency who quoted numerous defects. After a few weeks laid up at Southampton, she returned to Greece and was chartered to Acciona Trasmediterranea, becoming the *Saronic Star*. Plans for the new route appear to have been abandoned.

LD Lines' single ship Portsmouth - Le Havre service continued unchanged but a new ship was ordered from Singapore Technologies Marine for delivery in 2010, with an option for a second ship. The new ship will offer similar facilities to the *Norman Spirit* but will have more cabins.

The Channel Islands saw two new operators. New company HD Ferries introduced a car-carrying service between Jersey and Guernsey and St Malo using a Hong Kong-built Incat 80 metre K50 catamaran. She had a rather turbulent year, with a number of 'prangs' in St Helier harbour, but re-established competition following the demise of Emeraude Lines in 2006. Later twice-weekly calls at Cherbourg were introduced but plans to serve Alderney had to be dropped. In addition, well-established Compagnie Corsaire started a new passenger service between St Malo and Jersey with the brand-new 232 ton catamaran *Jacques Cartier*. Manche Iles Express introduced their new fast ferry, the monohull *Tocqueville*, on the subsidised Granville - Jersey - Sark - Guernsey route. Condor Ferries' services remained much as before.

Solent services were unchanged during 2007 but Wightlink exercised their option for a third new ferry for the Lymington - Yarmouth link from Croatia. The names of *Wight Light*, *Wight Sky* and *Wight Sun* were announced for the new vessels which are to replace the *Cenred*, *Cenwulf* and *Cuthred*, the last remaining ships bearing names from the Sealink 'Dark Ages' era, during 2008. During the autumn a pressure group started a scare campaign, attempting to have the new ferries banned on the grounds that

Jean Nicoli (*Mike Louagie*)

Pride of Bilbao (*John Bryant*)

they would damage Lymington Harbour, ignoring the fact that, although bigger, they had been designed not to displace any more water than the older ships.

In June, Red Funnel Ferries was purchased by Infracapital Partners LD, part of the Prudential Insurance Group from previous owners HBOS (Halifax Bank of Scotland)

IRISH SEA

Irish Ferries introduced the new *Oscar Wilde* on the service from Rosslare to Roscoff and Cherbourg at the end of November. She had something of a 'baptism of fire', making her maiden voyage in one of the worst storms of the autumn but all were impressed by the quality of her décor and service.

The Swansea-Cork passenger service did not operate during 2007 as the company, having sold the *Superferry* in 2006, could not find a suitable replacement. A new company, HJ Lines, was set up by entrepreneur Howard Jones to operate a freight service between the two ports and the small trailer ferry *Victoria* (later *Victoria VI*) was chartered. However, it was not successful and ceased after a couple of months.

There were no changes for Stena Line at Holyhead, but towards the end of the year the return of an old friend was announced, albeit only for a few weeks. This was the *Stena Nordica* which, as the *European Ambassador*, had operated between Liverpool and Dublin and later Mostyn and Dublin for P&O Irish Sea. She was to operate on the Holyhead - Dublin and Fishguard - Rosslare routes in 2008 to cover for refits.

Celtic Link Ferries, having started a Dublin - Liverpool service in 2006, rather belatedly brought in a second vessel in early 2007. The Japanese-built *Celtic Sun* entered service in January but left the fleet after a few weeks. In the autumn, the one-ship service, operated by the *Celtic Star*, was taken over by Seatruck Ferries and the promised two-ship service eventually started on a more permanent basis with the transfer of *Challenge* from the Heysham - Warrenpoint service in January 2008. She was initially replaced on the Heysham - Warrenpoint route short term by the chartered *Merchant Brilliant*.

The need for the above charter was because Seatruck's new ships, the *Clipper Pace* and *Clipper Point*, due in 2007, were delayed. During the year, plans to order five ships of this class, with the last two being longer, were changed to an order for four vessels, all at the 'Heysham max' length of 142 metres. In October 2007 Seatruck purchased two of the *Challenge*'s sisters - the *RR Arrow* and *RR Triumph*, both of which were on long-term charters. In January 2008 the other two ships in the series were also purchased - the *Challenge* and *Shield*. By early 2008 all four ships had lost the 'RR' prefix in their names. The *Arrow* and *Shield* remained on charter to rival operator Norfolkline and the *Triumph* to Balearia of Spain.

Norfolkline said farewell to the chartered *Merchant Bravery* and *Merchant Brilliant* during the year, both ships attracting some notoriety due to disputes between owners and crew over unpaid wages. Only one replacement was secured - the *CFF Seine*, which came directly from her suddenly terminated charter to Ferryways - and the Heysham - Belfast service continued as a two-ship operation for most of the year. In November the *CFF Seine* had new owners and was renamed the *East Express*. Norfolkline's Irish Sea passenger services continued unchanged.

At the start of the year, P&O Ferries replaced the small trailer ferry *RR Triumph* with the older but larger *Global Freighter* as back-up to the ro-pax vessels on the Liverpool - Dublin service. The route also saw the return of an old friend (well almost) in the autumn with the arrival of P&O's *European Endeavour*. The one-time *Midnight Merchant* - sister vessel of the two ships NorseMerchant Ferries operated on the route - was acquired by P&O to act as a relief vessel on various routes operated by P&O Ferries and P&O Irish Sea and her first job was to act as stand-in for the refits of the *Norbank* and *Norbay* on the Dublin - Liverpool run.

The Isle of Man Steam Packet Company's *Sea Express 1* was involved in a collision in fog in the Mersey with the bulk carrier *Alaska Rainbow* on 3rd February. The aluminium-hulled vessel was badly damaged but fortunately there were no casualties. The company had planned to operate two fast ferries during the summer period and it was clear that repairs - if considered worthwhile - would take some months. Accordingly, sister vessel the *Emeraude France* was brought from lay-up at Tilbury in March - although she did not enter service until the end of May. She operated until early September. In the event the company decided to repair the *Sea Express 1* and at the end of the year she was given the traditional

Caedmon (*Miles Cowsill*)

Steam Packet name of *Snaefell*. The company decided not to operate fast ferries through Winter 2007/08 and instead served Merseyside at weekends through the diversion of the ro-pax *Ben-my-Chree* to the Twelve Quays terminal at Birkenhead, the berths used by Norfolkline. Running directly to the Pier Head terminal at Liverpool was not an option as the vessel would not fit the linkspan but, hopefully, by next winter modifications will have been carried out to enable Liverpool to be served.

Merseyside saw two unusual arrivals in the autumn when the two ex-NordöLink ferries *Lübeck Link* and *Malmö Link* arrived from the Baltic. They had been purchased by Channel Ferries, a company which had bought them not to operate a cross-channel service but to sell or charter them to other operators. The *Malmö Link* was renamed the *Ropax 1* and the *Lübeck Link* the *Ropax 2*. They remained at Birkenhead until January 2008 when they went on charter to Mediterranean operators.

SCOTLAND

Plans for Stena Line to move their operations at Stranraer to an extended P&O terminal at Cairnryan were dropped in the autumn due to escalating costs. What will happen in the future is unclear; the elderly *Stena Caledonia* cannot go on for ever, yet she cannot be replaced at present as larger ships are too big for Stranraer. In addition the HSS *Stena Voyager* is forced to proceed up Loch Ryan very slowly and would benefit from serving a terminal nearer the mouth of the loch.

Caledonian MacBrayne was divided into a number of companies to fit into the tendering environment forced on the company (and the Scottish Government) by the European Commission. At the end of the tendering process only one candidate remained - Caledonian MacBrayne - and was duly awarded the contract for six years. One aspect unresolved, however, was the Gourock Pier- Dunoon Pier service. This was the subject of a separate tendering exercise, for which, ultimately, there were no takers. This is hardly surprising as no subsidy was offered. A complicating factor is that, although the service is more viable if cars are conveyed, this would compete with the commercial service operated by Western Ferries between McInroy's Point and Hunter's Quay. During the year construction continued on a second linkspan for each of Western Ferries' terminals. It came into use in December. Caledonian MacBrayne introduced a second new ferry on the Wemyss Bay - Rothesay route - the Polish-built *Argyle*, a near sister to the *Bute* of 2005. The new and much-delayed end-loading linkspan at Rothesay finally came into service in December, replacing the side-loading linkspan used previously and permitting bow/stern operation by the two new ferries. The Scottish-built *Loch Shira* entered service on the Largs - Cumbrae Slip route and an order was placed - in Poland again - for a new ship for Islay; this route now requires two ships for most of the year.

A third new vessel entered service on the Clyde in 2007, namely the passenger ferry *Seabus*, which replaced the *Kenilworth* on the Strathclyde Partnership for Transport Gourock to Kilcreggan service operated by Clyde Marine.

In July Stagecoach ran a two-week trial service between Kirkcaldy and Portobello using the hovercraft *Solent Express*, chartered from Hovertravel at Ryde, with a view to demonstrating the potential for a ferry crossing to ease congestion on the Forth Road Bridge. It is possible that a new cross-Forth will start later this year.

In January Superfast Ferries replaced the *Superfast X* on the Rosyth - Zeebrugge route by the *Blue Star 1* from associated company Blue Star Ferries.

Faroese operator Smyril Line announced the ending of their service to Lerwick in Shetland and the last call was made on 28th September. Ironically *Norröna* had to make an emergency call at Lerwick after suffering heavy weather damage (including damage to 60 cars) on passage from Bergen to Tórshavn on 12th November. Temporary repairs were carried out and she left for Tórshavn next day.

Following the closure of the Color Line service from Bergen to Hirtshals in January 2008, *Norröna* began a more intensive winter programme between Bergen and Frederikshavn with Hanstholm as an alternative port in the event of weather diversion.

Although the Shetland Development Agency was a major shareholder in the company, they were unable to persuade the management to change their minds. Instead the company's vessel, the *Nörrona* will, in June, July and August 2008, make weekly calls at Scrabster on the Scottish mainland.

Nick Widdows

European Endeavour (*Gordon Hislip*)

Stena Explorer (*Gordon Hislip*)

SCANDINAVIAN AND NORTHERN EUROPE REVIEW

The following geographical review again takes the form of a voyage along the coast of The Netherlands and Germany, round the southern tip of Norway, down the Kattegat, through the Great Belt and into the Baltic then up to the Gulf of Finland and Gulf of Bothnia.

FRISIAN ISLANDS

Rederij Doeksen acquired the 660 ton fast catamaran *Supercat 2002* from Philippines operator Supercat to operate between Harlingen, Terschelling and Vlieland. She started operations in Spring 2008 as the *Tiger*.

TESO disposed of the 1980-built *Molengat* to Indian operators; she had been laid up since 2005.

Wagenborg acquired their first catamaran passenger ferry - the 1999-built *Esonborg*.

SCANDINAVIA -GENERAL

Danish/German state-owned company Scandlines was sold to a consortium consisting of Allianz Capital Partners (Danish company) (40%), 3i Group (UK company) (40%) and Deutsche Seereederei (German company) (20%) for 1.56 billion Euro on 19th June. Deutsche Seereederei took over operational control of the company and jobs were safeguarded until 2010. The new owners later sold their Danish subsidiary, Scandlines Sydfyenske A/S, to the Copenhagen-based Clipper Group. They similarly disposed of their 30% share in Mols-Linien. Clipper Group is primarily a bulk carrier and cruise operator but has owned Seatruck Ferries following their acquisition of UK-based Crescent Shipping a few years ago.

NORWEGIAN DOMESTIC

The Hurtigruten newbuilding *Fram* was christened at the Akershus fortress in Oslo on 19th May by the Norwegian Crown Princess Mette-Marit. Due to late completion, her delivery cruise started at Barcelona rather than Venice; she called into London on 11th May. During 2007 she operated cruises around Greenland and then moved to South America but winter service on the Hurtigruten will possibly take place in future years.

SKAGERRAK AND KATTEGAT

Color Line operated the *Kronprins Harald* for the last time on the Oslo - Kiel service on 31st August and she was delivered to Irish Ferries at Oslo the following day. The new *Color Magic* took over the service between Oslo and Kiel on 17th September. The 27 knot *Superspeed 1* was floated out of her building dock at Aker Yards in Rauma on 1st August. She was due to be delivered in December and start operations on the Hirtshals - Kristiansand route in January 2008, replacing both the *Christian IV* and fast mono-hull *Silvia Ana L*. However, she was not delivered until February 2008 and entered service in March. The *Silvia Ana L* was sold back to Buquebus of Argentina.

Color Line announced that they would cease their Bergen - Stavanger - Hirtshals service operated by the *Prinsesse Ragnhild* at the beginning of 2008. The 1981 vessel would move to the Oslo - Hirtshals route replacing the newer *Color Festival*, which was to be sold to the owners of Corsica Sardinia Ferries of Italy. The Danish terminus moved to Frederikshavn during 2006 but, at 205.3 metres, the 1992 lengthening had made the *Prinsesse Ragnhild* too long for this port and so a return to Hirtshals was necessary. The service ended in May 2008.

On Monday 10th September Kystlink's *Pride of Telemark* lost power upon entering the port of Hirtshals and, after hitting the quay, started taking on water. Noone was hurt but the engine room was flooded. She was towed to CityVarvet at Gothenburg for repairs and Tallink's *Fantaasia* was chartered as a replacement. However, on arrival in Gothenburg from her Algerian charter, for what was presumably hoped would be a brief tidy-up, she was detained for various safety violations and her general condition was reported as being poor. She eventually entered service on 11th December. With *Fantaasia* on a six-month charter it was then decided to give the *Pride of Telemark* a major engine rebuild so she would not re-enter service until May 2008. In April 2008 Kystlink purchased the *Fantaasia*.

Master Ferries' plans to replace the *Master Cat* with a larger craft were frustrated when the craft they

Europalink (*FotoFlite*)

Polonia (*Mike Louagie*)

wanted was secured by the Government of Trinidad and Tobago. There were also problems in finding yard capacity to undertake the necessary conversion work. This meant that the *Master Cat* could not be chartered to SpeedFerries at Dover as their second vessel. At the end of the year it was announced that Master Ferries was to merge with Fjord Line. The company would trade as Fjord Line and that company's *Atlantic Traveller* (now renamed the *Bergensfjord*) would operate some sailings between Hanstholm and Kristiansand. The latter company's *Master Cat* was renamed *Fjord Cat* in 2008.

In the autumn, the Swedish Orvelin Group acquired the small Greek car ferry *Andreas II* and brought her to the shipyard at Frederikstad for refurbishment. The company's intention was to start a ferry service to bring Norwegian shoppers to their shopping complex near Strömstad (Swedish prices being lower than Norwegian ones) and also buy duty-free alcohol. The attractive little vessel was given the rather less attractive name of *Mr Shoppy One*. Services started in April 2008.

DANISH DOMESTIC

A new specification was drawn up for the future service to the island of Bornholm from 2011. Instead of the current pattern of two ro-pax ferries and one fast ferry there will be a single ro-pax and two fast ferries. Since the opening of the Øresund bridge, there has been a major switch to the overland route to the Swedish port of Ystad, which is much closer to Bornholm than anywhere in Denmark. The single-ship service was mooted a few years ago but modified after local objections, hence the hurried purchase of the *Ben-My-Chree* clones *Dueodde* and *Hammerodde*. One of them is likely to be sold and the other lengthened. Incumbent operator Bornholmstrafikken felt unable to bid in its own right and teamed up with the Clipper Group to form a new company called Nordic Ferry Services. Other bidders were Mols-Linien, Scandlines Sydfyenske and Rederi AB Gotland of Sweden; following its acquisition of Scandlines Sydfyenske and a share of Mols-Linien in 2008, the Clipper Group now has an interest in three of the four contenders.

Nordic Ferry Services partner Bornholmstrafikken won the concession to operate services from Sælvig on the island of Samsø and Hou In Jutland from October 2008. The other Samsø route   that between Kolby Kås and Kalundborg on Sealand - was won by incumbent operator Samsø-Linien but they later decided that running just one route was not viable and they are to hand over the franchise to Nordic Ferry Services in October.

SOUTH BALTIC

Scandlines chartered the *Thjelvar* from Rederi AB Gotland for the increasingly busy Rostock - Gedser service. She was renamed the *Rostock* and, from 1st October, provided back-up to the two former train ferries *Kronprins Frederik* and *Prins Joachim*. Later in the autumn, the company closed their Karlshamn (Sweden) - Ventspils (Latvia) service, operated by the chartered ro-pax *Fellow*. The *Fellow* was moved to the Rostock - Ventspils route to operate alongside the *Ask* and *Urd* to provide six departures per week in each direction.

In May, DFDS LISCO placed the *Envoy* on the Lübeck - Riga service to supplement the *Mermaid II*. The vessel had been undergoing long-term repairs since her withdrawal from the Nedlines IJmuiden - Harwich service in early 2006. Later, they started a direct train ferry service between Sassnitz and Baltijsk (Kaliningrad) in cooperation with Railion and the Russian national railway RZD. The service used the *Vilnius* which also operates between Sassnitz and Klaipeda. With booming traffic on the Karlshamn and Klaipeda route, a third vessel was introduced in the form of the trailer ferry *Tor Neringa*. On the other hand, in June, the company ended the once-weekly Klaipeda - Baltijsk service, operated by the *Lisco Patria*.

The former Finnlines Travemünde - Helsinki ship the *Finntrader*, was delivered to Finnlines NordöLink on 17th February and entered service soon afterwards. This enabled the *Finnsailor* to be moved to the Naantali - Kapellskär Finnlink route. The company's first brand-new ferry, the *Europalink*, then entered service on 31st March, replacing the 1996-built *Finnarrow*. Sister ship the *Nordlink* was delivered in July and replaced the *Malmö Link* on the Travemünde - Malmö service. The following month the *Finnpartner* returned from modifications at Gdansk and replaced the *Lübeck Link*. Both of the old ships were purchased by the British company Channel Ferries for charter and were taken to Northwestern Shiprepairers & Shipbuilders, Birkenhead. They were given the names *Ropax 1* and *Ropax 2* and subsequently chartered to Mediterranean operators.

In early May, the *Finnarrow* was chartered for three years to Stena Line to operate on their Karlskrona - Gdynia service as third ship; she is not advertised as being available for ordinary passengers.

Polish Unity Line partner Polsteam purchased the *Sky Wind* from Tallink subsidiary Sea Wind Line; she became their *Wolin* and was placed on the Swinoujscie - Trelleborg route. At the end of the year Polsteam ordered a second 300-passenger ro-pax vessel from New Szczecin Shipyard, Szczecin, Poland. She will be delivered in 2011. The other partner, Euroafrica Shipping Lines, purchased the *Vironia* (ex *Sky Wind*) from Narva Line. The ship was renamed the *Kopernick* and was due to replace the *Mikolaj Kopernik* on the Swinoujscie - Ystad route in the spring.

Polferries placed their new ro-pax ship, the *Baltivia* on the Gdansk - Nynäshamn route in January. The former *Dieppe* of Transmanche Ferries runs opposite the passenger ship, the *Scandinavia*.

CROSS BALTIC

Finnlines' third new ro-pax, the *Finnlady*, arrived in February, but things were not quite as they seemed. She was in fact the vessel launched as the *Europalink*, for the Finnlines NordöLink service. The *Europalink*, launched as the *Finnlady*, was delivered shortly afterwards. A three-ship fast service started on 17th March but two of the older Hansa class, the *Finnhansa* and the *Transeuropa*, were retained due to growing freight traffic and continued to offer an alternative, slower passenger service. The *Finnpartner* entered the Remontowa shipyard to be converted for two-level through-deck operation for Finnlines NordöLink and entered service in August. Finnlines ordered six ro-ro vessels from the Jinling Shipyard in Nanjing, China for delivery in 2010-11. They will replace chartered tonnage on the company's Baltic and North Sea services and will be similar to the *Finnmill* and *Finnpulp*.

At the end of April, Tallink placed the *Vana Tallinn* on the Stockholm - Riga service to run alongside the *Regina Baltica* and thus provide a daily service. A daily service was initially promised in 2006, but the proposed vessel, the *Fantaasia*, was chartered out instead. Former Stockholm - Riga vessel *Baltic Kristina* was sold in February by her owners, the Freeport of Riga, to Turkish-owned but Hamburg-based Euro 7 Fernseh & Marketing.

The UK-registered *Baltic Eager*, for 20 years a familiar sight at Felixstowe on the joint United Baltic Corporation/Finncarriers service to Finland as the *Baltic Eagle*, returned to the Baltic and was placed on the joint Finnlines/JSC Baltic Transport Systems TransRussia Express service between Lübeck and St Petersburg. She was joined by the Irish-owned *Kilmore*, one of the 12-strong Stena SeaRunner class, formerly the *Graip* of Gotlandslinjen and then the Chinese-owned *Chong Ming Dao*. She was converted back to a freight-only role in 2006.

Transfennica took delivery in June of their third combined ro-ro and container carrier, the *Genca*, from the New Szczecin Shipyard. The *Genca* joined the 2006-delivered *Kraftca* and *Timca*. She was followed in October by the *Trica*. More ships of this class are to be delivered in 2008 and 2009.

Scandlines started a new Rostock - Hanko freight service in October with the chartered *Merchant Brilliant*. This vessel was replaced in January 2008 by their own *Aurora* and the former Finnlines' *Merchant* which was acquired during the year.

SWEDISH DOMESTIC

Destination Gotland started a new service between Grankullavik on the Swedish island of Öland and Visby on Gotland. The vessel used was the fast ferry *Gotlandia* of 1996, laid up since her replacement by the *Gotlandia II* in 2006. Later in the year the company retained the contract to operate services from the Swedish mainland to the island.

NORTH BALTIC

From 1st January, Tallink's 'Superfast' service switched from Hanko to Helsinki and the ships undertook a round trip to Tallinn after each morning arrival. The new *Star* entered service on 5th April with a crossing time of two hours. Three crossings per day were operated with 90-minute turn-rounds. She replaced the *Vana Tallinn* which was transferred to the Stockholm - Riga route but the daily round trip by the 'Superfast' ship continued. It was announced that the near sister being built by Fincantieri was to be called the *Superstar*. In February, Tallink sold the *Tallink Autoexpress 3* to Arab Bridge Maritime Co of Jordan to operate between Egypt and Saudi Arabia as the *Queen Nefertiti*, and

Tom Sawyer (*FotoFlite*)

Schleswig-Holstein (*FotoFlite*)

Translandia (*Mike Louagie*)

Viking Xprs (*Bruce Peter*)

the following month the *Tallink Autoexpress 4* was sold to Jaywick Shipping of Greece to operate in the Aegean as the *Speedrunner 2*. This left the *Tallink Autoexpress 2* which remained laid up until October when she was chartered to Conferry of Venezuela. Tallink also sold the *Meloodia* to the Singaporean company Equinox Offshore Accommodation Ltd. for conversion to an offshore accommodation and repair vessel. She had been on charter to Eurolineas Maritimas SA (trading as Balearia) since the beginning of the year, her Helsinki-Tallinn service being covered by the *Vana Tallinn* until the *Star* was delivered.

Tallink announced that the *Galaxy* would move to the Silja Line Stockholm - Turku service in 2008, coinciding with the delivery of the new *Baltic Princess* from Aker Yards for the Tallinn - Helsinki service. She would replace the *Silja Festival*, which would move to the Stockholm - Riga route. A fifth cruise ferry was ordered from Aker Yards for delivery in 2009. It seems likely that she will take over the Tallinn - Stockholm service from the *Romantika*, which will in turn replace the *Silja Europa* on the Turku route.

Tallink subsidiary SeaWind Line sold their *Star Wind* to Unity Line partner, Euroafrica Shipping and at the end of the year ceased to carry ordinary passengers. The company is now back to a single vessel - the *Sea Wind*.

Despite the ending of all other Sea Containers ferry activities, the Helsinki - Tallinn SuperSeaCat service continued to operate unchanged. When it was announced in January 2008 that the two craft had been sold to Aegean Speed Lines of Greece it was assumed they would move to the Mediterranean; however, a few days later the company announced their intention of maintaining the Baltic service for 2008. It later transpired that 50% of the company remained in Sea Containers' ownership.

Birka Line - operators of the Åland cruise ship *Birka Princess* and six ro-ro ships on charter to Finnlines - took-over fellow Åland operator Rederi AB Eckerö. This company disposed of its last 'Papenburger' - the *Roslagen* - to Agoudimos Lines of Greece. The ship has been renamed the *Ionian Spirit*.

Viking Line named their new fast ship to operate between Helsinki and Tallinn the *Viking XPRS* (pronounced 'Viking Express'). XPRS was the project name and the company decided that this 'text message' style title should continue. Viking Line also ordered a new vessel for the Kapellskär - Mariehamn route to replace the 1972-built *Ålandsfärjan*. She is to be built by Astilleros de Sevilla in Seville, Spain and will be delivered in 2009. The project name is 'Viking ADCC' (which one hopes will not be her final name!).

The *Finnsailor* moved back to the Finnlines-owned FinnLink service between Naantali (Finland) and Kapellskär (Sweden) in March. The move was originally planned for October 2006 but was delayed due to the late delivery of Finnlines' new ships. Unlike the other vessels on the route, she conveys freight drivers only. Capacity on this route was also boosted by the fitting of an extra deck to the *Finnclipper* which now makes her similar to the 2000-built *Finnfellow* (ex *Stena Britannica*).

Estonian operator Saaremaa Laevakompanii signed a letter of intent with Fiskerstrand Verft of Norway for the construction of a new ferry with an option for a sister ship. A third ship is likely to be ordered in due course. The ship will be similar to the *Sylt Express* of Rømø-Sylt Linie and will be delivered in 2009. The first vessel will be operated on the Rohukula - Heltermaa service. In the autumn, the company ceased their Sillamäe (Estonia) - Kotka (Finland) 'Narva Line' service due to problems in utilising Russian waters to make the most direct crossing. The vessel used - the *Vironia* - was sold to Euroafrica Shipping Lines for Unity Line service.

In the spring, Baltic Scandinavian Line chartered the *Gute* from Rederi AB Gotland for their Kapellskar - Paldiski service. The former Sally Line ship joined the *Via Mare*, originally the *European Clearway* with Townsend Thoresen at Dover.

Gulf of Bothnia operators RG-Line disposed of the laid-up *Casino Express* to Indian breakers. On a happier note, the future of their route looks more assured following the decision of Swedish authorities to support the service; previously only the Finns provided financial assistance.

Nick Widdows

Bergen
Stavanger
Egersund
Kristiansand
Hanstholm
Kalundl
Esbjerg
Cuxhaven
Norddeich
Harlingen
Emden
North
Sea
N
Sa
H
DE
S
IJmuiden
Scheveningen
Hoek van Holland
NETH.
Harwich
Vlissingen
Rotterdam
Plymouth
Portsmouth
Ramsgate
Dover
Ostend
Zeebrugge
Newhaven
Dunkerque
U. K.
Calais
BELGIUM
GE
English Channel
Cherbourg
LUX.
Roscoff
Dieppe
Le Havre
Caen
St Malo

Umeå
Vaasa
FINLAND
Rauma
Naantali
Turku
Kotka
ÅLAND
Helsinki
Mariehamn
Långnäs
Hanko
Oslo
SWEDEN
Tallinn
Kapellskär
Paldiski
Moss
Södertälje
Stockholm
ESTONIA
Strömstad
Nynäshamn
Gothenburg
Västervik
Oskarshamn
Visby
Ventspils
Riga
shavn
Varberg
GOTLAND
LATVIA
ÖLAND
Liepaja
eltott
Helsingborg
Karlskrona
Klaìpeda
lsingør
Karlshamn
n
Malmö
LITHUANIA
openhagen
Ystad
Trelleborg
Rønne
Tars
BORNHOLM
y
Gedser
Sassnitz
Gdynia
den
Rostock
Gdansk
BYEL
ravemünde
beck
Swinoujscie
POLAND
UKR
CZECH

BRETAGNE
BRETAGNE

Bretagne (*Miles Cowsill*)

SECTION 1 GB & IRELAND - INTERNATIONAL PASSENGER OPERATIONS

BRITTANY FERRIES

THE COMPANY *Brittany Ferries* is the trading name of *BAI SA*, a French private sector company and the operating arm of the *Brittany Ferries Group*. The UK operations are run by *BAI (UK) Ltd*, a UK private sector company, wholly owned by the *Brittany Ferries Group*.

MANAGEMENT Group Managing Director Jean-Michel Giguet, **Managing Director UK & Ireland** David Longden.

ADDRESS Millbay Docks, Plymouth, Devon PL1 3EW.

TELEPHONE Administration *Plymouth* +44 (0)8709 010500, ***Portsmouth*** +44 (0)8709 011300, **Reservations *All Services*** +44 (0)871 244 1400.

FAX Administration & Reservations +44 (0)8709 011100.

INTERNET Website www.brittanyferries.com (*English, French, Spanish, German, Dutch*)

ROUTES OPERATED Conventional Ferries *All year* Plymouth - Roscoff (6 hrs (day), 6 hrs - 7 hrs 30 mins (night); *6,7*; up to 3 per day (Summer), 1 per day (Winter)), Portsmouth - St Malo (8 hrs 45 mins (day), 10 hrs 30 mins - 11 hrs 30 mins (night); *2*; 1 per day), Portsmouth - Caen (Ouistreham) (6 hrs (day), 6 hrs 15 mins - 8 hrs (night); *3,4*; 3 per day), Plymouth - Santander (Spain) (20 hrs 30 mins; *6*; 2 per week (March - November)), Poole - Cherbourg (4 hrs 15 mins; *1*; up to 2 per day), **15th March-1st November** Cork - Roscoff (14 hrs; *6*; 1 per week). **Fast Ferries 13th March-26th October** Portsmouth – Cherbourg (3 hrs; *5*; 1 or 2 per day), **14th March-26th October** Portsmouth - Caen (Ouistreham) (3 hrs 45 mins; *5*; 3 per week), **19th May-28th September** Poole - Cherbourg (2 hrs 15 mins; ***CONDOR VITESSE of Condor Ferries***; 1 per day). **Note:** The Poole - Cherbourg fast ferry service is operated from May to September by *Condor Ferries* jointly with *Brittany Ferries*.

1	BARFLEUR	20133t	92	19.3k	158.0m	1212P	590C	112T	BA2	FR	9007130
2	BRETAGNE	24534t	89	21.0k	151.0m	1926P	580C	84T	BA	FR	8707329
3	MONT ST MICHEL	35592t	02	21.5k	173.0m	2200P	880C	166T	BA2	FR	9238337
4	NORMANDIE	27541t	92	20.5k	161.0m	2120P	600C	126T	BA2	FR	9006253
5»	NORMANDIE EXPRESS	6581t	00	42.0k	97.2m	900P	260C	-	A	FR	8814134
6	PONT-AVEN	41748t	04	27.0k	184.3m	2400P	650C	85L	BA	FR	9268708
7	PONT L'ABBE	19589t	78	20.5k	152.9m	1120P	375C	45T	BA	FR	7615414

BARFLEUR Built by Kvaerner Masa-Yards, Helsinki for the *Truckline* Poole - Cherbourg service to replace two passenger vessels and to inaugurate a year-round passenger service. In 1999 the *Truckline* branding was dropped for passenger services and she was repainted into full *Brittany Ferries* livery. In 2005 operated partly Cherbourg - Poole and partly Cherbourg - Portsmouth but in 2006 returned to operating mainly to Poole.

BRETAGNE Built by Chantiers de l'Atlantique, St Nazaire for the Plymouth - Santander and Cork - Roscoff services (with two sailings per week between Plymouth and Roscoff). In 1993 she was transferred to the Portsmouth - St Malo service. In 2004 also operated between Portsmouth and Cherbourg. In 2005 operated between Plymouth and Roscoff. In 2006 returned to the Portsmouth - St Malo route.

MONT ST MICHEL Built by Van der Giessen-de Noord, Krimpen aan den IJssel, Rotterdam for *Brittany Ferries* to replace the DUC DE NORMANDIE on the Portsmouth - Caen route.

NORMANDIE Built by Kvaerner Masa-Yards, Turku, Finland for the Portsmouth - Caen route.

NORMANDIE EXPRESS Incat Evolution 10 catamaran built as the INCAT TASMANIA. In November 2000 chartered to *TranzRail* of New Zealand and renamed THE LYNX. Placed on the Wellington – Picton service. In July 2003 replaced by 1997-built Incat 86m craft INCAT 046, given the marketing name 'The Lynx' and laid up. In Spring 2005 chartered to *Brittany Ferries* to operate on their

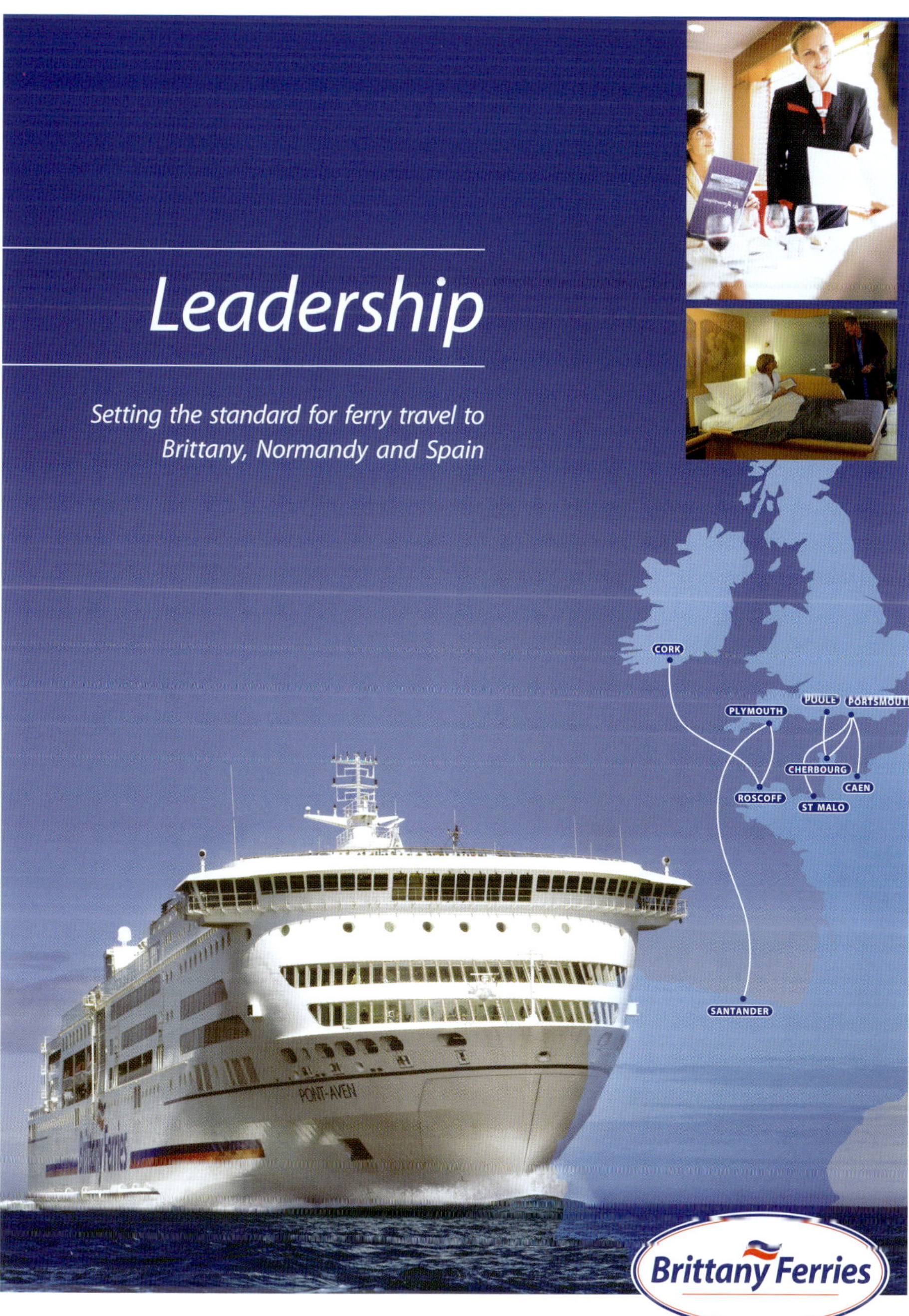
Leadership

Setting the standard for ferry travel to
Brittany, Normandy and Spain

CORK
PLYMOUTH
POOLE
PORTSMOUTH
CHERBOURG
CAEN
ROSCOFF
ST MALO
SANTANDER

PONT-AVEN

Brittany Ferries

brittanyferries.com

Cherbourg – Portsmouth and Caen – Portsmouth services and renamed the NORMANDIE EXPRESS. In 2007 purchased by *Brittany Ferries*.

PONT-AVEN Built by Jos L Meyer Werft, Papenburg, Germany to operate on the Plymouth - Roscoff, Plymouth - Santander and Cork - Roscoff routes.

PONT L'ABBE Built by Aalborg Værft A/S, Aalborg, Denmark for *DFDS* as the DANA ANGLIA for the Harwich - Esbjerg service and seldom operated elsewhere. In Autumn 2002, renamed the DUKE OF SCANDINAVIA and inaugurated a new Copenhagen - Trelleborg - Gdansk service. In 2003 moved to the Newcastle – IJmuiden service. In 2006 chartered to *Brittany Ferries*, placed on the Plymouth –Roscoff route and renamed the PONT L'ABBE. In 2007 purchased by *Brittany Ferries*.

Under Construction

8	ARMORIQUE	33500t	09	23.0k	167.0m	1500P	470C	65L	BA	FR	-

ARMORIQUE Under construction by Aker Yards, Helsinki, Finland for *Brittany Ferries* to operate between Plymouth and Roscoff.

CELTIC LINK FERRIES

THE COMPANY *Celtic Link Ferries Ltd* is an Irish Republic private sector company.

MANAGEMENT Marketing Manager Paul Tyrrell.

ADDRESS Kilmore Quay, Co Wexford, Republic of Ireland.

TELEPHONE Administration +353 (0)402 38091, **Reservations *Passenger* UK** +44 (0)870 458 0401, **Irish Republic** +353 (0)402 38091, ***Freight*** +353 (0)402 38091, **Ship Management** +353 (0)53 917 8789.

FAX Administration & Reservations +353 (0)402 38086, **Ship Management** +35 (0)53 917 8798.

INTERNET Website www.celticlinkferries.com (*English*)

ROUTE OPERATED Rosslare - Cherbourg (18 hrs; *1*; 3 per week).

1	DIPLOMAT	16776t	78	17.0k	151.0m	74P	-	122T	A2	BM	7528661

DIPLOMAT Built by Hyundai Shipbuilders & Heavy Industries, Ulsan, South Korea as the STENA TRANSPORTER, for *Stena Rederi* of Sweden. In 1979 she was renamed the FINNROSE and chartered to *Finnlines*. She later served with Atlanticargo on their service between Europe and USA/Mexico. In 1980 she returned to *Stena Line* and resumed her original name. Later in 1980 she was chartered to *European Ferries* for their Felixstowe - Rotterdam freight-only service and renamed the BALTIC FERRY. In 1982 she served in the Falkland Islands Task Force. In 1986 she was converted to ro-pax format and moved to the Felixstowe - Zeebrugge passenger service. In 1992 she was renamed the PRIDE OF SUFFOLK. In 1994 she was purchased by *P&O European Ferries*. In 1995 the Felixstowe - Zeebrugge passenger service ceased, most of her additional passenger accommodation was removed, passenger capacity was reduced and she was transferred to the Felixstowe - Rotterdam freight service. In 2001 transferred to *P&O Irish Sea's* Liverpool - Dublin route and renamed the EUROPEAN DIPLOMAT. In 2002 transferred to the Rosslare - Cherbourg route; this service ended in December 2004. In 2004 purchased by *Celtic Link Ferries*, renamed the DIPLOMAT and, in February 2005, re-launched the Rosslare – Cherbourg link.

Celtic Link Ferries Ltd also own the FINNFOREST which is on long-term charter to *Finnlines* and operates between Helsinki and Gdynia. See Section 3.

CONDOR FERRIES

THE COMPANY *Condor Ferries Ltd* is a Channel Islands private sector company owned by the *Condor Group*, Guernsey which is owned by the *Royal Bank of Scotland*.

MANAGEMENT Group Chief Executive Robert Provan, **Managing Director** David Harbord, **General Manager, Sales & Marketing** Nicholas Dobbs.

ADDRESS Head Office PO Box 10, New Jetty Offices, White Rock, St Peter Port, Guernsey GY1 3AF, **Sales and Marketing** Condor House, New Harbour Road South, Hamworthy, Poole BH15 4AJ.

TELEPHONE Administration *Guernsey* +44 (0)1481 728620, *Poole* +44 (0)1202 207207, **Reservations** +44 (0)870 2435100.

FAX Administration *Guernsey* +44 (0)1481 728521, *Poole* +44 (0)1202 685184, **Reservations** +44(0)1305 760776.

INTERNET Email reservations@condorferries.co.uk **Website** www.condorferries.com (*English, French*)

ROUTES OPERATED Conventional Ferry *All year* Portsmouth - St Peter Port (Guernsey) (7 hrs) - St Helier (Jersey) (10 hrs 30 mins) (return overnight Guernsey via Jersey, 12 hrs 30 mins, Jersey - Portsmouth; *1*; daily except Sunday), **Summer only (May to September)** Portsmouth - Cherbourg (France) (5 hrs; *1*; Sundays), **Fast Ferries** Weymouth - St Peter Port (2 hrs 10 mins) - St Helier (3hrs 25 mins) – St Malo (5hrs 15 mins): *3,4*; 2 sailings per week (Winter), daily (rest of year)(Weymouth to St Malo service does not operate from 19th May to 28th September, a link is possible via a change of vessel in Jersey or Guernsey), Poole - St Peter Port (2 hrs 30 mins) - St Helier (3 hrs); *3,4*; daily (April-September), Mon, Wed, Fri (October)), Poole - St Malo (France) (with call at either Guernsey of Jersey; *3,4*; daily (19th May–28th September), St Malo - St Helier (1 hr 15 min; *2*; Thu, Fri, Sat up to 2 sailings per day (Spring, Summer, Autumn)), St Malo - St Peter Port (2 hrs 45 mins; *2*; selected dates until 20th March and from 31st October - 31st December, daily 24th March – 31st October), Poole - Cherbourg (2 hrs 15 mins; *3,4*; daily 19th May – 28th September) (service operated on behalf of *Brittany Ferries*).

1	COMMODORE CLIPPER	14000t	99	18.25k	129.1m	500P	100C	92T	A	BS	9201750
2»	CONDOR 10	3241t	93	37.0k	74.3m	572P	80C	-	BA	BS	9001526
3»	CONDOR EXPRESS	5005t	96	39.0k	86.6m	741P	185C	-	A2	BS	9135896
4»	CONDOR VITESSE	5005t	97	39.0k	86.6m	741P	185C	-	A2	BS	9151008

COMMODORE CLIPPER Ro-pax vessel built by Van der Giessen-de Noord, Krimpen aan den IJssel, Rotterdam for *Commodore Ferries* to operate between Portsmouth and the Channel Islands. She replaced the ISLAND COMMODORE, a freight-only vessel. Her passenger capacity is normally restricted to 300 but is increased to 500 when the fast ferries are unable to operate.

CONDOR 10 Incat 74m catamaran. Built at Hobart, Tasmania, Australia for the *Holyman Group* for use by *Condor Ferries*. In Summer 1995 she was chartered to *Viking Line* to operate between Helsinki and Tallinn under the name 'VIKING EXPRESS II' (although not officially renamed). In Summer 1996 she was chartered to *Stena Line* to operate between Fishguard and Rosslare. During northern hemisphere winters she served for *TranzRail* of New Zealand for the service between Wellington (North Island) and Picton (South Island). In May 1997 she was transferred to *Holyman Sally Ferries* and inaugurated a new Ramsgate - Dunkerque (Est) service, replacing the Ramsgate - Dunkerque (Ouest) service of *Sally Ferries*. After further service in New Zealand during Winter 1997/98, in Summer 1998 she was due to operate between Weymouth, Guernsey and St Malo, but in the event the CONDOR VITESSE was chartered for that route and she was laid up in Australia. Refurbished during 2001, she returned to the UK in Spring 2002 replacing the passenger-only CONDOR 9 between St Malo and Guernsey and Jersey. She is now owned by *Condor Ferries*.

CONDOR EXPRESS Incat 86m catamaran built at Hobart, Tasmania, Australia. She was delivered in December 1996 and entered service in 1997.

CONDOR VITESSE Incat 86m catamaran built at Hobart. Built speculatively and launched as the INCAT 044. Moved to Europe in Summer 1997 and spent time in both the UK and Denmark but was

Be better connected

Only Condor Ferries offer passenger & freight services to France, UK & the Channel Islands

Condor Ferries offer the most comprehensive conventional and fast car ferry and freight services between the UK, Channel Islands and the French port of St. Malo.

So whether you're moving passengers, cars or freight, you can be sure of the same high standards of quality, care and attention that have made Condor Ferries so consistently successful.

So if you'd like to be better connected call or click today.

01202 207 207   www.**Condorferries**.com

Normandie Express (*Andrew Cooke*)

Condor Express (*Andrew Cooke*)

not used. In 1998 she was chartered to *Condor Ferries* and renamed the CONDOR VITESSE. During Winter 1999/2000 she was chartered to *TranzRail* of New Zealand. Returned to UK in Spring 2000.

DFDS SEAWAYS

THE COMPANY *DFDS Seaways* is the passenger division of *DFDS A/S*, a Danish private sector company. *DFDS Seaways Ltd* is a UK subsidiary.

MANAGEMENT Chairman and CEO DFDS A/S Niels Smedegaard, **Managing Director DFDS Seaways Ltd** John Crummie.

ADDRESS International Ferry Terminal, Royal Quays, North Shields, Tyne and Wear, NE29 6EE.

TELEPHONE Administration +44 (0)1255 243456, **Reservations *National*** 08705 333000 (from UK only), ***Harwich*** +44 (0)1255 240240, ***Newcastle*** +44 (0)191-293 6283.

FAX Administration & Reservations *Harwich* +44 (0)1255 244370, ***Newcastle*** +44 (0)191-293 6245.

INTERNET Email john.crummie@dfds.co.uk **Website** www.dfds.co.uk *(English)*

www.dfds.com *(Danish, Dutch, German, Norwegian, Swedish)*

ROUTES OPERATED *All year* Harwich - Esbjerg (Denmark) (17 hrs; *1*; 3 per week), Newcastle - Stavanger - Bergen (21 hrs 15 mins; *4*; Summer 3 sailings per week, Winter 2 sailing per week - ends August 2008), Newcastle (North Shields) - IJmuiden (Netherlands) (15 hrs; *2,3*; daily).

1	DANA SIRENA	22382t	03	23.0k	199.4m	602P	316C	154T	A	DK	9212163
2	KING OF SCANDINAVIA	31788t	87	21.0k	161.6m	2140P	600C	104T	BA	DK	8502406
3	PRINCESS OF NORWAY	31356t	86	21.0k	161.0m	1600P	600C	100T	BA	DK	8502391
4	QUEEN OF SCANDINAVIA	34093t	81	20.0k	168.1m	1638P	360C	54T	A	DK	7911533

DANA SIRENA Built by Stocznia Szczecinska, Szczecin, Poland for *Lloyd Sardegnu* of Italy as the GOLFO DEI DELFINI for service between Italy and Sardinia. However, due to late delivery the order was cancelled. In 2002 purchased by *DFDS Seaways*, and, during Winter 2002/03, passenger accommodation was enlarged and refitted, increasing passenger capacity from 308 to 600. In June 2003, renamed the DANA SIRENA, she replaced unmodified sister vessel, the DANA GLORIA (now with *DFDS LISCO* – see Section 6), on the Esbjerg – Harwich service. She is branded *DFDS Tor Line*.

KING OF SCANDINAVIA Built by Schichau Seebeckwerft AG, Bremerhaven, Germany as the NILS HOLGERSSON for *Rederi AB Swedcarrier* of Sweden for their service between Trelleborg and Travemünde, joint with *TT-Line* of Germany (trading as *TT-Line*). In 1992 purchased by *Brittany Ferries* for entry into service in Spring 1993. After a major rebuild, she was renamed the VAL DE LOIRE and introduced onto the Plymouth - Roscoff, Plymouth - Santander and Cork - Roscoff routes. In 2004 transferred to the Portsmouth - St Malo and Portsmouth – Cherbourg services. In 2005 operated mainly Portsmouth - St Malo. In 2006 sold to *DFDS*, renamed the KING OF SCANDINAVIA and placed on the Newcastle – IJmuiden route.

PRINCESS OF NORWAY Built by Schichau Seebeckwerft AG, Bremerhaven, Germany as the PETER PAN for *TT-Line* for the service between Travemünde and Trelleborg. In 1992 sold to *TT Line* of Australia (no connection) for use on their service between Port Melbourne (Victoria) and Hobart (Tasmania) and renamed the SPIRIT OF TASMANIA. In 2002 sold to *Nordsjøferger K/S* of Norway and renamed the SPIR. After modification work she was, in 2003, renamed the FJORD NORWAY and chartered to *Fjord Line*. Placed on the Bergen - Egersund - Hanstholm route. In 2005 placed on the Bergen - Stavanger - Newcastle route, but operated once a week to Hanstholm. In October 2006 sold to *DFDS* and renamed the PRINCESS OF NORWAY, remaining on the Newcastle - Norway service but no longer serving Hanstholm. In May 2007 moved to the Newcastle - IJmuiden route.

QUEEN OF SCANDINAVIA Built by Oy Wärtsilä Ab, Turku, Finland as the FINLANDIA for *EFFOA* of Finland for *Silja Line* services between Helsinki and Stockholm. In 1990 she was sold to *DFDS*, renamed the QUEEN OF SCANDINAVIA and introduced onto the Copenhagen - Helsingborg - Oslo service. In 2001 transferred to the Newcastle - IJmuiden route. In May 2007 moved to the Newcastle - Norway route.

HD FERRIES

THE COMPANY *HD Ferries* is a Jersey private sector company, part of the *2morrow Group*.

MANAGEMENT Managing Director Chris Howe-Davis, **Marketing Director** Yvie Corkery.

ADDRESS Elizabeth Terminal, La route du Port Elizabeth, St Helier, Jersey JE2 3NW.

TELEPHONE Passenger Reservations & Administration 0844 576 8831, **Freight** 0844 576 8832.

INTERNET Email mail@hdferries.com **Website** www.hdferries.com *(English, French)*

ROUTES OPERATED St Helier (Jersey) - St Malo (France) (1 hr; *1*; 2 per day), St Helier - St Peter Port (Guernsey) (1 hr; *1*; 1 per day).

1	HD1	2357t	98	45.0k	80.1m	383P	100C	-	A	BS	9160114

HD1 Incat 80m K50 catamaran built by *Afai Ships*, Hong Kong for *Incat Afai (HK9, Ltd)*, Nassau, Bahamas as the AFAI 08. Initially laid up in Portland, Dorset. In 1999 sold to *The Cat Ltd* of the Bahamas, renamed the INCAT K3 and chartered to *Bay Ferries*. Operated between Miami (USA), Freeport (Bahamas) and Nassau (Bahamas). After one season she was sold to *Savory Industries* of the Bahamas and laid up until 2002 when she was sold to *Incat Chartering* of The Bahamas. In 2003 chartered to *Caribbean Ferries* and operated between Guadeloupe and Martinique. In 2006 she was chartered to *Acciona Trasmediterránea* and operated between Palma (Mallorca), Ibiza and Alicante. In 2007 sold to *HD Ferries* and renamed the HD1.

IRISH FERRIES

THE COMPANY *Irish Ferries* is an Irish Republic private sector company, part of the *Irish Continental Group*. It was originally mainly owned by the state-owned *Irish Shipping* and partly by *Lion Ferry AB* of Sweden. *Lion Ferry* participation ceased in 1977 and the company was sold into the private sector in 1987. Formerly state owned *B&I Line* was taken over in 1991 and from 1995 all operations were marketed as *Irish Ferries*.

MANAGEMENT Group Managing Director Eamonn Rothwell, **Group Marketing Director** Tony Kelly.

ADDRESS PO Box 19, Ferryport, Dublin 1, Republic of Ireland.

TELEPHONE Administration + 353 (0)1 855 2222, **Reservations Ireland** + 353 (0)818300 400, **Rosslare Harbour** + 353 (0)53 913 3158, **Holyhead** + 44 (0)8705 329129, **Pembroke Dock** + 44 (0)8705 329543, **National** 08705 171717, **24 hour information** + 353 (0)1 661 0715 (Ireland) or 08705 171717 (UK).

FAX Administration & Reservations Dublin + 353 (0)1 819 3942, **Rosslare** + 353 (0)53 913 3544.

INTERNET Email info@irishferries.com **Website** www.irishferries.com *(English, French, German)*

ROUTES OPERATED Conventional Ferries Dublin - Holyhead (3 hrs 15 mins; *5*; 2 per day), Rosslare - Pembroke Dock (3 hrs 45 mins; *1*; 2 per day), Rosslare - Cherbourg (France) (17 hrs 30 mins; *4*; 1 or 2 per week), Rosslare - Roscoff (France) (16 hrs; *4*; 1 or 2 per week). **Fast Ferry** Dublin - Holyhead (1 hr 49 min; *2*; 2 per day) marketed as 'DUBLIN*Swift*'.

1	ISLE OF INISHMORE	34031t	97	21.5k	182.5m	2200P	802C	152T	BA2	CY	9142605
2»	JONATHAN SWIFT	5909t	99	39.5k	86.6m	800P	200C	-	BA	CY	9188881
3	KAITAKI	22365t	95	22k	181.6m	1650P	600C	130T	BA	UK	9107942
4	OSCAR WILDE	31914t	87	23.5k	166.3m	1458P	730C	90T	DA	BS	8506311
5	ULYSSES	50938t	01	22.0k	209.0m	1875P	1342C	300T	BA2	CY	9214991

ISLE OF INISHMORE Built by Van der Giessen-de Noord, Krimpen aan den IJssel, Rotterdam for *Irish Ferries* to operate on the Holyhead - Dublin service. In 2001 replaced by the ULYSSES and moved to the Rosslare - Pembroke Dock route. She also relieves on the Dublin – Holyhead route when the ULYSSES receives her annual overhaul. In 2006 transferred to Cypriot registry.

JONATHAN SWIFT Austal Auto-Express 86 catamaran built at Fremantle, Australia for *Irish Ferries* for the Dublin - Holyhead route. In 2006 transferred to Cypriot registry.

KAITAKI Built by Van der Giessen-de Noord, Krimpen aan den IJssel, Rotterdam as the ISLE OF INNISFREE for *Irish Ferries* to operate on the Holyhead - Dublin route. In 1997 transferred to the Rosslare - Pembroke Dock service; for a short period, before modifications at Pembroke Dock were completed, she operated between Rosslare and Fishguard. In Spring 2001 she was replaced by the ISLE OF INISHMORE and laid up. In July 2002 she was chartered to *P&O Portsmouth* for 5 years and renamed the PRIDE OF CHERBOURG. Entered service in October 2002. Withdrawn in October 2004. In January 2005, chartered to *Stena Line*, renamed the STENA CHALLENGER and operated on the Karlskrona - Gdynia route. In June 2006 chartered to *Toll Shipping* of New Zealand and renamed the CHALLENGER. In August 2006 she arrived in New Zealand and was placed on the Wellington - Picton route. In 2007 renamed the KAITAKI.

OSCAR WILDE Built by Oy Wärtsilä AB, Turku, Finland for *Jahre Line* of Norway as the KRONPRINS HARALD for the Oslo - Kiel service. In 1991 ownership was transferred to *Color Line*. In 2007 sold to *Irish Ferries* for delivery in September 2007. Chartered back to *Color Line* until that date. When delivered, renamed the OSCAR WILDE and in November placed on the Rosslare - Roscoff/Cherbourg routes.

ULYSSES Built by Aker Finnyards, Rauma, Finland for *Irish Ferries* for the Dublin - Holyhead service. In 2006 transferred to Cypriot registry.

Irish Continental Group also owns the PRIDE OF BILBAO, on charter to *P&O Ferries* until 2010.

ISLE OF MAN STEAM PACKET COMPANY

THE COMPANY The *Isle of Man Steam Packet Company Limited* is an Isle of Man-registered company owned by Australian investment and pension funds under the management of *Macquarie Bank Limited* of Australia. It was purchased from *Montagu Private Equity Limited* of the UK in 2005.

MANAGEMENT Chief Executive Officer Mark Woodward.

ADDRESS Imperial Buildings, Douglas, Isle of Man IM1 2BY.

TELEPHONE Administration + 44 (0)1624 645645, **Reservations *From UK*** 0871 222 1333, ***From elsewhere*** + 44 (0)1624 661661, **Freight Bookings** + 44 (0)1624 645620.

FAX Administration + 44 (0)1624 645609.

INTERNET Email res@steam-packet.com **Website** www.steam-packet.com (*English*)

ROUTES OPERATED Conventional Ferries *All year* Douglas (Isle of Man) - Heysham (3 hrs 30 mins; *1*; up to 2 per day), **November-February** Douglas (Isle of Man) - Liverpool (4 hrs 15 mins; *1*; 2 per week), **Fast Ferries (*March-October only*)** Douglas - Liverpool (2 hrs 30 mins; *2,3*; up to 3 per day), Douglas - Belfast (2 hrs 45 mins; *2,3*; up to 3 per week), Douglas - Dublin (2 hrs 45 mins; *2,3*; up to 3 per week), Douglas - Heysham (2 hrs; *2,3*; occasional).

1	**BEN-MY-CHREE**	12504t	98	19.0k	124.9m	630P	-	90T	A	IM	9170705
2»	**SNAEFELL**	3003t	91	37.0k	74.3m	516P	80C	-	BA	UK	8900012
3»	**VIKING**	4662t	97	38.0k	100.0m	694P	140C	-	A	UK	9141845

BEN-MY-CHREE Built by Van der Giessen-de Noord, Krimpen aan den IJssel, Rotterdam for the *IOMSP Co* and operates between Douglas and Heysham. Additional passenger accommodation was added at her Spring 2004 refit. In 2005 passenger certificate was increased from 500 to 630. During Winter 2007/08 operated some sailings between Douglas and Birkenhead; it is likely that she will operate these sailings to Liverpool during Winter 2008/09.

SNAEFELL Incat 74m catamaran built at Hobart, Tasmania, Australia. Built as the HOVERSPEED FRANCE, the second SeaCat. She inaugurated a Dover - Calais/Boulogne service in 1991. In 1992 she was chartered to *Sardinia Express* of Italy and renamed the SARDEGNA EXPRESS; she did not operate on the Channel that year. This charter was terminated at the end of 1992 and in 1993 she was renamed the SEACAT BOULOGNE and operated on the Dover - Calais and Folkestone - Boulogne

Ulysses (*Gordon Hislip*)

Ben-my-Chree (*Miles Cowsill*)

services. In 1994 she was chartered to *IOMSP Co*, renamed the SEACAT ISLE OF MAN and replaced the LADY OF MANN on services between Douglas (Isle of Man) and Britain and Ireland. During Winter 1994/5 she operated for *SeaCat Scotland* between Stranraer and Belfast. She returned to *IOMSP Co* in June 1995. During Spring 1995 she was chartered to *Condor Ferries*; she was then chartered again to *IOMSP Co* and returned to *Sea Containers* in the Autumn. In 1996 she was chartered to *ColorSeaCat KS*, renamed the SEACAT NORGE and inaugurated a new service between Langesund (Norway) and Frederikshavn (Denmark). During Winter 1996/97 she operated between Dover and Calais. In early 1997 she was again renamed the SEACAT ISLE OF MAN. During Summer 1997 she operated for *IOMSP Co*, serving on Liverpool, Dublin and Belfast seasonal services to Douglas (May to September) plus a weekly Liverpool - Dublin service when the LADY OF MANN operated from Fleetwood. In late 1997 she was transferred to the *Hoverspeed* Dover - Calais route and operated on this route throughout 1998. In 1999 she operated between Douglas and Liverpool and Douglas and Dublin for *IOMSP Co*. In 2000, 2001 and 2002 she also operated between Douglas and Belfast and Douglas and Heysham (plus providing some additional sailings between Liverpool and Dublin in 2002). In early 2003 she replaced the SEACAT SCOTLAND on the Belfast – Troon service. Returned to Isle of Man services in March 2003. At the end of the 2004 Summer season laid up. In 2005 chartered to *Irish Sea Express* and renamed the SEA EXPRESS 1. In October 2005 the service ceased and she was laid up. Re-entered service with *IOMSP Co* in Winter 2006 as relief vessel; it was planned that she would operate during 2007 as a second fast ferry with the SUPERSEACAT TWO. However, in February 2007 she was damaged in a collision and laid up for repairs. In December 2007 renamed the SNAEFELL and re-entered service in Spring 2008.

VIKING Fincantieri MDV1200 monohull vessel built at Riva Trigoso, Italy. Built as the SUPERSEACAT TWO for *Sea Containers*. In 1997 operated on the *Hoverspeed* Dover - Calais route. She was withdrawn from this route at the end of 1997 and in March 1998 she inaugurated a Liverpool - Dublin fast ferry service, operated by *IOMSP Co*. In Summer 1999 she operated for *Hoverspeed* between Newhaven and Dieppe. In 2000 she returned to the Irish Sea, operating on the Belfast - Heysham service. In Summer 2001 she operated between Dover and Calais and Dover and Ostend. In 2002 she was laid up for sale or charter. Since 2003 she has been on charter to the *IOMSP Co*. In 2008 renamed the VIKING.

LD LINES

THE COMPANY *LD Lines* is a French private sector company, a subsidiary of *Louis Dreyfus Armateurs*.

MANAGEMENT Managing Director Christophe Santoni, **Marketing Manager** *Passenger* Nadine Corbel, *Freight* Stéphane Boyer.

ADDRESSES HQ 87, Avenue de la Grande Armée, F 75782 Paris, CEDEX 16, **Le Havre** Terminal de la Citadelle, BP 90746, F-76060 Le Havre, **Portsmouth** Continental Ferry Port, Wharf Road, Portsmouth PO2 8QW.

TELEPHONE Administration + 33 (0)1 70 38 60 00.

Reservations UK *Passenger* + 44 (0) 870 428 4335, *Freight* + 44 (0) 870 428 4336, **France** *Passenger* + 33(0)2 35 19 78 78, *Freight* + 33(0)2 35 19 78 77.

FAX Administration + 33 (0)1 70 99 33 76, **Reservations UK** *Passengers* + 44 (0)1235 84 56 08, *Freight* + 44 (0)1235 84 56 08, **France** *Passenger* + 33(0)2 35 19 78 82, *Freight* + 33(0)2 35 19 78 93.

INTERNET Email ferry@ ldlines.com **Website** www.ldlines.com (*English, French*)

ROUTES OPERATED *Until November 2008* Le Havre - Portsmouth (5 hrs 30 mins (day), 7 hrs 30 mins (night); *1*; 1 per day), *From November 2008* Le Havre - Portsmouth (5 hrs 30 mins (day), 7 hrs 30 mins (night); *1,2*; up to 2 per day), Le Havre - Rosslare (20 hrs; *2*; 1 per week), *Summer only* Le Havre - Newhaven (5 hrs; *SEVEN SISTERS* of Transmanche Ferries; 1 per day).

1	NORMAN SPIRIT	28833t	91	21.0k	163.6m	1850P	600C	100L	BA2	UK	8908466

NORMAN SPIRIT Built by NV Boelwerf SA, Temse, Belgium as the PRINS FILIP for *Regie voor Maritiem Transport (RMT)* of Belgium for the Ostend - Dover service. Although completed in 1991, she did not enter service until May 1992. In 1994 the British port became Ramsgate. Withdrawn in 1997 and laid

ISLE OF MAN
STEAM PACKET COMPANY

Get surfing for some

GREAT SAVINGS!

We offer year round sailings across the Irish Sea to both Liverpool and Heysham, as well as seasonal services to Belfast and Dublin.

Steam Packet Holidays can help you enjoy a welcome break with our range of special event weekends and inclusive packages.

We offer a regular and reliable freight service that acts as a lifeline to the people and businesses on the Island.

Belfast
(seasonal)

Isle of Man

Heysham
(year round)

Dublin
(seasonal)

Liverpool
(year round)

ACKET.COM

for the best ferry deals visit STEAM-PACKET.COM
or for the best inclusive packages visit STEAMPACKETHOLIDAYS.COM

up for sale. In 1998 she was sold to *Stena RoRo* and renamed the STENA ROYAL. In November 1998 she was chartered to *P&O Stena Line* to operate as a freight-only vessel on the Dover - Zeebrugge route. In Spring 1999 it was decided to charter the vessel on a long-term basis and she was repainted into *P&O Stena Line* (later *P&O Ferries*) colours and renamed the P&OSL AQUITAINE. In Autumn 1999 she was modified to make her suitable to operate between Dover and Calais and was transferred to that route, becoming a passenger vessel again. In 2002 renamed the PO AQUITAINE and in 2003 the PRIDE OF AQUITAINE. In September 2005 sold to *LD Lines* and, in October, inaugurated a Le Havre - Portsmouth service, replacing that previously operated by *P&O Ferries*. Renamed the NORMAN SPIRIT.

Under Construction

2	**NORMAN VOYAGER**	26500t	08	24.0k	186.5	800P	185C	120L	A	UK	9417919
3	**NEWBUILDING 2**	25000t	10	22.0k	160.0m	1300P	450C	100L	BA2	UK	-

NORMAN VOYAGER Under construction by CN Visentini, Donada, Italy for *Epic Shipping* of the UK and to be chartered to *LD Lines*. To operate between Le Havre and Portsmouth and Le Havre and Rosslare from November 2008.

NEWBUILDING 2 Under construction by Singapore Technologies Marine (ST Marine) for *LD Lines*. An option for a sister ship has been attached to the contract.

NORFOLKLINE

THE COMPANY *Norfolkline* (before 1st January 1999 *Norfolk Line*) is a Dutch private sector company owned by the *A P Møller - Maersk Group* of Denmark. *Norse Merchant Ferries Limited* was taken over in November 2005 and the operations integrated in Spring 2006.

MANAGEMENT Managing Director Thomas Woldbye, **Director Ferry Division** Kell Robdrup.

ADDRESSES *Netherlands* **Scheveningen** Kranenburgweg 180, 2583 ER Scheveningen, The Netherlands.

United Kingdom **Felixstowe** Norfolk House, The Dock, Felixstowe, Suffolk IP11 3UY, **Dover:** Export Freight Plaza, Eastern Dock, Dover, Kent CT16 1JA, **Birkenhead** Twelve Quays Terminal, Tower Road, Birkenhead, Wirral CH41 1FE, **Harwich** Norfolkline Shipping BV, Container Terminal Offices, East Crossing, Harwich International Port, Harwich, Essex, CO12 4SR, **Belfast** Units 1-4 Victoria Business Park, 9 West Bank Road, Belfast, BT3 9JL, *Irish Republic* **Dublin** Alexandra Road Extension, Dublin Port, Dublin 1, Ireland, *Denmark* **Esbjerg** Adgangsvejen 1, 6700, Denmark, *France* **Dunkerque** Terminal Roulier du Port Ouest F-59279, Loon-Plage,Dunkerque.

TELEPHONE Administration *Belfast* +44 (0)28 9077 9090, **Reservations** *Irish Sea Services* **(UK and Northern Ireland)** +44 (0)870 600 4321, **(Ireland)** +353 (0)1 819 2988, *English Channel* 0870 870 1020.

FAX Administration *Belfast* +44 (0)28 9077 1286, **Reservations** *Irish Sea Services* +44 (0)28 9078 6061, **(Heysham Services)** +44 (0)28 9078 6073, *English Channel* +44 (0)1304 218415.

INTERNET Email *Irish Sea Services* irishpax@norfolkline.com, *English Channel* doverpax@norfolkline.com **Website** www.norfolkline.com *(English)*

ROUTES OPERATED Dover - Dunkerque (France) (1 hr 45 mins; *4,5,6*; up to 12 per day), Port of Liverpool (Twelve Quays River Terminal, Birkenhead) - Belfast (8 hrs; *2,7*; 1 per day (Mon), 2 per day (Sun, Tue-Sat)), Port of Liverpool (Twelve Quays River Terminal, Birkenhead) - Dublin (7 hrs; *1,3*; 1 per day (Sun, Mon), 2 per day (Tue-Sat)).

1	**DUBLIN VIKING**	21856t	97	20.0k	186.0m	320P	100C	135T	A	UK	9136022
2	**LAGAN VIKING**	27510t	05	23k	186.46m	980P	160C	135T	A	IT	9329849
3	**LIVERPOOL VIKING**	21856t	96	20.0k	186.0m	320P	100C	135T	A	UK	9136034
4	**MAERSK DELFT**	35923t	06	25.8k	187.0m	780P	200C	120L	BA2	NL	9293088
5	**MAERSK DOVER**	35923t	06	25.8k	187.0m	780P	200C	120L	BA2	NL	9318345
6	**MAERSK DUNKERQUE**	35923t	05	25.8k	187.0m	780P	200C	120L	BA2	NL	9293076

Norman Spirit (*Mike Louagie*)

Lagan Viking (*Miles Cowsill*)

| 7 | MERSEY VIKING | 27510t | 05 | 23k | 186.46m | 980P | 160C | 135T | A | IT | 9329851 |

DUBLIN VIKING Built as the MERSEY VIKING by CN Visentini, Donada, Italy for *Levantina Trasporti* of Italy and chartered to *Norse Irish Ferries*, operating between Liverpool and Belfast. In 1999 the charter was taken over by *Merchant Ferries*. Purchased by *NorseMerchant Ferries* in 2001. In 2002 service transferred to Twelve Quays River Terminal, Birkenhead. In September 2005 renamed the DUBLIN VIKING and in December moved to the Birkenhead – Dublin route.

LAGAN VIKING, MERSEY VIKING Built by CN Visentini for *Levantina Trasporti* of Italy. Chartered to *NorseMerchant Ferries* and placed on the Birkenhead - Belfast route.

LIVERPOOL VIKING Built by CN Visentini, Donada, Italy as the LAGAN VIKING. VIKING for *Levantina Trasporti* of Italy and chartered to *Norse Irish Ferries*, operating between Liverpool and Belfast. In 1999 charter was taken over by *Merchant Ferries*. Purchased by *NorseMerchant Ferries* in 2001. In 2002 service transferred to Twelve Quays River Terminal, Birkenhead. In January 2005 renamed the LIVERPOOL VIKING and in December moved to the Birkenhead – Dublin route. Other details as the DUBLIN VIKING.

MAERSK DELFT, MAERSK DOVER, MAERSK DUNKERQUE Built by Samsung Heavy Industries, Koje (Geoje) Island, South Korea for *Norfolkline* to operate between Dover and Dunkerque.

P&O FERRIES

THE COMPANY *P&O Ferries Holdings Ltd* is a private sector company, a subsidiary of *Dubai World*, owned by the Government of Dubai. In Autumn 2002 *P&O North Sea Ferries*, *P&O Portsmouth* and *P&O Stena Line* (*Stena Line* involvement having ceased) were merged into a single operation. Irish sea operations are operated by *P&O European Ferries (Irish Sea) Ltd*, trading as *P&O Irish Sea*.

MANAGEMENT Chief Executive Officer Helen Deeble, **Fleet and Ports Director** John Garner, **Communications Director** Chris Laming, **Freight Director** Ronald Daelman, **Human Resources Director** Clive Mowatt, **Chief Information Officer (IT)** Andrew Reeves, **Managing Director Irish Sea** Terry Cairns, **Director of Tourist Marketing** Simon Johnson, **Director of On-Board Services** Mike O'Dwyer, **Company Secretary** Susan Kitchin.

ADDRESSES *Head Office and Dover/ Portsmouth Services* Channel House, Channel View Road, Dover, Kent CT17 9TJ, *Hull* King George Dock, Hedon Road, Hull HU9 5QA, *Larne* P&O Irish Sea, Larne Harbour, Larne, Co Antrim BT40 1AW *Rotterdam* Beneluxhaven, Rotterdam (Europoort), Postbus 1123, 3180 Rozenburg, Netherlands, *Zeebrugge* Leopold II Dam 13, Havendam, 8380 Zeebrugge, Belgium.

TELEPHONE Administration UK + 44 (0)1304 863000, **Reservations Passenger UK** 08716 64 64 64, *France* + 33 (0)825 12 01 56, *Belgium* + 32 (0)70 70 77 71, *Netherlands* + 31 (0)20 20 13333, *Spain* + 34 (0)902 02 04 61, *Luxembourg* + 34 (0)20 80 82 94, *Freight (Dover)* + 44 (0)1304 862539.

FAX UK Passenger UK East and South Coast + 44 (0)1304 863464, *West Coast* 44 (0)02828 872195, *Netherlands* + 31 (0)118 1225 5215, *Belgium* + 32 (0)50 54 71 12.

INTERNET Email customer.services@poferries.com **Website** www.poferries.com (*English, French, Dutch, German*) www.poirishsea.com (*English*)

ROUTES OPERATED *P&O Ferries Branded routes* Dover - Calais (1 hr 15 mins - 1 hr 30 mins; *8,9,10,11,13*; up to 25 per day), Hull - Zeebrugge (Belgium) (from 12 hrs 30 mins; *7,15*; 1 per day), Hull - Rotterdam (Beneluxhaven, Europoort) (Netherlands) (from 10 hrs; *12,14*; 1 per day), Portsmouth - Bilbao (Santurzi) (34 hrs 15 mins (UK - Spain), 29 hrs (Spain - UK); *6*; every 3 days), *P&O Irish Sea Branded Routes* **Conventional Ferries** Cairnryan - Larne (1 hr 45 min; *1,2*; 7 per day), Liverpool - Dublin (8 hrs; *4,5*; up to 2 per day), **Fast Ferry** (March–October) Cairnryan - Larne (1 hr; *3*; 1 per day), Troon – Larne (1 hr 49 min; *3*; 2 per day).

1	EUROPEAN CAUSEWAY	20646t	00	23.0k	156.2m	410P	375C	107T	BA2	BS	9208394
2	EUROPEAN HIGHLANDER	21188t	02	23.0k	162.7m	410P	375C	107T	BA2	BS	9244116
3»	EXPRESS	5902t	98	41.0k	91.3m	920P	225C	-	A	BS	9176046
4	NORBANK	17464t	93	22.0k	166.7m	114P	-	150T	A	NL	9056583

dover calais
hull rotterdam / zeebrugge
portsmouth bilbao
teesport rotterdam / zeebrugge
tilbury zeebrugge
larne cairnryan / troon
dublin liverpool
this is my P&O
the UK's largest freight and passenger service
POferries.com
POferriesfreight.com
P&O Ferries
SECTION I – GB & IRELAND PASSENGER OPERATIONS

European Causeway (*Gordon Hislip*)

5	NORBAY	17464t	94	22.0k	166.7m	114P	-	150T	A	BM	9056595
6	PRIDE OF BILBAO	37583t	86	22.0k	177.0m	2553P	600C	77T	BA	UK	8414582
7	PRIDE OF BRUGES	31598t	87	18.5k	179.0m	1000P	850C	166T	A	NL	8503797
8	PRIDE OF BURGUNDY	28138t	93	21.0k	179.7m	1420P	600C	120L	BA2	UK	9015254
9	PRIDE OF CALAIS	26433t	87	22.0k	169.6m	2290P	650C	100L	BA2	UK	8517748
10	PRIDE OF CANTERBURY	30365t	92	21.0k	179.7m	2000P	650C	120L	BA2	UK	9007295
11	PRIDE OF DOVER	26433t	87	22.0k	163.5m	2290P	650C	100L	BA2	UK	8517736
12	PRIDE OF HULL	59925t	01	22.0k	215.1m	1360P	250C	240T	AS	UK	9208629
13	PRIDE OF KENT	30635t	92	21.0k	179.7m	2000P	650C	120L	BA2	UK	9015266
14	PRIDE OF ROTTERDAM	59925t	01	22.0k	215.1m	1360P	250C	240T	AS	NL	9208617
15	PRIDE OF YORK	31785t	87	18.5k	179.0m	1000P	850C	166T	A	UK	8501957

EUROPEAN CAUSEWAY Built by Mitsubishi Heavy Industries, Shimonoeki, Japan for *P&O Irish Sea* for the Cairnryan - Larne service.

EUROPEAN HIGHLANDER Built by Mitsubishi Heavy Industries, Shimonoeki, Japan for *P&O Irish Sea* for the Cairnryan - Larne service.

EXPRESS Incat 91m catamaran built at Hobart, Tasmania, Australia for *Buquebus* of Argentina as the CATALONIA I and used by *Buquebus España* on their service between Barcelona (Spain) and Mallorca. In April 2000 chartered to *P&O Portsmouth* and renamed the PORTSMOUTH EXPRESS. During Winter 2000/01 she operated for *Buquebus* between Buenos Aires (Argentina) and Piriapolis (Uruguay) and was renamed the CATALONIA. Returned to *P&O Portsmouth* in Spring 2001 and was renamed the PORTSMOUTH EXPRESS. Returned to *Buquebus* in Autumn 2001 and then returned to *P&O Portsmouth* in Spring 2002. Laid up in Europe during Winter 2002/03 and renamed the CATALONIA. She returned to *P&O Ferries* in Spring 2003 trading under the marketing name 'Express'. In November she was renamed the EXPRESS. In 2004 she operated as the 'Cherbourg Express'. In 2005 transferred to *P&O Irish Sea* and operated on the Larne - Cairnryan/Troon service. Additionally she is chartered to the *Isle of Man Steam Packet* to operate some Larne - Douglas sailings during the TT motor cycle races period.

NORBANK Built by Van der Giessen-de Noord, Krimpen aan den IJssel, Rotterdam, The Netherlands for *North Sea Ferries* for the Hull - Rotterdam service. She was originally built for and chartered to *Nedlloyd* but the charter was taken over by *P&O* in 1996 and she was bought by *P&O* in 2003. She retains Dutch crew and registry. In May 2001 moved to the Felixstowe - Europoort route. In January 2002 transferred to *P&O Irish Sea* and operated on the Liverpool – Dublin route.

NORBAY Built by Van der Giessen-de Noord, Krimpen aan den IJssel, Rotterdam, The Netherlands for *North Sea Ferries* for the Hull - Rotterdam service. Owned by *P&O*. In January 2002 transferred to *P&O Irish Sea* and operated on the Liverpool – Dublin route.

PRIDE OF BILBAO Built by Oy Wärtsilä Ab, Turku, Finland as the OLYMPIA for *Rederi AB Slite* of Sweden for *Viking Line* service between Stockholm and Helsinki. In 1993 she was chartered to *P&O European Ferries* to inaugurate a new service between Portsmouth and Bilbao. During the Summer period she also operated, at weekends, a round trip between Portsmouth and Cherbourg. In 1994 she was purchased by the *Irish Continental Group* and re-registered in the Bahamas. *P&O* have since entered her into the British bareboat register. In 2002 her charter was extended for a further five years and again for a further three years from October 2007. The Cherbourg service ended at the end of 2004.

PRIDE OF BRUGES Built as the NORSUN by NKK, Tsurumi, Japan for the Hull - Rotterdam service of *North Sea Ferries*. She was owned by *Nedlloyd* and was sold to *P&O* in 1996 but retains Dutch crew and registry. In May 2001 replaced by the PRIDE OF ROTTERDAM and in July 2001, after a major refurbishment, she was transferred to the Hull - Zeebrugge service, replacing the NORSTAR (26919t, 1974). In 2003 renamed the PRIDE OF BRUGES.

PRIDE OF BURGUNDY Built by Schichau Seebeckwerft AG, Bremerhaven, Germany for *P&O European Ferries* for the Dover - Calais service. When construction started she was due to be a sister vessel to the EUROPEAN HIGHWAY, EUROPEAN PATHWAY and EUROPEAN SEAWAY (see Section 3) called

P&O
drive to freedom
With 3 convenient routes
Troon - Larne
Cairnryan - Larne
Liverpool - Dublin
For more information
log on to our website
or call 0871 66 44 777
Troon
Cairnryan
Larne
Dublin
Liverpool
EXPRESS
P&O
POirishsea.com
P&O
Irish Sea
www.poirishsea.com

the EUROPEAN CAUSEWAY and operate on the Zeebrugge freight route. However, it was decided that she should be completed as a passenger/freight vessel (the design allowed for conversion) and she was launched as the PRIDE OF BURGUNDY. In 1998, transferred to *P&O Stena Line* and renamed the P&OSL BURGUNDY. In 2002 renamed the PO BURGUNDY and in 2003 renamed the PRIDE OF BURGUNDY. In 2004 she operated mainly in freight-only mode. In 2005 returned to full passenger service.

PRIDE OF CALAIS Built by Schichau Seebeckwerft AG, Bremerhaven, Germany for *European Ferries* as the PRIDE OF CALAIS for the Dover - Calais service. In 1998 transferred to *P&O Stena Line*. In 1999 renamed the P&OSL CALAIS. In 2003 renamed PO CALAIS and in 2003 renamed the PRIDE OF CALAIS.

PRIDE OF CANTERBURY Built by Schichau Seebeckwerft AG, Bremerhaven, Germany for *P&O European Ferries* as the EUROPEAN PATHWAY for the Dover - Zeebrugge freight service. (Sister vessel EUROPEAN SEAWAY is shown in Section 3). In 1998 transferred to *P&O Stena Line*. In 2001 car/foot passengers were again conveyed on the route. In 2002/03 rebuilt as a full passenger vessel and renamed the PRIDE OF CANTERBURY; now operates between Dover and Calais.

PRIDE OF DOVER Built by Schichau Seebeckwerft AG, Bremerhaven, Germany for *European Ferries* as the PRIDE OF DOVER for the Dover - Calais service. In 1998 transferred to *P&O Stena Line*. In 1999 renamed the P&OSL DOVER. In 2002 renamed PO DOVER and in 2003 renamed the PRIDE OF DOVER.

PRIDE OF HULL Built by Fincantieri-Cantieri Nav Italiani SpA, Venice, Italy for *P&O North Sea Ferries* to replace (with the PRIDE OF ROTTERDAM) the NORSEA and NORSUN plus the freight vessels NORBAY and NORBANK on the Hull - Rotterdam service.

PRIDE OF KENT Built by Schichau Seebeckwerft AG, Bremerhaven, Germany for *P&O European Ferries* as the EUROPEAN HIGHWAY for the Dover - Zeebrugge freight service. In 1998 transferred to *P&O Stena Line*. In Summer 1999 she operated full-time between Dover and Calais. She returned to the Dover - Zeebrugge route in the Autumn when the P&OSL AQUITAINE was transferred to the Dover - Calais service. In 2001 car/foot passengers were again conveyed on the route. In 2002/03 rebuilt as a full passenger vessel and renamed the PRIDE OF KENT; now operates between Dover and Calais.

PRIDE OF ROTTERDAM Built by Fincantieri-Cantieri Nav Italiani SpA, Venice, Italy. Keel laid as the PRIDE OF HULL but launched as the PRIDE OF ROTTERDAM. Owned by Dutch interests until 2006 when she was sold to *P&O Ferries*. Further details as the PRIDE OF HULL.

PRIDE OF YORK Built as the NORSEA by Govan Shipbuilders Ltd, Glasgow, UK for the Hull - Rotterdam service of *North Sea Ferries* (jointly owned by *P&O* and *The Royal Nedlloyd Group* of The Netherlands until 1996). In December 2001 she was replaced by the new PRIDE OF HULL and, after a two-month refurbishment, in 2002 transferred to the Hull - Zeebrugge service, replacing the NORLAND (26290t, 1974). In 2003 renamed the PRIDE OF YORK.

SEAFRANCE

THE COMPANY *SeaFrance SA* (previously *SNAT (Société Nouvelle Armement Transmanche)*) is a French state-owned company. It was originally jointly owned by *Société Nationale des Chemins de fer Français (French Railways)* and *Compagnie Générale Maritime Français (French National Shipping Company)*. SNAT was established in 1990 to take over the services of *SNCF Armement Naval*, a wholly-owned division of *SNCF*. At the same time a similarly constituted body called *Société Proprietaire Navires (SPN)* was established to take over ownership of the vessels; *Sealink British Ferries* (and later *Stena Line Ltd*) also had involvement in this company. Joint operation of services with *Stena Line* ceased at the end of 1995 and *SeaFrance SA* was formed. *Stena Line* involvement in *SPN* ended in 1999. In 2000, *SeaFrance* became 100% owned by *SNCF (French Railways)*. At the same time, *SeaFrance* absorbed *SPN* and took over the ownership of its vessels.

MANAGEMENT Président du Directoire Eudes Riblier, **Directeur SeaFrance Calais** Gérard Jachet, **Managing Director (UK)** Robin Wilkins.

ADDRESS *France* 1 Avenue de Flandre, 75019 Paris, France, **UK** Whitfield Court, Honeywood Close, Whitfield, Dover, Kent CT16 3PX.

TELEPHONE Administration *France* +33 1 53 35 11 00, **UK** +44 (0)871 222 5888, **Reservations** *France* +33 3 21 17 70 20, **UK (Passenger)** 0871 22 22 500 (from UK only), **UK (Freight)** +44 (0)871 282 8518.

FAX Administration *France* +33 1 53 35 11 76, **UK** +44 (0)8700 664775.

INTERNET Email *France* sfadmin@seafrance.fr **UK** admin@seafrance.fr

Website www.seafrance.com *(English, French)*

ROUTE OPERATED Calais - Dover (1 hr 15 mins - 1 hr 30 mins; *1,2,3,4,5*; up to 30 per day).

1	SEAFRANCE BERLIOZ	33940t	05	25.0k	186.0m	1900P	700C	120L	BA2	FR	9305843
2	SEAFRANCE CEZANNE	25122t	80	18.0k	163.5m	1800P	480C	65L	BA2	FR	7806099
3•	SEAFRANCE MANET	15093t	84	18.0k	134.0m	1650P	280C	50L	BA2	FR	8208763
4	SEAFRANCE RENOIR	15612t	81	18.0k	133.0m	1650P	280C	45L	BA2	FR	7920534
5	SEAFRANCE RODIN	33796t	01	25.0k	186.0m	1900P	700C	120L	BA2	FR	9232527

SEAFRANCE BERLIOZ Built by Chantiers de l'Atlantique, St Nazaire for *SeaFrance*.

SEAFRANCE CEZANNE Built by Kockums Varv AB, Malmö, Sweden as the ARIADNE for *Rederi AB Nordö* of Sweden. Renamed the SOCA before entering service on *UMEF* freight services (but with capacity for 175 drivers) in the Mediterranean. In 1981 she was sold to *SO Mejdunaroden Automobilen Transport (SOMAT)* of Bulgaria and renamed the TRAPEZITZA. She operated on *Medlink* services between Bulgaria and the Middle East. In 1988 she was acquired by *Sealink British Ferries*, re-registered in the Bahamas and in 1989 renamed the FANTASIA. Later in 1989 she was modified in Bremerhaven, renamed the CHANNEL SEAWAY and, in May, she inaugurated a new freight-only service between Dover (Eastern Docks) and Calais. During Winter 1989/90 she was modified in Bremerhaven to convert her for passenger service. In Spring 1990 she was renamed the FIESTA, transferred to *SNAT*, re-registered in France and replaced the CHAMPS ELYSEES (now the SEAFRANCE MANET) on the Dover - Calais service. In 1996 she was renamed the SEAFRANCE CEZANNE.

SEAFRANCE MANET Built by Chantiers Dubigeon SA, Nantes, France for *SNCF* as the CHAMPS ELYSEES to operate Calais - Dover and Boulogne - Dover services, later operating Calais - Dover only. In 1990 transferred to the Dieppe - Newhaven service. Chartered to *Stena Sealink Line* in June 1992 when they took over the operation of the service. She was renamed the STENA PARISIEN and carried a French crew. In 1997 the charter was terminated; she returned to *SeaFrance* and was renamed the SEAFRANCE MANET. In recent years used mainly in freight-only mode. At the end of April 2008 laid up for sale.

SEAFRANCE RENOIR Built by Ateliers et Chantiers du Havre, Le Havre, France for *SNCF* as the COTE D'AZUR for the Dover - Calais service. She also operated Boulogne - Dover in 1985. In 1996 she was renamed the SEAFRANCE RENOIR. Following the delivery of the SEAFRANCE RODIN she became the reserve vessel. During Summer 2002 she operated her own roster at peak periods with reduced passenger facilities. During Summer 2003 she operated a full roster to enable 20 passenger sailings per day to operate. This happened again in Summer 2004. In 2005 operated a full roster. In 2006 she shared a roster with the SEAFRANCE CEZANNE and this was repeated in 2007. To be laid up for sale when the SEAFRANCE MOLIERE enters service.

SEAFRANCE RODIN Built by Aker Finnyards, Rauma, Finland for *SeaFrance*.

Undergoing Rebuild

6	SEAFRANCE MOLIERE	30285t	02	27.9k	203.3m	1200P	660C	110L	BA2	FR	9211511

SEAFRANCE MOLIERE Built by Howaldtswerke Deutsche Werft AG, Kiel, Germany as SUPERFAST X for *Attica Enterprises* (now *Attica Group*) for use by *Superfast Ferries*. In May 2002 she and the SUPERFAST IX (see *Tallink*, Section 6) began operating between Rosyth and Zeebrugge. In 2004 fitted with additional cabins and conference/seating areas. In 2007 sold to *Veolia Transportation* and renamed the JEAN NICOLI. Chartered to *Cotunav* of Tunisia and operated between France/Italy and Tunisia. Later chartered to *ANEK Lines* of Greece and operated on the Patras Korfu - Igoumenitsa -

Venedig route. In 2008 sold to *SeaFrance* and renamed the SEAFRANCE MOLIERE. After modifications she will be placed on the Dover - Calais route in Summer 2008

SMYRIL LINE

THE COMPANY *Smyril Line* is a Faroe Islands company.

MANAGEMENT Managing Director Thomas Magnussen, **Financial Manager** Joannes A Vali.

ADDRESS Jonas Bronksgöta 37, PO Box 370, FO-100 Tórshavn, Faroe Islands.

TELEPHONE Administration +298-345900, **Reservations** *Faroe Islands* +298-345900, *UK* +44 (0)1595 690845 (Smyril Line Shetland).

FAX *Smyril Line* +298-343950.

INTERNET Email office@smyril-line.fo **Website** www.smyril-line.com *(English)*

ROUTES OPERATED Tórshavn (Faroes) - Hanstholm (Denmark) (31 hrs; *1*; 1 per week), Tórshavn - Scrabster (Scotland) (40 hrs; *1*; 1 per week) - Bergen (Norway) (via Lerwick) (24 hrs - 27 hrs 30 mins; *1*; 1 per week), Tórshavn - Seydisfjordur (Iceland) (15 hrs - 18 hrs; *1*; 1 per week).

1	NORRÖNA	35966t	03	21.0k	164.0m	1482P	800C	134T	BA	FA	9227390

NORRÖNA Built by Flender Werft, Lübeck, Germany for *Smyril Line*, to replace the existing NORRÖNA. Originally due to enter service in Summer 2002, start of building was delayed by financing difficulties. Originally to have been built at Flensburger Schiffbau-Gesellschaft, Flensburg, Germany but delays led to change of shipyard.

SPEEDFERRIES

THE COMPANY *SpeedFerries Ltd* is a UK company wholly owned by *SpeedFerries A/S* of Denmark.

MANAGEMENT Managing Director Curt Stavis, **Marketing & Communications** Marianne Illum, **Commercial Director** Annemette Stavis, **General Manager, UK & France Operations** Nick Dunn, **Commercial Manager** Nick Standing.

ADDRESS Hoverport, Western Docks, Dover, Kent CT17 9TG.

TELEPHONE Main Office +44 (0)1304 202420, **Reservations** *UK* 0871 222 7456, *Elsewhere* +44 (0)8702 200 570.

FAX +44 (0)1304 240280.

INTERNET Email customer service@speedferries.com **Website** www.speedferries.com *(English, French)*

ROUTE OPERATED Dover – Boulogne (50 mins; *1*; up to 5 per day).

1»	SPEED ONE	5007t	97	40.0k	86.1m	870P	200C	-	A	UK	9161560

SPEED ONE Incat 86m catamaran built at Hobart, Tasmania, Australia as the INCAT 045. Chartered to *Transport Tasmania* of Australia and operated between Melbourne (Victoria) and Devonport (Tasmania). In 1999 she was chartered to the *Royal Australian Navy*, renamed the HMAS JERVIS BAY and took part in moving Australian troops from Darwin to Dili (East Timor) as part of the United Nations operation. She operated over 73 trips between the two points carrying personnel and equipment for the United Nations Transitional Administration in East Timor (UNTAET). The charter ended in May 2001 and she was renamed the INCAT 045 and laid up. In Spring 2003 she was chartered to *Tirughetti Isole Sarde* (TRIS) of Italy, renamed the WINNER and operated between Genoa and Palau (Sardinia). In Autumn 2003 the charter ended, she resumed the name INCAT 045 and was laid up at Portland, Dorset. In 2004 chartered to *SpeedFerries* and renamed the SPEED ONE. In 2008 purchased by *SpeedFerries*.

STENA LINE

THE COMPANY *Stena Line Limited* is incorporated in Great Britain and registered in England and Wales. *Stena Line BV* is a Dutch company. The ultimate parent undertaking is *Stena AB* of Sweden.

MANAGEMENT Area Director, North Sea Pim de Lange, **Area Director, Irish Sea** Michael McGrath, **Sales Manager UK and Ireland** Dermot Cairns.

ADDRESS *UK* 1 Suffolk Way, Sevenoaks, Kent TN13 1YL, ***Netherlands*** PO Box 2, 3150 AA, Hook of Holland, Netherlands.

TELEPHONE Administration *UK* +44 (0)1732 585858, ***Netherlands*** +31 (0)174 389333, **Reservations *UK*** 08075 707070 (from UK only), ***Netherlands*** +31 (0)174 315811.

FAX Administration & Reservations *UK* +44 (0)1407 606811, ***Netherlands*** +31 (0)174 387045, **Telex** 31272.

INTERNET Email info@stenaline.com **Website** www.stenaline.com (*English, Danish, Dutch, German, Norwegian, Polish, Swedish*)

ROUTES OPERATED Conventional Ferries Stranraer - Belfast (3 hrs 15 mins; *3*; 2/3 per day (passengers carried on some sailings)), Holyhead - Dublin (3 hrs 15 mins; *1*; 2 per day), Fishguard - Rosslare (3 hrs 30 mins; *4*; 2 per day), Harwich - Hook of Holland (Netherlands) (7 hrs 30 mins; *2,6*; 2 per day), **Ro-pax Ferries** Fleetwood - Larne (7 hrs; *7,9,10*; 3 per day) (car passengers only conveyed - no foot passengers). **Fast Ferries** Stranraer - Belfast (1 hr 45 mins; *11*; up to 4 per day), Holyhead - Dún Laoghaire (1 hr 39 mins; *5*; up to 4 per day), Fishguard - Rosslare (Summer only) (1 hr 50 mins; *8*; up to 2 per day).

1	**STENA ADVENTURER**	43532t	03	22.0k	210.8m	1500P	-	250T	BA2	UK	9235529
2	**STENA BRITANNICA**	55050t	02	22.0k	240.8m	900P	-	264L	BA	UK	9235517
3	**STENA CALEDONIA**	12619t	81	19.5k	129.6m	1000P	280C	56L	BA2	UK	7910917
4	**STENA EUROPE**	24828t	81	19.0k	149.0m	2076P	456C	60T	BA	UK	7901760
5»	**STENA EXPLORER**	19638t	96	40.0k	126.6m	1500P	375C	50L	A	UK	9080194
6	**STENA HOLLANDICA**	44372t	01	22.0k	238.3m	900P	-	264L	BA	NL	9145176
7	**STENA LEADER**	12879t	75	17.0k	157.2m	50P	-	114T	A	BM	7361582
8»	**STENA LYNX III**	4113t	96	35.0k	81.1m	620P	181C	-	A	BS	9129328
9	**STENA PIONEER**	14426t	75	17.7k	141.8m	76P	-	114T	A	BM	7361570
10	**STENA SEAFARER**	10957t	75	18.0k	141.8m	50P	-	80T	A	BM	7361594
11»	**STENA VOYAGER**	19638t	96	40.0k	126.6m	1500P	375C	50L	A	UK	9080209

STENA ADVENTURER Ro-pax vessel built by Hyundai Heavy Industries, Ulsan, South Korea, for *Stena RoRo* and chartered to *Stena Line* to operate between Holyhead and Dublin.

STENA BRITANNICA Ro-pax vessel built by Hyundai Heavy Industries, Ulsan, South Korea, for *Stena RoRo*. Launched and delivered as the STENA BRITANNICA II. Chartered to *Stena Line* for use on the Hook of Holland - Harwich service, replacing the 2000-built STENA BRITANNICA, now the FINNFELLOW of *FinnLink*. A month after delivery renamed the STENA BRITANNICA. In 2007 lengthened at Lloyd Werft, Bremerhaven.

STENA CALEDONIA Built by Harland & Wolff Ltd, Belfast, UK for *Sealink* as the ST DAVID for the Holyhead - Dún Laoghaire and Fishguard - Rosslare services. It was originally planned that she would replace the chartered STENA NORMANDICA (5607t, 1975) but it was subsequently decided that an additional large vessel was required for the Irish Sea routes. Until 1985 her normal use was, therefore, to substitute for other Irish Sea vessels as necessary (including the Stranraer - Larne route) and also to operate additional summer services on the Holyhead - Dún Laoghaire route. During the Spring of 1983 she operated on the Dover - Calais service. From March 1985 she operated between Dover and Ostend, a service which ceased in December 1985 with the decision of *RMT* to link up with *Townsend Thoresen*. During the early part of 1986 she operated between Dover and Calais and then moved to the Stranraer - Larne route (later Stranraer – Belfast) where she became a regular vessel. In 1990 she was renamed the STENA CALEDONIA. In September 1996 she became mainly a freight-only vessel but passengers were carried on certain sailings and when the STENA VOYAGER was

Speed One (*John Bryant*)

SeaFrance Renoir (*Mike Louagie*)

unavailable; cars and passengers are now conveyed on most sailings.

STENA EUROPE Built by Götaverken Arendal AB, Gothenburg, Sweden as the KRONPRINSESSAN VICTORIA for *Göteborg-Frederikshavn Linjen* of Sweden (trading as *Sessan Linjen*) for their Gothenburg - Frederikshavn service. Shortly after delivery, the company was taken over by *Stena Line* and services were marketed as *Stena-Sessan Line* for a period. In 1982 she was converted to an overnight ferry by changing one vehicle deck into two additional decks of cabins and she was switched to the Gothenburg - Kiel route (with, during the summer, daytime runs from Gothenburg to Frederikshavn and Kiel to Korsør (Denmark)). In 1989 she was transferred to the Oslo - Frederikshavn route and renamed the STENA SAGA. In 1994, transferred to *Stena Line BV*, renamed the STENA EUROPE and operated between Hook of Holland and Harwich. She was withdrawn in June 1997, transferred to the *Lion Ferry* (a *Stena Line* subsidiary) Karlskrona - Gdynia service and renamed the LION EUROPE. In 1998 she was transferred back to *Stena Line* (remaining on the same route) and renamed the STENA EUROPE. In early 2002 the cabins installed in 1982 were removed and other modifications made and she was transferred to the Fishguard - Rosslare route.

STENA EXPLORER Finnyards HSS1500 built at Rauma, Finland for *Stena RoRo* and chartered to *Stena Line*. Operates on the Holyhead - Dún Laoghaire route.

STENA HOLLANDICA Ro-pax ferry built by Astilleros Españoles, Cadiz, Spain for *Stena RoRo* and chartered to *Stena Line BV* to operate between Hook of Holland and Harwich. In 2007 lengthened by 50m at Lloyd Werft, Bremerhaven. Passenger capacity increased to 900.

STENA LEADER Built by J J Sietas KG Schiffswerke, Hamburg, Germany for *Stena AB* as the BUFFALO and due to be chartered to *P&O* for *Pandoro* Irish Sea services. Before completion she was purchased by *P&O*. In 1989 she was lengthened by 12.5m and in 1998 she was further lengthened by 15m and renamed the EUROPEAN LEADER. In 2004 sold to *Stena Line* and renamed the STENA LEADER. Used on the Fleetwood - Larne service.

STENA LYNX III Incat 81m catamaran built at Hobart, Tasmania, Australia. Chartered new by *American Fast Ferries* of Argentina to *Stena Line* in June 1996 and named the STENA LYNX III. Initially used on the Dover - Calais service. From Summer 1997 until Autumn 1998 she operated between Newhaven and Dieppe. In March 1998 she was transferred to *P&O Stena Line* and renamed the ELITE. She was then renamed the P&O STENA ELITE (although only carrying the name ELITE on the bow). In late 1998 she was transferred back to *Stena Line* and renamed the STENA LYNX III. In 1999 she was placed on the Fishguard - Rosslare service, replacing the STENA LYNX (3231t, 1993). The charter ended in Autumn 2000 but was immediately renewed as a summer-only operation (with winter lay-up). The charter ended again in Autumn 2003 and she resumed the name ELITE. Later in 2003 purchased by *Stena Ropax*. In 2004 renamed the STENA LYNX III and resumed service on the Fishguard – Rosslare route, marketed as the 'Stena Express'.

STENA PIONEER Built by J J Sietas KG Schiffswerke, Hamburg, Germany for *Stena AB* as the BISON and due to be chartered to *P&O* for *Pandoro* Irish Sea services. Before completion she was purchased by *P&O*. Between 1989 and 1993 she was operated by *B&I Line* of Ireland on a joint service with *Pandoro* between Dublin and Liverpool. An additional deck was added in 1995. In late 1997 she was renamed the EUROPEAN PIONEER. In 2004 sold to *Stena Line* and renamed the STENA PIONEER. Used on the Fleetwood - Larne service.

STENA SEAFARER Built by J J Sietas KG Schiffswerke, Hamburg, Germany. Ordered by *Stena AB* as the UNION TRADER but completed as the UNION MELBOURNE for *Northern Coasters Ltd* of the UK and lengthened before entering service. Chartered to the *Union Steamship Company* of New Zealand and used on services to Australia. In 1980 she was sold to another *P&O* subsidiary and renamed the PUMA. In early 1998 she was renamed the EUROPEAN SEAFARER. Used on the Fleetwood - Larne service in subsequent years, in 2001 she was transferred to the Rosslare - Cherbourg service. In 2002 replaced by the EUROPEAN DIPLOMAT and returned to the Fleetwood - Larne service. In 2004 sold to *Stena Line* and renamed the STENA SEAFARER.

STENA VOYAGER Finnyards HSS1500 built at Rauma, Finland for *Stena RoRo* and chartered to *Stena Line*. Operates on the Stranraer - Belfast route.

Stena Britannica *(Mike Louagie)*

Blue Star 1 *(Miles Cowsill)*

Under Construction

12	NEWBUILDING 1	63600t	10	22.0k	240.0m	1200P	-	400T	BA2	-	-
13	NEWBUILDING 2	63600t	10	22.0k	240.0m	1200P	-	400T	BA2	-	-

NEWBUILDING 1, NEWBUILDING 2 Under construction by Aker Yards, in Wismar and Warnemünde, Germany, for *Stena Rederi*. To replace the existing vessels on the Harwich - Hook of Holland service. The existing vessels are likely to move to the Karlskrona - Gdynia route.

SUPERFAST FERRIES

THE COMPANY *Superfast Ferries* is a Greek car-passenger ferry operator, owned by the *Attica Group*.

MANAGEMENT Managing Director Petros Vettas, **Corporate Relations and Development Director/Director North Sea** Yannis Criticos.

ADDRESS *Greece* 157 C Karamanli Avenue, Voula 16673, Greece, ***Scotland*** Attica Premium S.A., The Terminal Building, Port of Rosyth, Fife KY11 2XP, ***Belgium*** ZSB, The Terminal Building, Doverlaan 7 BUS 9, 8380 Zeebrugge, Belgium.

TELEPHONE Administration *Greece & North Sea* + 30 210 89 19 500, **Reservations *Scotland*** + 44 (0)1383 608003, ***Belgium*** + 32 (0)50 252 252.

FAX Administration *Greece & North Sea* + 30 210 89 19 509.

INTERNET Email criticos@attica-group.com **Website** www.superfast.com (*English, Dutch, French, German*)

ROUTE OPERATED Rosyth (Scotland) - Zeebrugge (Belgium) (17 hrs 30 mins; *1*; 3 per week).

1	BLUE STAR 1	29858t	00	28.0k	176.1m	900P	640C	100L	BA	GR	9197105

BLUE STAR 1 One of two vessels built by Van der Giessen-de Noord at Krimpen aan den IJssel, Netherlands for *Strintzis Lines* (a company today called Blue Star Ferries and controlled by the *Attica Group* which owns 48.8% with the rest floated on the Athens Exchange) and initially used on a service between Ancona, Brindisi and Patras. The direct route from Ancona to Patras was later recognised as a more profitable use of the ships and the southern Italian port is no longer served. In Summer 2002 they were replaced by new vessels from the *Superfast* fleet and she was placed on a new Piraeus - Rhodes service. In 2005 she transferred to the Patras – Bari route. In 2007 she was transferred to the Zeebrugge-Rosyth route operating in a code-share service with *Superfast Ferries* replacing SUPERFAST X which operated the Zeebrugge – Rosyth service until then.

TRANSEUROPA FERRIES

THE COMPANY *TransEuropa Ferries NV* is a Belgian subsidiary of *TransEuropa Shipping Lines*, a Slovenian private sector company. Channel operations started in 1997, in conjunction with *Sally Ferries*, replacing them on November 1998. Passenger operations started in 2004. The company traded as *TransEuropa Shipping Lines (TSL)* until 2000. Note that all the current owning companies listed here are associated companies of *TSL*.

MANAGEMENT *TransEuropa Shipping* Managing Director Stergulc Rihard, ***TransEuropa Ferries NV*, General Manager Belgium & UK** Mr Dominique Penel, **Sales Manager, Europe** Peter Sys.

ADDRESS *TSL Slovenia* Vojkovo nabrezje 38, 6000 Koper, Slovenia, ***TEF UK*** Ferry Terminal, Ramsgate New Port, RAMSGATE, Kent CT11 8RP ***TEF Belgium*** Slijkensesteenweg 2, 8400 Ostend, Belgium.

TELEPHONE Admin *TSL Slovenia* + 386 (0)5 664 17 77, ***TEF UK*** + 44 (0)1843 853833, **Reservations *TEF Belgium*** + 32 (0)59 34 02 60, ***TEF UK*** + 44 (0)1843 595522.

FAX *TSL Slovenia* + 386 (0)5 639 50 36, ***TEF UK*** + 44 (0)1843 594663, ***TEF Belgium*** + 32 (0)59 34 02 61.

INTERNET Website www.transeuropaferries.com (*English*)

ROUTE OPERATED Ramsgate - Ostend (Belgium) (4 hrs; *1,2,3,4*; up to 4 per day).

1	EUROVOYAGER	12110t	78	22.0k	118.4m	1250P	348C	45L	BA2	CY	7613882
2	LARKSPUR	14458t	76	17.5k	143.8m	1150P	314C	55L	BA2	BS	7500451
3	OLEANDER	13728t	80	23.0k	132.5m	1326P	350C	44L	BA2	CY	7820497
4	PRIMROSE	12046t	75	22.0k	118.4m	1250P	348C	45L	BA2	CY	7357567

EUROVOYAGER Built by NV Cockerill Yards, Hoboken, Belgium as the PRINS ALBERT for *RMT* of Belgium for the Ostend - Dover service. During 1986 she had an additional vehicle deck added. In 1994 the British port became Ramsgate. Withdrawn after 28th February 1997 and laid up. In 1998 she was sold to *Hawthorn Shipping Co Ltd* and renamed the EUROVOYAGER. In July, she was chartered to *Sally Freight*. In November the *Sally Freight* service ended and she immediately began operating for *TSL* with no break in service. From 2004 began operating in passenger mode when the LARKSPUR, OLEANDER or PRIMROSE were unavailable.

LARKSPUR Built by Schichau-Unterweser AG, Bremerhaven, Germany as the GEDSER for *Gedser-Travemünde Ruten* of Denmark for their service between Gedser (Denmark) and Travemünde (Germany). In 1986 she was purchased by *Thorsviks Rederi A/S* of Norway and chartered to *Sally Ferries*, re-registered in the Bahamas, renamed the VIKING 2 and entered service on the Ramsgate - Dunkerque service. In early 1989 she was renamed the SALLY SKY and during Winter 1989/90 she was 'stretched' to increase vehicle capacity. At the end of 1996 she was withdrawn from the Dunkerque service. In 1997 she was renamed the EUROTRAVELLER, transferred to *Holyman-Sally Ferries* and, in March, was introduced onto the Ramsgate - Ostend route. In 1998, when *Holyman-Sally Ferries* came to an end, she operated in a freight-only role for *Sally Line* under the *Sally Freight* name. Passenger services were resumed in May, under the name of *Sally Direct*. All *Sally Line* operations ended in November 1998 and she was withdrawn for sale and laid up. In 1999 sold to *Forsythia Maritime Co Ltd* and renamed the LARKSPUR. She was given a major refit at Dunkerque, including the provision of 60 drivers' cabins with private facilities. She entered service with *TEF* in August 2000. Passengers were conveyed from July 2004.

OLEANDER Built by Schichau-Unterweser AG, Bremerhaven, Germany for *European Ferries (Townsend Thoresen)* as the PRIDE OF FREE ENTERPRISE for the Dover - Calais service, also operating on the Dover - Zeebrugge service during the winter. In 1988 she was renamed the PRIDE OF BRUGES and, following the delivery of the new PRIDE OF CALAIS, she was transferred all year to the Dover - Zeebrugge service. In 1992, after the closure of that route to passengers, she returned to the Dover - Calais route. Plans to operate her in a freight-only mode in 1997 were changed and she ran as a full passenger vessel. In 1998, transferred to *P&O Stena Line*; plans to transfer her to the Newhaven - Dieppe route were dropped and she remained at Dover. In 1999 renamed the P&OSL PICARDY. In early 2000 she was laid up for sale in Dunkerque. In 2001 she was sold to *Seaborne Navigation Co Ltd* and renamed the OLEANDER. Entered service with *TEF* in July 2002 after major renovation work in Dunkerque, including the provision of 60 drivers' cabins with private facilities. Passengers were conveyed from July 2004.

PRIMROSE Built by NV Cockerill Yards Hoboken, Hoboken, Belgium as the PRINCESSE MARIE-CHRISTINE for *Regie voor Maritiem Transport* of Belgium for the Ostend - Dover service. During 1985 she had an extra vehicle deck added, increasing vehicle capacity. Passenger capacity was increased by 200 by the conversion of an upper deck 'garage' into passenger accommodation. In January 1994 the British port became Ramsgate. In 1994 chartered briefly to *Sally Ferries* and operated between Ramsgate and Dunkerque. From then a spare vessel and withdrawn in early 1997. In 1998 sold to *Dianthus Maritime Co Ltd* of the UK and renamed the PRIMROSE. In 1999 she began operating for *TSL* between Ramsgate and Ostend after a major refit at Dunkerque. She normally operates in freight-only mode but can be used on the passenger roster if necessary.

TRANSMANCHE FERRIES

Transmanche Ferries is a French company, a subsidiary of *Louis Dreyfus Armateurs* operating under a franchise awarded by *Syndicat Mixte de L'Activité Transmanche* in Dieppe.

ADDRESS Transmanche Ferries, Quai Gaston Lalitte, 76200 Dieppe, France.

TELEPHONE Administration + 33 02 32 14 47 22, **Reservations *UK*** 0800 917 1201, ***France*** 0800 650 100.

FAX Administration + 33 02 32 14 52 00.

INTERNET Website www.transmancheferries.com (*English, French*)

ROUTE OPERATED Newhaven - Dieppe (4 hrs; *1,2*; up to 3 per day).

1	COTE D'ALBATRE	18425t	06	22.0k	112.0m	600P	300C	62L	BA	FR	9320128
2	SEVEN SISTERS	18425t	06	22.0k	112.0m	600P	300C	62L	BA	FR	9320130

COTE D'ALBATRE, SEVEN SISTERS Built by Astilleros Barreras SA, Vigo, Spain for *Transmanche Ferries*.

Eurovoyager *(John Hendy)*

Cote D'Albatre *(Mike Louagie)*

RED FUNNEL

Red Falcon (Miles Cowsill)

GB & IRELAND - DOMESTIC SERVICES

ARGYLL AND BUTE COUNCIL

THE COMPANY *Argyll and Bute Council* is a British local government authority.

MANAGEMENT Director of Operations Andrew Law, **Head of Roads & Amenity** Stewart Turner, **Assistant Operations Manager** Martin Gorringe.

ADDRESS Manse Brae, Lochgilphead, Argyll PA31 8RD.

TELEPHONE Administration + 44 (0)1546 604614.

FAX Administration + 44 (0)1546 606443.

INTERNET Email martin.gorringe@argyll-bute.gov.uk **Website** www.argyll-bute.gov.uk (*English*)

ROUTES OPERATED Vehicle ferries Seil - Luing (5 mins; *1*; approx half-hourly), Port Askaig (Islay) - Feolin (Jura) (5 mins; *3*; approx hourly). **Passenger-only ferries** Port Appin – Lismore (10 mins; *4*; approx hourly), Ellenabeich – Easdale (5 mins; *2*; approx quarter-hourly).

1	BELNAHUA	35t	72	8.0k	17.1m	40P	5C	1L	BA	UK
2p	EASDALE	-	93	6.5k	6.4m	11P	0C	0L	-	UK
3	EILEAN DHIURA	86t	98	9.0k	25.6m	50P	13C	1L	BA	UK
4p	LISMORE	12t	88	8.0k	9.7m	20P	0C	0L	-	UK

BELNAHUA Built by Campbeltown Shipyard, Campbeltown, UK for *Argyll County Council* for the Seil - Luing service. In 1975, following local government reorganisation, transferred to *Strathclyde Regional Council*. In 1996, transferred to *Argyll and Bute Council*.

EASDALE Built for *Strathclyde Regional Council* for the Ellenabeich - Easdale passenger-only service. In 1996, following local government reorganisation, transferred to *Argyll and Bute Council*.

EILEAN DHIURA Built by McTay Marine, Bromborough, Wirral, UK for *Argyll and Bute Council* to replace the *Western Ferries (Argyll)* SOUND OF GIGHA on the Islay - Jura route. *ASP Ship Management* manage and operate this vessel on behalf of *Argyll and Bute Council*.

LISMORE Built for *Strathclyde Regional Council* for the Port Appin – Lismore passenger-only service. In 1996, following local government reorganisation, transferred to *Argyll and Bute Council*.

ARRANMORE ISLAND FERRY SERVICES

THE COMPANY *Arranmore Island Ferry Services (Bád Farrantoireacht Arainn Mhór)* is an Irish Republic company, supported by *Roinn na Gaeltachta (The Gaeltacht Authority)*, a semi-state-owned body responsible for tourism and development in the Irish-speaking areas of The Irish Republic.

MANAGEMENT Managing Director Cornelius Bonner.

ADDRESS Bridge House, Leabgarrow, Arranmore, County Donegal, Republic of Ireland.

TELEPHONE Administration & Reservations + 353 (0)7495 20532.

FAX Administration & Reservations + 353 (0)7495 20750.

INTERNET Email: arranmoreferry@arainnmhor.com **Website** www.arranmoreferry.com (*English*)

ROUTE OPERATED Burtonport (County Donegal) - Leabgarrow (Arranmore Island) (20 mins; *1,2,3*; up to 8 per day (Summer), 5 per day (Winter)) (**Note**: Only one vessel is generally in use at any one time).

1	ÁRAINN MHÓR	64t	72	8.0k	23.8m	138P	6C	-	B	IR
2	COLL	69t	74	8.0k	25.3m	152P	6C	-	B	IR
3	RHUM	69t	73	8.0k	25.3m	164P	6C	-	B	IR

ÁRAINN MHÓR Built by James Lamont & Co Ltd, Port Glasgow, UK as the KILBRANNAN for

Hrossey (*Miles Cowsill*)

Caledonian MacBrayne. Used on a variety of routes until 1977, she was then transferred to the Scalpay (Harris) - Kyles Scalpay service. In 1990 she was replaced by the CANNA and, in turn, replaced the CANNA in her reserve/relief role. In 1992 sold to *Arranmore Island Ferry Services* and renamed the ÁRAINN MHÓR. She was subsequently sold to *Údarás na Gaeltachta* and leased back to *Arranmore Island Ferry Services*.

COLL Built by James Lamont & Co Ltd, Port Glasgow, UK for *Caledonian MacBrayne*. For several years she was employed mainly in a relief capacity. In 1986 she took over the Tobermory (Mull) - Kilchoan service from a passenger-only vessel; the conveyance of vehicles was not inaugurated until 1991. In 1996 she was transferred to the Oban - Lismore route. In 1998 she was sold to *Arranmore Island Ferry Services*.

RHUM Built by James Lamont & Co Ltd, Port Glasgow, UK for *Caledonian MacBrayne*. Until 1987, she was used primarily on the Claonaig - Lochranza (Arran) service. After that time she served on various routes. In 1994 she inaugurated a new service between Tarbert (Loch Fyne) and Portavadie. In 1997 operated between Kyles Scalpay and Scalpay until the opening of the new bridge on 16th December 1997. In 1998 she was sold to *Arranmore Island Ferry Services*.

ATLANTIC FERRIES

THE COMPANY *Atlantic Ferries Ltd* is a UK company.

MANAGEMENT Managing Director Angus Grains.

ADDRESS Gronnack, Whiteness, Shetland ZE2 9LL.

TELEPHONE Administration & Reservations +44 (0)7881 823732, **Sailing information voice bank** +44 (0)1595 743976.

FAX Administration & Reservations +44 (0)1595 840880.

INTERNET Email bookings@atlanticferries.co.uk **Website** www.atlanticferries.co.uk (English)

ROUTE OPERATED *All year* Foula - Walls (Mainland) (2 hours; *1*; 2 per week (Winter), 3 per week (Summer)), *Summer only* Foula - Scalloway (3 hrs 30 mins; *1*; alternate Thursdays).

1	NEW ADVANCE	25t	96	8.7k	9.8m	12P	1C	0L	C	UK

NEW ADVANCE Built by Richardson's, Stromness, Orkney, UK for *Shetland Islands Council* for the Foula service. Although built at Penryn, Cornwall, she was completed at Stromness. She has a Cygnus Marine GM38 hull and is based on the island where she can be lifted out of the water. Vehicle capacity is to take residents' vehicles to the island - not for tourist vehicles. In 2004 it was announced that the vessel and service would be transferred to the *Foula Community*. However, it was then found that under EU rules the route needed to be put out to competitive tender. In July 2006 the tender was awarded to *Atlantic Ferries Ltd* who began operations in October 2006.

BERE ISLAND FERRIES

THE COMPANY *Bere Island Ferries Ltd* is an Irish Republic private sector company.

MANAGEMENT Operator Colm Harrington.

ADDRESS Ferry Lodge, West End, Bere Island, County Cork, Republic of Ireland.

TELEPHONE Administration +353 (0)27 75009, **Reservations** Not applicable.

INTERNET Email info@bereislandferries.com **Website** www.bereislandferries.com (*English*)

ROUTE OPERATED Castletownbere (County Cork) - Bere Island (10 mins; *1,2*; up to 10 per day).

1F	MORVERN	64t	73	8.0k	23.8m	0P	6C	-	B	IR
2	OILEAN NA H-OIGE	69t	80	7.0k	18.6m	35P	4C	-	B	IR

MORVERN Built by James Lamont & Co Ltd, Port Glasgow, UK for *Caledonian MacBrayne*. After service on a number of routes she was, after 1979, the main vessel on the Fionnphort (Mull) - Iona service.

In 1992 replaced by the LOCH BUIE and became a spare vessel. In 1995 sold to *Arranmore Island Ferry Services*. In 2001 sold to *Bere Island Ferries*. In 2006 ceased to carry passengers and is now used in freight-only mode.

OILEAN NA H-OIGE Built by Lewis Offshore Ltd, Stornoway, UK as the EILEAN NA H-OIGE for *Western Isles Islands Council* (from 1st April 1996 the *Western Isles Council* and from 1st January 1998 *Comhairle Nan Eilean Siar*) for their Ludaig (South Uist) - Eriskay service. From 2000 operated from a temporary slipway at the Eriskay causeway. This route ceased in July 2001 following the full opening of the causeway and she was laid up. In 2002 she started operating between Eriskay and Barra. In 2003 replaced by the LOCH BHRUSDA of *Caledonian MacBrayne* and laid up. Later sold to *Bere Island Ferries* and renamed the OILEAN NA H-OIGE (same name in Irish rather than Scots Gaelic).

The SANCTA MARIA (formerly the EILEAN BHEARNARAIGH of *Comhairle Nan Eilean Siar*, a sister vessel to OILEAN NA H-OIGE) is expected to join the fleet later in the year,

CALEDONIAN MACBRAYNE

THE COMPANY *Caledonian MacBrayne* is the trading name of *CalMac Ferries Limited*, a subsidiary of *David MacBrayne Limited*, a British state-owned company, the responsibility of the First Minister of Scotland. Until 1990 it was part of the state-owned *Scottish Transport Group* (formed in 1969). *Caledonian MacBrayne Limited* was formed in 1973 by the merger of the *Caledonian Steam Packet Company Ltd* (which had been formed in 1889) and *David MacBrayne Ltd* (whose origins go back to 1851). *CalMac Ferries Ltd* was created and *David MacBrayne Ltd* reactivated in 2006. Ships are now owned by *Caledonian Maritime Assets Limited*, which is also a subsidiary of *David MacBrayne Ltd*.

MANAGEMENT Managing Director Lawrie Sinclair, **Marketing Manager** Susan Paterson, **Head of Communication & Customer Care** Hugh Dan MacLennan.

ADDRESS Ferry Terminal, Gourock PA19 1QP.

TELEPHONE Administration +44 (0)1475 650100, **Vehicle Reservations** +44 (0)8705 650000.

FAX Administration +44 (0)1475 650336, **Vehicle Reservations** +44 (0)1475 635235.

INTERNET Email hugh.maclennan@calmac.co.uk **Website** www.calmac.co.uk (*English*)

ROUTES OPERATED All year vehicle ferries (frequencies are for Summer) Ardrossan - Brodick (Arran) (55 mins; *4,32** (**June-August only*; up to 9 per day), Largs - Cumbrae Slip (Cumbrae) (10 mins; *17,26*; every 30 or 15 mins), Wemyss Bay - Rothesay (Bute) (35 mins; *2,3*; up to 18 per day), Colintraive - Rhubodach (Bute) (5 mins; *20*; frequent service), Tarbert (Loch Fyne) - Portavadie (25 mins; *12*; up to 12 per day), Gourock - Dunoon (23 mins; *16*; hourly service), Kennacraig - Port Ellen (Islay) (2 hrs 20 mins; *9,11*; up to 3 per day), Kennacraig - Port Askaig (Islay) (2 hrs 5 mins (*9,11*; 1 or 2 per day), Tayinloan - Gigha (20 mins; *24*; up to 10 per day), Oban - Lismore (50 mins; *8*; up to 4 per day), Oban - Colonsay (2 hrs 15 mins; *6,30*; 5 per week), Oban - Craignure (Mull) (45 mins; *14*; up to 7 per day), Oban - Coll - Tiree (2 hrs 45 min to Coll, 3 hrs 50 min to Tiree via Coll; *6,30*; 1 per day), Oban - Castlebay (Barra) (5 hrs (direct); *6,30*; 1 per day), Oban - Lochboisdale (South Uist) (5 hrs (if direct), 7 hrs (via Barra); *6,30*; 4 per week), Leverburgh (Harris) - Berneray (1 hr 10 mins; *23*; 3-4 per day), Lochaline - Fishnish (Mull) (15 mins; *21*; up to 14 per day), Tobermory (Mull) - Kilchoan (35 mins; *22*; up to 7 per day), Eriskay - Ard Mhor (Barra) (40 mins; *17*; up to 5 per day), Mallaig - Armadale (Skye) (23 mins; *7* (Summer), *29* (Winter); up to 9 per day (2 in Winter)), Sconser (Skye) - Raasay (15 mins; *27*; up to 11 per day), Uig (Skye) - Tarbert (Harris) (1 hr 40 mins; *10*; 1 or 2 per day), Uig (Skye) - Lochmaddy (North Uist) (1 hr 45 mins; *10*; 1 or 2 per day), Ullapool - Stornoway (Lewis) (2 hrs 45 mins; *13*; up to 3 per day). **All year passenger and restricted vehicle ferries** (frequencies are for Summer) Fionnphort (Mull) - Iona (5 mins; *19*; frequent), Mallaig - Eigg - Muck - Rum - Canna - Mallaig (round trip 7 hrs (all islands); *29*; at least 1 sailing per day most islands visited daily). **Note:** Although these services are operated by vehicle ferries, special permission is required to take a vehicle and tourist cars are not normally conveyed. **Summer-only vehicle ferries** Claonaig - Lochranza (Arran) (30 mins; *28*; up to 9 per day), Kennacraig - Port Askaig - Colonsay - Oban (3 hrs 35 mins; *11*; 1 per week). **Winter-only vehicle ferry** Tarbert (Loch Fyne) - Lochranza (Arran) (1 hr; *varies*; 1 per day). **All year passenger-only ferry** Gourock - Dunoon (20 mins; *1*; 3 per day (peak hours only)).

SECTION 2 – DOMESTIC SERVICES

Argyle (*John Hendy*)

Coruisk (*CalMac*)

1p	ALI CAT	74t	99	-	19.8m	250P	0C	0L	-	UK	
2	ARGYLE	2643t	07	13.0k	69.0m	450P	60C	-	BAS	UK	9365178
3	BUTE	2612t	05	13.0k	69.0m	450P	60C	-	AS	UK	9319741
4	CALEDONIAN ISLES	5221t	93	15.0k	94.3m	1000P	120C	10L	BA	UK	9051284
5	CANNA	69t	76	8.0k	24.3m	140P	6C	-	B	UK	7340423
6	CLANSMAN	5499t	98	16.5k	99.0m	638P	90C	6L	BA	UK	9158953
7	CORUISK	1599t	03	14.0k	65.0m	250P	40C	-	BA	UK	9274836
8	EIGG	69t	75	8.0k	24.3m	75P	6C	-	B	UK	7340411
9	HEBRIDEAN ISLES	3040t	85	15.0k	85.1m	494P	68C	10L	BAS	UK	8404812
10	HEBRIDES	5506t	00	16.5k	99.0m	612P	110C	6L	BA	UK	9211975
11	ISLE OF ARRAN	3296t	84	15.0k	85.0m	446P	68C	8L	BA	UK	8219554
12	ISLE OF CUMBRAE	201t	77	8.5k	37.7m	139P	18C	-	BA	UK	8219554
13	ISLE OF LEWIS	6753t	95	18.0k	101.2m	680P	123C	10L	BA	UK	9085974
14	ISLE OF MULL	4719t	88	15.0k	90.1m	962P	80C	20L	BA	UK	8608339
15•	JUNO	902t	74	13.0k	69.0m	381P	40C	-	AS	UK	7341063
16	JUPITER	898t	74	13.0k	69.0m	381P	40C	-	AS	UK	7341051
17	LOCH ALAINN	396t	98	10.0k	43.0m	150P	24C	-	BA	UK	9147722
18	LOCH BHRUSDA	246t	96	8.0k	35.4m	150P	18C	-	BA	UK	9129483
19	LOCH BUIE	295t	92	9.0k	35.5m	250P	9C	-	BA	UK	9031375
20	LOCH DUNVEGAN	549t	91	9.0k	54.2m	200P	36C	-	BA	UK	9006409
21	LOCH FYNE	549t	91	9.0k	54.2m	200P	36C	-	BA	UK	9006411
22	LOCH LINNHE	206t	86	9.0k	35.5m	199P	12C	-	BA	UK	8512308
23	LOCH PORTAIN	950t	03	10.5k	50.0m	200P	32C	-	BA	UK	9274824
24	LOCH RANZA	206t	87	9.0k	35.7m	199P	12C	-	BA	UK	8519887
25	LOCH RIDDON	206t	86	9.0k	35.5m	199P	12C	-	BA	UK	8519875
26	LOCH SHIRA	1024t	07	13.0k	43.0m	250P	24C	-	BA	UK	9376919
27	LOCH STRIVEN	206t	86	9.0k	35.7m	199P	12C	-	BA	UK	8512293
28	LOCH TARBERT	211t	92	9.0k	34.5m	149P	18C	-	BA	UK	9039389
29	LOCHNEVIS	941t	00	13.0k	49.1m	190P	14C	-	A	UK	9209063
30	LORD OF THE ISLES	3504t	89	16.0k	84.6m	506P	56C	16L	BAS	UK	8710869
31	RAASAY	69t	76	8.0k	24.3m	75P	6C	-	B	UK	7340435
32	SATURN	899t	78	13.0k	69.5m	381P	40C	-	AS	UK	7615490

Note: In the following list, Gaelic names are shown in parenthesis.

ALI CAT Catamaran built for *Solent & Wight Line Cruises* of Ryde, Isle of Wight. Operated a passenger service from Cowes to Hamble and Warsash and cruises from Cowes. At times chartered to *Wightlink* to cover for the fast catamarans when there were only two in their fleet. In 2002 chartered to *Red Funnel Ferries* who have contracted with *Caledonian MacBrayne* to operate passenger-only services between Gourock and Dunoon in the morning and evening peaks.

ARGYLE (*EARRA-GHÀIDHEAL*) Built by Stocznia Remontowa, Gdansk, Poland to operate on the Wemyss Bay - Rothesay route.

BUTE (*EILEAN BHÒID*) Built by Stocznia Remontowa, Gdansk, Poland to operate on the Wemyss Bay – Rothesay route.

CALEDONIAN ISLES (*EILEANAN CHALEDONIA*) Built by Richards Shipyard, Lowestoft, UK for the Ardrossan - Brodick (Arran) service.

CANNA (*EILEAN CHANNAIGH*) Built by James Lamont & Co Ltd, Port Glasgow, UK. She was the regular vessel on the Lochaline - Fishnish (Mull) service. In 1986 she was replaced by the ISLE OF CUMBRAE and until 1990 she served in a relief capacity in the north, often assisting on the Iona service. In 1990 she replaced the KILBRANNAN (see the ÁRAINN MHÓR, *Arranmore Island Ferry Services*) on the Kyles Scalpay (Harris) - Scalpay service (replaced by a bridge in Autumn 1997). In Spring 1997 she was transferred to the Ballycastle - Rathlin Island route. In June 2008 chartered to

Ciarán O'Driscoll of Cape Clear Island, Republic of Ireland who took over the operation of the service on behalf of the *NI Department of Regional Development*.

CLANSMAN *(FEAR-CINNIDH)* Built by Appledore Shipbuilders Ltd, Appledore, UK to replace the LORD OF THE ISLES on the Oban - Coll and Tiree and Oban - Castlebay and Lochboisdale services in the summer. She also serves as winter relief vessel on the Stornoway, Tarbert, Lochmaddy, Mull/Colonsay and Brodick routes.

CORUISK *(COIR' UISG')* Built by Appledore Shipbuilders Ltd, Appledore, UK to replace the LORD OF THE ISLES on the Mallaig - Armadale route during the summer. She operates on the Upper Clyde during the winter.

EIGG *(EILEAN EIGE)* Built by James Lamont & Co, Port Glasgow, UK. Since 1976 she has been employed mainly on the Oban - Lismore service. In 1996 she was transferred to the Tobermory (Mull) - Kilchoan route, very occasionally making sailings to the Small Isles (Canna, Eigg, Muck and Rum) for special cargoes. In 1999 her wheelhouse was raised to make it easier to see over taller lorries and she returned to the Oban - Lismore route.

HEBRIDEAN ISLES *(EILEANAN INNSE GALL)* Built by Cochrane Shipbuilders, Selby UK for the Uig - Tarbert/Lochmaddy service. She was used initially on the Ullapool - Stornoway and Oban - Craignure/Colonsay services pending installation of link-span facilities at Uig, Tarbert and Lochmaddy. She took up her regular role in May 1986. Since May 1996 she no longer operated direct services in summer between Tarbert and Lochmaddy, this role being taken on by the new Harris - North Uist services of the LOCH BHRUSDA. In 2001 replaced by the HEBRIDES and transferred to the Islay service. In Autumn 2002 she operated between Scrabster and Stromness for *NorthLink Orkney and Shetland Ferries* before port modifications at Scrabster enabled the HAMNAVOE to enter service in Spring 2003. She then returned to the Islay service. She also relieved on the *NorthLink* Pentland Firth service between 2004 and 2007.

HEBRIDES *(INNSE GALL)* Built by Ferguson Shipbuilders Ltd, Port Glasgow, UK for the Uig - Tarbert and Uig - Lochmaddy services.

ISLE OF ARRAN *(EILEAN ARAINN)* Built by Ferguson Ailsa, Port Glasgow, UK for the Ardrossan - Brodick service. In 1993 transferred to the Kennacraig - Port Ellen/Port Askaig service, also undertaking the weekly Port Askaig - Colonsay - Oban summer service. From then until 1997/98 she also relieved on the Brodick, Coll/Tiree, Castlebay/Lochboisdale, Craignure and Tarbert/Lochmaddy routes in winter. In 2001 replaced by the HEBRIDEAN ISLES and became a reserve for the larger vessels. She has operated on the two-ship Islay service in summer since 2003; this service is now all-year-round.

ISLE OF CUMBRAE *(EILEAN CHUMRAIGH)* Built by Ailsa Shipbuilding Ltd, Troon, UK for the Largs - Cumbrae Slip (Cumbrae) service. In 1986 she was replaced by the LOCH LINNHE and the LOCH STRIVEN and transferred to the Lochaline - Fishnish (Mull) service. She used to spend most of the winter as secondary vessel on the Kyle of Lochalsh - Kyleakin service; however, this ceased following the opening of the Skye Bridge in 1995. In 1997 she was transferred to the Colintraive - Rhubodach service. In Summer 1999 she was transferred to the Tarbert - Portavadie service.

ISLE OF LEWIS *(EILEAN LEÒDHAIS)* Built by Ferguson Shipbuilders Ltd, Port Glasgow, UK for the Ullapool - Stornoway service.

ISLE OF MULL *(AN T-EILEAN MUILEACH)* Built by Appledore Ferguson, Port Glasgow, UK for the Oban - Craignure (Mull) service. She also operates some Oban - Colonsay sailings and until 1997/98 was the usual winter relief vessel on the Ullapool - Stornoway service. She has also deputised on the Oban - Castlebay/Lochboisdale and Oban - Coll/Tiree routes.

JUNO *(IÙNO)*, JUPITER *(IUPADAR)*, SATURN *(SATHARN)* Built by James Lamont & Co Ltd, Port Glasgow, UK (SATURN Ailsa Shipbuilding, Troon) for the Gourock - Dunoon, Gourock - Kilcreggan and Wemyss Bay - Rothesay services. The SATURN was upgraded to Class III standard in 2005 for the Ardrossan - Brodick service. Before 1986, the JUNO and JUPITER operated mainly on the Gourock - Dunoon and Gourock - Kilcreggan (now withdrawn) services and the SATURN on the Wemyss Bay - Rothesay service. Between 1986 and 2005 they have usually rotated on these services; until 2000 this, in summer, included Clyde cruising but this was not repeated in 2001. In Summer 2005, 2006

Hebrides (*CalMac*)

Hoy Head (*Miles Cowsill*)

SECTION 2 – DOMESTIC SERVICES

and 2007 following the delivery of the new BUTE, the SATURN has operated additional sailings between Ardrossan and Brodick with a maximum capacity of 250 passengers. This will be repeated in 2008. JUNO was withdrawn in April 2007.

LOCH ALAINN *(LOCH ÀLAINN)* Built by Buckie Shipbuilders Ltd, Buckie, UK for the Lochaline - Fishnish service. Launched as the LOCH ALINE but renamed the LOCH ALAINN before entering service. After a brief period on the service she was built for, she was transferred to the Colintraive - Rhubodach route. In Summer 1998 she was transferred to the Largs - Cumbrae Slip service. In July 2007 took over the Sound of Barra service.

LOCH BHRUSDA *(LOCH BHRÙSTA)* Built by McTay Marine, Bromborough, Wirral, UK to inaugurate a new Otternish (North Uist) - Leverburgh (Harris) service. In 2001 the service became Berneray - Leverburgh. In 2003 moved to the Eriskay - Barra service, previously operated by *Comhairle Nan Eilean Siar* vessels. In 2007 became a spare vessel on the Clyde. Note 'Bhrusda' is pronounced "Vroosta".

LOCH BUIE *(LOCH BUIDHE)* Built by J W Miller & Sons Ltd, St Monans, Fife, UK for the Fionnphort (Mull) - Iona service to replace the MORVERN (see *Arranmore Island Ferry Services*) and obviate the need for a relief vessel in the summer. Due to height restrictions, loading arrangements for vehicles taller than private cars are bow-only. Only islanders' cars and service vehicles (eg. mail vans, police) are carried; no tourist vehicles are conveyed.

LOCH DUNVEGAN *(LOCH DÙNBHEAGAN)* Built by Ferguson Shipbuilders Ltd, Port Glasgow, UK for the Kyle of Lochalsh - Kyleakin service. On the opening of the Skye Bridge in October 1995 she was withdrawn from service and put up for sale. In Autumn 1997, returned to service on the Lochaline - Fishnish route. In 1998 she was due to be transferred to the Colintraive - Rhubodach route but this was delayed because of problems in providing terminal facilities. She operated on the Clyde and between Mallaig and Armadale during the early Summer and spent the rest of that Summer laid up. In 1999 she was transferred to the Colintraive - Rhubodach route.

LOCH FYNE *(LOCH FINE)* Built by Ferguson Shipbuilders Ltd, Port Glasgow, UK for the Kyle of Lochalsh - Kyleakin service (see the LOCH DUNVEGAN). In Autumn 1997, she also served on the Lochaline - Fishnish route and was transferred to this route as regular vessel in 1998.

LOCH LINNHE *(AN LINNE DHUBH)* Built by Richard Dunston (Hessle) Ltd, Hessle, UK. Until 1997 she was used mainly on the Largs - Cumbrae Slip (Cumbrae) service and until Winter 1994/95 she was usually used on the Lochaline - Fishnish service during the winter. Since then she has relieved on various routes in winter. In Summer 1998 she operated mainly on the Tarbert - Portavadie route. In 1999 she was transferred to the Summer only Tobermory - Kilchoan service. In 2003 she launched the new Sound of Barra service before delivery of the LOCH PORTAIN allowed the LOCH BHRUSDA to be moved to that route.

LOCH PORTAIN *(LOCHPORTAIN)* Built by McTay Marine, Bromborough, Wirral, UK (hull constructed in Poland) to replace the LOCH BHRUSDA on the Berneray - Leverburgh service.

LOCH RANZA *(LOCH RAONASA)* Built by Richard Dunston (Hessle) Ltd, Hessle, UK for the Claonaig - Lochranza (Arran) seasonal service and used a relief vessel in the winter. In 1992 she was replaced by the LOCH TARBERT and transferred to the Tayinloan - Gigha service.

LOCH RIDDON *(LOCH RAODAIN)* Built by Richard Dunston (Hessle) Ltd, Hessle, UK. Until 1997 she was used almost exclusively on the Colintraive - Rhubodach service. In 1997, she was transferred to the Largs - Cumbrae Slip service and is often to be found on the Tarbert-Portavadie/Lochranza service in winter. Now a spare vessel.

LOCH SHIRA *(LOCH SIORA)* Built by Ferguson Shipbuilders, Port Glasgow, UK for the Largs - Cumbrae Slip route.

LOCH STRIVEN *(LOCH SROIGHEANN)* Built by Richard Dunston (Hessle) Ltd, Hessle, UK. Used mainly on the Largs - Cumbrae Slip service until 1997. In Winter 1995/96 and 1996/97 she was used on the Tarbert - Portavadie and Claonaig - Lochranza routes. In 1997 she took over the Sconser - Raasay service.

LOCH TARBERT *(LOCH AN TAIRBEIRT)* Built by J W Miller & Sons Ltd, St Monans, Fife, UK for the

Claonaig - Lochranza service. She has been the winter relief vessel on the Largs - Cumbrae Slip route since Winter 1994/95.

LOCHNEVIS (*LOCH NIBHEIS*) Built by Ailsa Shipbuilding, Troon, UK to replace the LOCHMOR on the Mallaig - Small Isles service and the winter Mallaig - Armadale service. Although a vehicle ferry, cars are not normally carried to the Small Isles; the ro-ro facility is used for the carriage of agricultural machinery and livestock and it is possible to convey a vehicle on the ferry from which goods can be unloaded directly onto local transport rather than transhipping at Mallaig.

LORD OF THE ISLES (*RIGH NAN EILEAN*) Built by Appledore Ferguson, Port Glasgow, UK to replace the CLAYMORE on the Oban - Castlebay and Lochboisdale services and also the COLUMBA (1420t, 1964) on the Oban - Coll and Tiree service. She took over the Mallaig - Armadale and Mallaig - Outer Isles services in July 1998 but returned to her previous routes during the winter period. In Spring 2003 the Mallaig – Armadale service was taken over by the PIONEER standing in for the new CORUISK and she operated services from Oban to South Uist and Barra.

RAASAY (*EILEAN RATHARSAIR*) Built by James Lamont & Co Ltd, Port Glasgow, UK for and used primarily on the Sconser (Skye) - Raasay service. In 1997 she was replaced by the LOCH STRIVEN, became a spare/relief vessel and inaugurated in October 2003 the winter service between Tobermory (Mull) and Kilchoan (Ardnamurchan).

Under Construction

33	NEWBUILDING		-	10	16.5k	98.9m	550P	88C	-	BA	UK	-

Under construction by Stocznia Remontowa, Gdansk, Poland for the Kennacraig - Islay service.

CROMARTY FERRY COMPANY

THE COMPANY The *Cromarty Ferry Company* operate under contract to *The Highland Council*.

MANAGEMENT Managing Director John Henderson.

ADDRESS Udale Farm, Poyntzfield, by Dingwall, IV7 8LY.

TELEPHONE +44 (0)1381 610269, Mobile +44 (0)7768 653674.

FAX +44 (0)1381 610408.

INTERNET Email info@cromarty-ferry.co.uk **Website** www.cromarty-ferry.co.uk (*English*)

ROUTE OPERATED *June-October* Cromarty - Nigg (Ross-shire) (10 mins; *1*; half-hourly - 0800 to 1800 ex Cromarty (19.00 in July and August)).

1	CROMARTY ROSE	28t	87	8.0k	14.0m	50P	2C	-	B	UK

CROMARTY ROSE Built by McCrindle Shipbuilding Ltd, Ardrossan, UK for *Seaboard Marine (Nigg) Ltd* who operated the service until 2001, supported by *The Highland Council*. In 2002, after a tendering exercise held in 2001, the contract was awarded to the *Cromarty Ferry Company*. The new company purchased the CROMARTY ROSE from *Seaboard Marine (Nigg) Ltd*.

CROSS RIVER FERRIES

THE COMPANY *Cross River Ferries Ltd* is an Irish Republic company, jointly owned by *Marine Transport Services Ltd* of Cobh and *Arklow Shipping Ltd* of Arklow, County Wicklow.

MANAGEMENT Operations Manager Eoin O'Sullivan.

ADDRESS Westlands House, Rushbrooke, Cobh, County Cork, Republic of Ireland.

TELEPHONE Administration +353 (0)21 481 1223, **Reservations** Not applicable.

FAX Administration +353 (0)21 481 2645, **Reservations** Not applicable.

ROUTE OPERATED Carrigaloe (near Cobh, on Great Island) - Glenbrook (Co Cork) (4 mins; *1,2*; frequent service 07.00 - 00.15 (one or two vessels used according to demand)).

1	CARRIGALOE	225t	70	8.0k	49.1m	200P	27C	-	BA	IR	7028386
2	GLENBROOK	225t	71	8.0k	49.1m	200P	27C	-	BA	IR	7101607

CARRIGALOE Built by Newport Shipbuilding and Engineering Company, Newport (Gwent), UK as the KYLEAKIN for *Caledonian Steam Packet Company* (later *Caledonian MacBrayne*) for the Kyle of Lochalsh - Kyleakin service. In 1991 sold to *Marine Transport Services Ltd* and renamed the CARRIGALOE. She entered service in March 1993. In Summer 2002 chartered to the *Lough Foyle Ferry Company*, returning in Spring 2003.

GLENBROOK Built by Newport Shipbuilding and Engineering Company, Newport (Gwent), UK as the LOCHALSH for *Caledonian Steam Packet Company* (later *Caledonian MacBrayne*) for the Kyle of Lochalsh - Kyleakin service. In 1991 sold to *Marine Transport Services Ltd* and renamed the GLENBROOK. She entered service in March 1993.

THE HIGHLAND COUNCIL

THE COMPANY *The Highland Council* (previously *Highland Regional Council*) is a British local government authority.

MANAGEMENT Area Transport, Environment & Community Works Services Manager James C Tolmie, **Ferry Foremen** Allan McCowan and Donald Dixon.

ADDRESS *Area Office* Lochybridge Depot, Carr's Corner Industrial Estate, Fort William PH33 6TQ, *Ferry Office* Ferry Cottage, Ardgour, Fort William PH33 7AA.

TELEPHONE Administration *Area Office* +44 (0)1397 709000, *Corran* +44 (0)1855 841243, *Camusnagaul* – Now run by private operator *Geoff Ward* by vessel RIVE GAUCHE.

FAX Administration *Area Office* +44 (0)1397 705735, *Corran* +44 (0)1855 841243, **Reservations** Not applicable.

INTERNET Email tecs@highland.gov.uk **Website** lochabertransport.org.uk/corranferry.html (*English - external site reproducing official ferry leaflet*)

ROUTES OPERATED Vehicle Ferries Corran - Ardgour (5 mins; *2,3*; half-hourly), **Passenger-only Ferry** Fort William - Camusnagaul (10 mins; ***chartered vessel***; Frequent)).

1p•	CAILIN AN AISEAG	-	80	7.5k	9.8m	26P	0C	0L	-	UK	
2	CORRAN	351t	01	10.0k	42.0m	150P	30C	2L	BA	UK	9225990
3	MAID OF GLENCOUL	166t	75	8.0k	32.0m	116P	16C	1L	BA	UK	7521613

CAILIN AN AISEAG Built by Buckie Shipbuilders Ltd, Buckie, UK for *Highland Regional Council* and used on the Fort William - Camusnagaul passenger-only service. In 2006 service transferred to *Geoff Ward* under contract. Vessel laid up for sale.

CORRAN Built by George Prior Engineering Ltd, Hull, UK for *The Highland Council* to replace the MAID OF GLENCOUL as main vessel.

MAID OF GLENCOUL Built by William McCrindle Ltd, Shipbuilders, Ardrossan, UK for *Highland Regional Council* for the service between Kylesku and Kylestrome. In 1984 the ferry service was replaced by a bridge and she was transferred to the Corran - Ardgour service. In April 1996, ownership transferred to *The Highland Council*. In 2001 became the reserve vessel.

ISLES OF SCILLY STEAMSHIP COMPANY

THE COMPANY *Isles of Scilly Steamship Company* is a British private sector company.

MANAGEMENT Chief Executive J Marston, **Marketing Manager** Jackie Gwennap.

ADDRESS *Scilly* PO Box 10, Hugh Town, St Mary's, Isles of Scilly TR21 0LJ, *Penzance* Steamship House, Quay Street, Penzance, Cornwall, TR18 4BZ.

TELEPHONE Administration & Reservations +44 (0)845 710 5555.

FAX Administration & Reservations + 44 (0)1736 334228.

INTERNET Email sales@islesofscilly-travel.co.uk **Website** www.ios-travel.co.uk (*English*)

ROUTES OPERATED Penzance - St Mary's (Isles of Scilly) (2 hrs 40 mins; *1,4*; 1 per day), St Mary's - Tresco/St Martin's/St Agnes/Bryher; *2,3,4*; irregular).

1	GRY MARITHA	590t	81	10.5k	40.3m	6P	5C	1L	C	UK	8008462
2	ISLAND LADY	-	86	-	27.4m	12P	6C	2L	B	UK	
3	LYONESSE LADY	40t	91	9.0k	15.5m	12P	1C	0L	AC	UK	
4	SCILLONIAN III	1346t	77	15.5k	67.7m	600P	5C	-	C	UK	7527796
5F	SWIFT LADY	-	04	-	8.4m	12P	0C	0C	-	UK	

GRY MARITHA Built by Moen Slip AS, Kolvereid, Norway for *Gjofor* of Norway. In design she is a coaster rather than a ferry. In 1990 sold to *Isles of Scilly Steamship Company*. She operates a freight and passenger service all year (conveying most goods to and from the Islands). During the winter she provides the only sea service to the islands, the SCILLONIAN III being laid up.

ISLAND LADY Built by McTay Marine, Bromborough, UK, for the *British MoD*. In 2007 sold to *Isles of Scilly Steamship Company*. Currently used to support the off-island quay reconstruction project being undertaken by Nuttall John Martin. Also used for inter-island transport as required.

LYONESSE LADY Built at Fort William, UK, for inter-island ferry work.

SCILLONIAN III Built by Appledore Shipbuilders Ltd, Appledore, UK for the Penzance-St Mary's service. She operates from late March to November and is laid up in the winter. Last major conventional passenger/cargo ferry built for UK waters and probably Western Europe. Extensively refurbished during Winter 1998/99. She can carry cars in her hold and on deck, as well as general cargo/perishables, boats, trailer tents and passenger luggage.

SWIFT LADY Built by Redbay Boats of Cushendall, Co Antrim, Northern Ireland for inter-island ferry work conveying mail.

KERRERA FERRY

THE COMPANY The *Kerrera Ferry* is privately operated.

MANAGEMENT Ferry Master Duncan MacEachen.

ADDRESS The Ferry, Isle of Kerrera, by Oban PA34 4SX.

TELEPHONE Administration + 44 (0)1631 563665.

ROUTE OPERATED Gallanach (Argyll) - Kerrera (5 mins; *1*; on demand 10.30 - 12.30 and 14.00 - 18.00, Easter - October, other times by arrangement).

1	GYLEN LADY	9t	99	8.0k	10.0m	12P	1C	-	B	UK

GYLEN LADY Built by Corpach Boatyard, Corpach, UK to inaugurate a vehicle ferry service to the Isle of Kerrera, replacing open passenger boat.

LOUGH FOYLE FERRY COMPANY

THE COMPANY *Lough Foyle Ferry Company Ltd* is an Irish Republic Company.

MANAGEMENT Managing Director Jim McClenaghan.

ADDRESS The Pier, Greencastle, Co Donegal, Republic of Ireland.

TELEPHONE Administration + 353 (0)74 93 81901.

FAX Administration: + 353 (0)74 93 81903.

INTERNET Email: info@loughfoyleferry.com **Website:** www.loughfoyleferry.com (*English*)

ROUTES OPERATED *Lough Foyle Service* Greencastle (Inishowen, Co Donegal, Republic of Ireland)

SECTION 2 – DOMESTIC SERVICES

Pentalina-B (*FotoFlite*)

Hrossey (*Miles Cowsill*)

- Magilligan (Co Londonderry, Northern Ireland) (10 mins; *2*; about every 20 mins), **Lough Swilly Service (1st April - 30th September)** Buncrana (Inishowen, Co Donegal) - Rathmullan (Co Donegal) (20 mins; *1*; hourly).

| 1 | FOYLE RAMBLER | 122t | 72 | 10.0k | 35.0m | 100P | 20C | - | BA | IR | 8985531 |
| 2 | FOYLE VENTURE | 324t | 78 | 10.0k | 47.9m | 300P | 44C | - | BA | IR | 7800033 |

FOYLE VENTURE Built by Scott & Sons (Bowling) Ltd, Bowling, Glasgow, UK as the SHANNON WILLOW for *Shannon Ferry Ltd*. In 2000 replaced by the SHANNON BREEZE and laid up for sale. In 2003 sold to the *Lough Foyle Ferry Company Ltd* and renamed the FOYLE VENTURE.

FOYLE RAMBLER Built by Abeking & Rasmussen, Lemwerder, Germany as the STEDINGEN for *Schnellastfähre Berne-Farge GmbH* (later *Fähren Bremen-Stedingen GmbH*) to operate across the River Weser (Vegesack - Lemwerder and Berne - Farge). In 2004 sold to the *Lough Foyle Ferry Company Ltd* and renamed the FOYLE RAMBLER.

MURPHY'S FERRY SERVICE

THE COMPANY *Murphy's Ferry Service* is privately operated.

MANAGEMENT Operator Patrick Murphy, **Finance/Marketing** Carol Murphy.

ADDRESS Anchorage, Lawrence Cove, Bere Island, Co Cork, Republic of Ireland.

TELEPHONE Administration + 353 (0)27 75014 **Mobile** + 353 (0)87 2386095.

FAX Administration + 353 (0)27 75014.

INTERNET Email info@murphysferry.com **Website** www.murphysferry.com (*English*)

ROUTE OPERATED Castletownbere (Pontoon - 3 miles to east of town centre) - Bere Island (Lawrence Cove, near Rerrin) (20 mins; *1*; up to 8 per day).

| 1 | IKOM K | 55t | 99 | 10.0k | 16.0m | 60P | 4C | 1L | B | IR | |

IKOM K Built by Arklow Marine Services, Arklow, Irish Republic for *Murphy's Ferry Service*.

NORTHLINK FERRIES

THE COMPANY *NorthLink Ferries Ltd* is a Scottish company, a subsidiary of *David MacBrayne Ltd*, a company owned by the First Minister of Scotland and the parent company of *Caledonian MacBrayne Ltd*.

MANAGEMENT Chief Executive Bill Davidson, **Commercial Director** Cynthia Spencer.

ADDRESS Kiln Corner, Ayre Road, Kirkwall, Orkney KW15 1QX.

TELEPHONE Administration + 44 (0)1856 885500, **Reservations** + 44 (0)845 6000 449.

FAX Administration + 44 (0)1856 879588.

INTERNET Email info@northlinkferries.co.uk **Website** www.northlinkferries.co.uk (*English*)

ROUTES OPERATED Scrabster - Stromness (Orkney) (1 hr 30 min; *1*; up to 3 per day), Aberdeen - Lerwick (Shetland) (direct) (12 hrs; *2,3*; 3 northbound/4 southbound per week), Aberdeen - Kirkwall, Hatston New Pier (Orkney) (5 hrs 45 mins) - Lerwick (14 hrs; *2,3*; 4 northbound/3 southbound per week).

1	HAMNAVOE	8780t	02	19.0k	112.0m	600P	95C	20L	BA	UK	9246061
2	HJALTLAND	11720t	02	24.0k	125.0m	600P	150C	30L	BA	UK	9244958
3	HROSSEY	11720t	02	24.0k	125.0m	600P	150C	30L	BA	UK	9244960

HAMNAVOE Built by Aker Finnyards, Rauma, Finland for *NorthLink Orkney and Shetland Ferries Ltd* to operate on the Scrabster - Stromness route. Did not enter service until Spring 2003 due to late completion of work at Scrabster to accommodate the ship. *Caledonian MacBrayne's* HEBRIDEAN ISLES covered between October 2002 and Spring 2003.

HJALTLAND, HROSSEY Built by Aker Finnyards, Rauma, Finland for *NorthLink Orkney and Shetland Ferries Ltd* to operate on the Aberdeen - Kirkwall - Lerwick route when services started in 2002.

ORKNEY FERRIES

THE COMPANY *Orkney Ferries Ltd* (previously the *Orkney Islands Shipping Company*) is a British company, owned by *Orkney Islands Council.*

MANAGEMENT Operations Director Capt N H Mills, **Ferry Services Manager** D I Sawkins.

ADDRESS Shore Street, Kirkwall, Orkney KW15 1LG.

TELEPHONE Administration + 44 (0)1856 872044, **Reservations** + 44 (0)1856 872044.

FAX Administration & Reservations + 44 (0)1856 872921.

INTERNET Email info@orkneyferries.co.uk **Website** www.orkneyferries.co.uk *(English)*

ROUTES OPERATED Kirkwall (Mainland) to Eday (1 hr 15 mins), Rapness (Westray) (1 hr 25 mins), Sanday (1 hr 25 mins), Stronsay (1 hr 35 mins), Papa Westray (1 hr 50 mins), North Ronaldsay (2 hrs 30 mins) ('North Isles service') (timings are direct from Kirkwall - sailings via other islands take longer; *1,2,9*; 1/2 per day except Papa Westray which is twice weekly and North Ronaldsay which is weekly), Pierowall (Westray) - Papa Westray (25 mins; *4*; up to six per day (Summer service - passenger-only)), Kirkwall - Shapinsay (25 mins; *7*; 6 per day), Houton (Mainland) to Lyness (Hoy) (35 mins; *6*; 5 per day), and Flotta (35 mins; *6*; 4 per day) ('South Isles service') (timings are direct from Houton - sailings via other islands take longer), Tingwall (Mainland) to Rousay (20 mins; *3*; 6 per day), Egilsay (30 mins; *3*; 5 per day) and Wyre (20 mins; *3*; 5 per day) (timings are direct from Tingwall - sailings via other islands take longer), Stromness (Mainland) to Moaness (Hoy) (25 mins; *5*; 2/3 per day) and Graemsay (25 mins; *5*; 2/3 per day) (passenger/cargo service - cars not normally conveyed).

1	**EARL SIGURD**	771t	90	12.0k	45.0m	190P	26C	-	BA	UK	8902711
2	**EARL THORFINN**	771t	90	12.0k	45.0m	190P	26C	-	BA	UK	8902723
3	**EYNHALLOW**	104t	87	10.5k	28.8m	95P	11C	-	BA	UK	8960880
4p	**GOLDEN MARIANA**	33t	73	9.5k	15.2m	40P	0C	-	-	UK	
5	**GRAEMSAY**	82t	96	10.0k	16.2m	73P	2C	-	C	UK	
6	**HOY HEAD**	358t	94	11.0k	39.5m	125P	18C	-	BA	UK	9081722
7	**SHAPINSAY**	199t	89	9.5k	26.6m	91P	12C	-	BA	UK	8814184
8	**THORSVOE**	385t	91	10.6k	35.0m	122P	16C	-	BA	UK	9014743
9	**VARAGEN**	928t	88	12.0k	49.9m	144P	33C	5L	BA	UK	8818154

EARL SIGURD, EARL THORFINN Built by McTay Marine, Bromborough, Wirral, UK to inaugurate ro-ro working on the 'North Isles' service (see above).

EYNHALLOW Built by David Abels Boat Builders, Bristol, UK to inaugurate ro-ro services from Tingwall (Mainland) to Rousay, Egilsay and Wyre. In 1991 she was lengthened by 5 metres, to increase car capacity.

GOLDEN MARIANA Built by Bideford Shipyard Ltd, Bideford, UK for *A J G England* of Padstow as a dual-purpose passenger and fishing vessel. In 1975 sold to *M MacKenzie* of Ullapool, then to *Pentland Ferries, Wide Firth Ferry* in 1982, and *Orkney Islands Council* in 1986. Passenger-only vessel. Generally operates summer-only feeder service between Pierowall (Westray) and Papa Westray.

GRAEMSAY Built by Ailsa Shipbuilding, Troon UK to operate between Stromness (Mainland), Moaness (Hoy) and Graemsay. Designed to offer an all year round service to these islands, primarily for passengers and cargo.

HOY HEAD Built by Appledore Shipbuilders Ltd, Appledore, UK to replace the THORSVOE on the 'South Isles' service (see below).

SHAPINSAY Built by Yorkshire Drydock Ltd, Hull, UK for the service from Kirkwall (Mainland) to Shapinsay.

THORSVOE Built by Campbeltown Shipyard, Campbeltown, UK for the 'South Isles' service (see above). In 1994 replaced by new HOY HEAD and became the main reserve vessel for the fleet.

VARAGEN Built by Cochrane Shipbuilders, Selby, UK for *Orkney Ferries*, a private company established to start a new route between Gills Bay (Caithness, Scotland) and Burwick (South Ronaldsay, Orkney). However, due to problems with the terminals it was not possible to maintain regular services. In 1991, the company was taken over by *Orkney Islands Shipping Company* and the VARAGEN became part of their fleet, sharing 'North Isles' services with the EARL SIGURD and the EARL THORFINN and replacing the freight vessel ISLANDER (494t, 1969).

PASSAGE EAST FERRY

THE COMPANY *Passage East Ferry Company Ltd* is an Irish Republic private sector company.

MANAGEMENT Managing Director Derek Donnelly, **Operations Manager** Conor Gilligan.

ADDRESS Barrack Street, Passage East, Co Waterford, Republic of Ireland.

TELEPHONE Administration + 353 (0)51 382480, **Reservations** Not applicable.

FAX Administration + 353 (0)51 382598, **Reservations** Not applicable.

INTERNET Email passageferry@eircom.net **Website** www.passageferry.com (*English*)

ROUTE OPERATED Passage East (County Waterford) - Ballyhack (County Wexford) (7 mins; *1*; frequent service).

1	FBD TINTERN	236t	71	9.0k	54.8m	130P	30C	-	BA	IR

FBD TINTERN Built by Schiffswerft Oberwinter, Oberwinter/Rhein, Germany as the STADT LINZ for *Rheinfähre Linz - Remagen GmbH* of Germany and operated on the Rhine between Linz and Remagen. In 1990 renamed the ST JOHANNES. In 1997 sold to *Fähren Bremen-Stedingen GmbH*, renamed the VEGESACK and operated across the Weser between Lemwerder and Vegesack. In 2003 she became a reserve vessel and in 2004 was renamed the STEDINGEN (the name previously carried by the ferry sold to *Lough Foyle Ferry Company*). Later sold to *Schraven BV* of the Netherlands and refurbished. In Autumn 2005 sold to *Passage East Ferry* and renamed the FBD TINTERN. Entered service in December 2005.

PENTLAND FERRIES

THE COMPANY *Pentland Ferries* is a UK private sector company.

MANAGEMENT Managing Director Andrew Banks, **Marketing Manager** Linda Knott.

ADDRESS Pier Road, St Margaret's Hope, South Ronaldsay, Orkney KW17 2SW.

TELEPHONE Administration & Reservations + 44 (0)1856 831226.

FAX Administration & Reservations + 44 (0)1856 831614.

INTERNET Email sales@pentlandferries.co.uk **Website** www.pentlandferries.co.uk (*English*)

ROUTE OPERATED Gills Bay (Scotland) - St Margaret's Hope (South Ronaldsay, Orkney) (***Until Summer** 2008* 1 hr; *1or 2*; 3 per day, ***from late Summer 2008*** 45 min; *3*; up to 4 per day).

1	CLAYMORE	1871t	70	14.0k	77.2m	160P	50C	8T	AS	UK	7715434
2	PENTALINA B	1908t	70	16.0k	74.3m	250P	46C	7L	BAS	UK	7009653

CLAYMORE Built by Robb Caledon Shipbuilders Ltd, Leith, UK for *Caledonian MacBrayne* for the Oban - Castlebay/Lochboisdale service, also serving Coll and Tiree between October and May, replacing the IONA (see the PENTALINA B). In 1989 she was transferred to the Kennacraig - Port Ellen/Port Askaig (Islay) route, again replacing the IONA. In summer she also operated a weekly service from Port Askaig (Islay) to Colonsay and Oban. She relieved on the Ardrossan - Brodick service during Winter 1990. In Autumn 1993 she was replaced by the ISLE OF ARRAN and became a spare vessel. Her summer duties in 1994, 1995 and 1996 included Saturday sailings from Ardrossan to Douglas

Red Jet 3 (Miles Cowsill)

Red Osprey (Miles Cowsill)

(Isle of Man), returning on Sundays plus standby duties and charter to the *Isle of Man Steam Packet Company* to provide extra sailings between Heysham and Douglas during the TT season. During the winter she was general relief vessel, spending several months on Islay sailings. In 1997 she was sold to *Sea Containers* to operate for *Sea Containers Ferries Scotland Ltd* (trading as the *Argyll and Antrim Steam Packet Company*) between Campbeltown (Scotland) and Ballycastle (Northern Ireland) (Summer only). During Winter 1997/98 she was chartered back to *Caledonian MacBrayne* to cover during the refit period. The Campbeltown - Ballycastle service did not resume in 2000 and during the summer she was chartered to *Strandfaraskip Landsins* of the Faroe Islands and used on the Tórshavn - Suderoy service. She was then laid up for sale. In 2002 she was sold to *Pentland Ferries* and inaugurated a new Invergordon - St Margaret's Hope service. This service was withdrawn after a short period and she was laid up until the Summer period when it was planned she would operate alongside the PENTALINA B. However, a passenger certificate was not granted until 2004, so at the times she operated only 12 passengers were allowed. Winter passenger capacity is 71. She has also at various times been chartered to a farmers' co-operative to operate livestock sailings between Dover and Dunkerque.

PENTALINA B Built by Ailsa Shipbuilding Co Ltd, Troon, UK as the IONA for *David MacBrayne*. She was built to operate the Islay service. However, shortly after the order was placed, plans to build a new pier at Redhouse, near the mouth of West Loch Tarbert, were abandoned, so she was not able to operate on this route until *Caledonian MacBrayne* acquired the pier used by *Western Ferries* in deeper water at Kennacraig in 1978. She operated on the Gourock - Dunoon service in 1970 and 1971, between Mallaig and Kyle of Lochalsh and Stornoway in 1972 and between Oban and Craignure in 1973. From 1974 until 1978 she operated mainly on the Oban to Castlebay/Lochboisdale service and in addition the Winter Oban - Coll/Tiree route. From 1978 until 1989 she operated mainly on the Islay service. In 1989 she was replaced by the CLAYMORE and then replaced the PIONEER as the Summer Mallaig - Armadale vessel. Full ro-ro working was introduced on the route in 1994; she also operated a twice-weekly sailing between Mallaig, Lochboisdale and Castlebay and, in 1997, a weekly Mallaig - Coll and Tiree sailing. She was withdrawn in October 1997 and sold to *Pentland Ferries*. In 1998 she was renamed the PENTALINA B. In Spring 1998 she was chartered back to *Caledonian MacBrayne* to operate between Oban and Craignure following the breakdown of the ISLE OF MULL. *Pentland Ferries'* services started in Summer 2001. She has also at various times been chartered to a farmers' co-operative to operate livestock sailings between Dover and Dunkerque.

Under Construction

3	PENTALINA	1250t	08	18.0k	64.0m	350P	85C	9L	BA	UK	9437969

PENTALINA Catamaran under construction by FBMA Marine, Cebu, Philippines for *Pentland Ferries*. To be delivered in Summer 2008.

RED FUNNEL FERRIES

THE COMPANY *Red Funnel Ferries* is the trading name of the *Southampton, Isle of Wight and South of England Royal Mail Steam Packet Company Limited*, a British private sector company. The company was acquired by *JP Morgan International Capital Corporation* in 2000; it was purchased by the management in 2004 and in 2007 it was sold to *Infracapital Partners LP* – the infrastructure fund of the *Prudential Group*.

MANAGEMENT Managing Director Tom Docherty, **Commercial Director** Colin Hetherington.

ADDRESS 12 Bugle Street, Southampton SO14 2JY.

TELEPHONE Administration 0844 844 2699, **Reservations UK** 0844 844 9988, *Elsewhere* +44 845 155 2442.

FAX Administration & Reservations 0844 844 9998.

INTERNET Email post@redfunnel.co.uk **Website** www.redfunnel.co.uk (*English*)

ROUTES OPERATED Conventional Ferries Southampton - East Cowes (55 mins; *1,2,7*; hourly), **Fast Passenger Ferries** Southampton - West Cowes (22 mins; *3,4,5,6*; every half hour).

1	RED EAGLE	3953t	96	14.0k	93.2m	895P	200C	18L	BA	UK	9117337
2	RED FALCON	3953t	94	14.0k	93.2m	895P	200C	18L	BA	UK	9064047
3»p	RED JET 1	168t	91	34.0k	32.5m	138P	0C	0L	-	UK	9001679
4»p	RED JET 2	168t	91	34.0k	32.5m	138P	0C	0L	-	UK	9011681
5»p	RED JET 3	213t	98	34.0k	32.9m	190P	0C	0L	-	UK	9182758
6»p	RED JET 4	342t	03	35.0k	39.8m	277P	0C	0L	-	UK	9295854
7	RED OSPREY	3953t	94	14.0k	93.2m	895P	200C	18L	BA	UK	9064059

RED EAGLE Built by Ferguson Shipbuilders, Port Glasgow, UK for the Southampton - East Cowes service. During Winter 2004/05 stretched by 10 metres and height raised by 3 metres at Gdansk, Poland.

RED FALCON Built by Ferguson Shipbuilders, Port Glasgow, UK for the Southampton - East Cowes service. In 2004 stretched by 10 metres and height raised by 3 metres at Gdansk, Poland.

RED JET 1, RED JET 2, RED JET 3 FBM Marine catamarans built at Cowes, UK for the Southampton - West Cowes service.

RED JET 4 North West Bay Ships Pty Ltd catamaran built in Hobart, Tasmania, Australia for the Southampton - West Cowes service.

RED OSPREY Built by Ferguson Shipbuilders, Port Glasgow, UK for the Southampton - East Cowes service. In 2003 stretched by 10 metres and height raised by 3 metres at Gdansk, Poland.

SHANNON FERRY LTD

THE COMPANY *Shannon Ferry Group Ltd* is an Irish Republic private company owned by six families on both sides of the Shannon Estuary.

MANAGEMENT Managing Director Eugene Maher.

ADDRESS Ferry Terminal, Killimer, County Clare, Republic of Ireland.

TELEPHONE Administration + 353 (0)65 9053124, **Reservations** Not applicable.

FAX Administration + 353 (0)65 9053125, **Reservations** Not applicable.

INTERNET Email enquiries@shannonferries.com **Website** www.shannonferries.com (*English*)

ROUTE OPERATED Killimer (County Clare) - Tarbert (County Kerry) (20 mins; *1,2*; hourly (half-hourly during May, June, July, August and September)).

1	SHANNON BREEZE	611t	00	10.0k	80.8m	350P	60C	-	BA	IR	9224910
2	SHANNON DOLPHIN	501t	95	10.0k	71.9m	350P	52C	-	BA	IR	9114933

SHANNON BREEZE, SHANNON DOLPHIN Built by Appledore Shipbuilders, Appledore, UK for *Shannon Ferry Ltd.*

SHETLAND ISLANDS COUNCIL

THE COMPANY *Shetland Islands Council* is a British local government authority.

MANAGEMENT Ferry Services Manager Alistair Christie-Henry, **Marine Superintendent** Capt. Colin Reeves.

ADDRESS Port Administration Building, Sella Ness, Mossbank, Shetland ZE2 9QR.

TELEPHONE Administration +44(0)1806 244234, 244266, **Reservations Yell Sound & Bluemull** +44(0)1957 722259, *Fair Isle* +44(0)1595 760222, *Whalsay* +44(0)1806 566259, *Skerries* +44(0)1806 515266, *Papa Stour* +44 (0)1957 722259.

VOICEBANK *Bluemull Sound* +44 (0)1595 743971, *Bressay* +44 (0)1595 743974, *Fair Isle* +44 (0)1595 743978, *Papa Stour* +44 (0)1595 743977, *Skerries* +44 (0)1595 743975, *Whalsay* +44 (0)1595 743973, *Yell Sound* +44 (0)1595 743972.

FAX + 44 (0)1806 244232.

INTERNET Email ferries@sic.shetland.gov.uk **Website:** www.shetland.gov.uk/ferries (*English*)

ROUTES OPERATED Yell Sound Service Toft (Mainland) - Ulsta (Yell) (20 mins; *2,3*; up to 26 per day), **Bluemull Sound Service** (Gutcher (Yell) - Belmont (Unst) (10 mins; *1,5,6*; up to 28 per day), Gutcher – Hamars Ness (Fetlar) (25 mins; *1,5,6*; up to 8 per day), **Bressay** Lerwick (Mainland) - Maryfield (Bressay) (5 mins; *9*; up to 23 per day), **Whalsay** Laxo/Vidlin (Mainland) - Symbister (Whalsay) (30-45 mins; *8,10*; up to 18 per day), **Skerries** Vidlin (Mainland) – Out Skerries (1 hr 30 mins; *4*; up to 10 per week), Out Skerries – Lerwick (3 hours; *4*; 2 per week), **Fair Isle** (Grutness (Mainland) - Fair Isle (3 hrs; *7*; 2 per week), **Papa Stour** West Burrafirth (Mainland) – Papa Stour (40 mins; *11*; up to 7 per week).

1	BIGGA	274t	91	11.0k	33.5m	96P	21C	4L	BA	UK	9000821
2	DAGALIEN	1861t	04	12.0k	61m	145P	30C	4L	BA	UK	9291626
3	DAGGRI	1861t	04	12.0k	61m	145P	30C	4L	BA	UK	9291614
4	FILLA	356t	03	12.0k	35.5m	30P	10C	2L	BA	UK	9269192
5	FIVLA	230t	85	11.0k	29.9m	95P	15C	4L	BA	UK	8410237
6	GEIRA	226t	88	10.8k	29.9m	95P	15C	4L	BA	UK	8712489
7	GOOD SHEPHERD IV	76t	86	10.0k	18.3m	12P	1C	0L	C	UK	
8	HENDRA	248	82	11.0k	33.8m	100P	18C	4L	BA	UK	8200254
9	LEIRNA	420t	92	9.0k	35.1m	100P	20C	4L	BA	UK	9050199
10	LINGA	658t	01	11.0k	35.8m	100P	16C	2L	BA	UK	9242170
11	SNOLDA	130t	83	9.0k	24.4m	12P	6C	1L	A	UK	8302090
12	THORA	147t	75	8.5k	25.3m	93P	10C	2L	BA	UK	7347354

BIGGA Built by JW Miller & Sons Ltd, St Monans, Fife, UK. Used on the Toft - Ulsta service. In 2005 moved to the Bluemull Sound service.

DAGALIEN, DAGGRI Built by Stocznia Polnócna, Gdansk, Poland to replace the BIGGA and HENDRA on Toft - Ulsta service.

FILLA Built by Stocznia Polnócna, Gdansk, Poland for the Lerwick /Vidlin - Out Skerries service. She looks like an oil rig supply vessel and is capable of transporting fresh water for replenishing the tanks on the Skerries in case of drought.

FIVLA Built by Ailsa Shipbuilding, Troon, UK. Now a spare vessel, though often used on the Bluemull service.

GEIRA Built by Richard Dunston (Hessle), Hessle, UK. Formerly used on the Laxo - Symbister route. Replaced by the HENDRA in 2005 and moved to the Bluemull Sound service.

GOOD SHEPHERD IV Built by JW Miller & Sons Ltd, St Monans, Fife, UK. Used on the service between Grutness (Mainland) and Fair Isle. Vehicles conveyed by special arrangement and generally consist of agricultural vehicles. She is pulled up on the marine slip on Fair Isle at the conclusion of each voyage.

HENDRA Built by McTay Marine, Bromborough, Wirral, UK for the Laxo - Symbister service. In 2002 transferred to the Toft - Ulsta service. In 2004 replaced by new vessels DAGGRI and DAGALIEN and moved to the Bluemull Sound service. In May 2005 returned to the Laxo - Symbister service as second vessel.

LEIRNA Built by Ferguson Shipbuilders, Port Glasgow, UK. Used on the Lerwick - Maryfield (Bressay) service.

LINGA Built by Stocznia Polnócna, Gdansk, Poland. Used on the Laxo - Symbister service.

SNOLDA Built by Sigbjorn Iversen, Flekkefjord, Norway as the FILLA. Used on the Lerwick (Mainland) - Out Skerries and Vidlin (Mainland) - Out Skerries services. At other times she operated freight and charter services around the Shetland Archipelago. She resembles a miniature oil rig supply vessel. Passenger capacity was originally 20 from 1st April to 31st October inclusive but is now 12 all year. In 2003 renamed the SNOLDA; replaced by the new FILLA and, in 2004, transferred to the West

Burrafirth - Papa Stour route.

THORA Built by Tórshavnor Skipasmidja, Tórshavn, Faroe Islands. After a period as a spare vessel, in 1998 she took over the Laxo - Symbister service from the withdrawn KJELLA (158t, 1957). Withdrawn again in 2001 and became a spare vessel.

SKYE FERRY

THE COMPANY The *Skye Ferry* is owned by the *Isle of Skye Ferry Community Interest Company*, a company limited by guarantee.

ADDRESS 6 Coulindune, Glenelg, Kyle, Ross-shire, IV40 8JU.

TELEPHONE Administration & Reservations + 44 (0)1599 522313.

FAX Administration & Reservations + 44 (0)1599 522313.

INTERNET Email info@skyeferry.co.uk **Website** www.skyeferry.co.uk (*English*)

ROUTE OPERATED *Easter - October only* Glenelg - Kylerhea (Skye) (10 mins; *1*; frequent service).

| 1 | GLENACHULISH | 44t | 69 | 9.0k | 20.0m | 12P | 6C | - | BSt | UK | |

GLENACHULISH Built by Ailsa Shipbuilding Company, Troon, UK for the *Balachulish Ferry Company* for the service between North Ballachulish and South Ballachulish, across the mouth of Loch Leven. In 1975 the ferry was replaced by a bridge and she was sold to *Highland Regional Council* and used on a relief basis on the North Kessock - South Kessock and Kylesku - Kylestrome routes. In 1983 she was sold to *Murdo Mc Kenzie*, who had operated the Glenelg – Skye route as ferryman since 1959. The vessel was eventually bought by *Roddy MacLeod* and the service resumed in September 1990. The *Isle of Skye Ferry Community Interest Company* reached agreement with *Mr MacLeod* that he would operate the ferry in 2006 and in 2007 she was sold to the Company. She is the last turntable ferry in operation.

STRANGFORD LOUGH FERRY SERVICE

THE COMPANY The *Strangford Lough Ferry Service* is operated by the *DRD (Department for Regional Development)*, a Northern Ireland Government Department (formerly operated by *Department of the Environment (Northern Ireland)*).

MANAGEMENT Ferry Manager D Pedlow.

ADDRESS Strangford Lough Ferry Service, Strangford, Co Down BT30 7NE.

TELEPHONE Administration + 44 (0)28 4488 1637, **Reservations** Not applicable.

FAX Administration + 44 (0)28 4488 1249, **Reservations** Not applicable.

INTERNET Website www.roadsni.gov.uk/Strangford_Ferry/index.htm (*English*)

ROUTE OPERATED Strangford - Portaferry (County Down) (10 mins; *1,2*; half-hourly).

| 1 | PORTAFERRY II | 312t | 01 | 12.0k | 38.2m | 260P | 28C | - | BA | UK | 9237436 |
| 2 | STRANGFORD FERRY | 186t | 69 | 10.0k | 32.9m | 263P | 20C | - | BA | UK | 6926311 |

PORTAFERRY II Built by McTay Marine, Bromborough, Wirral, UK for *DRD (Northern Ireland)*.

STRANGFORD FERRY Built by Verolme Dockyard Ltd, Cork, Irish Republic for *Down County Council*. Subsequently transferred to the *DOE (Northern Ireland)* and then the *DRD (Northern Ireland)*. Following delivery of the PORTAFERRY II, she became reserve ferry.

C TOMS & SON LTD

THE COMPANY *C Toms & Son Ltd* is a British private sector company.

MANAGEMENT Managing Director Allen Toms.

Strangford Ferry (*Miles Cowsill*)

John Burns (*John Hendy*)

ADDRESS East Street, Polruan, Fowey, Cornwall PL23 1PB.

TELEPHONE Administration +44 (0)1726 870232.

FAX Administration +44 (0)1726 870318.

ROUTE OPERATED Fowey - Bodinnick (Cornwall) (5 mins; *1,2*; frequent).

1	GELLAN	50t	03	4.5k	36.0m	50P	10C	-	BA	UK
2	JENACK	60t	00	4.5k	36.0m	50P	15C	-	BA	UK

GELLAN, JENACK Built by *C Toms & Sons Ltd*, Fowey, UK.

VALENTIA ISLAND FERRIES

THE COMPANY *Valentia Island Ferries Ltd* is an Irish Republic private sector company.

MANAGEMENT Manager Richard Foran.

ADDRESS Valentia Island, County Kerry, Republic of Ireland.

TELEPHONE Administration +353 (0)66 76141, **Reservations** Not applicable.

FAX Administration +353 (0)66 76377, **Reservations** Not applicable.

INTERNET Email reforan@indigo.ie **Website** indigo.ie/%7ecguiney/ferry.html *(English)*

ROUTE OPERATED Reenard (Co Kerry) - Knightstown (Valentia Island) (5 minutes; *1*; frequent service, 1st April - 30th September).

1	GOD MET ONS III	95t	63	-	43.0m	95P	18C	-	BA	IR

GOD MET ONS III Built by BV Scheepswerven Vh HH Bodewes, Millingen, The Netherlands for *FMHE Res* of The Netherlands for a service across the River Maas between Cuijk and Middelaar. In 1987 a new bridge was opened and the service ceased. She was latterly used on contract work in the Elbe and then laid up. In 1996 acquired by *Valentia Island Ferries* and inaugurated a car ferry service to the island. **Note:** This island never had a car ferry service before. A bridge was opened at the south end of the island in 1970; before that a passenger/cargo service operated between Reenard Point and Knightstown.

WESTERN FERRIES

THE COMPANY *Western Ferries (Clyde) Ltd* is a British private sector company.

MANAGEMENT Managing Director Gordon Ross.

ADDRESS Hunter's Quay, Dunoon PA23 8HJ.

TELEPHONE Administration +44 (0)1369 704452, **Reservations** Not applicable.

FAX Administration +44 (0)1369 706020, **Reservations** Not applicable.

INTERNET Email enquiries@western-ferries.co.uk **Website** www.western-ferries.co.uk *(English)*

ROUTE OPERATED McInroy's Point (Gourock) - Hunter's Quay (Dunoon) (20 mins; *1,2,3,4*; every 20 mins (15 mins in peaks)).

1	SOUND OF SANDA	403t	64	10.0k	48.43m	220P	37C	4/5L	BA	UK	8928894
2	SOUND OF SCALPAY	403t	61	10.0k	48.43m	220P	37C	4/5L	BA	UK	8928882
3	SOUND OF SCARBA	489t	01	11.0k	49.95m	220P	40C	4/5L	BA	UK	9237424
4	SOUND OF SHUNA	489t	03	11.0k	49.95m	220P	40C	4/5L	BA	UK	9289441

SOUND OF SANDA Built by Gutehoffnungshulte Sterkrade AG, Rheinwerft, Walsum, Germany as the GEMEENTEPONT 24 for *Amsterdam City Council* and operated from Centraal Station to the other side of the River IJ. In 1996 purchased by *Western Ferries* and renamed the SOUND OF SANDA.

SOUND OF SCALPAY Built by Arnhemsche Scheepsbouw Maatschappij NV, Arnhem, The

Fastcat Ryde and **St Helen** (*Miles Cowsill*)

Caedmon (*John Hendy*)

SECTION 2 – DOMESTIC SERVICES

Netherlands as the GEMEENTEPONT 23 for *Amsterdam City Council*. In 1995 sold to *Western Ferries* and renamed the SOUND OF SCALPAY.

SOUND OF SCARBA, SOUND OF SHUNA Built by Ferguson Shipbuilders, Port Glasgow, UK for *Western Ferries*.

WIGHTLINK

THE COMPANY *Wightlink* is a British private sector company, owned by the *Macquarie Group* of Australia. The routes and vessels were previously part of *Sealink (British Rail)* but were excluded from the purchase of most of the *Sealink* operations by *Stena Line AB* in 1990. They remained in *Sea Containers'* ownership until purchased by *CINVen* Ltd, a venture capital company in 1995. The company was the subject of a management buy-out financed by the *Royal Bank of Scotland* in 2001 and sold to the *Macquarie Group* in 2005.

MANAGEMENT Chief Executive Andrew Willson, **Marketing Manager** Kerry Jackson, **Commercial Director** Clive Tilley.

ADDRESS PO Box 59, Portsmouth PO1 2XB.

TELEPHONE Administration +44 (0)23 9281 2011, **Reservations** 0871 376 1000 (from UK only), +44 (0)23 9281 2011 (from overseas).

FAX Administration & Reservations +44 (0)23 9285 5257, **Telex** 86440 WIGHTLG.

INTERNET Email info@wightlink.co.uk **Website** www.wightlink.co.uk (*English, Dutch, French, German*)

ROUTES OPERATED Conventional Ferries Lymington - Yarmouth (Isle of Wight) (approx 30 mins; *1,2,3*; half-hourly), Portsmouth - Fishbourne (Isle of Wight) (approx 40 mins; *7,8,9,10,11*; half-hourly or hourly depending on time of day). **Fast Passenger Ferries** Portsmouth - Ryde (Isle of Wight) (passenger-only) (approx 18 mins; *4,5,6*; half-hourly/hourly).

1	CAEDMON	764t	73	9.5k	57.9m	512P	58C	6L	BA	UK	7314888
2	CENRED	761t	73	9.5k	57.9m	512P	58C	6L	BA	UK	7324091
3	CENWULF	761t	73	9.5k	57.9m	512P	58C	6L	BA	UK	7320021
4»p	FASTCAT RYDE	478t	96	34.0k	40.0m	361P	0C	0L	-	UK	9144976
5»p	FASTCAT SHANKLIN	482t	96	34.0k	40.0m	361P	0C	0L	-	UK	8888513
6»p	OUR LADY PAMELA	312t	86	28.5k	29.5m	395P	0C	0L	-	UK	8508931
7	ST. CATHERINE	2036t	83	12.5k	77.0m	771P	142C	12L	BA	UK	8120557
8	ST. CECILIA	2968t	86	12.5k	77.0m	771P	142C	12L	BA	UK	8518546
9	ST. CLARE	5359t	01	13.0k	86.0m	878P	186C	-	BA	UK	9236949
10	ST. FAITH	3009t	89	12.5k	77.0m	771P	142C	12L	BA	UK	8907228
11	ST. HELEN	2983t	83	12.5k	77.0m	771P	142C	12L	BA	UK	8120569

CAEDMON Built by Robb Caledon Shipbuilders Ltd, Dundee, UK for *Sealink* for the Portsmouth - Fishbourne service. In 1983 transferred to the Lymington - Yarmouth service. To be withdrawn from service in Summer 2008 due to the introduction of the 'Wight Class'.

CENRED, CENWULF Built by Robb Caledon Shipbuilders Ltd, Dundee, UK for *Sealink* for the Lymington - Yarmouth service. To be withdrawn from service in Summer 2008/early 2009 due to the introduction of the 'Wight Class'.

FASTCAT RYDE Kværner Fjellstrand Flyingcat 40m built at Singapore as the WATER JET 1 for *Waterjet Netherlands Antilles* and operated in the Philippines. In 1999 renamed the SUPERCAT 17. In Summer 2000 sold to *Wightlink* and renamed the FASTCAT RYDE. After modifications, entered service on the Portsmouth - Ryde route in Autumn 2000.

FASTCAT SHANKLIN Kværner Fjellstrand Flyingcat 40m built at Singapore as the WATER JET 2 for *Waterjet Netherlands Antilles* and operated in the Philippines. In 1999 renamed the SUPERCAT 18. In Summer 2000 sold to *Wightlink* and renamed the FASTCAT SHANKLIN. After modifications, entered service on the Portsmouth - Ryde route in Autumn 2000.

OUR LADY PAMELA Incat 30m catamaran built at Hobart, Tasmania, Australia for *Sealink* for the Portsmouth - Ryde service. Now a reserve vessel.

ST CATHERINE, ST HELEN Built by Henry Robb Caledon Yard, Leith, UK for *Sealink* for the Portsmouth - Fishbourne service.

ST CECILIA, ST FAITH Built by Cochrane Shipbuilders, Selby, UK for *Sealink* for the Portsmouth - Fishbourne service.

ST CLARE Built by Stocznia Remontowa, Gdansk, Poland for the Portsmouth - Fishbourne service. She is a double-ended ferry with a central bridge.

Under Construction

12»p	NEWBUILDING 1	-	09	20.0k	40.9m	260P	0C	-	-	UK	
13»p	NEWBUILDING 2	-	09	20.0k	40.9m	260P	0C	-	-	UK	
14	WIGHT LIGHT	1500t	08	12.0k	62.4m	360P	65C	-	BA	UK	9446972
15	WIGHT SKY	1500t	08	12.0k	62.4m	360P	65C	-	BA	UK	9446984
16	WIGHT SUN	1500t	09	12.0k	62.4m	360P	65C	-	BA	UK	9490416

NEWBUILDING 1, NEWBUILDING 2 Catamarans under construction by FBMA Marine, Cebu, Philippines. To operate on the Portsmouth - Ryde service.

WIGHT LIGHT, WIGHT SKY Under construction by Brodogradilite Kraljevica, Croatia for the Lymington - Yarmouth route. To enter service in Summer 2008.

WIGHT SUN Under construction by Brodogradilište Kraljevica, Croatia for the Lymington - Yarmouth route. To enter service early 2009.

WOOLWICH FREE FERRY

THE COMPANY The *Woolwich Free Ferry* is operated by the *London Borough of Greenwich*, a British municipal authority on behalf of *Transport for London*.

MANAGEMENT Ferry Manager Capt. D Newcomb.

ADDRESS New Ferry Approach, Woolwich, London SE18 6DX.

TELEPHONE Administration +44 (0)20 8921 5786, +44 (0)20 8921 5967, **Reservations** Not applicable.

FAX Administration +44 (0)20 8316 6096, **Reservations** Not applicable.

INTERNET Email

Website www.greenwich.gov.uk/Greenwich/Travel/LocalTravelServices/WoolwichFerry.htm (*English*)

ROUTE OPERATED Woolwich - North Woolwich (free ferry) (5 mins; *1,2,3*; every 10 mins (weekdays - two ferries in operation), every 15 mins (weekends - one ferry in operation)). **Note:** One ferry is always in reserve/under maintenance.

1	ERNEST BEVIN	1194t	63	8.0k	56.7m	310P	32C	6L	BA	UK	5426998
2	JAMES NEWMAN	1194t	63	8.0k	56.7m	310P	32C	6L	BA	UK	5411905
3	JOHN BURNS	1194t	63	8.0k	56.7m	310P	32C	6L	BA	UK	5416010

ERNEST BEVIN, JAMES NEWMAN, JOHN BURNS Built by Robb Caledon Shipbuilders Ltd, Dundee, UK for the *London County Council* who operated the service when the vessels were new. In 1965 ownership was transferred to the *Greater London Council*. Following the abolition of the *GLC* in April 1986, ownership was transferred to the *Department of Transport* and in 2001 to *Transport for London*. The *London Borough of Greenwich* operate the service on their behalf. An alternative loading is 6 x 18m articulated lorries and 14 cars; lorries of this length are too high for the nearby northbound Blackwall Tunnel.

SECTION 2 – DOMESTIC SERVICES

Gardenia *(Mike Louagie)*

SECTION 3 -
GB & IRELAND - FREIGHT-ONLY FERRIES
BRITTANY FERRIES

THE COMPANY See Section 1. The freight division of *Brittany Ferries* traded as *Truckline Ferries* until 2002.

MANAGEMENT Managing Director David Longden, **Freight Director** John Clarke.

ADDRESS New Harbour Road, Poole, Dorset BH15 4AJ.

TELEPHONE Administration & Enquiries +44 (0)8709 013300, **Reservations** +44 (0)8709 040200.

FAX Administration & Reservations +44 (0)1202 679828, **Telex** 41744, 41745.

INTERNET Website www.brittanyferriesfreight.co.uk (*English*)

ROUTES OPERATED Cherbourg (***Winter** dep: 00.45 Tue, 09.30 Wed, Fri, 18.30 Tue, Thu, 23.45 Wed, Fri, **Summer** 00.45 Tue-Sat, 14.15 Tue-Fri*) - Poole (***Winter** dep: 08.30 Tue, Thu, 16.00 Wed, Fri, 18.30 Mon, 23.45 Tue, Thu, **Summer** dep: 08.00 Tue-Fri, 18.30 Mon-Fri*) (4 hrs 30 mins; *1*; 1/2 per day) (operates with passenger vessel BARFLEUR to give 3/4 sailings per day), Poole (*dep: 08.30 Sat*) - Santander (*dep: 15.15 Sun*) (27 hrs; *1*; 1 per week).

1	COTENTIN	22542t	07	23.0k	167.0m	160P	-	140L	BA	FR	9364978
2•	COUTANCES	6507t	78	17.0k	125.2m	58P	-	58T	BA	FR	7528477

COTENTIN Built by Aker Finnyards, Rauma, Finland for *Brittany Ferries*. Operates from Poole to Cherbourg and also operates a weekend service to Santander.

COUTANCES Built by Ateliers et Chantiers du Havre, Le Havre, France for *Truckline Ferries* for their Cherbourg - Poole service. In 1986 lengthened to increase vehicle capacity by 34%. In December 2007 transferred to the Portsmouth - Caen service and operated at weekends between Poole and Cherbourg when the COTENTIN was operating to Santander. In May 2008 these sailings were withdrawn. Sold June 2008.

CALEDONIAN MACBRAYNE

THE COMPANY, MANAGEMENT, ADDRESS, TELEPHONE & INTERNET See Section 2.

ROUTE OPERATED Ullapool - Stornoway (Lewis) (3 hours; *1*; 1 per day) (no fixed schedule - run according to demand).

1	MUIRNEAG	5801t	79	15.5k	105.6m	0P	-	54T	AS	UK	7725362

MUIRNEAG Built by Frederikshavn Værft A/S, Frederikshavn, Denmark as the MERCANDIAN CARRIER II for *Mercandia* of Denmark and used on a variety of services. In 1983 she was briefly renamed ALIANZA and between 1984 and 1985 she carried the name CARRIER II. In 1985 sold to *P&O*, renamed the BELARD and used on *Northern Ireland Trailers'* services between Ardrossan and Belfast (later Larne), subsequently becoming part of *Pandoro*. In 1993 she was chartered to *IOMSP* subsidiary *Mannin Line* to inaugurate a new service between Great Yarmouth and IJmuiden. In 1994 she was purchased by *IOMSP*; however, in 1995 the *Mannin Line* service ceased and she was chartered back to *Pandoro*. At the end of 1995 she was returned to *IOMSP*. In 1996, after deputising for the PEVERIL, she was briefly chartered to *Exxtor Ferries* (operating between Immingham and Rotterdam) and then laid up. In 1997, she again deputised for the PEVERIL, followed by a short period of charter to *P&O European Ferries*. In 1997 she returned to *IOMSP* and replaced the PEVERIL as the main freight vessel. In 1998 she was sold to the *Aabrenaa Rederi* and operated between Åbenrå and Klaìpeda. This service ended in 1999 and she was used on a number of short- term charters. In Spring 2002 chartered to *Ferryways* and operated between Ipswich and Ostend. In Autumn 2002 she was chartered to *Caledonian MacBrayne*, renamed the MUIRNEAG and placed on the Ullapool – Stornoway service, replacing the HASCOSAY (see *NorthLink*). She was subsequently sold to *Harrisons (2002) Ltd* and chartered back.

Cotentin (*Miles Cowsill*)

Coutances (*Miles Cowsill*)

Yasmine (*Mike Louagie*)

COBELFRET FERRIES

THE COMPANY *Cobelfret Ferries NV* is a Belgian private sector company, a subsidiary of *Cobelfret NV* of Antwerp. *Dart Line* of the UK was taken over by the company in 2006.

MANAGEMENT Operations Manager (Belgium) Marc Vandersteen, **UK *Purfleet, Dartford and Dagenham services*** Cobelfret Ferries UK Ltd - **General Manager, Line & Agency Division** Nick Kavanagh, ***Killingholme Services*** Cobelfret Ferries UK Ltd (Killingholme Branch) - **General Manager** Peter Kirman, ***Rotterdam Services*** Cobelfret Ferries UK Ltd (Rotterdam Branch) – **General Manager** Henk In'tveen, ***Vlissingen Service*** Cobelfret Ferries BV – **General Manager**, Hugo Von Aesch.

ADDRESSES *Belgium* Sea-Ro Terminal, Britannia Quay, 8380 Zeebrugge, Belgium **UK *Purfleet*** CdMR Terminal, London Road, Purfleet, Essex RM19 1RP, **UK – *Dartford*** Dartline Ltd, Thames Europort, Clipper Boulevard, Crossways, Dartford, Kent DA2 6QB **UK *Killingholme*** CdMR Terminal, Clough Lane, North Killingholme, Immingham DN40 3JS, ***The Netherlands - Rotterdam*** CdMR Terminal, Merseyweg 70, Port no:5230 Rotterdam, Botlek, ***The Netherlands – Vlissingen*** CdMR Terminal, 4389 PA Ritthem, Harbour No. 1125, Vlissingen Oost.

TELEPHONE Administration & Reservations *Belgium* + 32 (0)50 502243, **UK *(Purfleet)*** + 44 (0)1708 891199, ***(Killingholme)*** + 44 (0)1469 542500, **The Netherlands *(Rotterdam)*** + 31 (0) 181 234022, ***(Vlissingen)*** + 31 118480005.

FAX Administration & Reservations *Belgium* + 32 (0)50 502219, **UK *(Purfleet)*** + 44 (0)1708 890853, ***(Killingholme)*** + 44 (0)1469 542501, **The Netherlands *(Rotterdam)*** + 31 (0) 181 216699, ***(Vlissingen)*** + 31 118480009.

INTERNET Website www.cobelfret.com *(English)*

ROUTES OPERATED Zeebrugge *(dep: 04.00 Tue-Fri, 10.00 Mon-Fri, 16.00 Mon-Fri, 22.00 Mon-Fri)* - Purfleet *(dep: 06.00 Tue-Fri, 12.00 Mon-Fri, 18.00 Mon-Fri, 23.00 Mon-Fri* (**Note:** *weekend services run subject to demand and are liable to vary))* (9 hrs; **4,5,7,13,25**; 4 per day), Ostend *(dep: 01.00 Mon-Fri, 13.00 Mon-Fri)* - Dartford *(dep: 00.01 Mon-Fri, 12.00 Mon-Fri)* (9 hrs; 2 per day), Ostend *(dep:22.00 Mon-Fri)* - Killingholme *(dep: 00.01 Tue-Sat)* (21 hours; 1 per day), Ostend *(dep: 10.00 Tue-Fri, 22.00 Sun-Fri)* - Ipswich *(dep: 09.00 Tue-Fri, 11.45 Sat, 21.00 Mon-Fri)* (7 hrs; 2 per day). **Note:** Ostend services are operated by **1,6,11,12,15,17**; they are often switched between routes. Vlissingen *(dep: 02.00 Tue-Fri, 10.00 Mon-Fri, 18.00 Mon-Fri)* - Dagenham *(dep: 01.00 Tue-Fri, 09.00 Mon-Fri, 17.00 Mon-Fri)* (contract service for Ford Motor Company) (11 hrs; **8,9,22,23**; 3 per day), Zeebrugge *(dep: 17.00 Sat, 20.30 Mon-Fri)* - Killingholme *(dep: 17.00 Sat, 20.00 Mon-Fri)* (14 hrs; **16,27**) (*Sunday sailings as required*); 1/2 per day), Vlissingen *(dep: Sat)* – Southampton *(dep: Sun)* (**8,9,22,23**; 1 or 2 per week - for Ford Motor Company – runs as required), Rotterdam *(dep: 17.00 Sat, 20.00 Mon-Fri)* - Dartford *(dep: 16.00 Sat, 19.30 Mon-Fri)* (14 hrs; **2,24**; 1 per day), Rotterdam *(dep: 17.30)* - Killingholme *(dep: 17.30)* (14 hrs; **3,14**; 1 per day), Zeebrugge *(dep: 18.00 Fri)* - Esbjerg *(dep: 00.01 Sun)* (24 hrs; **4,5,7,13,25**; 1 per week), Zeebrugge *(dep: 03.00 Sun, 10.00 Mon, 12.00 Tue, 20.00 Wed, 20.00 Thu, 22.00 Fri, 10.00 Sat)* - Gothenburg *(dep: 16.00 Sun, 04.00 Mon, 00.01 Tue, 00.01 Wed, 04.00 Thu, 13.00 Fri, 13.00 Sat)* (33-38 hrs; **18,20,21**; 6 per week). **Note:** The Gothenburg service is operated for the *Stora-Enso* paper and board group, for the conveyance of their products. *Cobelfret Ferries* act as handling agents at Zeebrugge and Gothenburg and market the surplus capacity on the vessels, which is available for general ro-ro traffic. Although this route is strictly outside the scope of this book it is included for the sake of completeness.

1	ANGLIAN WAY	7628t	78	15.0k	141.3m	12P	55C	84T	A	MT	7613404
2	AQUILINE	22748t	80	18.0k	178.5m	12P	-	155T	A	BM	7822196
3	CATHERINE	21287t	02	20.0k	182.2m	12P	-	200T	A2	LU	9209453
4	CELANDINE	23987t	00	18.0k	162.5m	12P	630C	157T	A	BE	9183904
5	CELESTINE	23986t	96	17.8k	162.5m	24P	630C	157T	A	BE	9125372
6	CERVINE	9088t	84	15.0k	121.5m	12P	-	90T	A2	BM	8009076
7	CLEMENTINE	23986t	97	17.8k	162.5m	24P	630C	157T	A	BE	9125384
8	CYMBELINE	11866t	92	14.5k	147.4m	8P	350C	100T	A2	LU	9007764
9	EGLANTINE	10035t	89	14.5k	147.4m	8P	350C	100T	A2	LU	8302806

10	EQUINE	16948t	79	15.0k	170.3m	12P	180C	160T	A	BE	7800760
11	FLANDERS WAY	7635t	77	16.0k	141.3m	12P	55C	84T	A	MT	7720477
12	IPSWICH WAY	6568t	80	15.0k	136.0m	12P	-	84T	A	MT	7816496
13	LOUISE RUSS	18265t	00	23.5k	174.0m	12P	-	171T	A	GI	9226360
14	MELUSINE	23987t	99	18.0k	162.5m	12P	630C	157T	A	BE	9166637
15	OSTEND WAY	6568t	80	15.0k	136.1m	12P	-	84T	A	MT	7816501
16	PAULINE	49166t	06	21.7k	200.0m	12P	656C	258T	A	LU	9324473
17	PHOCINE	9088t	84	15.0k	121.5m	12P	-	90T	A2	BM	8009064
18	SCHIEBORG	21005t	00	17.0k	183.4m	12P	-	180T	A	NL	9188233
19	SERPENTINE	22748t	80	18.0k	178.5m	12P	-	155T	A	BE	7822201
20	SLINGEBORG	21005t	00	17.0k	183.4m	12P	-	180T	A	NL	9188245
21	SPAARNEBORG	21005t	00	17.0k	183.4m	12P	-	180T	A	NL	9188221
22	SYMPHORINE	10030t	88	14.5k	147.4m	8P	350C	100T	A2	LU	8302791
23	UNDINE	11854t	91	14.5k	147.4m	8P	350C	100T	A2	LU	9006112
24	VALENTINE	23987t	99	18.0k	162.5m	12P	630C	157T	A	BE	9166625
25	VICTORINE	23987t	00	18.0k	162.5m	12P	630C	157T	A	BE	9184029
26	VULPINE	16947t	78	15.0k	170.3m	12P	180C	160T	A	PA	7800758
27	YASMINE	49166t	07	21.7k	200.0m	12P	656C	258T	A	LU	9337353

ANGLIAN WAY Built by Rickmers Werft GmbH, Bremerhaven, Germany as the THOMAS WEHR for *Wehr Transport* of Germany as THOMAS WEHR but on delivery chartered to *Wacro Line* and renamed the WACRO EXPRESS. In 1978 the charter ended and she was renamed the THOMAS WEHR. Over the next few years she was chartered to several operators. In 1982 she was chartered to *Tor Lloyd* (later *Tor Line*) for North Sea service and renamed the TOR NEERLANDIA. In 1985 the charter was transferred to *DFDS* and she was renamed the DANA GERMANIA. This charter terminated in 1985 and she resumed her original name. In early 1986 she was chartered to *North Sea Ferries* for their Hull - Zeebrugge service. This charter ended in Summer 1987. Subsequent charters included *Cobelfret* and *Elbe-Humber RoLine* and a twelve-month period with *North Sea Ferries* again - this time on the Hull - Rotterdam and Teesport - Zeebrugge routes. In 1993 she was renamed the MANA, then the SANTA MARIA and finally chartered to *TT-Line* and renamed the FULDATAL. In 1994 she was chartered to *Horn Line* for service between Europe and the Caribbean and renamed the HORNLINK. Later that year she was chartered to *P&O European Ferries* for the Portsmouth - Le Havre freight service and resumed the name THOMAS WEHR. In late 1995 transferred to the Felixstowe - Zeebrugge freight service. In Autumn 1999 the charter was ended. In 2000 she was chartered to *Ferryways*. In 2001 she was purchased by *Ferryways* and renamed the ANGLIAN WAY. Generally operated between Ostend and Ipswich. In June 2007 acquired by *Cobelfret Ferries*. In July inaugurated a new Ostend - Dartford service, then switched to the Ostend - Dartford route, becoming Ostend - Harwich in Spring 2008. Operates on all routes from Ostend.

AQUILINE Built by Kawasaki Heavy Industries, Sakaide, Japan as the GU BEI KOU, a deep sea ro-ro/container ship for *China Ocean Shipping Company* of the People's Republic of China for service between the USA, Australia and New Zealand. In 1999, purchased by *Jacobs Holdings*. After delivery, she was converted in Nantong, China to short sea ro-ro specification, including the fitting of a stern ramp (replacing the quarter ramp) and luxury accommodation for 12 drivers. Renamed the DART 9 and entered service in September 1999 on the Dartford - Zeebrugge service. In 2003 chartered to the *British MoD* for service in the Persian Gulf. Returned in September 2003 and resumed service on the Dartford – Zeebrugge route. In 2006 renamed the AQUILINE. In 2008 moved to the Rotterdam - Dartford service.

CATHERINE Built as the ROMIRA by Zhonghua Shipyard, Zhonghua, China for *Dag Engström Rederi* of Sweden. For six months engaged on a number of short-term charters, including *Cobelfret Ferries* who used her on both the Rotterdam - Immingham and Zeebrugge - Purfleet routes. In September 2002 purchased by *Cobelfret Ferries* and, in November 2002, renamed the CATHERINE and started on the Rotterdam - Immingham service. In Spring 2003 chartered to the *US Defense Department* to convey materials to the Persian Gulf. Returned in late summer and has operated on the Rotterdam - Immingham service ever since.

CELANDINE, VALENTINE, VICTORINE Built by Kawasaki Heavy Industries, Sakaide, Japan for *Cobelfret*. Similar to the CLEMENTINE. The CELANDINE was originally to be called the CATHERINE and the VICTORINE the CELANDINE. The names were changed before delivery. The CELANDINE and VICTORINE are generally used on the Zeebrugge - Purfleet service and the VALENTINE on the Rotterdam - Dartford route.

CELESTINE Built by Kawasaki Heavy Industries, Sakaide, Japan as the CELESTINE. In 1996 chartered to the *British MoD* and renamed the SEA CRUSADER. She was originally expected to return to *Cobelfret Ferries* in early 2003 and resume the name CELESTINE; however, the charter was extended because of the Iraq crisis. Returned in September 2003 and placed on the Zeebrugge - Immingham service. In November 2006 moved to the Zeebrugge - Purfleet route.

CERVINE Built by Santierul Naval, Galatz, Romania as the BALDER BRE for *K/S A/S Balder RO/RO No 2* of Norway. Later in 1985 acquired by *Navrom* of Romania and renamed the BAZIAS 4. In 1991 chartered to *Sally Ferries* for the Ramsgate - Ostend freight service and subsequently purchased by *Rosal SA*, a joint *Sally Ferries/Romline* company. In 1993 renamed the SALLY EUROLINK and re-registered in The Bahamas. In 1997 *Sally Ferries'* interests in her were purchased by *Jacobs Holdings*. She was later transferred to *Dart Line* and renamed the DART 4. In 1998 she was chartered to *Belfast Freight Ferries*. She returned to *Dart Line* in February 1999. Generally operated on the Dartford - Vlissingen route. In June 2006 transferred to *Cobelfret Ferries* and operated mainly on the Zeebrugge - Purfleet and Zeebrugge - Killingholme services. In September 2006 renamed the CERVINE. Since July 2007 has operated mainly on the Ostend - Killingholme service.

CLEMENTINE Built by Kawasaki Heavy Industries, Sakaide, Japan for *Cobelfret*. Mainly used on the Zeebrugge - Immingham service. In 2007 moved to the Zeebrugge - Purfleet route.

CYMBELINE, EGLANTINE, SYMPHORINE, UNDINE Built by Dalian Shipyard, Dalian, China for *Cobelfret*. Currently used on the Dagenham - Vlissingen route.

EQUINE Built by Öresundsvarvet AB, Landskrona, Sweden as the EVA ODEN for *AB Norsjöfrakt* (later *Bylock & Norsjöfrakt*) of Sweden and chartered to *Oden Line* of Sweden for North Sea services, in particular associated with the export of Volvo cars and trucks from Gothenburg. In 1980 *Oden Line* was taken over by *Tor Lloyd AB*, a joint venture between *Tor Line* and *Broströms AB* and the charter transferred to them, moving to *Tor Line* in 1981 when *DFDS* took over. In 1987 she was enlarged and on re-entry into service in early 1988 was renamed the TOR BELGIA, becoming a regular vessel on the Gothenburg - Ghent (Belgium) service. In 1998 renamed the EVA ODEN and in 1999 the charter was terminated. In 2000 she was chartered to *Cobelfret Ferries*. Until 2003, generally used on the Zeebrugge - Purfleet service. In 2003 transferred to the Rotterdam - Immingham service, replacing the CATHERINE. In July 2003 transferred to the Rotterdam - Purfleet route. In September replaced by the BRITTA ODEN and, on return from refit, placed on the Zeebrugge - Purfleet route. In 2004 transferred to the Immingham - Gothenburg route. In 2005 the service was taken over by *DFDS Tor Line* and chartered to them. She returned to Zeebrugge in December 2005. Used on the Zeebrugge - Purfleet and Zeebrugge - Gothenburg (weekend) services. In 2006 renamed the EQUINE. In 2007 transferred to the Dartford - Vlissingen service and later used on the Zeebrugge - Purfleet route In January 2008 chartered to *P&O Irish Sea* to operate between Liverpool and Dublin. In April she was chartered to *RMR Shipping Agency* to operate between Antwerp and Lagos (Nigeria) via Harwich.

FLANDERS WAY Built by Rickmers Werft GmbH, Bremerhaven, Germany as the GABRIELE WEHR for *Wehr Transport* of Germany and chartered to several operators. In 1982, chartered to *Tor Lloyd* (later *Tor Line*) for North Sea service and renamed the TOR ANGLIA. This charter terminated in 1985 when she resumed her original name and, in early 1986, she was chartered to *North Sea Ferries* for their Hull - Zeebrugge service. This charter ended in Summer 1987 when the lengthened NORLAND and NORSTAR entered service. Subsequent charters included *Kent Line* and *Brittany Ferries* In 1989 she was chartered to *P&O European Ferries* for the Portsmouth - Le Havre freight service. Her charter was terminated following the transfer of the EUROPEAN TRADER to the route in late 1992 but in 1993 it was renewed, following the transfer of the EUROPEAN CLEARWAY (now the VIA MARE) to *Pandoro*. In 1996, she was transferred to the Felixstowe - Zeebrugge service. In Autumn 1999 the charter was ended. In 2000 she was chartered to *Ferryways*. In 2001 she was purchased by *Ferryways* and renamed the FLANDERS WAY. Generally operates between Ostend and Ipswich. In June 2007 acquired by *Cobelfret Ferries*. In late July inaugurated a new Ostend - Harwich service. Generally operates on

Ostend services.

IPSWICH WAY Built by Karlskronavarvet AB, Karlskrona, Sweden as the BALDER DONA for *Dag Engström Rederi* of Sweden and undertook a number of charters in the Caribbean and Mediterranean. In 1984 she was renamed the RODONA and chartered to *Seaboard Shipping* of the USA and used on Caribbean services. In 1987 she was chartered to the *Ford Motor Company* for conveyance of privately-owned trailers between Dagenham and Zeebrugge. In 1995 *Cobelfret Ferries* took over the operation of this service and she was used on both the Purfleet - Zeebrugge and Dagenham - Zeebrugge services. In 1999 she was chartered to *P&O North Sea Ferries* to operate between Felixstowe and Zeebrugge. In 2002 this service ceased and she was chartered to *Ferryways*. In 2003 purchased by *Ferryways* and renamed the IPSWICH WAY. Generally operated between Ostend and Tilbury. In June 2007 acquired by *Cobelfret Ferries*. In July inaugurated a new Ostend - Dartford service. Generally operates on Ostend services.

LOUISE RUSS Launched by J J Sietas Schiffswerft, Hamburg, Germany as the LOUISE RUSS for *Ernst Russ* of Germany. On completion, renamed the PORTO EXPRESS and chartered to *ROROExpress* to operate between Southampton, Oporto and Tangier. The service ceased in Autumn 2001 when she was returned to her owners and resumed the name LOUISE RUSS. In 2002 chartered to *Cobelfret Ferries* and placed on the Rotterdam - Immingham service. In 2004 transferred to the Rotterdam - Purfleet service. In January 2005 temporarily transferred to the Zeebrugge - Gothenburg route to replace the fire-damaged SCHIEBORG. Returned to the Purfleet - Rotterdam service in June 2005. In 2006 her charter was extended for three years. In January 2008 the service became Dartford - Rotterdam.

MELUSINE Built by Kawasaki Heavy Industries, Sakaide, Japan for *Cobelfret*. Similar to the CLEMENTINE. Currently used on the Rotterdam - Immingham service.

OSTEND WAY Built by Karlskronavarvet AB, Karlskrona, Sweden as the BALDER VINGA for *Dag Engström Rederi* of Sweden and undertook a number of charters in the Caribbean and Mediterranean. In 1984 she was renamed the ROVINGA, chartered to *Seaboard Shipping* of the USA and used on Caribbean services. In 1985 she was renamed the AZUA. In 1987 she briefly reverted to the name ROVINGA before being renamed the SAPPHIRE and chartered to the *Ford Motor Company* for conveyance of privately-owned trailers between Dagenham and Zeebrugge. In 1995 *Cobelfret Ferries* took over the operation of this service and she was used on both the Purfleet - Zeebrugge and Dagenham - Zeebrugge services. In 1999 she was chartered to *P&O North Sea Ferries* to operate between Felixstowe and Zeebrugge. In 2003 purchased by *Ferryways* and renamed the OSTEND WAY. Generally operated between Ostend and Tilbury. In June 2007 acquired by *Cobelfret Ferries*. In July inaugurated a new Ostend - Dartford service. Generally operates on Ostend services.

PAULINE, YASMINE Built by Flensburger Schiffbau-Gesellschaft, Flensburg, Germany to operate on the Zeebrugge - Killingholme route.

PHOCINE Built by Santierul Naval, Galatz, Romania as the BALDER STEN for *K/S A/S Balder RO/RO No 2* of Norway (part of the *Parley Augustsson* group). In 1995 acquired by *Navrom* of Romania and renamed the BAZIAS 3. In 1991 chartered to *Sally Ferries* for the Ramsgate - Ostend freight service and subsequently purchased by a joint *Sally Ferries/Romline* company. In 1993 renamed the SALLY EUROROUTE and re-registered in The Bahamas. In October 1996 she was chartered to *Belfast Freight Ferries* and renamed the MERLE. In 1997 *Sally Ferries'* interests in her were purchased by *Jacobs Holdings*. In January 2000 she joined *Dart Line* and was placed on the Vlissingen service, being renamed the DART 3. In Autumn 2000 she was chartered to *NorseMerchant Ferries* and placed again on the Heysham - Belfast service. In Autumn 2001 returned to *Dart Line*. Generally operated on the Dartford - Vlissingen route. In June 2006 transferred to *Cobelfret Ferries* and operated mainly on the Zeebrugge - Purfleet and Zeebrugge - Killingholme services. In September 2006 renamed the PHOCINE. Since July 2007 has operated mainly on the Ostend - Killingholme service.

SCHIEBORG, SLINGEBORG, SPAARNEBORG Built by Flender Werft AG, Lübeck, Germany for *Wagenborg* of The Netherlands and time-chartered to *Stora-Enso* to operate between Zeebrugge and Gothenburg.

SERPENTINE Built by Kawasaki Heavy Industries, Sakaide, Japan as the XI FENG KOU, a deep sea ro-ro/container ship for *China Ocean Shipping Company* of the People's Republic of China for service

Louise Russ *(Mike Louagie)*

Ipswich Way *(John Bryant)*

between the USA, Australia and New Zealand. In 1999, purchased by *Jacobs Holdings*. After delivery, she was converted in Nantong, China to short sea ro-ro specification, including the fitting of a stern ramp (replacing the quarter ramp) and luxury accommodation for 12 drivers. Renamed the DART 8 and entered service in August 1999 on the Dartford - Zeebrugge service. In 2003 chartered to the *British MoD* for service in the Persian Gulf. Returned in September 2003 and resumed service on the Dartford – Zeebrugge route. In 2006 renamed the SERPENTINE. In February 2008 chartered to *DFDS Tor Line* to operate between Immingham and Cuxhaven.

VULPINE Built by Öresundsvarvet Ab, Landskrona, Sweden as the ANNA ODEN for *AB Norsjöfrakt* of Sweden and chartered to *Oden Line* of Sweden for North Sea services, in particular associated with the export of Volvo cars and trucks from Gothenburg. In 1980 *Oden Line* was taken over by *Tor Lloyd AB*, a joint venture between *Tor Line* and *Broströms AB* and the charter transferred to them, moving to *Tor Line* in 1981 when *DFDS* took over. In 1987 she was lengthened; on re-entry into service in early 1988 she was renamed the TOR FLANDRIA and became regular vessel on the Gothenburg - Ghent (Belgium) service, largely operated for Volvo. In 1999 the charter was ended and she was renamed the SOUTHERN CARRIER. She was chartered to a number of operators including *Cobelfret Ferries* and *Flota Suardiaz*. In 2002 she was renamed the ANNA ODEN. In 2003 she was sold to *Cobelfret Ferries*. In 2004 inaugurated a new Immingham – Gothenburg service. In 2005 moved to the Zeebrugge – Purfleet route. In 2006 renamed the VULPINE. In 2007 chartered to *RMR Shipping Agency* to operate between Antwerp and Lagos (Nigeria) via Harwich.

Cobelfret Ferries also own the URSINE which is currently on charter to *P&O Ferries*.

Under Construction

28	NEWBUILDING 1	23200t	09	19.0k	182.6m	12P	-	180T	A	-	-
29	NEWBUILDING 2	23200t	09	19.0k	182.6m	12P	-	180T	A	-	-
30	NEWBUILDING 3	23200t	10	19.0k	182.6m	12P	-	180T	A	-	-
31	NEWBUILDING 4	23200t	10	19.0k	182.6m	12P	-	180T	A	-	-
32	NEWBUILDING 5	23200t	10	19.0k	195.4m	12P	-	180T	A	-	-
33	NEWBUILDING 6	23200t	11	19.0k	195.4m	12P	-	180T	A	-	-

NEWBUILDING 1, NEWBUILDING 2, NEWBUILDING 3, NEWBUILDING 4, NEWBUILDING 5 and NEWBUILDING 6 On order from Flensburger Schiffbau-Gesellschaft, Flensburg, Germany. An improved version of the CATHERINE.

CONDOR FERRIES

THE COMPANY *Condor Ferries Ltd* is a Channel Islands private sector company owned by the *Condor Group*, Guernsey which is owned by the *Royal Bank of Scotland*.

MANAGEMENT Group Chief Executive Robert Provan, **Managing Director** David Harbord.

ADDRESS *Head Office* PO Box 10, New Jetty Offices, White Rock, St Peter Port, Guernsey GY1 3AF, *Sales and Marketing* New Jetty Offices, White Rock, St Peter Port, Guernsey GY1 3AF.

TELEPHONE Administration +44 (0)1481 728620.

FAX Administration +44 (0)1481 728521.

INTERNET Email jeff.vidamour@condorferries.co.uk **Websites:** www.condorferries.co.uk (*English*)

www.condorferries.fr (*French, English, Dutch, German*)

ROUTES OPERATED Portsmouth (*dep: 09.00*, 19.30*) - Guernsey (*dep: 04.00, 17.30**) (6 hrs 30 min) - Jersey (*dep: 08.15, 21.30**) (10 hrs 30 min; 1; 2 per day) (*operated by ro-pax ferry COMMODORE CLIPPER - see Section 1), Guernsey (*dep: 04.00 Sat*) - Jersey (*dep: 08.15 Sat*) - St Malo (*arr: 14.00 Sat, dep: 17.00 Sat*) - Jersey (*arr: 06.00 Sun*) - Guernsey (*arr: 03.00 Mon*); 1; 1 per week).

1	COMMODORE GOODWILL	11166t	96	18.3k	126.4m	12P	-	92T	A	BS	9117985

COMMODORE GOODWILL Built by Koninklijke Scheldegroep BV, Vlissingen, The Netherlands for *Commodore Ferries*.

DFDS TOR LINE

THE COMPANY *DFDS Tor Line* is primarily a ro-ro operator on the North Sea and Baltic Sea. It is part of *DFDS A/S* which was formed in 1866 and is today quoted on the Copenhagen Stock Exchange. The *DFDS A/S* group consists of companies in Denmark, Sweden, Norway, the United Kingdom, the Netherlands, Belgium, Germany and Lithuania.

MANAGEMENT Managing Director Björn Petrusson, **Managing Director DFDS Tor Line plc** Jens Skibsted Nielsen.

ADDRESS *Denmark (Head Office)* Sundkrogsgade 11, DK-2100 Copenhagen Ø, **UK** Nordic House, Western Access Road, Immingham Dock, Immingham, South Humberside DN40 2LZ.

TELEPHONE Administration & Reservations *Denmark (Head Office)* + 45 33 42 33 00, **UK** + 44 (0)1469 575231.

FAX Administration & Reservations *Denmark* + 45 33 42 33 01, **UK** + 44 (0)1469 552662.

INTERNET Email info@dfdstorline.com **Website** www.dfdstorline.com (*English*)

ROUTES OPERATED Esbjerg (*dep: 21.30 Mon-Sat*) - Immingham (*dep: 20.30 Mon-Sat*) (18 hrs; *6,19*; 6 per week), Cuxhaven (*dep: 19.00 Mon, 19.00 Tue, 02.00 Thu, 19.00 Fri, 09.00 Sat*) - Immingham (*dep: 11.00 Sun, 22.30 Tue, 22.30 Wed, 04.30 Fri, 22.30 Sat*) (22 hrs; *4,8*; 5 per week), Immingham (*dep: 16.00 Sun*) - Antwerp (*arr: 14.00 Mon*) (21 hrs; *4,8*; 3-4 times per month), Gothenburg (*dep: 19.00 Tue, 19.00 Thu, 16.00 Sat*) - Tilbury (*dep: 19.00 Tue, 19.00 Thu, 16.00 Sat; 37 hrs; 1,18*; 2 per week), Gothenburg (*dep: 21.00 Sun-Fri, 18.00 Sat*) - Immingham (*dep: 04.00 Sun-Fri, 10.00 Sat*) - (26 hrs; *3,9,10*; 7 per week), Rotterdam (Maasvlakte) (*dep: 20.00 Mon -Fri, 17.00 Sat*) - Immingham (*dep: 19.00 Mon-Fri, 17.00 Sat*) (12 hrs; *13,15*; 6 per week), Gothenburg (*dep: 20.00 Sun, 22.00 Mon, 23.00 Tue, 03.00 Thu, 04.00 Fri, 08.00 Sat*) - Brevik (Norway) (*dep: 07.00 Sun*) - Ghent (Belgium) (*dep: 22.00 Sun, 10.00 Tue, 12.00 Wed, 16.00 Thu, 18.00 Fri*, 18.00 Sat (*Brevik served by Fri departure)*) (Gothenburg 32 hrs, Brevik 32 hrs; *12,14,16,17*; 6 per week) (*calls at Brevik before Gothenburg), Brevik (*dep: 15.30 Mon, 02.30 Fri*) - Kristiansand (*dep: 12.30 Thu*) - Immingham (*dep: 05.30 Wed, 16.00 Sat*) (approx 27-29 hours Norwegian Port - Immingham; *5*; 2 per week) (**Note:** Wed ex Immingham operates Immingham - Kristiansand - Brevik - Immingham, Sat ex Immingham operates Immingham - Brevik - Immingham), Fredericia (*dep: 21.00 Tue, 02.30 Sat*) – Copenhagen (*dep: 08.30 Wed, Sat 15.00*) - Klaìpeda (Lithuania) (*dep: 21.00 Sun, 13.00 Thu*); *7*; 2 per week).

Space is also used for freight on *DFDS Seaways/DFDS Tor Line* passenger vessels between Harwich and Esbjerg (3 per week or alternate days during the summer), Bergen - Stavanger - Newcastle (2-3 per week) and IJmuiden - Newcastle (daily).

Note: Non-UK routes shown above are strictly outside the scope of this book but are shown for the sake of completeness.

1	ARK FORWARDER	21104t	98	22.0k	182.6m	12P	-	196T	A	UK	9138783
2	TOR ANGLIA	17492t	77	16.0k	171.9m	12P	-	180T	A	DK	7707736
3	TOR BEGONIA	32289t	04	22.5k	199.8m	12P	-	280T	AS	SE	9262089
4	TOR BELGIA	21491t	78	18.5k	193.3m	12P	200C	194T	AS	SE	7624063
5	TOR BELLONA	22748t	80	18.0k	178.5m	12P	-	155T	A	NO	7822213
6	TOR BRITANNIA	24196t	00	21.1k	197.5m	12P	-	200T	A	DK	9153032
7	TOR CORONA	25548t	08	20.0k	184.8m	12P	-	250T	AS	UK	9357597
8	TOR DANIA	21850t	70	19.5k	183.6m	12P	200C	192T	AS	UK	7624051
9	TOR FICARIA	32289t	06	22.5k	199.8m	12P	-	280T	AS	DK	9320568
10	TOR FREESIA	32289t	05	22.5k	199.8m	12P	-	280T	AS	SE	9274848
11	TOR FUTURA	18725t	96	19.7k	183.3m	12P	-	164T	AS	DK	9129598
12	TOR HAFNIA	25548t	08	20.0k	184.8m	12P	-	250T	AS	UK	9357602
13	TOR HUMBRIA	20165t	78	17.5k	177.4m	12P	-	154T	A	NO	7430723
14	TOR MAGNOLIA	32289t	03	22.5k	199.8m	12P		280T	AS	SF	9259496
15	TOR MINERVA	21215t	78	18.5k	177.4m	12P	-	158T	A	NO	7430735
16	TOR PETUNIA	32289t	04	22.5k	199.8m	12P	-	280T	AS	DK	9259501

17	TOR PRIMULA	32289t	04	22.5k	199.8m	12P	-	280T	AS	DK	9259513
18	TOR SELANDIA	24196t	98	21.1k	197.5m	12P	-	206T	A	SE	9157284
19	TOR SUECIA	24196t	99	21.1k	197.5m	12P	-	206T	A	DK	9153020

ARK FORWARDER Launched as the STENA AUSONIA by Societa Esercizio Cantieri SpA, Viareggio, Italy. Completed by INMA, La Spezia, Italy and delivered to *Stena Ferries*, a UK subsidiary of *Stena AB*. Chartered to the *Royal Fleet Auxiliary* and renamed the SEA CENTURION (Naval pennant number A98). In 2003 chartered to *Sudcargo* and renamed the MONT VENTOUX. In 2005 renamed the STENA FORWARDER but continued to be chartered to *Sudcargo*. Later in 2005 chartered to *Trasmediterranea*. In November 2006 chartered to the *Danish MoD* for the ARK Project (strategic sealift for Danish and German military and other NATO countries) for five years but available for commercial charter when not required for military use. In January 2007 chartered to *DFDS Tor Line* and initially placed on the Rotterdam - Immingham service; in February renamed the ARK FORWARDER and in March transferred to the Gothenburg - Tilbury service.

TOR ANGLIA Built by Schiffswerft und Maschinenfabrik Paul Lindenau, Kiel, Germany as the MERZARIO GALLIA and chartered to *Merzario Line* of Italy for services between Italy and Saudi Arabia. In 1981 she was chartered to *Wilhelmsen*, renamed the TANA and used between USA and West Africa. In 1983 she was chartered to *Salenia AB* of Sweden and renamed the NORDIC WASA. In 1987 she had a brief period on charter to *Atlantic Marine* as the AFRICAN GATEWAY and in 1988 she was sold to *Tor Line* and renamed the TOR ANGLIA. In 1989 an additional deck was added. In subsequent years she operated on the Gothenburg - Ghent service but in late 1998 she was switched to the Immingham - Rotterdam service. In 2001 transferred back to the Gothenburg - Ghent service. In January 2003 chartered to the *British MoD* for three months. Later chartered to the *Danish MoD* for NATO service (ARK Project - see above) but can be used on other short-term charters if not required. During 2004 she was chartered to *Van-Uden Ro-Ro* for their service from Northern Europe to the Western Mediterranean. In February and June 2005 briefly chartered to *Cobelfret Ferries*. Between September and November 2006 chartered to *Cobelfret Ferries* to operate between Purfleet and Rotterdam.

TOR BEGONIA Built by Flensburger Schiffbau-Gesellschaft, Flensburg, Germany for *DFDS Tor Line*. Operates on the Gothenburg - Immingham route.

TOR BELGIA Built by Société Metallurgique & Navale Dunkerque-Normandie, Dunkerque, France as the VILLE DU HAVRE for *Société Française de Transports Maritimes* of France. Between 1979 and 1981 she was chartered to *Foss Line*, renamed the FOSS HAVRE and operated between Europe and the Middle East. In 1987 she was renamed the KAMINA. In 1990 she was chartered to *Maersk Line* of Denmark, renamed the MAERSK KENT and used on *Kent Line* services between Dartford and Zeebrugge. In 1992 she was chartered to and later purchased by *Tor Line*, placed on the Gothenburg - Immingham route and renamed the TOR BRITANNIA. In 1994 she was lengthened by 23.7m. In 1999 she was renamed the TOR BELGIA and was later transferred to the Gothenburg - Brevik - Ghent route. In 2003 she was sold to *Eidsiva Roro KS* of Norway and chartered back for four years. In 2004 moved to the new Gothenburg – Copenhagen – Gdansk route. Later chartered to *Trasmediterranea* to operate between Spain and the Canary Islands. Returned to *DFDS Tor Line* in late 2005. In 2006 briefly placed on the Immingham - Cuxhaven route in place of the TOR DANIA, following an accident, and then transferred to the Gothenburg – Tilbury service. In March 2007 transferred to the Cuxhaven - Immingham service.

TOR BELLONA Built by Kawasaki Heavy Industries, Sakaide, Japan as the ZHANG JIA KOU, a deep sea ro-ro/container ship for *China Ocean Shipping Company* of the People's Republic of China for service between the USA, Australia and New Zealand. In 1999, purchased by *Jacobs Holdings*. After delivery, she was converted in Nantong, China to short sea ro-ro specification, including the fitting of a stern ramp (replacing the quarter ramp) and luxury accommodation for 12 drivers. Rebuilt as the DART 10. On completion of rebuilding, chartered to *Sudcargo* of France, renamed the MONT VENTOUX and operated between France and North Africa. In December 2000 the charter ended. In January 2001 she briefly ran on the Dartford - Zeebrugge route in place of the DART 8. After two brief charters to the *British MoD* she was refitted and renamed the DART 10. She then entered long-term charter with the *British MoD*. Returned to *Dart Line* in August 2003 and operated between Dartford and Zeebrugge for about three weeks before going on another *MoD* charter to Iraq. She was then chartered to *CETAM* of France and renamed the MASSILIA. In early 2005 sold to a limited

Commodore Goodwill (*Miles Cowsill*)

Tor Primula (*Mike Louagie*)

partnership under control of *Eidsiva Rederi* of Norway; continued to be chartered to *CETAM*. In Autumn 2005 chartered to *DFDS Tor Line* and renamed the TOR BELLONA. Placed on the Immingham - Cuxhaven service.

TOR BRITANNIA Built by Fincantieri-Cantieri Navali Italiani SpA, Ancona, Italy for *DFDS Tor Line*. Operated on the Gothenburg - Immingham route until 2004 when she was transferred to the Esbjerg - Immingham route.

TOR CORONA Built by Jinling Shipyard in Nanjing, China for *Macoma Shipping Ltd* of the UK and time-chartered to *DFDS Tor Line* for ten years. Used on the Fredericia – Copenhagen - Klaìpeda service.

TOR DANIA Built by Société Metallurgique & Navale Dunkerque-Normandie, Dunkerque, France as the VILLE DE DUNKERQUE for *Société Française de Transports Maritimes* of France. Between 1979 and 1981 she was chartered to *Foss Line*, renamed the FOSS DUNKERQUE and operated between Europe and the Middle East. In 1986 she was chartered to *Grimaldi* of Italy and renamed the G AND C EXPRESS. In 1988 she was briefly chartered to *Elbe-Humber RoLine* and renamed the RAILRO. She was then chartered to *DFDS* where she was renamed the DANA HAFNIA. The following year she was chartered to *Maersk Line* of Denmark, renamed the MAERSK ESSEX and used on *Kent Line* services between Dartford and Zeebrugge. In 1992 she was chartered to and later purchased by *DFDS* and renamed the TOR DANIA. In 1993 she was renamed the BRIT DANIA but later in the year reverted to her original name. She was generally used on the Harwich - Esbjerg service, working in consort with the passenger ferry DANA ANGLIA. In 1994 she was lengthened by 23.7m, chartered to *Tor Line* and placed on the Gothenburg - Immingham route. In 2000 transferred to the Gothenburg - Ghent route. In 2003 she was sold to *Goliat RoRo KS* of Norway and chartered back. In 2004 moved to the Immingham – Cuxhaven route.

TOR FICARIA, TOR FREESIA Built by Flensburger Schiffbau-Gesellschaft, Flensburg, Germany for *DFDS Tor Line*. They operate on the Gothenburg - Immingham service.

TOR FUTURA Built by C N Visentini di Visentini Francesco & C, Donada, Italy as the DANA FUTURA for *DFDS*. In 2001 she was renamed the TOR FUTURA. Initially operated mainly between Esbjerg and Harwich, but latterly operated mainly between Esbjerg and Immingham. In 2004 chartered to *Toll Shipping* of Australia. Later time-chartered to the *Danish MoD* for 5.5 years. However, when not required for military service she has been chartered to other operators such as *P&O Ferries* and *Cobelfret Ferries* and used on *DFDS Tor Line* services. In 2006 sold to *DFDS Lys Line Rederi A/S* of Norway, a *DFDS* subsidiary and chartered back.

TOR HAFNIA Built by Jinling Shipyard in Nanjing, China for *Macoma Shipping Ltd* of the UK and time-chartered to *DFDS Tor Line* for ten years. Delivered in late May 2008 and deployed initially on the Gothenburg - Tilbury service.

TOR HUMBRIA Built by Oskarshamns Varvs Ab, Oskarshamn, Sweden as the EMIRATES EXPRESS for *A/S Skarhamns Oljetransport* of Norway and chartered to *Mideastcargo* for services between Europe and the Middle East. In 1981 chartered to *OT West Africa Line* for services between Europe and West Africa and renamed the ABUJA EXPRESS. In 1983 chartered to *Foss Line*, renamed the FOSSEAGLE and returned to Middle East service. In 1985 she was renamed the FINNEAGLE, chartered briefly to *Finncarriers* and then to *Fred. Olsen Lines*. In 1987 they purchased her and renamed her the BORAC. In 1999 purchased by *DFDS Tor Line* and renamed the TOR HUMBRIA. In 2000 she was chartered to *Costa Container Lines spa* of Italy, operating between Savano and Catania. This service ended in early 2001 and she was then chartered to *CoTuNav* of Tunisia. Returned in April 2001. In 2003 sold to Norwegian interests and chartered back. She currently operates on the Rotterdam - Immingham service. In 2007 sold to *Cs & Partners* of Denmark; *DFDS Tor Line* charter continued.

TOR MAGNOLIA Built by Flensburger Schiffbau-Gesellschaft, Flensburg, Germany for *DFDS Tor Line*. Initially operated on the Gothenburg - Immingham route. In 2005 moved to the Gothenburg – Ghent route.

TOR MINERVA Built by Oskarshamns Varvs Ab, Oskarshamn, Sweden as the BANDAR ABBAS EXPRESS for *A/S Skarhamns Oljetransport* of Norway and chartered out. In 1980 renamed the SAUDI EXPRESS. During the early 1980s she undertook a number of charters including *Mideastcargo* for services between Europe and the Middle East, *Atlanticargo* for services from Europe to USA and

Mexico and *OT West Africa Line* from Europe to West Africa. In 1983 she was chartered to *Ignazio Messina* of Italy, renamed the JOLLY AVORIO and used on services from Italy to the Middle East. In 1986 this charter ended and she briefly reverted to the name SAUDI EXPRESS before being chartered again to *OT West Africa Line* and renamed the KARAWA. In 1987 she was sold to *Fred. Olsen Lines* who renamed her the BORACAY; she operated between Norway and Northern Europe. In 1998 she was sold to *DFDS*, renamed the DANA MINERVA and placed on the Esbjerg - Immingham route. In 2001 she was renamed the TOR MINERVA. In 2003 she was sold to *Goliat RoRo KS* of Norway. In 2007 sold to *Cs & Partners* of Denmark; *DFDS Tor Line* charter continued. She currently operates between Rotterdam and Immingham.

TOR PETUNIA Built by Flensburger Schiffbau-Gesellschaft, Flensburg, Germany for *DFDS Tor Line*. Initially operated on the Gothenburg - Immingham route. In July 2006 moved to the Gothenburg – Ghent route.

TOR PRIMULA Built by Flensburger Schiffbau-Gesellschaft, Flensburg, Germany for *DFDS Tor Line*. Initially operated on the Gothenburg - Immingham route. Later in 2004 moved to the Gothenburg – Ghent route.

TOR SELANDIA Built by Fincantieri-Cantieri Navali Italiani SpA, Ancona, Italy for *DFDS Tor Line*. Operated on the Gothenburg - Immingham route until 2004 when she was moved to the Gothenburg – Ghent route. In 2005 she moved to the Gothenburg – Harwich route. In July UK terminal moved to Tilbury.

TOR SUECIA Built by Fincantieri-Cantieri Navali Italiani SpA, Ancona, Italy for *DFDS Tor Line*. Operated on the Gothenburg - Immingham route until 2004 when she was transferred to the Esbjerg - Immingham route. Later transferred to the Danish flag.

In Spring 2009 *DFDS Tor Line* will take possession of the FINNMASTER and FINNREEL, currently operated by *Finnlines*. They will be renamed and operated on a North Sea route.

Under Construction

| 20 | **TOR FINONIA** | 25548t | 09 | 20.0k | 184.8m | 12P | - | 250T | AS | UK | - |
| 21 | **TOR JUTLANDIA** | 25548t | 09 | 20.0k | 184.8m | 12P | - | 250T | AS | UK | - |

TOR FINONIA, TOR JUTLANDIA Under construction by Jinling Shipyard in Nanjing, China for *Macoma Shipping Ltd* of the UK. The vessels will be time-chartered to *DFDS Tor Line* for ten years (with an option on a further three). They will be delivered in March and November 2009.

FINNLINES

THE COMPANY *Finnlines PLC* is a Finnish private sector company. Services to the UK are marketed by *Finnlines UK Ltd*, a British private sector company. From 1st January 2001, *Finncarriers* was merged into the parent company, trading as *Finnlines Cargo Service*.

MANAGEMENT *Finnlines* **President** Antti Lageroos, **Vice-President** Simo Airas.

ADDRESS *Finnlines* PO Box 197, Salmisaarenkatu 1, 00181 Helsinki, Finland, *Finnlines UK Ltd* 8 Heron Quay, London E14 4JB.

TELEPHONE Administration & Reservations *Finnlines* + 358 (0)10 34350, *Finnlines UK Ltd* + 44 (0)20 7519 7300.

FAX Administration *Finnlines* + 358 (0)10 3435200, *Finnlines UK Ltd* + 44 (0)20 7536 0255.

INTERNET Email *Finnlines* info@finnlines.fi *Finnlines UK Ltd* london@finnlines.co.uk (*English*)

Website www.finnlines.fi (*English, Finnish, German*)

ROUTES OPERATED *Circuit 1* Helsinki (*dep: Tue*) - Kotka (*dep: Wed*) - Rauma (*dep: Fri*) - Hull (*arr/dep: Tue*) - Antwerp (*arr/dep: Wed*) - Turku (*dep: Sun*) - Rauma (*dep: Mon*) - Hull (*dep: Fri*) - Helsinki (*arr: Tue*); *4,6,8*. **Note:** Each ship operates two round trips between Finland and NW Europe every three weeks. *Circuit 2* Helsinki (*dep: Tue*) - Kotka (*dep: Wed*) - Hull (*arr: Sat, dep: Sun*) - Helsinki (*arr/dep: Wed*) - Antwerp (*arr/dep: Sat*) - Helsinki (*arr: Tue*); *7,15*. **Note:** Each ship operates two round trips between Finland and NW Europe every two weeks, alternating between Hull and Antwerp).

Circuit 3 Helsinki *(dep: Sun)* - Hull *(arr/dep: Wed)* - Amsterdam *(arr/dep: Thu)* - Helsinki *(arr: Sun)*; *12*.

In view of the fact that ships are liable to be transferred between routes, the following is a list of all *Finnlines Cargo Service* ro-ro vessels, including those which currently do not serve the UK. Ro-pax vessels (none of which normally serve the UK) are listed in Section 6.

1	**ANTARES**	19963t	88	20.3k	157.6m	18P	-	154T	A	NO	8500680
2	**BALTICA**	21224t	90	19.0k	157.7m	0P	-	163T	A	GE	8813154
3	**BIRKA CARRIER**	12251t	98	20.0k	155.5m	12P	-	124T	A2	FI	9132002
4	**BIRKA EXPORTER**	6620t	91	16.5k	122.0m	0P	-	90T	A	FI	8820860
5	**BIRKA EXPRESS**	12251t	97	20.0k	154.5m	12P	-	124T	A2	FI	9131993
6	**BIRKA SHIPPER**	6620t	91	16.5k	122.0m	0P	-	90T	A	FI	8911748
7	**BIRKA TRADER**	12251t	98	20.0k	154.5m	12P	-	124T	A2	FI	9132014
8	**BIRKA TRANSPORTER**	6620t	91	16.5k	122.0m	0P	-	90T	A	FI	8820858
9	**FINNFOREST**	15525t	78	17.0k	155.9m	0P	-	155T	A	SE	7528623
10	**FINNHAWK**	11530t	01	20.0k	162.2m	12P	-	140T	A	FI	9207895
11	**FINNKRAFT**	11530t	00	20.0k	162.2m	12P	-	140T	A	FI	9207883
12	**FINNMASTER**	11530t	00	20.0k	162.2m	12P	-	140T	A	UK	9192129
13	**FINNMILL**	25654t	02	20.0k	184.8m	12P	-	190T	A	SW	9212656
14	**FINNPULP**	25654t	02	20.0k	184.8m	12P	-	190T	A	SW	9212644
15	**FINNREEL**	11530t	00	20.0k	162.2m	12P	-	140T	A	UK	9198721
16	**INOWROCLAW**	14786t	80	15.0k	137.2m	12P	-	96T	A	PL	7804053
17	**RUNNER**	20729t	90	18.9k	189.7m	12P	-	144t	A	FI	8807416
18	**VASALAND**	20203t	84	14.0k	155.0m	0P	-	160T	A	UK	8222111

ANTARES Built by Gdansk Shipyard, Gdansk, Poland as the FINNFOREST for *Neste* of Finland and chartered to *Finncarriers*. In 1988 renamed the ANTARES. In 2002 chartered to *Stena Line* to operate between Harwich and Rotterdam. In 2003 chartered to the *British MoD* for service to the Gulf. Currently operates on the Helsinki - Gdynia route; she returns via Travemünde, offering an additional northbound service.

BALTICA Built by Hyundai Heavy Industries, Ulsan, South Korea as the AHLERS BALTIC for *Ahlers Line* and chartered to *Finncarriers*. In 1995 acquired by *Poseidon Schiffahrt AG* of Germany and renamed the TRANSBALTICA. She continued to be chartered to *Finncarriers* and was acquired by them when they purchased *Poseidon Schiffahrt AG* (now *Finnlines Deutschland AG*) in 1997. In 2003 sold to Norwegian interests and chartered back. She was renamed the BALTICA. In recent years she operated on the Helsinki - St Petersburg - Hamina - Helsinki - Zeebrugge - Tilbury – Amsterdam - Antwerp - service with the MERCHANT. During 2007 she operated Helsinki - Turku - Antwerp on a one-week cycle. In January 2008 moved to the Rauma - Rostock - Lübeck - Travemünde route.

BIRKA CARRIER, BIRKA EXPRESS, BIRKA TRADER Built by Fosen Mekaniske Verksteder A/S, Rissa, Norway as the UNITED CARRIER, UNITED EXPRESS and UNITED TRADER for *United Shipping* (a subsidiary of *Birka Shipping*) of Finland and chartered to *Transfennica*. During 2000 they were used on their Kemi - Oulu - Antwerp - Felixstowe service. In 2001 the route was transferred to *Finnlines* and the vessels used sub-chartered to them (charter later transferred to *Finnlines*. In 2002 *United Shipping* was renamed *Birka Cargo* and the ships were renamed the BIRKA CARRIER, BIRKA EXPRESS and BIRKA TRADER. In 2006 the service ceased. The BIRKA CARRIER and BIRKA EXPRESS were transferred to the Helsinki - Bilbao service and the BIRKA TRADER to the Helsinki - Hull - Amsterdam service. In 2007 the BIRKA TRADER was transferred to the Rauma - Hull service and in 2008 to the Kotka - Hull - Antwerp service. In 2008 charter was extended a further four years.

BIRKA EXPORTER Built as the GRANÖ by Brodogradiliste Sava, Macvanska Mitrovica, Yugoslavia (fitted out by Fosen Mekaniske Verksteder of Rissa, Norway) for *Rederi AB Gustav Erikson* of Finland and chartered to *Transfennica* for service between Finland and Germany. In 1995 the owning company became *United Shipping* and in 2002 *Birka Cargo AB*. In 2000 she was chartered to the *Korsnäs Paper Group* to carry their traffic from Gävle (Sweden) to Chatham and Terneuzen (The Netherlands). In 2002 she was renamed the BIRKA EXPORTER. In 2005 the charter and operation of the services were taken over by *DFDS Tor Line*. The northbound Terneuzen - Gävle section became a ferry route marketed as part of the *DFDS Tor Line* network. This arrangement ended in 2006. In 2008 chartered to *Finnlines*. Operates Helsinki/Rauma/Turku - Antwerp/Hull service undertaking two round trips every three weeks.

BIRKA SHIPPER Built as the STYRSÖ and renamed the BIRKA SHIPPER In 2002. Otherwise as the BIRKA EXPORTER.

BIRKA TRANSPORTER Built as the HAMNÖ and renamed the BIRKA TRANSPORTER in 2002. Otherwise as the BIRKA EXPORTER.

FINNFOREST Laid down by Hyundai Heavy Industries, Ulsan, South Korea as the STENA PROJECT, completed as ATLANTIC PROJECT for *Stena Rederi* and chartered to *ACL* (see above). In 1981 chartered to *Merzario Line* of Italy for services between Italy and Saudi Arabia and renamed the MERZARIO HISPANIA. In 1983 returned to *Stena Line* and renamed the STENA HISPANIA. In 1984 chartered to *Kotka Line* of Finland, renamed the KOTKA VIOLET and used on their services between Finland, UK and West Africa. This charter ended in 1985 and she was again named the STENA HISPANIA. In 1986 she was renamed the STENA BRITANNICA and used on the *Stena Portlink* (later *Stena Tor Line*) service between Sweden and Britain. In 1988 she was chartered to *Bore Line* of Finland, renamed the BORE BRITANNICA and used on services between Finland and Britain. In 1992 chartered to *Finncarriers*. In 1997 renamed the FINNFOREST. In 1997 she began operating a service between Hull and Zeebrugge on charter to *P&O North Sea Ferries* in the course of her normal two-week circuit from Finland. This ceased in 1999. In 2000 transferred to the Helsinki - Århus service. In 2007 transferred to the Helsinki - Gdynia service. In 2008 purchased by *Celtic Link Ferries* but currently remains on charter to *Finnlines*.

FINNHAWK Built by Jinling Shipyard, Nanjing, China for the *Macoma Shipping Group* and chartered to *Finnlines*. Currently operates Helsinki - Århus. In 2008 purchased by *Finnlines*.

FINNKRAFT Built by Jinling Shipyard, Nanjing, China for the *Macoma Shipping Group* and chartered to *Finncarriers*. Currently operates Helsinki - Århus. In 2008 purchased by *Finnlines*.

FINNMASTER Built by Jinling Shipyard, Nanjing, China for the *Macoma Shipping Group* and chartered to *Finncarriers*. Operates on Helsinki - Kotka - Hull/Amsterdam route. To be sold to *DFDS Tor Line* in Spring 2009.

FINNMILL Built by Jinling Shipyard, Nanjing, China for the *Macoma Shipping Group* and chartered to *Finnlines*. Currently used on the Turku - Helsinki – Hanko - Kotka - Malmö - Lübeck/Travemünde service. In 2008 purchased by *Finnlines*.

FINNPULP Built by Jinling Shipyard, Nanjing, China for the *Macoma Shipping Group* and chartered to *Finnlines*. Currently used on the Turku - Helsinki – Hanko - Kotka - Malmö - Lübeck/Travemünde service. In 2008 purchased by *Finnlines*.

FINNREEL Launched as the FINNMAID but renamed before delivery. Built by Jinling Shipyard, Nanjing, China for the *Macoma Shipping Group* and chartered to *Finncarriers*. Currently operating on the Helsinki - Hull - Amsterdam service. To be sold to *DFDS Tor Line* in Spring 2009.

INOWROCLAW Built by Rauma Repola Oy, Rauma, Finland for *Polish Ocean Lines*. Operated between Gdynia and Felixstowe and later Gdynia - Felixstowe - Middlesbrough. In 1998 she was replaced by a container ship and she was transferred to the joint *POL/Euroafrica Shipping/Finnlines Polfin* service between Helsinki and Gdynia. At the end of 2006 the joint service was ended, it became a solely *Finnlines* operation and she was chartered to *Finnlines*.

RUNNER Built by Schichau Seebeckwerft GmbH, Bremerhaven, Germany as the RAILSHIP III for *Railship*, later taken over by *Finnlines*. In 2002 her role changed from rail ferry to truck and trailer ferry; renamed the FINNRUNNER. In 2003 sold to *Finland Roro* of Norway and chartered back. In 2004 renamed the RUNNER. Operates between Travemünde and Turku.

VASALAND Built by Rauma Repola Oy, Rauma, Finland as the OIHONNA for *Finncarriers*. In 2003 sold to *Stena RoRo*. Later sold to *Imperial RoRo*, chartered back to *Stena RoRo* and then time-chartered to *Finnlines*. In 2004 transferred to *TranRussia Express*. In 2005 transferred back to *Finnlines* and operated on the Rauma – Rostock - Lübeck Travemünde service. In 2006 chartered to *Transfennica*.

Under Construction

19	NEWBUILDING 1	25654t	10	20.0k	184.8m	12P	-	190T	A	-	-
20	NEWBUILDING 2	25654t	10	20.0k	184.8m	12P	-	190T	A	-	-
21	NEWBUILDING 3	25654t	10	20.0k	184.8m	12P	-	190T	A	-	-
22	NEWBUILDING 4	25654t	11	20.0k	184.8m	12P	-	190T	A	-	-
23	NEWBUILDING 5	25654t	11	20.0k	184.8m	12P	-	190T	A	-	-
24	NEWBUILDING 6	25654t	11	20.0k	184.8m	12P	-	190T	A	-	-

NEWBUILDING 1, NEWBUILDING 2 NEWBUILDING 3 NEWBUILDING 4 NEWBUILDING 5 NEWBUILDING 6 Under construction by Jinling Shipyard, Nanjing, China for *Finnlines*.

FORELAND SHIPPING

THE COMPANY *Foreland Shipping Limited* (formerly *AWSR Shipping Limited*) is a UK private sector company jointly owned by *Bibby Line, James Fisher, The Hadley Shipping Company* and *Andrew Weir*.

MANAGEMENT Managing Director Max J Gladwyn.

ADDRESS Dexter House, 2 Royal Mint Court, London EC3N 4XX.

TELEPHONE Administration + 44 (0)20 7480 4140.

FAX Administration + 44 (0)20 7481 9940.

INTERNET Email max.gladwyn@foreland-shipping.co.uk

ROUTES OPERATED No routes are operated. The ships are for charter to the UK *Ministry of Defence* for their 'Strategic Sealift Capability'. Normally two of the ships are chartered commercially but can be recalled in times of emergency.

1	ANVIL POINT	23235t	03	18.0k	193.0m	12P	-	180T	A	UK	9248540
2	EDDYSTONE	23235t	02	21.0k	193.0m	12P	-	180T	A	UK	9234070
3	HARTLAND POINT	23235t	03	18.0k	193.0m	12P	-	180T	A	UK	9248538
4	HURST POINT	23235t	02	18.0k	193.0m	12P	-	180T	A	UK	9234068

ANVIL POINT, HARTLAND POINT Built by Harland & Wolff, Belfast, UK for *AWSR Shipping*.

EDDYSTONE, HURST POINT Built by Flensburger Schiffbau-Gesellschaft, Flensburg, Germany for *AWSR Shipping*.

Foreland Shipping Limited also owns the BEACHY HEAD and the LONGSTONE, currently on charter to *Transfennica*.

MANN LINES

THE COMPANY *Mann Lines* is owned by *Mann & Son (London) Ltd* of Great Britain. It replaced in 2001 *ArgoMann Ferry Service*, a joint venture between *Argo Reederei* of Germany and *Mann & Son*.

MANAGEMENT Managing Director Bill Binks.

ADDRESS *UK* Mann & Son (London) Ltd, The Naval House, Kings Quay Street, Harwich CO12 3JJ, *Germany* Mann Lines GmbH, Birkenstrasse 15, 28195 Bremen.

TELEPHONE Administration & Reservations *UK* + 44 (0)1255 245200, *Germany* + 49 (0)421 163850, *Finland* + 352 (0)22750000, *Estonia* + 372 (0)679 1450.

FAX Administration & Reservations *UK* + 44 (0)1255 245219, *Germany* + 49 (0)421 1638520

INTERNET Email Michael.footitt@mannlines.co.uk **Website** www.mannlines.com (*English, German, Finnish, Estonian, Russian*)

ROUTES OPERATED *Borden* Killingholme - Harwich - Vlissingen - Paldiski - Turku (approx every 10 days), *Estraden* Harwich (Navyard) (*dep: 22.00 Fri*) - Cuxhaven (*arr: 17.00 Sat, dep: 19.00 Sat*) - Paldiski (*arr: 15.00 Mon, dep: 21.00 Mon*) - Turku (*arr: 08.00 Tue, dep: 17.00 Tue*) - Bremerhaven (*arr:*

18.00 Thu, dep: 21.00 Thu) – Harwich *(arr: 16.00 Fri)*; ***Balticborg & Bothniaborg*** Piteå (Sweden) *(dep: Thu)* – Bremen (Germany) *(arr/dep: Mon)* – Sheerness (UK) *(arr/dep: Wed)* – Terneuzen (The Netherlands) *(arr/dep: Thu)* – Vlissingen *(arr/dep: Fri)* – Paldiski (Estonia) *(arr/dep: Mon)* – Piteå *(arr: Thu)*. **Note:** Southbound capacity (Piteå - Vlissingen) is taken by private traffic for *Smurfit Kappa Group*. Northbound capacity (Vlissingen - Paldiski - Piteå) is marketed by *Mann Lines*.

1	BALTICBORG	12460t	04	16.5 k	153.1m	0P	-	104T	A	NL	9267716
2	BORDEN	10100t	77	17.5k	142.3m	12P	800C	105T	A	FI	7521950
3	BOTHNIABORG	12460t	04	16.5 k	153.1m	0P	-	104T	A	NL	9267728
4	ESTRADEN	18205t	99	20.0k	162.7m	12P	130C	170T	A	FI	9181077

BALTICBORG, BOTHNIABORG Built by Bodewes Volharding, Volharding, The Netherlands (hull built by Daewoo Mangalia Heavy Industries SA, Mangalia, Romania) for *Wagenborg Shipping* of The Netherlands. Time-chartered to *Kappa Packaging* (now *Smurfit Kappa Group*). Placed on service between Piteå and Northern Europe. Northbound journeys (Terneuzen - Piteå) marketed as *RORO2 Stockholm*, with a call at Södertälje (Sweden (near Stockholm)) and, from 2005, the section between Bremen and Terneuzen marketed as *RORO2London*. In 2007 these arrangements ceased and *Mann Lines* took over the marketing of northbound traffic, the Södertälje call being replaced by a call at Paldiski in Estonia.

BORDEN Built at Frederikstad, Norway as the BORE SKY for *Bore Line* of Finland and used on services between Finland, Northern Europe and Britain; subsequently sold and chartered back. In 1991 when *Bore Line* began to pull out of regular shipping services, she was renamed BLUE SKY and undertook charters for *Tor Line* and *North Sea Ferries*. Sold in 1992 to *Rederi Ab Engship* of Finland and renamed BORDEN she spent the next 10 years undertaking charters to *Finncarriers*, *ArgoMann*, *Transfennica* and *Finnlines*. In 2002 chartered to *Cetam* and renamed CETAM VICTORIAE for use between Southampton and Santander. In 2004 renamed BORDEN and chartered to *UECC*. She has been fitted with hoistable mezzanine decks to increase car capacity and is generally used on the Baltic or Iberian services. In 2006 *Rederi AB Engship* was taken over by *Rettig Group Bore* and she remained on charter to *UECC*. In 2007 chartered to *Mann Lines* and placed on a Killingholme - Harwich - Vlissingen - Paldiski   Turku schedule.

ESTRADEN Built by Aker Finnyards, Rauma, Finland as the ESTRADEN for *Rederi Ab Engship* (later *Bore Shipowners*) of Finland and chartered to *ArgoMann*. Later in 1999 renamed the AMAZON. In 2001 the charter was taken over by *Mann Lines* and later in the year she resumed the name ESTRADEN. In 2006 *Rederi AB Engship* was taken over by *Rettig Group Bore* and she remained on charter to *Mann Lines*.

Under Construction

5	NEWBUILDING 1	23200t	11	19.0k	195.0m	12P	-	210T	A2	FI	-
6	NEWBUILDING 2	23200t	11	19.0k	195.0m	12P	-	210T	A2	FI	-

NEWBUILDING 1, NEWBUILDING 2 To be built by Flensburger Schiffsbau, Flensburg, Germany for *Bore Shipowners* (*Rettig Group Bore*) of Finland. To be chartered to *Mann Lines*.

NORFOLKLINE

THE COMPANY, MANAGEMENT, ADDRESSES See Section 1.

TELEPHONE Administration *Belfast* +44 (0)28 9077 9090, **Reservations** *Belfast (Liverpool Services)* +44 (0)870 6099 299, **(Heysham Services)** +44 (0)870 6099 299, *Liverpool (Belfast Services)* +44 (0)870 6099 299, **(Dublin Services)** +44 (0)870 6099 299, *Heysham* +44 (0)1524 865050, **Dublin** +353 (0)1 819 2955, *Felixstowe & Killingholme Services (Felixstowe office)* +44 1394 603767, **(Vlaardingen office)** +31 (0)102 081 302/3, **Dover (English Channel Services)**, +44 (0)1304 218400 **Dunkerque (English Channel Services)** +33 32828 9550.

FAX Administration *Belfast* +44 (0)28 9077 1286, **Reservations** *Belfast (Liverpool Services)* +44 (0)28 9077 5520, **(Heysham Services)** +44 (0)28 9078 6073, *Heysham* +44 (0)1524 865070, *Liverpool (Belfast Services)* +44 (0)151 906 2718, **(Dublin Services)** +44 (0)151 906 2718, *Dublin* +353 (0)1 819 2941, *Felixstowe & Killingholme Services (Felixstowe office)* + 44 (0)1394 603705,

(Vlaardingen office) + 31 (0)102084 321, **Dover *(English Channel Services)*** +44 (0)1304 218420/218421, **Dunkerque *(English Channel Services)*** + 33 32828 9544.

INTERNET Email *General Information* info@norfolkline.com, **Irish Sea Services *(Belfast, Liverpool, Heysham & Dublin)*** irishseabooking@norfolkline.com, **North Sea Services *(Felixstowe & Killingholme)*** ferryfelix@norfolkline.com, ***(Vlaardingen)*** ferryschev@norfolkline.com, **English Channel Services *(Dover)*** doverbooking@norfolkline.com, ***(Dunkerque)*** dunkerquebooking@norfolkline.com

Website www.norfolkline.com *(English)*

ROUTES OPERATED Vlaardingen *(dep: 07.00 Tue-Fri, 13.00 Sun, 14.00 Sat, 14.30 Mon-Fri, 19.00 Sat, 19.30 Mon-Fri, 22.00 Sun, 00.01 Tue-Sat)* - Felixstowe *(dep: 06.00 Tue-Fri, 12.00 Daily, 19.00 Mon-Fri, 00.01 Daily)* (7 hrs; **3,4,5,6**; 4 per day), Vlaardingen *(dep: 20.00 Mon-Sat)* - Killingholme *(dep: 20.00 Mon-Fri, 18.00 Sat)* (14 hrs; **7,8**; 1 per day), Immingham - Esbjerg (6 per week), Harwich - Esbjerg (3 per week) (UK - Denmark services operated in conjunction with *DFDS Tor Line* who provide all vessels), Heysham *(dep: 08.00 Tue-Sat, 20.00 Mon-Sat, 20.30 Sun,)* - Dublin *(dep: 09.00 Tue-Sat, 21.00 Daily)* (8 hrs; **1,10**; 2 per day), Heysham *(dep: 11.00 Tue-Sat, 20.00 Sun, 23.30 Mon-Sat)* - Belfast *(dep: 11.00 Tue-Sat, 20.00 Sun, 23.30 Mon-Sat)* (7 hrs; **2,9**; 2 per day). Note: Heysham based ships are sometimes moved between the two routes.

1	ARROW	7606t	98	17.0k	122.3m	12P	-	84T	A	MT	9119414
2	EAST EXPRESS	9071t	84	15.0k	121.5m	12P	-	90T	A	MT	8009040
3	MAERSK ANGLIA	13073t	00	18.6k	142.5m	12P	-	114T	A	NL	9186649
4	MAERSK EXPORTER	13017t	96	18.6k	142.5m	12P	-	114T	A	NL	9121625
5	MAERSK FLANDERS	13073t	00	18.6k	142.5m	12P	-	114T	A	NL	9186637
6	MAERSK IMPORTER	13017t	96	18.6k	142.5m	12P	-	114T	A	NL	9121637
7	MAERSK VLAARDINGEN	22900t	01	21.6k	193.0m	12P	-	190T	A	NL	9207998
8	MAERSK VOYAGER	22900t	00	21.6k	193.0m	12P	-	190T	A	NL	9208007
9	SAGA MOON	7746t	84	15.0k	134.8m	12P	-	66T	A	GI	8411267
10	SHIELD	7606t	99	17.0k	122.3m	12P	-	84T	A	MT	9119426

ARROW Built by Astilleros de Huelva SA, Huelva, Spain as the VARBOLA for *Estonian Shipping Company*. On completion, chartered to *Dart Line* and placed on the Dartford - Vlissingen route. In 1999 she was renamed the DART 6. At the end of August 1999, the charter was terminated and she was renamed the VARBOLA. She undertook a number of short-term charters, including *Merchant Ferries*. In 2000 long-term chartered to *Merchant Ferries* to operate between Heysham and Dublin. In 2003 the charter ended and she was chartered to *Dart Line* to replace the DART 9; she was placed initially on the Dartford - Vlissingen route but later transferred to the Dartford - Dunkerque route. Later sub-chartered to *NorseMerchant Ferries* and placed on the Heysham – Dublin route. In 2004 the charter transferred to *NorseMerchant Ferries*. In 2005 sold to *Elmira Shipping* of Greece and renamed the RR ARROW. In October 2007 sold to *Seatruck Ferries* but the charter to *Norfolkline* continued. Renamed the ARROW.

EAST EXPRESS Built by Santierul Naval SA, Galatz, Romania as the BALDER FJORD for *K/S A/S Balder RO/RO No 2* of Norway. In 1986 acquired by *Navrom* of Romania and renamed the BAZIAS 1. In 1990 transferred to *Romline* of Romania and subsequently sold to *Octogon Shipping* of Romania. In 1996 chartered to *Ignazio Messina* of Italy and later renamed the JOLLY ARANCIONE. In late 1997 chartered to *Dart Line* and renamed the DART 1. In late 1999 the charter ended, and she was briefly chartered to *Merchant Ferries*, although she was taken back on short-term charter by *Dart Line* in February 2000. In 2001 renamed the BAZIAS 1 and in April chartered to *11 Ferries* to operate between Rotterdam and Purfleet. In that autumn she transferred to the Zeebrugge -Purfleet service. In March 2002 chartered to *Dart Line* to operate between Dartford and Dunkerque (not inter-worked with the Vlissingen service). In Summer 2002 the charter ended. Re-chartered in Autumn 2002 and worked additional sailings from Dartford to Zeebrugge. From November 2002 she operated a triangular Dartford - Dunkerque - Zeebrugge - Dartford service. From January 2003 resumed service between Dartford and Zeebrugge only. Later operated mainly between Dartford and Dunkerque. In 2004 chartered to *Channel Freight Ferries* and renamed the CFF SEINE. Later in 2004 purchased by *Clarksons* (owners of *Channel Freight Ferries*) and re-registered in The Bahamas. *Channel Freight Ferries* ceased trading in

Maersk Voyager (*FotoFlite*)

Shield (*Miles Cowsill*)

December 2005. In 2006 briefly chartered to *Cobelfret Ferries* and used on the Vlissingen – Dagenham service. Then chartered to *Ferryways* to operate between Ostend and Immingham. In September transferred to the Ostend - Ipswich route but operated one round trip to Immingham over Friday and Saturday. In June 2007 chartered to *Norfolkline* to operate between Heysham and Dublin. In November sold to *Express Shipping A/S* of Denmark and renamed the EAST EXPRESS.

MAERSK ANGLIA Built by Guangzhou Shipyard International, Guangzhou, China for *Norfolkline*. Entered service as the GUANGZHOU 7130011 (unofficially the 'China II') but renamed shortly afterwards. Operates on the Vlaardingen - Felixstowe service.

MAERSK EXPORTER, MAERSK IMPORTER Built by Miho Shipyard, Shimizu, Japan for *Norfolkline*. Used on the Vlaardingen - Felixstowe service.

MAERSK FLANDERS Built by Guangzhou Shipyard International, Guangzhou, China for *Norfolkline*. Used on the Vlaardingen - Felixstowe service.

MAERSK VLAARDINGEN Built as the UND AKDENIZ by Flensburger Schiffsbau, Flensburg, Germany for *UND Roro* of Turkey and operated between Istanbul and Trieste. In 2005 sold to *Norfolkline* and chartered back. In July 2005 delivered to *Norfolkline* and renamed the MAERSK VLAARDINGEN. In 2006 entered service for *Norfolkline* between Vlaardingen and Killingholme.

MAERSK VOYAGER Built as the UND KARADENIZ by Flensburger Schiffsbau, Flensburg, Germany for *UND Roro* of Turkey and operated between Istanbul and Trieste. In 2005 sold to *Norfolkline* and chartered back. In November delivered to *Norfolkline* and renamed the MAERSK VOYAGER. In 2006 entered service for *Norfolkline* between Vlaardingen and Killingholme.

SAGA MOON Built by Schlichting Werft GmbH, Travemünde, Germany as the LIDARTINDUR for *Trader Line* of the Faroe Islands for services between Tórshavn and Denmark. In 1986 chartered to *Belfast Freight Ferries* and renamed the SAGA MOON. In 1990 she was purchased by *Belfast Freight Ferries*. In 1995 she was lengthened by 18m to increase capacity for trailers from 52 to 72 units and trade cars from 25 to 50; the lift was replaced by an internal fixed ramp. In 1998 she was transferred to *Merchant Ferries'* Heysham - Dublin service and in 2001 back to the Heysham - Belfast service. Resumed service between Heysham and Dublin in 2002. In 2004 transferred to the Heysham - Belfast service.

SHIELD Built by Astilleros de Huelva SA, Huelva, Spain as the LEILI for *Estonian Shipping Company*. Used on Baltic services. In 2002 chartered to *Crowley Maritime* of the USA and renamed the PORT EVERGLADES EXPRESS. In 2004 resumed the name LEILI and chartered to *NorseMerchant Ferries* to operate between Birkenhead and Dublin. In July 2005 moved to the Heysham - Belfast route and at the same time sold to *Elmira Shipping* of Greece and renamed the RR SHIELD. In 2007 sold to *Attica Group* of Greece and renamed the SHIELD. In January 2008 sold to *Seatruck Ferries* but continued to be chartered to *Norfolkline*. Now normally operates on the Heysham - Dublin route.

NORTHLINK FERRIES

THE COMPANY, MANAGEMENT, ADDRESS, FAX & INTERNET See Section 2.

TELEPHONE Freight Reservations + 44 (0)845 6060 449.

ROUTES OPERATED Aberdeen - Kirkwall (Orkney), Aberdeen - Lerwick (Shetland). Timings vary; see www.northlinkferries.co.uk/freight-timetables.html for details.

1	CLARE	5617t	72	17.0k	114.9m	12P	-	62T	A	NO	7214727
2	HASCOSAY	6136t	71	17.0k	118.4m	12P	-	50T	A	UK	7120768

CLARE Built by Rickmers Werft, Bremerhaven, Germany as the WESERTAL for *J A Reinecke & Co* of Germany. After delivery she was renamed the MEYER EXPRESS and resumed the name WESERTAL in 1973. She was chartered out to a number of operators including *North Sea Ferries* and *Olau Line*. In 1993 she was sold to *CO.NA.TIR. SpA* of Italy and renamed the VINZIA E. She was chartered to *Stena Sealink Line* and operated between Newhaven and Dieppe. In 1994 she was chartered to *DFDS* subsidiary *Dan-Let Line* (later *DFDS Baltic Line*) and renamed the DANA BALTICA. She operated between Denmark and Lithuania. In 1996 she was renamed the CLARE and again placed on the charter market. In 1997 she briefly served on *NorSea Link*, a joint venture between *Scandlines (DSB Rederi)* and *Norse Irish Ferries* between Kristiansand and Eemshaven in the north of The Netherlands. In 1998 she was again chartered to *DFDS* to institute freight-only services between Newcastle and IJmuiden. After further brief charters she was, in 1999, briefly chartered to *CargoConnect Transport + Logistics* and placed on a new service between Hull and Hamburg. In 2001, she was chartered to *Smyril Line* to operate between Tórshavn and Hanstholm. In 2002, Lerwick was added to her winter itinerary. From September 2002 Aberdeen was added to a year-round roster but dropped at the beginning of 2003. In Autumn 2003, the charter was ended. In December 2003 chartered to *NorthLink*.

HASCOSAY Built by Kristiansands M/V A/S, Kristiansand, Norway as the JUNO for *Finska Ångfartygs AB* of Finland. In 1979 sold to *Finnfranline* of France, renamed the NORMANDIA and chartered to *Finncurriers* for service between Finland and France. In 1982 chartered to *Sudcargo* and used on services between France and Algeria and the Middle East. In 1986 sold to *Mikkola* of Finland, renamed the MISIDIA and chartered to *Transfennica* for services between Finland and Northern Europe. In 1990 sold to *Kristiania Eiendom* of Norway and renamed the EURO NOR. In 1991 she was chartered to *Commodore Ferries* and renamed the COMMODORE CLIPPER. In 1996 she was replaced by the COMMODORE GOODWILL and renamed the SEA CLIPPER. She was placed on the charter market. In 1998 she was chartered to the *Estonian Shipping Company (ESCO)* and operated between Germany and Estonia; she was renamed the TRANSBALTICA. In 2001 she resumed the name SEA CLIPPER and was chartered to *Fjord Line*. In 2002 she was sold to *NorthLink* and renamed the HASCOSAY. She was modified to enable her to accommodate *NorthLink's* cassette system for livestock transport in addition to commercial vehicles. She was chartered to *Caledonian MacBrayne* to operate between Ullapool and Stornoway during Summer 2002. In October 2002 entered service with *NorthLink*.

P&O FERRIES

THE COMPANY, MANAGEMENT, ADDRESS, TELEPHONE See Section 1.

INTERNET Websites www.poferriesfreight.com *(English)*

MANAGEMENT Managing Director Terry Cairns, **Marketing Manager** Tracy Robb.

TELEPHONE Administration +44 (0)1253 615700, **Reservations UK** 0870 6000 868, **Irish Republic** +353 (0)1 855 0522.

FAX Administration & Reservations *Cairnryan* +44 (0)1581 200282, *Larne* +44 (0)28 2827 2477, *Fleetwood* +44 (0)1253 615740.

ROUTES OPERATED P&O Ferries branded routes Dover (1hr 20 mins; *3,5*; up to 9 freight only sailings per day when both ships are in operation (times vary). Freight is also conveyed on up to 25 passenger sailings), Tilbury *(dep: 18.00 Mon, 10.00, 22.00 Tue, 14.00 Wed, 11.00, 18.00 Thu, 15.00, 22.00 Fri, 19.00 Sat, 18.00 Sun)* - Zeebrugge *(dep: 20.00 Mon, 10.00 Tue, 01.00, 19.00 Wed, 05.00 Thu, 02.00, 09.00 Fri, 06.00, 19.00 Sat, 21.00 Sun)* (10 hrs; *1,8*; 1/2 per day), Hull *(dep: 18.00 Tue, 16.00 Thu, 21.00+ Daily)* - Rotterdam *(dep: 23.00 Mon, 16.00 Wed, 21.00 Daily+)* (15 hrs; *13* + *passenger ship*; 10 per week), Hull *(dep: 19.00+ Daily, 20.00 Mon, Wed, Fri)* - Zeebrugge *(dep: 19.00+ Daily, 21.00 Tue, Thu, Sat)* (13 hrs; *6* + *passenger ship*; 11 per week), Middlesbrough (Teesport) *(dep: 21.00 Mon-Fri, 18.00 Sat)* - Rotterdam (Beneluxhaven, Europoort) *(dep: 23.00 Mon-Fri, 19.00 Sat)* (15 hrs; *9,10*; 6 per week), Middlesbrough (Teesport) *(dep: 21.00 Mon-Fri, 17.00 Sat)* - Zeebrugge *(dep: 21.00 Mon-Sat)* (15 hrs 30 mins; *11,12*; 6 per week).

P&O Irish Sea branded routes Troon *(dep: 02.00 Mon-Sat)* - Larne *(dep: 19.00 Sun-Fri)* (4 hrs 30 mins; *4*, 1 per day), Liverpool *(dep: 03.00 (Sun, Tue-Sat) 10.00 (Tue-Sat), 22.00 (Daily))* – Dublin *(dep: 10.00 (Tue-Sat), 15.00 (Mon-Sat), 22.00 (Daily))* (7 hrs 30 mins; *2* + NORBANK and NORBAY *(see Section 1)*; 18 per week).

1	CALIBUR	9737t	76	16.0k	126.4m	12P	-	95T	A	MT	7427752
2	CELTIC STAR	11086t	91	20.8k	136.0m	12P	-	86T	A	CY	9009633
3	EUROPEAN ENDEAVOUR	22152t	00	22.5k	180.0m	210P	-	130L	BA2	UK	9181106
4	EUROPEAN MARINER	5897t	77	15.0k	116.3m	12P	-	62T	A	BS	7636092
5	EUROPEAN SEAWAY	22986t	91	21.0k	179.7m	200P	-	120L	BA2	UK	9007283

6	EUROPEAN TRADER	17068t	78	17.0k	176.2m	12P	-	194T	A	NO	7708778
7	HOBURGEN	9080t	86	15.0k	121.5m	12P	-	100T	A	BS	8009088
8	NORCAPE	14807t	79	19.4k	151.0m	12P	-	124T	A	NL	7716086
9	NORKING	17884t	80	19.0k	170.9m	12P	-	155T	A	FI	7902635
10	NORQUEEN	17884t	80	19.0k	170.9m	12P	-	155T	A	FI	7902647
11	NORSKY	20296t	99	20.0k	180.0m	12P	-	194T	A	NL	9186182
12	NORSTREAM	20296t	99	20.0k	180.0m	12P	-	194T	A	NL	9186194
13	URSINE	16947t	79	15.0k	170.3m	12P	180C	160T	A	BE	7800746

CALIBUR Built by Trosvik Verksted A/S, Brevik, Norway as the SEASPEED DANA for *Seaspeed Ferries* of Greece and chartered to *Fred. Olsen Seaspeed Ferries* for service in the Middle East. In 1979 chartered to *Roto Line* and used on services between Sweden and the UK, renamed the DANA. In 1983 she was sold to *Stena Line* and embarked on a number of charters, mainly in the Caribbean. In 1990 she was chartered to *CoTuNav* of Tunisia, renamed the SALAH L and used on services from Tunisia to Southern Europe. In 1993 she was chartered to *Olympic Ferries* of Greece, renamed the SENATOR, operating between Greece and Italy. In 1995 she was sold to *Exxtor Ferries* and renamed the EXCALIBUR. She operated between Immingham and Rotterdam. The service was taken over by *Cobelfret Ferries* in 1997 and she was sold to *Kaliningrad Key Line* of Malta, renamed the CALIBUR and placed on their Køge (Denmark) – Aabenraa (Denmark) – Kaliningrad service. In 1998 she was sold to *V Ships* of Monaco and placed on the charter market, undertaking a number of short charters. In 2003 she was chartered to *Ferryways* and placed on their Ostend – Killingholme service. In Summer 2005 she went to Turkey for a major refit. She returned in January 2006 and resumed service on the Killingholme/Immingham service. In June 2007 laid up following the liquidation of *Ferryways*. In July chartered to *P&O Ferries* and on 16th July inaugurated a new Tilbury - Zeebrugge service. In November she moved to the Hull - Zeebrugge service but returned to the Tilbury service in January 2008.

CELTIC STAR Built at Kawajiri, Japan as the KOSEI MARU for *Kanko Kisen KK Line* of Japan for domestic services. In 1998 she was sold to *Jay Management Corporation* of Cyprus and renamed the IOLAOS. In November 1998 she was chartered to *East Coast Ferries*, renamed the LOON-PLAGE and placed on their Hull - Dunkerque service. The service ceased in January 1999 and after a brief charter to *DFDS Tor Line*, she was renamed the CELTIC STAR, chartered to *P&O European Ferries (Irish Sea)* and placed on the Liverpool - Dublin route. In January 2002 she was renamed the NORTHERN STAR and inaugurated a new Liverpool - Larne service. In 2003 chartered to *Dart Line* to replace the DART 8; placed on the Dartford - Vlissingen route. In 2004 chartered *CoTuNav* of Tunisia to operate between Tunis and Livorno (Italy). In 2006 chartered to *Celtic Link Ferries* to inaugurate a new service between Dublin and Liverpool. Renamed the CELTIC STAR. In September 2007 the charter of the vessel and the service were taken over by *Seatruck Ferries*. In 2008 chartered to *P&O Ferries* to operate on the same route.

EUROPEAN ENDEAVOUR Built as the MIDNIGHT MERCHANT by Astilleros Españoles SA, Seville, Spain for *Cenargo* (then owners of *NorseMerchant Ferries*). On delivery, chartered to *Norfolkline* to operate as second vessel on the Dover - Dunkerque (Ouest) service. In 2002 modified to allow two-deck loading. In 2006 chartered to *Acciona Trasmediterranea* of Spain and renamed the EL GRECO. Used on Mediterranean and Canary Island services. In 2007 sold to *P&O Ferries* and renamed the EUROPEAN ENDEAVOUR. Operates on the Dover - Calais route and as a winter relief vessel on Irish Sea routes.

EUROPEAN MARINER Built at Rickmers Werft, Bremerhaven, Germany as the SALAHALA and chartered to *Gilnavi* of Italy for Mediterranean services. In 1990 she was purchased by *Cenargo* and chartered to *Merchant Ferries* who renamed her the MERCHANT VALIANT. She was used on their Fleetwood - Warrenpoint service until 1993 when she was chartered to *Pandoro* and placed on their Ardrossan - Larne service. Purchased by *P&O* in 1995 and renamed the LION. In early 1998 renamed the EUROPEAN HIGHLANDER. In July 2001, the service moved to Troon and she was renamed the EUROPEAN MARINER. In 2002 replaced by the EUROPEAN NAVIGATOR. After a brief charter to *Seatruck Ferries* she went on a two-month charter to *Color Line*, operating between Kristiansand and Hirtshals. On return she went on a short charter to *Commodore Ferries* and in late September was transferred to the Larne - Troon route replacing the EUROPEAN NAVIGATOR. Later she was chartered to *Norse Island Ferries*; she returned to *P&O Irish Sea* in late 2002. Expected to be replaced by the NORCAPE later in 2008.

EUROPEAN SEAWAY Built by Schichau Seebeckwerft AG, Bremerhaven, Germany for *P&O European Ferries* for the Dover - Zeebrugge freight service. In 2000 a regular twice-daily freight-only Dover-Calais service was established, using this vessel which continued to operate to Zeebrugge at night. In 2001 car passengers (not foot or coach passengers) began to be conveyed on the Dover - Zeebrugge service. In 2003 the Zeebrugge service ended and she operated only between Dover and Calais in a freight-only mode. In 2004 withdrawn and laid up. In January 2005 returned to the Dover - Calais route.

EUROPEAN TRADER Built by Hitachi Zosen, Osaka Works, Sakai, Japan as the DANA MAXIMA for *DFDS* for their North Sea services. Until 1995 generally used on the Esbjerg - Grimsby and North Shields services. In Summer 1995 she was lengthened to increase trailer capacity. In 2000 she was renamed the TOR MAXIMA. In 2001 sold to *Goliat Shipping AS* of Norway and chartered back. In 2008 sold to *P&O Ferries* to operate between Hull and Zeebrugge and renamed the EUROPEAN TRADER.

HOBURGEN Launched at Galatz, Romania as the BALDER RA for *K/S A/S Balder RO/RO No 2* of Norway. On completion acquired by *Navrom* of Romania, renamed the BAZIAS 5 and used on Mediterranean services; subsequently transferred to *Romline* of Romania. In 1995 she was chartered to *Grimaldi* of Italy and renamed the PERSEUS; she was later chartered to *Sudcargo* of France. In 1996 she was chartered to *Dart Line* and renamed the DART 5. In 1999 she was arrested in respect of a claim against *Romline* and laid up in Zeebrugge. In 2000 she was sold at auction to *Rederi AB Gotland* of Sweden. She was placed on the charter market. In 2001 she was chartered to *Cobelfret Ferries* and placed on the Purfleet - Rotterdam service, initially on a short-term basis and, after a short break, on a longer-term basis. Later operated on the Zeebrugge - Purfleet service. In Autumn 2003 the charter ended. She was chartered to *DFDS Tor Line*. In January and February 2004 chartered to the *Isle of Man Steam Packet Company* to operate between Heysham and Douglas whilst the BEN-MY-CHREE was having additional accommodation built. In 2005 chartered to *Transfennica* and placed on a new route between Halmstad and Travemünde. In August chartered to *Ferryways* and placed on the Ostend - Immingham service. In December chartered to *Norfolkline* followed in 2007 by charters to the *Isle of Man Steam Packet Company* and *Smyril Line*. In September 2007 she was sold to *Rederi Ab Lillgaard* of Finland and chartered to *P&O Ferries*. She normally operated on the Zeebrugge - Tilbury service.

NORCAPE Built by Mitsui Engineering and Shipbuilding, Tamano, Japan. Launched as the PUMA but on completion chartered to *B&I Line* and renamed the TIPPERARY for their Dublin - Liverpool service. In 1989 sold to *North Sea Ferries*, renamed the NORCAPE and introduced onto the Ipswich - Rotterdam service. In 1995 that service ceased and she was moved to the Hull - Zeebrugge freight service. She retains Dutch crew and registry. Until early 2008 operated on the Hull – Zeebrugge and Hull – Rotterdam routes. In May 2008 given a major rebuild. Then she will be placed on the Zeebrugge - Tilbury route.

NORKING, NORQUEEN Built by Rauma-Repola Oy, Rauma, Finland as the BORE KING and the BORE QUEEN for *Bore Line* of Finland for Baltic services. In 1991 chartered to *North Sea Ferries* for their Teesport - Zeebrugge service and renamed the NORKING and NORQUEEN respectively. During Winter 1995/96 they were lengthened by 28.8 metres and re-engined. In 1999 transferred to the Teesport - Rotterdam service.

NORSKY, NORSTREAM Built by Aker Finnyards, Rauma, Finland for *Bore Line* of Finland and chartered to *P&O North Sea Ferries*. They generally operate on the Teesport - Zeebrugge service.

URSINE Built by Öresundsvarvet Ab, Landskrona, Sweden as the BRITTA ODEN for *AB Norsjöfrakt* (later *Bylock & Norsjöfrakt*) of Sweden and chartered to *Oden Line* of Sweden for North Sea services, in particular associated with the export of Volvo cars and trucks from Gothenburg. In 1980 *Oden Line* was taken over by *Tor Lloyd AB*, a joint venture between *Tor Line* and *Broströms AB* and the charter transferred to them, moving to *Tor Line* in 1981 when *DFDS* took over. In 1987 she was enlarged, on re-entry into service in early 1988 she was renamed the TOR SCANDIA and became regular vessel on the Gothenburg - Ghent (Belgium) service. In 1998 renamed the BRITTA ODEN. In 1999 the charter was ended and she was chartered to *Flota Suardiaz*. In September 2003 she was chartered to *Cobelfret Ferries* and placed on the Rotterdam - Purfleet service. In October 2003 purchased by

Cobelfret Ferries. In 2004 she inaugurated a new Killingholme - Gothenburg service. In Spring 2005 the service was taken over by *DFDS Tor Line* and she was chartered to them but returned to the Zeebrugge - Purfleet service in August 2005. In June 2006 placed on a new Dartford - Vlissingen service. In October 2006 renamed the URSINE and in November 2006 chartered to *P&O Ferries* to operate on the Hull - Rotterdam route.

SCA TRANSFOREST

THE COMPANY *SCA Transforest* is a Swedish company.

MANAGEMENT Managing Director (UK) Bo Frölander.

ADDRESS Interforest Terminal London Ltd, 44 Berth, Tilbury Dock, Essex RM18 7HR.

TELEPHONE Administration & Reservations *Sweden* +46 (0)60-19 35 00, *UK* +44 (0)1375 48 85 00.

FAX Administration & Reservations *Sweden* +46 (0)60-19 35 74 *UK* +44 (0)1375 48 85 03.

INTERNET Email *Sweden* info@transforest.sca.com *UK* bo.frolander@sca.com

Website www.transforest.sca.se *(English)*

ROUTE OPERATED Umeå *(dep: 11.00 Mon, 16.00 Thu)* - Husum *(dep: 20.00 Mon, 22.00 Thu)* - Sundsvall *(dep: 12.00 Tue, 12.00 Fri)* - Iggesund *(dep: 19.00 Tue, 19.00 Fri)* - Tilbury *(arr: 11.00 Tue, 13.00 Sat, dep: 16.00 Tue, 18.00 Sat)* - Rotterdam (Eemhaven) *(dep: 13.00 Sun, 12.00 Wed)* - Helsingborg *(arr: 07.00 Fri)* (8/9 day round trip; *1,2,3*; 2 per week).

1	OBBOLA	20168t	96	16.0k	170.6m	0P	-	-	A	SE	9087350
2	ORTVIKEN	20154t	97	16.0k	170.4m	0P	-	-	A	SE	9087374
3	ÖSTRAND	20171t	96	16.0k	170.6m	0P	-	-	A	SE	9087362

OBBOLA, ORTVIKEN, ÖSTRAND Built by Astilleros Españoles, Seville, Spain for *Gorthon Lines* and chartered to *SCA Transforest*. They are designed for the handling of forest products in non-wheeled 'cassettes' but can also accommodate ro-ro trailers; however, no trailer capacity is quoted. The ORTVIKEN was lengthened during Autumn 2000 and the OBBOLA and ÖSTRAND were lengthened during 2001.

SEA-CARGO

THE COMPANY *Sea-Cargo AS* of Norway is a joint venture between *Nor-Cargo AS* (a Norwegian company jointly owned by *Det Stavangerske Dampskipsselskab* and *Hurtigruten Group ASA*) and *SeaTrans DS* of Norway.

MANAGEMENT *Sea-Cargo UK Ltd* Managing Director Barry Jenks.

ADDRESS *Norway* Sea-Cargo AS, PO Box 353, Nesttun, 5853 Bergen, Norway, ***Immingham*** Sea-Cargo UK, West Riverside Road, Immingham Dock, Immingham DN40 2NT, ***Aberdeen*** Nor-Cargo Ltd, Matthews Quay, Aberdeen Harbour, Aberdeen, AB11 5PG.

TELEPHONE Administration & Bookings *Bergen* +47 85 02 82 16, ***Immingham*** +44 (0)1469 577119, ***Aberdeen*** +44 (0)1224 596481.

FAX Administration & Reservations *Bergen* +47 85 02 82 16, ***Immingham*** 44 (0)1469 577708, ***Aberdeen*** +44 (0)1224 582360.

INTERNET Email mail@sea-cargo.no **Website** www.sea-cargo.no *(English)*

ROUTES OPERATED Sea-Cargo operates a complex network of services between West Norway and Amsterdam, Aberdeen, Immingham and Esbjerg. The schedule varies from week to week and is shown on the company website.

1	AMBER	6719t	93	16.5k	122.0m	12P	-	86T	A	NO	8917871
2	ASTREA	9528t	91	13.5k	129.1m	0P	-	60T	A	NO	8917895

3	COMETA	4610t	81	15.0k	102.2m	0P	-	20T	AS	NO	7922166
4	NORDIA	7395t	91	16.5k	123.0m	12P	-	86T	A	GR	8912388
5	SC ABERDEEN	4234t	79	15.5k	109.0m	0P	-	24T	AS	BS	7800540
6	TRANS CARRIER	8476t	93	14.5k	125.2m	0P	-	78T	A	BS	9007879

AMBER Built by Brodogradiliste "Sava", Macvanska Mitrovica, Yugoslavia, completed by Fosen Mekaniske Verksteder, Rissa, Norway for *Brax Shipping* of Sweden and chartered to *Euroafrica Shipping Lines of Norway* (a subsidiary of the Polish company of the same name). Operated on the joint *POL/Euroafrica Shipping/Finnlines Polfin* service between Helsinki and Gdynia. Has also operated on other *Finnlines* services. From January 2007 operated on the *Finnlines* Helsinki - Gdynia service. Later chartered to *Sea-Cargo* to operate a new service to Esbjerg.

ASTREA Built by Tangen Verft Kragerø A/S, Tomrefjord, Norway for *Finncarriers*. Operated between Finland and Spain - Portugal via Antwerp. In 2006 chartered to *Danish MoD*. In 2007 chartered to *Sea-Cargo*.

COMETA Con-ro vessel (only the main deck can take trailers) built by Fosen Mekaniske Verksteder, Rissa, Norway for *Nor-Cargo*.

SC ABERDEEN Con-ro vessel built by Fosen Mekaniske Verksteder, Rissa, Norway for *Nor-Cargo*. Launched as the ERIC JARL but renamed the ASTREA before entering service. In 1986 she sank and, after raising and refitting, she was, in 1992, renamed the TUNGENES. In 2001 she was renamed the SC ABERDEEN.

NORDIA Built by Solheimsviken A/S at Bergen, Norway for *Oy Rettig AB* of Finland as the BORE NORDIA and used on *Bore Line* service between Turku - Kiel - Cuxhaven - Harwich. In 1992 chartered to *Finncarriers* and used on Baltic services. In 1997 she was renamed the FINNSEAL. In 2003 she was renamed the BORE NORDIA and chartered to *Transfennica*. In 2004 sold to *Attica Group* and renamed the NORDIA. In January 2005 inaugurated a new service between Rostock and Uusikaupunki. In 2007 the *Transfennica* charter was terminated, she was chartered to *Sea-Cargo* and inaugurated a service between Esbjerg and West Norway. In 2008 sold to *Compagnie Maritime Marfret* of France but the *Sea-Cargo* charter continued.

TRANS CARRIER Built by Brodogradiliste Kraljevica, Kraljevica, Croatia as the KORSNÄS LINK for *SeaLink AB* of Sweden and due to be time-chartered to *Korsnäs AB*, a Swedish forest products company. However, due to the war in Croatia, delivery was seriously delayed and she was offered for sale. In 1994 sold to the *Swan Group* and renamed the SWAN HUNTER. She was placed on the charter market. In 1997 she was chartered to *Euroseabridge* and renamed the PARCHIM. In 1999 the charter ended and she resumed the name SWAN HUNTER. In 1999 she was sold to *SeaTrans* and renamed the TRANS CARRIER. She operated for *Sea-Cargo*. In 2005 chartered to *Finnlines* and used on the Finland to Spain/Portugal service. In 2006 returned to *Sea-Cargo*.

Under Construction

| 7 | NEWBUILDING 1 | 6470t | 08 | 16.0k | 116.7m | 0P | - | 35T | AS | BS | 9358060 |
| 8 | NEWBUILDING 2 | 6470t | 08 | 16.0k | 116.7m | 0P | - | 35T | AS | BS | 9358072 |

NEWBUILDING 1, NEWBUILDING 2 Con-ro vessels under construction at Bharati Ratnagiri Ltd, Mumbai, India for *Sea-Cargo*.

SEAFRANCE

THE COMPANY, MANAGEMENT & ADDRESS See Section 1.

TELEPHONE Reservations + 44 (0)871 282 8518

FAX Reservations + 44 (0)871 282 8514.

INTERNET Email freightdover@wanadoo.fr **Website** www.seafrancefreight.com (*English, French, Dutch, German*)

ROUTE OPERATED Calais (*dep: 02.15 Mon-Sat, 09.15 Mon-Sat, 13.30, 17.45, 22.00 Sun-Fri*) - Dover *(dep: 06.00 Mon-Sat, 10.15 Mon-Sat, 14.30, 18.45, 23.00 Sun-Fri)* (1 hr 30 mins; *1*; 5 per day).

1	SEAFRANCE									
	NORD PAS-DE-CALAIS	7264t	87	21.5k	160.1m	80P	-	102L	BA2	FR 8512152

SEAFRANCE NORD PAS-DE-CALAIS Built by Chantiers du Nord et de la Mediterranée, Dunkerque, France as the NORD PAS-DE-CALAIS at Dunkerque, France for *SNCF* for the Dunkerque (Ouest) - Dover train ferry service. Before being used on this service (which required the construction of a new berth at Dover (Western Docks)) in May 1988, she operated road freight services from Calais to Dover Eastern Docks. The train ferry service continued to operate following the opening of the Channel Tunnel in 1994, to convey road vehicles and dangerous loads which were banned from the Tunnel. However, it ceased in December 1995 and, after a refit, in February 1996 she was renamed the SEAFRANCE NORD PAS-DE-CALAIS and switched to the Calais - Dover service, primarily for road freight vehicles and drivers but also advertised as carrying up to 50 car passengers. Since the entry into service of a third multi-purpose ferry, she has operated on a freight-only basis.

SEATRUCK FERRIES

THE COMPANY *Seatruck Ferries Ltd* is a British private sector company. It is part of the *Clipper Group*.

MANAGEMENT Managing Director Kevin Hobbs, **Sales Director** Alistair Eagles.

ADDRESS *Warrenpoint (HQ)* Seatruck House, The Ferry Terminal, Warrenpoint, County Down BT34 3JR. *Heysham* North Quay, Heysham Port, Heysham, Morecambe, Lancs LA3 2XF.

TELEPHONE Administration + 44 (0)28 4175 4411, **Reservations *Warrenpoint*** + 44 (0)28 4175 4400, *Heysham* + 44 (0)1524 853512.

FAX Administration + 44 (0)28 4175 4545, **Reservations *Warrenpoint*** + 44 (0)28 4177 3737, *Heysham* + 44 (0)1524 853549.

INTERNET Email alistair@seatruck-ferries.co.uk **Website** www.seatruckferries.com (*English*)

ROUTES OPERATED Heysham *(dep: 08.00 Tue-Sat, 19.00 Mon-Fri, 21.00 Sat, Sun, 23.00 Mon-Fri)* - Warrenpoint *(dep: 07.00 Tue-Sat, 10.30 Tue-Fri, 18.00 Sat, Sun, 22.00 Sun-Fri)* (7-8 hrs; *2,4,6*; 3 per day), Dublin *(dep: 09.45 (Tue-Sat), 21.45 (daily))* - Liverpool *dep: 09.45 (Tue-Sat), 21.45 (daily))* (7 hr 15 min; *1,5*; 2 per day).

1	CHALLENGE	7606t	98	17.0k	122.3m	12P	-	84T	A	MT	9119402
2	CLIPPER POINT	14759t	08	22.0k	142.0m	12P	-	120T	A	CY	9350666
3	LYGRA	7012t	79	14.0k	113.4m	0P	-	54T	A	NO	7704629
4	MOONDANCE	5881t	78	15.0k	116.3m	12P	-	62T	A	CY	7800112
5	TRIUMPH	7800t	98	17.0k	122.3m	12P	-	86T	A	MA	9119397
6	WEST EXPRESS	9368t	78	17.0k	134.8m	12P	-	94T	A	JM	7724253

CHALLENGE Built at Huelva, Spain as the LEMBITU for the *Estonian Shipping Company*. On completion chartered to *P&O European Ferries (Irish Sea)* and placed on their Liverpool - Dublin route. In Autumn 1998 she was chartered to *Dart Line* and placed on the Dartford - Vlissingen route. In 1999 she was renamed the DART 7. In Autumn 1999 the charter was ended and she was chartered to *Cetma* of France, resumed the name LEMBITU and was used on services between Marseilles and Tunis. In 2000 she was chartered to *P&O European Ferries (Irish Sea)* and renamed the CELTIC SUN; she operated between Liverpool and Dublin. In 2001 the chartered ended; she then reverted to the name LEMBITU and was chartered to *NorseMerchant Ferries* and placed on the Heysham - Dublin service. In late 2001 the charter ended and she returned to *ESCO* service in the Baltic. In 2003 chartered to *Scandlines AG* and placed on their Rostock - Helsinki - Muuga service. This service finished in December 2004 and she was chartered to *Channel Freight Ferries* in January 2005. In March 2005 chartered to *NorseMerchant Ferries* again and operated between Heysham and Belfast. Later purchased by *Elmira Shipping* of Greece and renamed the RR CHALLENGE. In June 2005 chartered to *Seatruck Ferries*. In October 2007 sold to *Attica Group* of Greece and renamed the CHALLENGE. She continued to be chartered to *Seatruck Ferries*. In January 2008 transferred to the Liverpool - Dublin route and sold to *Seatruck Ferries*.

CLIPPER POINT Built by Astilleros de Huelva SA, Huelva, Spain for *Seatruck Ferries*. Operates on the Heysham - Warrenpoint service.

LYGRA Built by Ankerløkken Verft Glommen A/S, Frederikstad, Norway as the CENTRO AMERICA for *Liniera Naviera Pan Atlantica SA* of Puerto Rico. In 1984 sold to *K/S Bergenske og Euro Trans I/S (K/S Seatrans)* of Norway and renamed the NORNEWS SERVICE. In 1992 sold to *K/S Eurotrans A/S* of the Bahamas. In 1994 renamed the TRANS FJORD, operating between Hamburg and Skien (Norway). In 1997 sold to *Fjord Line* and renamed the LYGRA. In 1994 sold to *Flores Holding AS* of Norway and chartered back. The charter ended in October 2006 and since then she has undertaken a number of short-term charters. In April 2008 chartered to *Seatruck Ferries* and operated between Heysham and Warrenpoint. The charter was ended in June 2008.

MOONDANCE Built by Rickmers Werft, Bremerhaven, Germany as the EMADALA for *Emadulu Shipping* and chartered to *Gilnavi Line* of Italy for Mediterranean services. In 1987 she was purchased by *Gilnavi Line*. In 1990 sold to *Cenargo* of Great Britain, chartered to *Merchant Ferries* for their Heysham - Warrenpoint service and renamed the MERCHANT VICTOR. She was withdrawn from that service in 1993 and was chartered out to a number of operators. In 1997 she was chartered to *Seatruck Ferries* and renamed the MOONDANCE. In 1998 she was purchased by *Seatruck Ferries*. Following the collapse of the ramp at Warrenpoint in January 2001, she briefly operated between Heysham and Larne.

TRIUMPH Built at Huelva, Spain as the LEHOLA for the *Estonian Shipping Company*. Initially used on *ESCO* Baltic services. In 1998 chartered to *Czar Peter Line* to operate between Moerdijk (The Netherlands) and Kronstadt (Russia). In 1999 chartered to *Delom* of France to operate between Marseilles and Sete and Tunis. In 2000 she returned to *ESCO*, operating between Kiel and Tallinn. In 2003 chartered to *Scandlines AG* and transferred to subsidiary *Scandlines Estonia AS*. Operated Rostock - Helsinki – Muuga initially and later Rostock – Helsinki. Service finished at the end of 2004 and in 2005 she was chartered to *P&O Ferries* to operate between Hull and Rotterdam and Hull and Zeebrugge. In 2005 sold to *Elmira Shipping* of Greece. Later renamed the RR TRIUMPH. In 2006 transferred to *P&O Irish Sea* to operate between Liverpool and Dublin. In 2007 chartered to *Balearia* of Spain and operated from Barcelona. In 2008 purchased by *Seatruck Ferries* and renamed the TRIUMPH. In Spring 2008 she was sub-chartered to *Condor Ferries* to cover for the refit period of the COMMODORE GOODWILL. In June 2008 placed on the Liverpool-Dublin route.

WEST EXPRESS Built by Nylands Verksted, Oslo, Norway. Launched as the STEVI for *Steineger & Wiik* of Norway and, on delivery, chartered to *Norient Line* of Norway, being renamed the NORWEGIAN CRUSADER. In 1980 chartered to *Ignazio Messina* of Italy for Mediterranean service and renamed the JOLLY GIALLO. In 1982 the charter ended and she was briefly renamed the NORWEGIAN CRUSADER before being purchased by *Ignazio Messina* and resuming the name JOLLY GIALLO. In 1993 sold to *Merchant Ferries*, renamed the MERCHANT BRAVERY and placed on the Heysham - Warrenpoint (Dublin since 1995) service. In 1999 transferred to *Belfast Freight Ferries'* Heysham - Belfast service. In 2004 moved to the Heysham - Dublin route. In 2004 sold to *Bravery International Shipping Ltd* of Latvia and chartered back to *NorseMerchant Ferries*. Re-registered in Jamaica. In January 2007 charter terminated. She then undertook a number of short-term charters. In April sold to *Express Shipping A/S* of Denmark and renamed the WEST EXPRESS. Later chartered to *Seatruck Ferries* to operate between Heyshaml and Warrenpoint.

Under Construction

7	CLIPPER PACE	14759t	08	22.0k	142.0m	12P	-	120T	A	CY	9350678
8	CLIPPER PANORAMA	14760t	08	22.0k	142.0m	12P	-	120T	A	CY	9372688
9	CLIPPER PENNANT	14759t	08	22.0k	142.0m	12P	-	120T	A	CY	9372676
10	NEWBUILDING 1	-	11	21.0k	142.0m	12P		151T	A	-	-
11	NEWBUILDING 2	-	12	21.0k	142.0m	12P		151T	A	-	-
12	NEWBUILDING 3	-	12	21.0k	142.0m	12P	-	151T	A	-	-
13	NEWBUILDING 4	-	12	21.0k	142.0m	12P	-	151T	A	-	-

CLIPPER PACE, CLIPPER PANORAMA Under construction by Astilleros de Huelva SA, Huelva, Spain for *Seatruck Ferries*.

CLIPPER PENNANT Under construction by Astilleros de Sevilla SA, Seville, Spain for *Seatruck Ferries*.

NEWBUILDING 1, NEWBUILDING 2, NEWBUILDING 3, NEWBUILDING 4 On order from Flensburger Schiffbau-Gesellschaft, Flensburg, Germany for *Seatruck Ferries*.

STENA LINE

THE COMPANY, MANAGEMENT, ADDRESS, TELEPHONE AND INTERNET See Section 1.

ROUTES OPERATED Harwich (*dep: 05.00 Tue-Sat, 11.00 Mon-Sat, 22.45 Sun-Fri*) - Rotterdam (*dep: 11.30 Mon-Sat, 19.00 Mon-Fri, 23.45 Sun-Fri*) (7 hrs 45 mins; *1,4,5*; 3 per day), Killingholme (*dep: 19.15*) - Hook of Holland (*dep: 19.00*) (13 hrs; *3,6*; 1 per day), Holyhead (*dep: 22.15*) - Dublin (*dep: 15.15*) (4 hrs 30 mins; *2*; 1 per day).

1	STENA PARTNER	21162t	77	16.5k	184.6m	166P	-	180T	A2	UK	7528635
2	STENA SEATRADER	17991t	73	17.5k	181.6m	221P	-	174T	AS2	UK	7301491
3	STENA TRADER	26660t	06	22.2k	212.0m	200P	-	220T	A	NL	9331177
4	STENA TRANSFER	21162t	77	16.5k	184.6m	166P	-	180T	A2	UK	7528570
5	STENA TRANSPORTER	16776t	78	17.0k	151.0m	74P	-	122T	A2	UK	7528659
6	STENA TRAVELLER	26660t	07	22.2k	212.0m	200P	-	220T	A	NL	9331189

STENA PARTNER Built by Hyundai Shipbuilders & Heavy Industries, Ulsan, South Korea for *Stena Rederi* as the ALPHA ENTERPRISE and chartered to *Aghiris Navigation* of Cyprus. In 1979 she was renamed the SYRIA and chartered to *Hellas Ferries* for services between Greece and Syria. In 1981 she was lengthened by 33.6m. In 1982 she was chartered to *European Ferries* and used on freight services between Felixstowe and Rotterdam. In 1983 she was renamed the STENA TRANSPORTER and in 1986 the CERDIC FERRY. In 1992 she was renamed the EUROPEAN FREEWAY and, in 1994, purchased by *P&O European Ferries*. In 2002 sold to *Stena Line* and renamed the FREEWAY. She initially operated between Felixstowe and Rotterdam and later Harwich and Rotterdam. In early 2003 she was renamed the STENA PARTNER.

STENA SEATRADER Built by A/S Nakskov Skipsværft, Nakskov, Denmark as the SVEALAND for *Lion Ferry AB* of Sweden and chartered to *Statens Järnvägar (Swedish State Railways)* for the train ferry service between Trelleborg (Sweden) and Sassnitz (Germany (DDR)). The charter ceased in 1980 and in 1982 she was sold to *Rederi AB Nordö* of Sweden. She was lengthened by 33.7 metres, renamed the SVEALAND AV MALMÖ and used on their lorry/rail wagon service between Malmö and Travemünde. In 1986 she was rebuilt with a higher superstructure and in 1987 she was renamed the SVEA LINK, the service being renamed *Nordö Link*. In 1990 she was sold to *Stena Line*, renamed the STENA SEATRADER and introduced onto the Hook of Holland - Harwich service. In Spring 2001 she replaced the chartered ROSEBAY (see TRANSLANDIA, *Eckerö Line*) on the Hook of Holland - Killingholme service. In 2006 transferred to the Holyhead - Dublin route.

STENA TRADER Built by Fosen Mekaniske Verksteder, Rissa, Norway (hull built by Baltiysky Zavod JSC, St Petersburg, Russia) for *Stena RoRo* and chartered to *Stena Line* to operate on the Hook of Holland - Killingholme service. Between January and May 2007 she operated between Hook of Holland and Harwich whilst the STENA BRITANNICA and STENA HOLLANDICA (see Section 1) were lengthened.

STENA TRANSFER Built by Hyundai Shipbuilders & Heavy Industries, Ulsan, South Korea. Launched as the STENA RUNNER for *Stena Rederi* of Sweden. On completion, renamed the ALPHA PROGRESS and chartered to *Aghiris Navigation* of Greece. In 1979 renamed the HELLAS and operated by *Soutos-Hellas Ferry Services* on services between Greece and Syria. In 1982 she was lengthened by 33.6m. In 1982 she was chartered to *European Ferries* and used on freight services between Felixstowe and Rotterdam. The following year she was returned to *Hellas Ferries*. In 1985 she returned to *European Ferries* and the Rotterdam service. In 1986 she was renamed the DORIC FERRY. In 1992 she was renamed the EUROPEAN TIDEWAY and, in 1994, purchased by *P&O European Ferries*. In 2001 replaced by the NORBANK and laid up. In 2002 returned to the Felixstowe - Rotterdam route when the NORBANK was transferred to *P&O Irish Sea*. In 2002 sold to *Stena Line* and renamed the IDEWAY. She initially operated between Felixstowe and Rotterdam and later Harwich and Rotterdam. Later in 2002 she was renamed the STENA TRANSFER.

Clipper Point (*Matthew Davies*)

Stena Seatrader (*Gordon Hislip*)

STENA TRANSPORTER Built by Hyundai Shipbuilders & Heavy Industries, Ulsan, South Korea as the MERZARIO ESPANIA for *Stena Rederi* of Sweden and immediately chartered to *Merzario Line* for their service between Italy and Saudi Arabia. In the same year she was renamed the MERZARIO HISPANIA. In 1979 she was chartered to *European Ferries* for their ro-ro freight service between Felixstowe and Rotterdam and renamed the NORDIC FERRY. In 1982 she served in the Falkland Islands Task Force. In 1986 she was modified to carry 688 passengers and, with sister vessel the BALTIC FERRY (now the EUROPEAN DIPLOMAT), took over the Felixstowe - Zeebrugge passenger service. In 1992 she was renamed the PRIDE OF FLANDERS. In 1994, purchased by *P&O European Ferries*. In 1995 the Felixstowe - Zeebrugge passenger service ceased, her additional passenger accommodation was removed, passenger capacity was reduced and she was transferred to the Felixstowe - Rotterdam freight service. In 2002 sold to *Stena Line* and renamed the FLANDERS. She initially operated between Felixstowe and Rotterdam and later Harwich and Rotterdam. In Autumn 2002 chartered to *Scandlines AB* of Sweden to operate between Travemünde and Trelleborg whilst the SVEALAND was undergoing a major rebuild. Later in 2002, after a refit, she returned to the Harwich - Rotterdam route and was renamed the STENA TRANSPORTER. She has also operated between Hook of Holland and Killingholme.

STENA TRAVELLER Built by Fosen Mekaniske Verksteder, Rissa, Norway (hull built by Baltiysky Zavod JSC, St Petersburg, Russia) for *Stena RoRo* and chartered to *Stena Line* to operate on the Hook of Holland - Killingholme service.

Under Construction

7	NEWBUILDING 1	37500t	11	23.0k	212.0m	300P	-	290T	A2	UK
8	NEWBUILDING 2	37500t	11	23.0k	212.0m	300P	-	290T	A2	UK

NEWBUILDING 1, NEWBUILDING 2 Under construction by Samsung Heavy Industries, Koje, South Korea. They are to be used on the Hook of Holland - Killingholme service, enabling the existing vessels to move to the Harwich - Rotterdam route.

TRANSEUROPA FERRIES

THE COMPANY *TransEuropa Ferries NV* is a Belgian subsidiary of *TransEuropa Shipping Lines*, a Slovenian private sector company. Channel operations started in 1997, in conjunction with *Sally Ferries*, replacing them on November 1998. The company traded as *TransEuropa Shipping Lines (TSL)* until 2000. Note that all the owning companies listed here are associated companies of *TSL*.

MANAGEMENT *TransEuropa Shipping* Managing Director Stergulc Rihard, ***TransEuropa Ferries NV*, General Manager Belgium & UK** Mr Dominique Penel, **Sales Manager, Europe** Peter Sys.

ADDRESSES *TSL Slovenia* Vojkovo nabrezje 38, 6000 Koper, Slovenia, ***TEF UK*** Ferry Terminal, Ramsgate New Port, Ramsgate, Kent CT11 8RP ***TEF Belgium*** Slijkensesteenweg 2, 8400 Ostend, Belgium.

TELEPHONE Admin *TSL Slovenia* +386 (0)5 664 17 77, ***TEF UK*** +44 (0)1843 853833, **Reservations *TEF Belgium*** +32 (0)59 34 02 50, ***TEF UK*** +44 (0)1843 853523, ***TEF Belgium*** +32 (0)59 340240.

FAX *TSL Admin Slovenia* +386 (0)5 639 50 36, ***TEF Belgium*** +32 (0)59 34 02 51, **Admin & Sales *TEF UK*** +44 (0)1843 853668, **Sales *TEF Belgium*** +32 (0)59 34 02 51.

INTERNET Website www.transeuropaferries.co.uk *(English)*

ROUTE OPERATED Ramsgate *(dep: 01.00 Sat, 02.00 Mon-Fri, 03.00 Sat, 03.30 Tue-Fri, 07.00 Daily, 09.30 Mon, 12.00 Sun, 13.30 Mon-Fri, 15.30 Sun, 16.30 Mon-Fri, 18.30 Daily, 20.30 Sun-Fri, 22.30 Daily, 23.45 Sun, 23.59 Mon-Thu)* - Ostend (Belgium) *(dep: 01.00 Daily, 03.00 Tue-Thu, 05.30 Mon, 07.00 Daily, 11.00 Sun-Fri, 13.30 Daily, 16.00 Sun-Fri, 18.00 Daily, 20.00 Sun-Thu, 21.30 Sun-Thu, 22.30 Fri, 23.00 Mon-Thu, 23.30 Sun)* (4 hrs; *1 plus passenger vessels* EUROVOYAGER, LARKSPUR, OLEANDER *and* PRIMROSE; *up to 10 per day).*

1	GARDENIA	8097t	78	18.4k	118.1m	105P	-	52L	BA2	CY	7711139

GARDENIA Built by Schichau-Unterweser AG, Bremerhaven, Germany as the EUROPEAN

Stena Partner (*Mike Louagie*)

ENTERPRISE for *European Ferries*. In 1988 she was renamed the EUROPEAN ENDEAVOUR. She was used on freight services between Dover and Calais and Dover and Zeebrugge. If space were available, a small number of passengers was sometimes conveyed on the Zeebrugge service, although the sailings were not advertised for passengers. This ceased with the withdrawal of passenger services on this route at the end of 1991. During the summer period she provided additional freight capacity on the Dover - Calais service and has also served on other routes. In Autumn 1995 she was transferred to the Cairnryan - Larne service. In 1998 her accommodation was raised to provide extra freight capacity. In March 1999 she also began operating from Larne to Ardrossan but this ceased later in the year. Withdrawn from service in July 2002 and sold to *Odyssy Maritime Co Ltd* and renamed the GARDENIA. In 2003 she began operating for *TEF* between Ramsgate and Ostend.

TRANSFENNICA

THE COMPANY *Transfennica Ltd* is a Finnish private sector company wholly owned by *Spliethoff Bevrachtingskantoor* of The Netherlands.

MANAGEMENT Managing Director Dirk P. Witteveen, **Director (UK)** Jim Deeprose.

ADDRESSES *Finland* Eteläranta 12, 00130 Helsinki, Finland, ***UK*** Finland House, 47 Berth, Tilbury Freeport, Tilbury, Essex RM18 7EH.

TELEPHONE Administration & Reservations *Finland* + 358 (0)9 13262, ***UK*** + 44 (0)1375 363 900.

FAX Administration & Reservations *Finland* + 358 (0)9 652377, ***UK*** + 44 (0)1375 840 888.

INTERNET Email *Finland* info@transfennica.fi ***UK*** info.uk@transfennica.com

Website www.transfennica.com *(English)*

ROUTES OPERATED *Circuit 1* Hamina *(dep: 18.00 Mon)* – Hanko *(arr: 07.00 Tue, dep: 15.00 Tue)* – Tilbury *(arr: 06.00 Fri, dep: 17.00 Fri)* – Hamina *(arr: 14.00 Mon)*. **Note:** 'dep' times are closure times for freight. Ship will actually leave a little later. Ships will often arrive at Tilbury before scheduled time - sometimes the night before if coming from Finland. All *Transfennica* ships are listed below as ships are sometimes moved between routes. At the time of going to press, the Tilbury service is normally operated by the SEAGARD. *Transfennica* also acts as London agent for the *UPM-Kymmene Seaways* Hamina - Amsterdam - Tilbury –Lübeck and vv service and sells northbound capacity.

1	**BEACHY HEAD**	23235t	03	21.0k	193.0m	12P	-	180T	A	UK	9234094
2	**CAROLINE RUSS**	10488t	99	21.0k	153.5m	12P	-	134T	A2	AG	9197533
3	**ELISABETH RUSS**	10471t	99	21.0k	153.5m	12P	-	120T	A2	AG	9186429
4	**FRIEDRICH RUSS**	10471t	99	21.0k	153.5m	12P	-	120T	A2	AG	9186429
5	**GENCA**	28289t	07	22.0k	205.0m	12P	-	200T	A	NL	9307372
6	**KRAFTCA**	28289t	06	22.0k	205.0m	12P	-	200T	A	NL	9307360
7	**LONGSTONE**	23235t	03	21.0k	193.0m	12P	-	180T	A	UK	9234082
8	**PAULINE RUSS**	10488t	99	21.0k	153.5m	12P	-	120T	A2	AG	9198989
9	**PULPCA**	28289t	08	22.0k	205.0m	12P	-	200T	A	NL	9345386
10	**SEAGARD**	10488t	99	21.0k	153.5m	12P	-	134T	A2	FI	9198977
11	**STENA FORECASTER**	24688t	03	22.5k	195.3m	12P	-	210T	A2	SE	9214666
12	**STENA FORERUNNER**	24688t	02	22.5k	195.3m	12P	-	210T	A2	SE	9214666
13	**TIMCA**	28300t	06	22.0k	205.0m	12P	-	200T	A	NL	9307358
14	**TRICA**	28289t	07	22.0k	205.0m	12P	-	200T	A	NL	9307384

BEACHY HEAD Built by Flensburger Schiffbau-Gesellschaft, Flensburg, Germany for *AWSR Shipping*. On delivery, chartered to *Transfennica* and operated between Hanko (Finland) and Lübeck (Germany). In July 2006 chartered to *Stora Enso* and placed on the Kotka - Gothenburg route. In late August transferred to the Antwerp - Gothenburg service. In 2007 chartered to *Transfennica*.

CAROLINE RUSS, ELISABETH RUSS, FRIEDRICH RUSS, PAULINE RUSS, Built by J J Sietas KG, Hamburg, Germany for *Ernst Russ* of Germany and chartered to *Transfennica*.

Timca (*FotoFlite*)

Auto Bay (*Mike Louagie*)

GENCA, KRAFTCA, PULPCA, TIMCA, TRICA Built by New Szczecin Shipyard (SSN), Szczecin, Poland for *Spliethoff Bevrachtingskantoor*, owners of *Transfennica*.

LONGSTONE Built by Flensburger Schiffbau-Gesellschaft, Flensburg, Germany for *AWSR Shipping*. Chartered to *Transfennica* and operated between Hanko (Finland) and Lübeck (Germany).

SEAGARD Built by J J Sietas KG, Hamburg, Germany for *Bror Hussell Chartering* of Finland (later acquired by *Bore Shipowning* of Finland) and chartered to *Transfennica*.

STENA FORECASTER, STENA FORERUNNER Built by Dalian Shipyard Co Ltd, Dalian, China for *Stena RoRo* and chartered to *Transfennica*.

Under Construction

15	PLYCA	28289t	08	22.0k	205.0m	12P	-	200T	A	NL	9345398
16	STEELCA	28289t	08	22.0k	205.0m	12P	-	200T	A	NL	9376153
17	WOODCA	28289t	08	22.0k	205.0m	12P	-	200T	A	NL	9376165

PLYCA, STEELCA, WOODCA Under construction by New Szczecin Shipyard (SSN), Szczecin, Poland for *Spliethoff Bevrachtingskantoor*, owners of *Transfennica*.

UECC

THE COMPANY *United European Car Carriers AS* is a Norwegian private sector company jointly owned in equal shares by *Nippon Yusen Kabushiki Kaisha (NYK)* of Tokyo and *Wallenius Lines* of Stockholm. *UECC* consists of companies in Norway, Germany, Spain, France, Portugal and the UK. The fleet technical department is based in Grimsby (UK).

MANAGEMENT Managing Director Jan Eyvin Wang, **Senior Commercial Manager UK** Peter Pegg.

ADDRESSES Norway Hasseldalen, PO Box 265, 4892 Grimstad, Norway, **UK** 17 St. Helen's Place, London EC3A 6DG.

TELEPHONE Norway + 47 37 25 11 00, **UK** + 44 (0)207 628 2855.

FAX Norway + 47 37 25 11 11, **UK** + 44 (0)207 628 2858.

INTERNET E-mail companymail@uecc.com **Website** www.uecc.com (*English*)

ROUTES OPERATED East Coast Line (3 circuits per week) Pasajes - Vlissingen – Zeebrugge – Killingholme – Sheerness – Santander – Pasajes. **Bristol Line** (every 4 days) Bristol – Pasajes. **Iberia Line 1** (weekly circuit) Southampton – Malaga – Vigo – Zeebrugge - Southampton. **Iberia Line 2** (weekly circuit) Sheerness - Zeebrugge - Vigo - Le Havre – Sheerness. **Setubal Line** (weekly circuit) Zeebrugge - Setubal - Vigo – Zeebrugge. **Cross Channel** (3 sailings per week) Southampton – Le Havre. **Ireland Service** (weekly circuit) Bristol – Dublin – Southampton – Ghent – Zeebrugge – Cork – Bristol. **North Sea Line** (twice weekly) Bremerhaven – Oslo – Drammen. **Baltic Service** (weekly circuit) Bremerhaven – Hanko – Kotka – Bremerhaven. **Sweden & Poland Service 1** (weekly circuit) Zeebrugge - Malmo - Gdynia – Zeebrugge. **Sweden & Poland Service 2** (weekly circuit) Zeebrugge - Malmö - Emden - Sheerness – Zeebrugge. **Mediterranean Service** (weekly circuit) Zeebrugge – Southampton – Vigo – Malaga - Livorno – Piraeus – Derince – Yenikoy – Vigo – Zeebrugge. **Black Sea Service** (weekly circuit) Piraeus - Derince - Ilichevsk - Constantza - Piraeus.

Services listed carry unaccompanied ro-ro cargo together with large volumes of trade cars. The Baltic routes are strictly outside the scope of this book but are shown for the sake of completeness. A large number of short-sea contract sailings for vehicle manufacturers and distributors are also operated and these serve many additional ports in Northern Europe. In view of the fact that vessels are regularly transferred between routes and contracts, the following is a list of all vessels in the *UECC* fleet at the present time including those that do not presently serve the UK.

1	AEGEAN BREEZE	27876t	83	17.0k	164.0m	0P	3070C	260T	QRS	SG	8202367
2	ARABIAN BREEZE	27876t	83	17.0k	164.0m	0P	3070C	260T	QRS	SG	8202355
3	ASIAN BREEZE	27876t	83	17.0k	164.0m	0P	3070C	260T	QRS	SG	8202381
4	AUTO BALTIC	18979t	96	20.0k	138.5m	12P	1452C	105T	A2	FI	9121998

5	AUTO BANK	19107t	96	20.0k	138.8m	12P	1610C	105T	A2	FI	9160774
6	AUTO BAY	19094t	96	20.0k	138.8m	12P	1610C	105T	A2	FI	9122007
7	AUTOCARRIER	6421t	82	13.5k	89.5m	0P	650C	-	AS	PT	8100519
8	AUTOLINE	7087t	83	14.0k	99.9m	0P	700C	-	AS	PT	8200565
9	AUTOPREMIER	11591t	97	20.0k	128.8m	0P	1220C	-	AS	PT	9131943
10	AUTOPRESTIGE	11591t	99	20.0k	128.8m	0P	1220C	-	AS	PT	9190157
11	AUTOPRIDE	11591t	97	20.0k	128.8m	0P	1220C	-	AS	PT	9131955
12	AUTOPROGRESS	11591t	98	20.0k	128.8m	0P	1220C	-	AS	PT	9131967
13	AUTORACER	9693t	94	20.0k	119.9m	0P	1060C	-	AS	PT	9079200
14	AUTOROUTE	7114t	79	14.5k	99.9m	0P	690C	-	AS	PT	7822079
15	AUTORUNNER	9693t	94	20.0k	119.9m	0P	1060C	-	AS	PT	9079212
16	AUTOSKY	21010t	00	20.0k	140.0m	0P	1220C	-	AS	PT	9206774
17	AUTOSTAR	21010t	00	20.0k	140.0m	0P	1220C	-	AS	PT	9206786
18	AUTOSUN	21094t	00	20.0k	140.0m	0P	1220C	-	AS	PT	9227053
19	AUTOTRANSPORTER	7069t	83	14.0k	99.9m	0P	700C	-	AS	PT	8200577
20	BALTIC BREEZE	29979t	83	17.0k	164.0m	0P	3070C	260T	QRS	SG	8312590
21	ELLA J	10762t	77	17k	150.9m	12P	930C	100T	A	VC	7521962
22	GRAN CANARIA CAR	9600t	01	16k	132.5m	0P	705C	42T	A	ES	9218014
23	LE CASTELLET	7930t	92	15.5k	116.5m	0P	900C	-	A	PT	8020044
24	MONTLHERY	7930t	82	15.5k	116.5m	0P	900C	-	A	PT	8006878
25	NOBLEZA	29933t	83	17.0k	164.0m	0P	3070C	260T	QRAS	LR	8300470
26	SETUDAL	20248t	78	16.0k	138.6m	0P	2155C	-	QRAS	PA	7812452
27	VELAZQUEZ	16021t	83	14.5k	138.0m	12P	955C	146T	A	ES	7728596
28	YOHJIN	29933t	83	16.5k	164.0m	0P	3100C	260T	QRAS	PA	8300468

AEGEAN BREEZE, ARABIAN BREEZE, ASIAN BREEZE Built by Kurushima Dockyard, Onishi, Japan for *Fuji Shipping* of Tokyo. Sold in 1988 to *Amon Shipping*. In 1990 sold to *Wallenius Lines*, Singapore and later chartered to *UECC*. Of deep sea ocean-going ro-ro design with quarter ramps, they are normally used on the Mediterranean service.

AUTO BALTIC Built by Sterkoder, Kristiansund, Norway as TRANSGARD for *Bror Husell Chartering* of Finland for long-term charter to *Transfennica* and used between Rauma and Antwerp and Hamina and Lübeck. Later chartered to *Finncarriers*. In 2005 she underwent conversion in Poland to add a garage on top of the original weather deck and was placed on long-term charter to *UECC* with options to purchase. Generally used on the Baltic or Iberian services. In 2006 *Rederi AB Engship* was taken over by *Rettig Group Bore* and she remains on charter to *UECC*. In 2007 renamed AUTO BALTIC.

AUTO BANK Built by Umoe Sterkoder AS, Kristiansund, Norway as SERENADEN for *Rederi AB Engship* of Finland and chartered to *Transfennica*. In 2006 *Rederi AB Engship* was taken over by *Rettig Group Bore*. In 2007 converted at COSCO Shipyard, Nantong, China to add a garage on top of the weather deck, renamed AUTO BANK and placed on long-term charter to *UECC*.

AUTO BAY Built by Umoe Sterkoder AS, Kristiansund, Norway as HERALDEN for *Rederi AB Engship* of Finland and chartered to *Transfennica*. In 2006 *Rederi AB Engship* was taken over by *Rettig Group Bore*. In 2007 converted at COSCO Shipyard, Nantong, China to add a garage on top of the weather deck, renamed AUTO BAY and placed on long-term charter to *UECC*.

AUTOCARRIER Built by Flender Werft, Lübeck, Germany as CASTORP for the *Lübeck Line*. In 1982 ownership passed to *Ahrenkiel* of Hamburg and she was chartered to *Carline*. In 1989 purchased by *UECC* upon the takeover of *Carline*. In 2001 she underwent major refurbishment to extend her lifespan by a further 10 to 15 years. Normally used on contract sailings between Sheerness and Calais and Killingholme and Calais.

AUTOLINE, AUTOTRANSPORTER Built by Kambara Marine, Numakuma, Japan for *UECC* to a Ramsgate Max specification which included a shallow draft to enter the port's inner harbour. Both are normally used on sailings between UK and France or Belgium. In 2001 each underwent major refurbishment to extend their lifespan by a further 10 to 15 years. Normally used on sailings between UK, France and Belgium.

AUTOPREMIER, AUTOPRESTIGE, AUTOPROGRESS, AUTOPRIDE Built by Frisian Shipyard Welgelegen, Harlingen, The Netherlands for *UECC*. Designated P-class, they are an enlarged version of the R-class and built to a 'Grimsby Max' specification with greater capacity for ro-ro cargo. Normally used on scheduled sailings between Iberia, Belgium, Ireland and UK.

AUTORUNNER, AUTORACER. Built by Brattvaag Skipsverft, Brattvaag, Norway for *UECC*. Designated as R-class, they are normally used on scheduled sailings between Iberia, Belgium, Ireland and UK.

AUTOROUTE Built by Mitsui Tamano, Tamano, Japan for *UECC*. Normally used on sailings between UK and France or Belgium.

AUTOSKY, AUTOSTAR, AUTOSUN Built by Tsuneishi Zosen, Tadotsu, Japan for *UECC*. Designated S-class, they are a further enlargement of the P-class and R-class designs and are normally used on the longer routes to Iberia and in the Baltic.

BALTIC BREEZE Built by Kurushima Dockyard, Onishi, Japan for *Fuji Shipping Co* of Tokyo. Sold in 1988 to *Amon Shipping*. Sold to *Wallenius Lines*, Singapore in 1990. Chartered to *Eukor* then to *UECC*. Of deep sea ocean-going ro-ro design with a quarter ramp, she is normally used on the Mediterranean service.

ELLA J Built at Fredrikstad, Norway as BORE SUN for *Bore Line* of Finland and used on services between Finland, Northern Europe and Britain. In 1989 sold to *Rederi Ab Liro* of Sweden and chartered back to *Bore Line*. In 1992 renamed LIRO SUN and chartered to *Finncarriers* for use between Finland, Germany and the UK. In 1993 sold to *Rederi Ab Engship* of Finland, renamed GARDEN and chartered to *ArgoMann* for use on their Turku - Cuxhaven – Harwich service. In 1999 chartered to *Transfennica* and used between Finland, Germany and the UK. In 2001 chartered to *UECC*. She was fitted with hoistable mezzanine decks to increase car capacity and is generally used on the Baltic or Iberian services. In 2006 *Rederi Ab Engship* was taken over by *Rettig Group Bore* who later sold her to *Dilys Carrier*. She remains on charter to *UECC*.

GRAN CANARIA CAR Built by Hijos de J. Barreras SA, Vigo, Portugal for *Flota Suardiaz* of Spain as HARALD FLICK for use on services in the Mediterranean and to the Canaries, UK and the Benelux countries. Renamed GRAN CANARIA CAR before entering service. In 2006 chartered to *UECC* for use between Bremerhaven and Drammen / Oslo.

LE CASTELLET, MONTLHERY Built by Ateliers et Chantiers, La Rochelle-Pallice for *Carline SA* of France. Both were acquired by *UECC* in 1989 when the *Carline* business was taken over.

NOBLEZA Built by Kanasashi, Shimizu City, Japan for *NYK Line* and to have been named CARIBBEAN BREEZE. Entered service as MEIJIN and renamed NOBLEZA in 1992. In 2002 placed on long-term charter to *UECC*. Of deep sea ocean-going ro-ro design with quarter ramp, she is generally used on the longer Mediterranean or Iberian services.

SETUBAL Built by Oshima Shipbuilding, Japan as ZUIJIN for *NYK Line*. In 1995 sold to *UECC* and renamed SETUBAL. Of deep sea ocean-going ro-ro design with quarter ramp, she is generally used on the longer Mediterranean or Iberian services.

VELAZQUEZ Built by Empresa Nacional Bazan, San Fernando, Spain for *Flota Suardiaz* of Spain for use on services in the Mediterranean and to the Canaries, UK and the Benelux countries. In 2007 chartered to *UECC*.

YOHJIN Built by Kanasashi, Shimizu City, Japan for *NYK Line* and to have been named ARAFURA BREEZE. Entered service as YOHJIN then renamed NOSAC YOHJIN in 1995. In 1999 again renamed the YOHJIN. In 2006 placed on long-term charter to *UECC*. Of deep sea ocean-going ro-ro design with quarter ramp, she is generally used on the longer Mediterranean or Iberian services.

UPM-KYMMENE SEAWAYS

THE COMPANY *UPM-Kymmene Seaways Oy Ltd* is a Finnish company, part of the *UPM-Kymmene* paper and card manufacturing group.

ADDRESS Kirkkokatu 1 A PL 224, 48100 Kotka, Finland.

TELEPHONE Administration & Reservations *Finland* + 358 (0)204 151 91, **Reservations** *UK*

+ 44 (0)1375 363 900 (*Transfennica*).

FAX Administration & Reservations *Finland* + 358 (0)204 151 90, ***Reservations (UK)*** + 44 (0)1375 840 888 (*Transfennica*).

INTERNET Website w3.upm-kymmene.com (*English*)

ROUTE OPERATED Kotka (*dep: Thu*) - Amsterdam (*arr: Sun, dep: Mon*) - Tilbury (*arr: Wed, dep: Wed*) - Lübeck (*arr: Sat, dep: Sat*) - Kotka (*arr: Mon*); *1,2*)

| 1 | MIRANDA | 10471t | 98 | 22.0k | 153.5m | 12P | - | 112T | A | FI | 9183790 |
| 2 | MISTRAL | 10471t | 98 | 22.0k | 153.5m | 12P | - | 112T | A | FI | 9183788 |

MIRANDA Built by J J Sietas KG, Hamburg, Germany for *Godby Shipping A/S* of Finland. Initially chartered to *Transfennica*. In 2000 she was chartered to *Finnlines*. Until the end of 2007 used on a Helsinki - Hamina - Zeebrugge service only available northbound for general traffic. From January 2008 operated on *UPM-Kymmene Seaways* service from Hamina to Lübeck, Amsterdam and Tilbury.

MISTRAL Built by J J Sietas KG, Hamburg, Germany for *Godby Shipping AB* of Finland. Chartered to *Transfennica*. In 2003 chartered to *UPM Kymmene Oy* of Finland and operated between Rauma and Santander. In 2005 chartered to *Finnlines*. Until the end of 2007 used on a Helsinki - Hamina - Zeebrugge service only available northbound for general traffic. From January 2008 operated on *UPM-Kymmene Seaways* service from Hamina to Lübeck, Amsterdam and Tilbury.

VAN UDEN RO-RO

THE COMPANY *Van Uden Ro-Ro* is division of *Van Uden Maritime BV*, a Dutch company.

ADDRESS Van Uden Maritime BV, Brielselaan 85, 3081 AB Rotterdam, The Netherlands.

TELEPHONE Administration & Reservations 31 (0)10 - 297 31 00.

FAX Administration & Reservations + 31 (0)10 - 297 31 51.

INTERNET Email roro@van-uden.nl **Website** www.van-uden.nl/home/index.php (*English*)

ROUTE OPERATED Moerdijk (The Netherlands), Antwerp, Immingham and Hamburg to Malta, Tunis, Lattakia, Mersin, Gemlik, Limassol, Alexandria, Beirut, Tripoli, Tyr, Piraeus and Thessalonica (*1,2,3*; approx 2/3 per month).

1	AMALIAHAVEN	8424t	80	15.0k	139.6m	0P	-	65T	B	MT	7946394
2	JULIANAHAVEN	9489t	85	14.4k	152.1m	0P	-	70T	B	PA	8623975
3	MAXIMAHAVEN	8548t	79	16.5k	139.1m	0P	-	65T	B	PA	7831018

AMALIAHAVEN Built at the Zhdanov Shipbuilding Yard, Leningrad, USSR as the MARJAN for *Jadroplov* of Yugoslavia. In 1990 sold to Gibraltar interests and renamed the VALENICA BRIDGE. She was chartered to *Grimaldi Lines*. In late 2004 she was renamed the EUROFEEDER. In 2006 chartered to *Van Uden Ro-Ro* and renamed the AMALIAHAVEN.

JULIANAHAVEN Built at the Zhdanov Shipbuilding Yard, Leningrad, USSR as the NIKOLAI JANSON for *ESCO* of the USSR (later the Republic of Estonia). In 1991 chartered to *Van Uden Ro-Ro* and renamed the EEMHAVEN. In 1993 sold to *Kegan Shipping Co* of Estonia and renamed the HAAPSALU. In 1998 sold back to *ESCO*. In 2002 sold to *Van Uden Ro-Ro* and renamed the JULIANAHAVEN.

MAXIMAHAVEN Built at the Zhdanov Shipbuilding Yard, Leningrad, USSR as the TIMUR FRUNZE for *ESCO* of the USSR (later the Republic of Estonia). In 1991 chartered to *Van Uden Ro-Ro* and renamed the NARVAHAVEN. In 1993 renamed the NARVA. In 2002 chartered again to *Van Uden Ro-Ro* and renamed MAXIMAHAVEN.

Note: The three ships above were part of two large series of ro-ro ships built by the Soviet Union. Unusually they were built with large bow visors and slewing ramps rather than the more conventional stern ramp. This was so they could be used as tank landing craft in the event of war. They had specially strengthened decks. The Soviet-owned ships were used commercially and for conveyance of Soviet army equipment.

SECTION 4 –
GB & IRELAND - CHAIN, CABLE ETC FERRIES

In addition to the ferries listed above, there are a number of short-distance chain ferries, cable ferries and ferries operated by unpowered floats.

BOURNEMOUTH-SWANAGE MOTOR ROAD AND FERRY COMPANY

Address *Company* Shell Bay, Studland, Swanage, Dorset BH19 3BA. **Tel** + 44 (0)1929 450203, **Fax** + 44 (0)1929 450498), *Ferry* Floating Bridge, Ferry Way, Sandbanks, Poole, Dorset BH13 7QN. **Tel** + 44 (0)1929 450203.

Internet Email email@sandbanksferry.co.uk **Website** www.sandbanksferry.co.uk (*English*)

Route Sandbanks - Studland (Dorset).

1	BRAMBLE BUSH BAY	125t	93	-	74.4m	400P	48C	-	BA	9072070

BRAMBLE BUSH BAY Chain ferry, built by Richard Dunston (Hessle) Ltd, Hessle, UK for the *Bournemouth-Swanage Motor Road and Ferry Company*.

CUMBRIA COUNTY COUNCIL

Address Community, Economy & Environment Department, The Courts, Carlisle CA3 8NA. **Tel** + 44 (0)1228 607653, **Fax** + 44 (0)1228 607658.

Internet Email john.robinson@cumbriacc.gov.uk

Route Bowness-on-Windermere - Far Sawrey.

1	MALLARD	-	90	-	25.9m	140P	18C	-	BA

MALLARD Chain ferry built by F L Steelcraft, Borth, Dyfed for *Cumbria County Council*.

DARTMOUTH – KINGSWEAR FLOATING BRIDGE CO LTD

Address Dart Marina, Sandquay Road, Dartmouth, Devon TQ6 9PH. **Tel** + 44 (0)1803 833351.

Route Dartmouth - Kingswear (Devon) across River Dart (higher route) (forms part of A379).

1	HIGHER FERRY	-	60	-	42.7m	136P	18C	-	BA

HIGHER FERRY Built by Philip & Son Ltd, Dartmouth, UK. Diesel-electric paddle-propelled vessel guided by cross-river cables.

ISLE OF WIGHT COUNCIL (COWES FLOATING BRIDGE)

Address Ferry Office, Medina Road, Cowes, Isle of Wight PO31 7BX. **Tel** + 44 (0)1983 293041.

Route West Cowes - East Cowes.

1	NO 5	-	76	-	33.5m	-	15C	-	BA

NO 5 Chain ferry built by Fairey Marine, East Cowes, UK for *Isle of Wight County Council*, now *Isle of Wight Council*.

KING HARRY STEAM FERRY COMPANY

Address Feock, Truro, Cornwall TR3 6QJ. **Tel** + 44 (0)1872 862312, **Fax** + 44 (0)1872 863355.

Internet Email info@kingharry.fq.co.uk **Website** www.kingharry-info.co.uk (*English*)

Bramble Bush Bay (*Miles Cowsill*)

Hotspur IV (*Miles Cowsill*)

Route Across River Fal, King Harry Ferry (Cornwall).

| 1 | **KING HARRY FERRY** | 500t | 06 | - | 55.2m | 150P | 34C | - | BA | UK | 9364370 |

KING HARRY FERRY Chain ferry built by Pendennis Shipyard, Falmouth (hull constructed at Ravenstein Shipyard, Ravenstein, The Netherlands) for *King Harry Steam Ferry Company* to replace the previous ferry. Unlike the previous ferry, she is registered as a 'Passenger/Ro-Ro Cargo' ship and thus has gross tonnage, nation of registry and, being over 100t, an IMO number.

REEDHAM FERRY

Address Reedham Ferry, Ferry Inn, Reedham, Norwich NR13 3HA. **Tel** +44 (0)1493 700429, **Fax** +44 (0)1493 700999.

Route Acle - Reedham - Norton (across River Yare, Norfolk).

| 1 | **REEDHAM FERRY** | - | 84 | - | 11.3m | 20P | 3C | - | BA |

REEDHAM FERRY Chain ferry built by Newsons, Oulton Broad, Lowestoft, UK for *Reedham Ferry*. Maximum vehicle weight: 12 tons.

SOUTH HAMS DISTRICT COUNCIL

Address Lower Ferry Office, The Square, Kingswear, Dartmouth, Devon TQ6 0AA. **Tel** +44 (0)1803 752342, **Fax** +44 (0)1803 752227.

Internet Website www.southhams.gov.uk/sp-dartmouthlowerferry.htm *(English)*

Route Dartmouth - Kingswear (Devon) across River Dart (lower route).

| 1 | **THE TOM AVIS** | - | 94 | - | 33.5m | 50P | 8C | - | BA |
| 2 | **THE TOM CASEY** | - | 89 | - | 33.5m | 50P | 8C | - | BA |

THE TOM AVIS Float (propelled by tugs) built by Alan Toms, Fowey, UK for *South Hams District Council*.

THE TOM CASEY Float (propelled by tugs) built Cozens, Portland, UK for *South Hams District Council*.

TORPOINT FERRY

Address 2 Ferry St, Torpoint, Cornwall PL11 2AX. **Tel** +44 (0)1752 812233, **Fax** +44 (0)1752 816873.

Internet Website www.torpointferry.org.uk *(English)*

Route Devonport (Plymouth) - Torpoint (Cornwall) across the Tamar. The three ferries operate in parallel, each on her own 'track'. Pre-booking is not possible and the above number cannot be used for that purpose.

1	**LYNHER II**	748t	06	-	73.0m	350P	73C	-	BA	UK	9310941
2	**PLYM II**	748t	04	-	73.0m	350P	73C	-	BA	UK	9310927
3	**TAMAR II**	748t	05	-	73.0m	350P	73C	-	BA	UK	9310939

LYNHER II, PLYM II, TAMAR II Chain ferries built by Ferguson Shipbuilders Ltd, Port Glasgow, UK to replace 1960s-built ships. Unlike previous ferries, they are registered as 'Passenger/Ro-Ro Cargo' ships and thus have gross tonnage, nation of registry and, being over 100t, an IMO number.

WATERFORD CASTLE HOTEL

Address The Island, Waterford, Irish Republic. **Tel** +353 (0)51 78203.

Internet Email info@waterfordcastle.com **Website** www.waterfordcastle.com *(English (mainly about hotel; little about ferry))*

Route Grantstown - Little Island (in River Suir, County Waterford).

| 1 | **LITTLE ISLAND FERRY** | - | 68 | - | - | 24P | 6C | - | BA |

LITTLE ISLAND FERRY Chain ferry built at Cork, Irish Republic for *Waterford Castle Hotel*.

SECTION 5 - GB & IRELAND - MAJOR PASSENGER-ONLY FERRIES

There are a surprisingly large number of passenger-only ferries operating in the British Isles, mainly operated by launches and small motor boats. There are, however, a few 'major' operators who operate only passenger vessels (of rather larger dimensions) and have not therefore been mentioned previously.

Aran Direct (trading name of Bád Árann Teoranta) ARAN PRINCESS (ex HARBOURLYNX, 2008, ex ANGEL OF FREEDOM, 2003) (472t, 1997, 37.0m, 300 passengers, IMO: 9154880), CLAN EAGLE 1 (170 tons, 2006), CLANN NA NOILEÁIN (170 tons, 2007). **Routes operated** Galway - Inis Mór, Rossaveal (Co Galway) – Inis Mór, Rossaveal - Inis Meáin, Rossaveal - Inisheer. **Tel** + 353 (0)91 566 535, **Fax** + 353 (0)91 534 315, **Email** info@arandirect.com, **Website** www.arandirect.com (*English*).

Aran Doolin Ferries HAPPY HOOKER (77t, 1989, 19.8m, 96 passengers), ROSE OF ARAN (113t, 1976, 20.1m, 96 passengers. IMO 7527916). **Routes operated** Doolin (Co Clare) - Inisheer, Doolin - Inishmor, Inisheer - Inishmor. **Tel** + 353 (0)65 7074455 & 7074189, **Fax** + 353 (0)65 7074914, **Email** doolinferries@eircom.net **Website** www.doolinferries.com (*English*)

Aran Island Ferries ARAN EXPRESS (117t, 1984, 27.4m, 180 passengers), ARAN FLYER (170t, 1988, 33.5m, 208 passengers), CEOL NA FARRAIGE (234t, 2001, 35.4m, 294 passengers, IMO 9246750), DRAÍOCHT NA FARRAIGE (318t, 1999, 35.4m, 294 passengers, IMO 9200897), BANRION CHOMAMARA (ex QUEEN OF ARAN II, 2007) (300t, 2001, 29.9m, 227 passengers, IMO 9231016). **Routes operated** Rossaveal (Co Galway) – Inishmor, Rossaveal - Inis Meáin, Rossaveal - Inisheer. **Tel** + 353 (0)91 568903 (572273 after 19.00), **Fax** + 353 (0)91 568538, **Email** island@iol.ie, **Website** www.aranislandferries.com (*English*)

Bruce Watt Cruises WESTERN ISLES (46t, 1969, 19.5m, 81 passengers). **Route Operated** Mallaig - Inverie (Knoydart) - Tarbet. **Tel/Fax** + 44 (0)1687 462320, **Email** brucewattcruises@aol.com, **Website** www.knoydart-ferry.co.uk (*English*)

Clyde Marine Services CRUISER (ex POOLE SCENE, 2001) (119t, 1974, 24.4m, 249 passengers), FENCER (18t, 1976, 11.0m, 33 passengers), KENILWORTH (ex HOTSPUR II - Southampton - Hythe ferry - 1979) (44t, 1936, 18.3m, 126 passengers), ROVER (48t, 1964, 19.8m, 120 passengers), SEABUS (2007, 19.5m, 100 passengers), THE SECOND SNARK (45t, 1938, 22.9m, 120 passengers). **Routes operated** Gourock - Kilcreggan - Helensburgh (generally the SEABUS) (operated on behalf of *Strathclyde Partnership for Transport*), Greenock - Helensburgh - Blairmore (for National Park) (generally the KENILWORTH). **Tel** + 44 (0)1475 721281, **Fax** + 44 (0)1475 888023, **Websites** www.clyde-marine.co.uk   www.clydecruiser.com (*English*)

Compagnie Corsaire JACQUES CARTIER (232t, 2007, 37.0m, 203 passengers, IMO 9447689). **Route operated (international)** St Malo - Jersey. **Tel:** + 33 08 25 13 81 00, **Fax:** + 33 02 23 18 02 97, **Website** www.compagniecorsaire.com (*French*)

Dart Pleasure Craft DARTMOUTH PRINCESS (22t, 1990, 18.3m, 156 passengers), KINGSWEAR BELLE (43t, 1972, 18.0m, 257 passengers). **Route operated** Dartmouth - Kingswear. EDGCUMBE BELLE (35t, 1957, 17.7m, 150 passengers), **Route operated** Dartmouth – Greenway (summer only). **Note:** Pleasure craft owned by this operator are also used for the ferry service on some occasions. **Tel** + 44 (0)1803 834488, **Fax** + 44 (0)1803 835248, **Email** sales@riverlink.co.uk **Website** www.riverlink.co.uk (*English*)

Doolin Ferry Company QUEEN OF ARAN (113t, 1976, 20.1m, 96 passengers, IMO 7327928), TRANQUILITY (62t, 1988, 15.8m, 100 passengers). **Routes operated** Doolin - Inisheer, Doolin - Inishmore. **Tel** + 353 (0)65 707 5555, **Fax** 00 353 (0)65 707 11 82, **Email** info@doolinferry.com **Website** www.doolinferry.com (*English*)

Fleetwood - Knott End Ferry (operated by *Wyre Waste Management Ltd*) WYRE ROSE (2005, 32 passengers). **Route operated** Fleetwood - Knott End. **Tel** + 44 (0)1253 878889 **Website** www.wyremarine.co.uk/Services/Ferry.html

G&T Ferries (trading name of Lower Thames & Medway Passenger Boat Co Ltd) DUCHESS M (ex VESTA 1979) (71t, 1956, 23.8m, 124 passengers), PRINCESS POCAHONTAS (ex FREYA II 1989, LABOE I 1985, LABOE 1984) (180t, 1962, 33.5m, 207 passengers, IMO 5201271). She is an excursion vessel operating regularly to Greenwich, Westminster, Chelsea and Southend, also occasionally to Rochester and Whitstable but sometimes covers the ferry roster. **Route operated** Gravesend (Kent) - Tilbury (Essex), **Tel** +44 (0)1732 353448, **Direct Line to Ferry** +44 (0)7973 390124, **Email** enquiry@princess-pocahontas.com **Website** www.princess-pocahontas.com *(English)*

Gosport Ferry GOSPORT QUEEN (159t, 1966, 30.5m, 250 passengers, IMO 8633700), PORTSMOUTH QUEEN (159t, 1966, 30.5m, 250 passengers, IMO 8633695), SOLENT PRINCE (ex FINGAL OF STAFFA, ex JENNY ANN) (12t, 1981, 43m, 60 passengers - mainly used on charter work), SPIRIT OF GOSPORT (300t, 2001, 32.6m, 300 passengers, IMO 8972089), SPIRIT OF PORTSMOUTH (377t, 2005, 32.6m, 300 passengers, IMO 9319894). **Route operated** Gosport - Portsmouth. **Tel** +44 (0)23 9252 4551, **Email** admin@gosportferry.co.uk **Website** www.gosportferry.co.uk *(English)*

Hayling Ferry PRIDE OF HAYLING (1989, 11.9m, 63 passengers). **Route operated** Eastney – Hayling Island. **Tel** +44 (0)23 9248 2868, **Website** www.langstoneharbour.org.uk/harbour/ferry.htm *(English)*

Hovertravel FREEDOM 90 (1990, 25.4m, 95 passengers, BHC AP1-88/100S hovercraft, converted from AP1-88/100 in 2000), ISLAND EXPRESS (ex FREJA VIKING 2002) (1985, 25.4m, 95 passengers, BHC AP1-88/100S hovercraft, converted from BHC AP1-88/100 in 2001), SOLENT EXPRESS (2006, 29.5m, 130 passengers, BHT 130 hovercraft). **Route operated** Southsea - Ryde. **Tel** +44 (0)1983 811000, **Fax** +44 (0)1983 812859, **Email** rbox@hoverwork.co.uk **Website** www.hovertravel.co.uk *(English)*

Hythe Ferry (White Horse Ferries) GREAT EXPECTATIONS (66t, 1992, 21.3m, 162 passengers - catamaran), HOTSPUR IV (50t, 1946, 19.5m, 125 passengers). **Route operated** Southampton - Hythe (Hants). *Head Office* **Tel.** +44 (0)1793 618566, **Fax** +44 (0)1793 488428, *Local Office* **Tel** +44 (0)23 8084 0722, **Fax** +44 (0)23 8084 6611, **Email** post@hytheferry.co.uk **Website** www.hytheferry.co.uk *(English)*

John O'Groats Ferries PENTLAND VENTURE (186t, 1987, 29.6m, 250 passengers, IMO 8834122). **Route operated** John O'Groats – Burwick (Orkney). **Tel** +44 (0)1955 611353, **Email** Office@jogferry.co.uk **Website** www.jogferry.co.uk *(English)*

Lundy Company OLDENBURG (294, 1958, 43.6m, 267 passengers, IMO 5262146). **Routes operated** Bideford - Lundy Island, Ilfracombe - Lundy Island. Also North Devon coastal cruises and River Torridge cruises. **Tel** +44 (0)1237 470074, **Fax** +44 (0)1237 477779, **Email** info@lundyisland.co.uk **Website** www.lundyisland.co.uk *(English)*

Manche Iles Express (trading name of Société Morbihannaise de Navigation) VICTOR HUGO (ex SALTEN 2003) (387t, 1997, 35.0m, 195 passengers, IMO 9157806 - catamaran), **Routes operated** Portbail or Carteret – Jersey, Guernsey and Sark, Dielette - Alderney - Guernsey, MARIN MARIE (ex AREMETI 3 2003) (608t, 1994, 40.0m, 243 passengers, IMO 9112478), TOCQUEVILLE (269t, 2007, 37m, 260 passengers, IMO 9442823). **Route operated** Granville – Jersey - Sark - Guernsey. **Tel *Jersey*** +44 (0)1534 880314, ***Guernsey*** +44 (0)1481 701 316, ***Granville, Carteret, Diélette*** +33 0825 133 050 **Email** mancheilesexpress@cwgsy.net **Website** www.manche-iles-express.com *(French, English)*

Mersey Ferries ROYAL DAFFODIL (ex OVERCHURCH 1999) (751t, 1962, 46.6m, 860 passengers, IMO 4900868), ROYAL IRIS OF THE MERSEY (ex MOUNTWOOD 2002) (464t, 1960, 46.3m, 750 passengers, IMO 8633712), SNOWDROP (ex WOODCHURCH 2004) (670t, 1960, 46.6m, 750 passengers, IMO 8633724). **Routes operated** Liverpool (Pier Head) - Birkenhead (Woodside), Liverpool - Wallasey (Seacombe) with regular cruises from Woodside and Seacombe to Salford along the Manchester Ship Canal. **Tel *Admin*** +44 (0)151 639 0609, ***Reservations*** +44 (0)151 330 1444, **Fax** +44 (0)151 639 0578, **Email** info@merseyferries.co.uk **Website** www.merseyferries.co.uk *(English)*

Mudeford Ferry (Derham Marine) FERRY DAME (4t, 1989, 9.1m, 48 passengers), JOSEPHINE (10t, 1997, 10.7m, 70 passengers - catamaran). **Route operated** Mudeford Quay - Mudeford Sandbank. **Tel** +44 (0)7968 334441 **Email** information@mudefordferry.co.uk **Website**

www.mudefordferry.co.uk *(English)*

Nexus (trading name of Tyne & Wear PTE) PRIDE OF THE TYNE (222t, 1993, 24.0m, 240 passengers, IMO 9062166), SHIELDSMAN (93t, 1976, 24.0m, 350 passengers (laid up for sale)), SPIRIT OF THE TYNE (174t, 2006, 25.0m, 200 passengers) **Route operated** North Shields - South Shields. Also cruises South Shields - Newcastle. **Tel** +44 (0)191 454 8183, **Fax** +44 (0)191 427 9510, **Website** www.nexus.org.uk *(English)*

SPT (trading name of Strathclyde Partnership for Transport) RENFREW ROSE (65t, 1984, 21.9m, 50 passengers), YOKER SWAN (65t, 1984, 21.9m, 50 passengers). **Route operated** Renfrew - Yoker. **Note:** Although this a passenger-only service, the vessels were built as small bow-loading car ferries and are able to convey one vehicle if necessary. This facility was sometimes used for the conveyance of ambulances but this practice has now ceased. **Tel** +44 (0)141 885 2123, **Fax** +44 (0)141 432 1025, **Email** john.mcdonnell@spt.co.uk **Website** www.spt.co.uk *(English)*

Thames Clippers (trading name of Collins River Enterprises) AURORA CLIPPER (181t, 2007, 37.8m, 27.5k, 220 passengers, IMO 9451824), CYCLONE CLIPPER (181t, 2007, 37.8m, 27.5k, 220 passengers, IMO 9451880), HURRICANE CLIPPER (181t, 2002, 37.8m, 27.5k, 220 passengers, IMO 9249702), METEOR CLIPPER (181t, 2007, 37.8m, 27.5k, 220 passengers, IMO 9451812), MONSOON CLIPPER (181t, 2007, 37.8m, 27.5k, 220 passengers, IMO 9451795), MOON CLIPPER (ex DOWN RUNNER 2005) (98t, 2001, 32.0m, 25.0k, 138 passengers, IMO 9245586), SKY CLIPPER (ex VERITATUM 1995, SD10 2000) (60t, 1992, 25.0m, 62 passengers), STAR CLIPPER (ex CONRAD CHELSEA HARBOUR SD9 2000) (60t, 1992, 25.0m, 62 passengers), STORM CLIPPER (ex DHL WORLDWIDE EXPRESS 1995, SD11 2000) (60t, 1992, 25.0m, 62 passengers), SUN CLIPPER (ex ANTRIM RUNNER 2005) (98t, 2001, 32.0m, 25.0k, 138 passengers, IMO 9232292), TORNADO CLIPPER (181t, 2007, 37.8m, 27.5k, 220 passengers, IMO 9451783), TWIN STAR (45t, 1974, 19.2m, 120 passengers), TYPHOON CLIPPER (181t, 2007, 37.8m, 27.5k, 220 passengers, IMO 9451771). **Routes operated** Savoy Pier (Embankment) - Canary Wharf - Woolwich, Bankside - Waterloo - Millbank, Canary Wharf - Rotherhithe (Hilton Hotel) (usually the TWIN STAR). **Tel** +44 (0)20 7977 6892, **Fax** +44(0) 20 7481 8300, **Email** sean@thamesclippers.com **Website** www.thamesclippers.com *(English)*. The 'Typhoon', 'Tornado', 'Cyclone' and 'Monsoon' Clippers were designed by AIMTEK and built by Brisbane Ship Constructions in Australia in 2007.

Waverley Excursions BALMORAL (735t, 1949, 62.2m, 800 passengers, IMO 5034927), WAVERLEY (693t, 1947, 73.2m, 950 passengers, IMO 5386954). **Routes operated** Excursions all round British Isles. However, regular cruises in the Clyde, Bristol Channel, South Coast and Thames provide a service which can be used for transport purposes and therefore both vessels are, in a sense, ferries. The WAVERLEY is the only seagoing paddle steamer in the world. **Tel** +44 (0)845 130 4647, **Fax** +44 (0)141 248 2150, **Email** info@waverleyexcursions.co.uk **Website** www.waverleyexcursions.co.uk *(English)*

Viking Cinderella (Miles Cowsill)

SECTION 6 - NORTHERN EUROPE

BALTIC SCANDINAVIAN LINE

THE COMPANY *Baltic Scandinavian Line* in an Estonian private sector company.

MANAGEMENT Manager Mart Loik, **Sales Manager** Anryo Raamat.

ADDRESS Narva mnt. 13, 10 151 Tallinn, Estonia.

TELEPHONE Administration + 372 666 1675, **Reservations *Estonia*** + 372 666 168, ***Sweden*** + 46 (0)855 925 297.

FAX Administration & Reservations + 372 652 5578.

INTERNET Email info@bsl.ee **Website** www.bsl.ee *(English, Estonian, Russia, Swedish)*

ROUTE OPERATED Paldiski (Estonia) - Kapellskär (Sweden) (10 hrs; *1*; 1 per day).

1	VIA MARE	8023t	76	18.5k	118.1m	105P	-	52L	BA	EE	7411258

VIA MARE Built by Schichau-Unterweser AG, Bremerhaven, Germany as the EUROPEAN CLEARWAY for *European Ferries'* ro-ro freight services. She was used on freight services between Dover and Calais and Dover and Zeebrugge. In 1992 she was moved to the Portsmouth - Le Havre route. In 1993 she was transferred to *Pandoro* to inaugurate a new Cherbourg - Rosslare service. In 1996 she was renamed the PANTHER. In early 1998 she was renamed the EUROPEAN PATHFINDER. In 2001 she was moved to the Cairnryan - Larne service to replace the EUROPEAN TRADER. In 2002 sold to *ERATO Shipping* and renamed the REGINA I. Before delivery, resold to *Abbey Trading SA Trust Co*, delivered to *TransEuropa Ferries* and renamed the BEGONIA. In 2004 began operating for *TransEuropa Ferries*. In 2005 sold to *Baltic Scandinavian Line* and renamed the VIA MARE.

BASTØ FOSEN

THE COMPANY *Bastø Fosen* is a Norwegian private sector company, a subsidiary of *Fosen Trafikklag* of Trondheim.

MANAGEMENT Managing Director Olav Brein.

ADDRESS PO Box 94, 3191 Horten, Norway.

TELEPHONE Administration + 47 33 03 17 40, **Reservations** + 47 33 03 17 40 (buses only).

FAX Administration + 47 33 03 17 49, **Reservations** + 47 33 03 17 49 (buses only).

INTERNET Email basto@fosen.no **Website** www.basto-fosen.no *(Norwegian)*

ROUTE OPERATED Moss - Horten (across Oslofjord, Norway) (30 mins; *1,2,3*; up to every 30 mins).

1	BASTØ I	5505t	97	16.0k	109.0m	550P	200C	18L	BA	NO	9144081
2	BASTØ II	5505t	97	16.0k	109.0m	550P	200C	18L	BA	NO	9144093
3	BASTØ III	7310t	05	18.0k	116.2m	540P	212C	18L	BA	NO	9299408

BASTØ I, BASTØ II Built by Fosen Mekaniske Verksteder, Frengen, Norway for *Bastø Fosen*.

BASTØ III Built by Stocznia Remontowa, Gdansk, Poland for *Bastø Fosen*.

BORNHOLMSTRAFIKKEN

THE COMPANY *Bornholmstrafikken A/S* is a Danish public sector joint-stock company.

MANAGEMENT Managing Director Mads Kofod, **Sales and Marketing Manager** Ole B Larsen.

ADDRESS Dampskibskajen 3-5, 3700 Rønne, Denmark.

TELEPHONE Administration + 45 56 95 18 66, **Reservations** + 45 56 95 18 66.

Christian IV (*Miles Cowsill*)

Superspeed 1 (*FERRY information*)

FAX Administration & Reservations + 45 56 91 07 66.

INTERNET Website www.Bornholmstrafikken.dk or www.bht.as *(Danish, German, Swedish, English)*

ROUTES OPERATED Conventional Ferries Rønne (Bornholm, Denmark) - Køge (6 hrs 30 mins; *1,2*; 1 per day), Rønne - Ystad (Sweden) (2 hrs 30 mins; *1,2,3*; 1 or 2 per day), *Summer only:* Rønne – Sassnitz (Germany) (3 hrs 30 mins; *1,2,3*; 1 or 2 per day). **Fast Ferry** Rønne - Ystad (Sweden) (1 hr 15 mins; *4*; up to 5 per day).

1	**DUEODDE**	13906t	05	18.5k	124.9m	400P	342C	88T	A	DK	9323704
2	**HAMMERODDE**	13906t	05	18.5k	124.9m	400P	342C	88T	A	DK	9323699
3	**POVL ANKER**	12131t	78	19.5k	121.0m	1500P	262C	26T	BA	DK	7633143
4»	**VILLUM CLAUSEN**	6402t	99	40.0k	86.6m	1055P	200C	-	BA	DK	9216250

DUEODDE Built by Volharding Shipyards, Westerbroek, The Netherlands.

HAMMERODDE Built by Merwede Shipyard, Hardinxveld-Giessendam, The Netherlands.

POVL ANKER Built by Aalborg Værft A/S, Denmark. Used on the Rønne - Copenhagen, Rønne - Ystad and Rønne - Sassnitz services. Now operates between Rønne and Sassnitz and Rønne and Ystad in the peak summer period.

VILLUM CLAUSEN Austal Auto-Express 86 catamaran built at Fremantle, Australia for *Bornholmstrafikken*. Used on the Rønne - Ystad service. Car capacity increased in 2005.

COLOR LINE

THE COMPANY *Color Line ASA* is a Norwegian private sector stock-listed limited company. The company merged with *Larvik Scandi Line* of Norway (which owned *Larvik Line* and *Scandi Line*) in 1996. *Larvik Line's* operations were incorporated into *Color Line* in 1997; *Scandi Line* continued as a separate subsidiary until 1999, when it was also incorporated into *Color Line*. The marketing name *Color Scandi Line* was dropped at the end of 2000.

MANAGEMENT Managing Director Trond Kleivdal, **Marketing Manager** Elisabeth Anspach.

ADDRESS *Commercial* Postboks 1422 Vika, 0115 Oslo, Norway, *Technical Management* Color Line Marine AS, PO Box 2090, 3210 Sandefjord, Norway.

TELEPHONE Administration + 47 22 94 42 00, **Reservations** + 47 810 00 811.

FAX Administration + 47 22 83 07 76.

INTERNET Email *Press* presse@colorline.no *Public* customerservice@colorline.com **Website** www.colorline.com *(Norwegian, Danish, English, Swedish, German)*

ROUTES OPERATED Conventional Ferries *All year* Oslo (Norway) - Kiel (Germany) (19 hrs 30 mins; *3,4*; 1 per day), Kristiansand (Norway) - Hirtshals (4 hrs 30 mins; *7*; 4 per day), Larvik (Norway) - Hirtshals (Denmark) (5 hrs 15 mins; *2 (until June)*, *8 (from June*; up to 2 per day), Sandefjord (Norway) - Strömstad (Sweden) (2 hrs 30 mins; *1,5*; up to 6 per day).

1	**BOHUS**	9149t	71	20.0k	123.4m	1165P	240C	34T	BA	NO	7037806
2	**CHRISTIAN IV**	21699t	81	19.0k	153.4m	1860P	530C	56T	BAS2	NO	8020642
3	**COLOR FANTASY**	75027t	04	22.3k	224.0m	2750P	750C	90T	BA	NO	9278234
4	**COLOR MAGIC**	75100t	07	22.3k	223.7m	2750P	550C	90T	BA	NO	9349863
5	**COLOR VIKING**	19763t	85	17.0k	134.0m	2000P	320C	40T	BA2	NO	8317942
6•	**PRINSESSE RAGNHILD**	35855t	81	22.0k	205.3m	1530P	600C	70T	BA	NO	7904891
7	**SUPERSPEED 1**	33500t	08	27.0k	211.3m	1800P	525C	121T	BA2	NO	9374519
8	**SUPERSPEED 2**	33500t	08	27.0k	211.3m	1800P	525C	121T	BA2	NO	9378682

BOHUS Built by Aalborg Værft A/S, Aalborg, Denmark as the PRINSESSAN DESIREE for *Rederi AB Göteborg-Frederikshavn Linjen* of Sweden (trading as *Sessan Linjen*) for their service between Gothenburg and Frederikshavn. In 1981 the company was taken over by *Stena Line* and she became surplus to requirements. During 1981 she had a number of charters including *B&I Line* of Ireland and

Sealink UK. In 1982 she was chartered to *Sally Line* to operate as second vessel on the Ramsgate - Dunkerque service between June and September. She bore the name 'VIKING 2' in large letters on her hull although she was never officially renamed. In September 1982 she returned to *Stena Line* and in 1983 she was transferred to subsidiary company *Varberg-Grenaa Line* for their service between Varberg (Sweden) and Grenaa (Denmark), renamed the EUROPAFÄRJAN. In 1985 she was renamed the EUROPAFÄRJAN II. In 1986, following a reorganisation within *Stena Line*, ownership was transferred to subsidiary company *Lion Ferry AB* and she was named the LION PRINCESS. In 1993 she was sold to *Scandi Line* and renamed the BOHUS. In 1999 *Scandi Line* operations were integrated into *Color Line.*

CHRISTIAN IV Built by AG Weser Seebeckwerft, Bremerhaven, Germany as the OLAU BRITANNIA for *Olau Line* of Germany for their service between Vlissingen (The Netherlands) and Sheerness (England). In 1989 sold to *Nordström & Thulin* of Sweden for delivery in Spring 1990. She was subsequently resold to *Fred. Olsen Lines* of Norway and, on delivery, renamed the BAYARD and used on their service between Kristiansand and Hirtshals. In December 1990 she was acquired by *Color Line* and in 1991 renamed the CHRISTIAN IV. In March 2008 replaced by the SUPERSPEED 1 and transferred to the Larvik - Hirtshals service until the delivery of SUPERSPEED 2 in June 2008 when she is due to be laid up for sale.

COLOR FANTASY Built by Kværner Masa-Yards, Turku, Finland for *Color Line* to replace the PRINSESSE RAGNHILD on the Oslo – Kiel service.

COLOR MAGIC Built by Aker Yards, Turku, Finland (hull construction) and Rauma, Finland (fitting out), for the Oslo - Kiel route.

COLOR VIKING Built by Nakskov Skibsværft A/S, Nakskov, Denmark as the PEDER PAARS for *DSB (Danish State Railways)* for their service between Kalundborg (Sealand) and Århus (Jutland). In 1990 purchased by *Stena Line* of Sweden for delivery in 1991. In that year renamed the STENA INVICTA and entered service on the *Sealink Stena Line* Dover - Calais service. She was withdrawn from the route in February 1998, before the formation of *P&O Stena Line*, but ownership was transferred to that company. In Summer 1998, she was chartered to *Silja Line* to operate between Vaasa and Umeå under the marketing name 'WASA JUBILEE'. In Autumn 1998 she was laid up at Zeebrugge. She remained there until Autumn 1999 when she was chartered to *Stena Line* to operate between Holyhead and Dublin. In 2000 she was chartered to *Color Line*, renamed the COLOR VIKING and in April entered service on the Sandefjord - Strömstad service. In 2002 purchased by *Color Line.*

PRINSESSE RAGNHILD Built by Kiel Howaldtswerke, Kiel, Germany for *Jahre Line* of Norway for the Oslo - Kiel service. In 1991 ownership transferred to *Color Line.* In 1992 rebuilt in Spain with an additional mid-ships section and additional decks. In 2005 started new Bergen - Stavanger - Hirtshals service. In January 2008 transferred to the Oslo - Hirtshals service. In May the route closed and she was laid up.

SUPERSPEED 1, SUPERSPEED 2 Built by Aker Yards, Rauma, Finland for the Kristiansand - Hirtshals and Larvik - Hirtshals routes.

DESTINATION GOTLAND

THE COMPANY *Destination Gotland AB* is a Swedish private sector company owned by *Rederi AB Gotland*. It took over the operation of services to Gotland from 1st January 1998 on a ten-year concession. Originally jointly owned by *Rederi AB Gotland* and *Silja Line*, *Silja Line* involvement in the company ceased at the end of 1998.

MANAGEMENT Managing Director Jan-Erik Rosengren, **Marketing Manager** Per-Erling Evensen.

ADDRESS PO Box 1234, 621 23 Visby, Gotland, Sweden.

TELEPHONE Administration + 46 (0)498-20 18 00, **Reservations** + 46 (0)771-22 33 00.

FAX Administration & Reservations + 46 (0)498-20 18 90.

INTERNET Email info@destinationgotland.se **Website** www.destinationgotland.se *(Swedish, English, Finnish, German)*

Gotland (Miles Cowsill)

Mermaid II (FotoFlite)

ROUTES OPERATED Fast Conventional Ferries Visby (Gotland) - Nynäshamn (Swedish mainland) (3 hrs 15 mins; *1,4*; 1/2 per day), Visby - Oskarshamn (Swedish mainland) (2 hrs 55 mins; *1,4*; 1/4 per day). **Fast Ferries (Summer only)** Visby - Nynäshamn (2 hrs 50 mins; *3*; up to 3 per day), Visby - Oskarshamn (Swedish mainland) (2 hrs 30 mins; *3*; occasional), Visby - Grankullavik (Öland) (2 hrs; *2*; 1 per day).

1	GOTLAND	29746t	03	28.5k	195.8m	1500P	500C	118T	BAS2	SE	9223796
2»	GOTLANDIA	5632t	99	32.0k	112.5m	700P	140C	-	A	SE	9171163
3»	GOTLANDIA II	6554t	06	32.0k	122.0m	780P	160C	-	A	SE	9328015
4	VISBY	29746t	03	28.5k	195.8m	1500P	500C	118T	BAS2	SE	9223784

GOTLAND Built by Guangzhou Shipyard International, Guangzhou, China for *Rederi AB Gotland* for use on *Destination Gotland* services.

GOTLANDIA Alstom Leroux Corsair 11500 monohull vessel built at Lorient, France, as the GOTLAND for *Rederi AB Gotland* and chartered to *Destination Gotland*. In 2003 renamed the GOTLANDIA. In 2006 laid up. In 2007 inaugurated a new route between Visby and Grankullavik (Öland).

GOTLANDIA II Fincantieri SF700 monohull fast ferry built at Riva Trigoso, Italy for *Rederi AB Gotland* for use by *Destination Gotland*.

VISBY Built by Guangzhou Shipyard International, Guangzhou, China for *Rederi AB Gotland* and used on *Destination Gotland* services.

DFDS LISCO

THE COMPANY *AB DFDS LISCO* (formerly *AB LISCO Baltic Service*) is a Lithuanian company, owned by *DFDS A/S of Denmark*; they purchased the company from the Lithuanian Government in 2001.

ADDRESS 24 J Janonio Str, Klaìpeda 92251, Lithuania.

TELEPHONE Administration *DFDS LISCO (Klaìpeda)* + 370 46 393600. **Reservations *LISCO (Klaìpeda)*:** + 370 46 393616 – passengers, + 370 46 395048 - cargo; ***LISCO/Krantas Travel*** + 370 46 395051/395050 - passengers; ***DFDS Tor Line (Karlshamn)*** + 46 (0)45433680 – passengers, + 46 (0)45433690 – cargo; ***DFDS LISCO GmbH (Kiel)*** + 49 (0)43120976480 – passengers, + 49 (0)431 2097 6444 - cargo.

FAX Administration + 370 46 395000. **Reservations *LISCO (Klaìpeda)*** + 370 46 393606; ***LISCO/Krantas Travel*** + 370 46 395053/395052 - passengers; ***DFDS Tor Line (Karlshamn)*** + 46 (0)45433688 - passengers, + 46 (0)454433689 – cargo; ***DFDS LISCO GmbH (Kiel)*** + 49 (0) 431 2097 6102 - passengers, + 49 (0)431 2097 6555 - cargo.

INTERNET Email - Administration info@dfdslisco.lt **Reservations *DFDS LISCO (Klaìpeda)*** **Passengers** booking@lisco.lt **Freight** cargo.dexp@lisco.lt ***DFDS LISCO/Krantas Travel*** passengers@lisco.lt ***DFDS Tor Line (Karlshamn)*** **Freight** Karlshamn@dfdstorline.com **Passengers** pax@dfdstorline.com ***DFDS LISCO GmbH(Kiel)*** **Freight** dlcargo@dfdslisco.com **Passengers** passage@dfdslisco.com

Websites www.dfdslisco.lt (*English*) www.dfdslisco.se (*English, Swedish*) www.dfdslisco.com (*English, German*)

ROUTES OPERATED Klaìpeda (Lithuania) - Kiel (Germany) (21 hrs; *3,4*; 6 per week), Klaìpeda - Karlshamn (Sweden) (14 hrs, *2,5*, 7 per week), Klaìpeda - Sassnitz (Germany) (18 hrs; *8*; 2 per week), Baltijsk (Kaliningrad) - Sassnitz (Germany) (18 hrs; *8*; 1 per week), Lübeck (Germany) - Riga (Latvia) (32 hrs; *1,6*; 4 per week).

1	ENVOY	18653t	79	18.2k	150.0m	107P	-	142T	A	NO	7716074
2	KAUNAS	25606t	89	16.3k	190.9m	262P	460C	93Tr	A2	LT	8311924
3	LISCO GLORIA	20140t	02	22.0k	199.4m	308P	316C	166T	A2	LT	9212151
4	LISCO OPTIMA	25206t	99	21.5k	186.25m	327P	164C	150T	A	LT	9188427
5	LISCO PATRIA	18332t	92	17.0k	154.0m	242P	-	114T	BA2	LT	8917390
6	MERMAID II	13730t	72	17.5k	137.3m	69P	170C	84T	A3	LV	7214002

| 7F | TOR NERINGA | 12494t | 75 | 19.0k | 168.0m | 12P | - | 122T | A | LV | 7411387 |
| 8 | VILNIUS | 22341t | 87 | 16.3k | 190.9m | 132P | 460C | 112Tr | A2 | LT | 8311900 |

ENVOY Built by Mitsui Engineering and Shipbuilding Co Ltd, Tamano, Japan as the IBEX for *P&O* for *Pandoro* Irish sea services. In 1980 chartered to *North Sea Ferries*, renamed the NORSEA and used on the Ipswich - Rotterdam service. In 1986 she was renamed the NORSKY. In 1995 she returned to *Pandoro* and was re-registered in Bermuda. Later in 1995 she resumed her original name of IBEX. An additional deck was added in 1996. In late 1997 she was renamed the EUROPEAN ENVOY. In November 2001 transferred to the Mostyn - Dublin service. In 2004 the Mostyn route closed and she was sold to *Stena RoRo* who resold her to *KystLink* who renamed her the ENVOY. In 2005 chartered to *Finnlines*. Sub-chartered to *P&O Irish Ferries* to operate between Liverpool and Dublin in July and August 2005. In September sub-chartered to *Nedlines*. In January 2005 she was sold to *Taubåtkompaniet* of Norway, remaining sub-chartered to *Nedlines*. In 2006 withdrawn for repairs and eventually the service ended. In 2007 chartered to *DFDS LISCO* and placed on the Lübeck - Riga service.

KAUNAS Train ferry built by VEB Mathias-Thesen-Werft, Wismar, Germany (DDR) for *LISCO* of the former Soviet Union and operated between Klaìpeda and Mukran in Germany (DDR). She was part of a series of vessels built to link the USSR and Germany (DDR), avoiding Poland. In 1994 she was modified to offer limited passenger facilities and placed on the Klaìpeda – Kiel service. In 2003 transferred to the Klaìpeda – Karlshamn route. Early in 2004 chartered to *DFDS Tor Line* to operate between Lübeck and Riga. In 2005 returned to the Klaìpeda – Karlshamn route.

LISCO GLORIA Built by Stocznia Szczecinska im A Warskiego, Szczecin, Poland for *Lloyd Sardegna* of Italy as the GOLFO DEI CORALLI for operating between Italy and Sardinia. However, due to late delivery the order was cancelled. In 2002 purchased by *DFDS Tor Line*, renamed the DANA GLORIA and, in Autumn 2002, placed on the Esbjerg – Harwich service. In June 2003 replaced by modified sister vessel DANA SIRENA (see Section 1), sold to *LISCO Baltic Service* and renamed the LISCO GLORIA. Operates between Klaìpeda and Kiel.

LISCO OPTIMA Ro-pax vessel built by C N Visentini di Visentini Francesco & C Donada, Italy as the ALYSSA for *Levantina Trasporti* of Italy for charter. She was initially chartered to *CoTuNav* of Tunisia for service between Marseilles, Genoa and Tunis and in 2000 to *Trasmediterranea* of Spain for service between Barcelona and Palma de Mallorca. In 2001 chartered to *Stena Line Scandinavia AB*, renamed the SVEALAND and placed as second vessel on the *Scandlines AB* freight-only Trelleborg - Travemünde service. In 2003 sub-chartered to *Scandlines AG* and placed on the Kiel - Klaìpeda route, replacing the ASK and PETERSBURG. In 2004 sold to *Rederia AB Hornet*, a *Stena* company. In late 2005 the *Scandlines* Kiel - Klaìpeda service ended. In early 2006 she was chartered to *TT-Line* to cover for the rebuilding of the engines of their four newest vessels. Later sold to *DFDS*, renamed the LISCO OPTIMA and placed on the Kiel - Klaìpeda route in Spring 2006.

LISCO PATRIA Ro-pax vessel built by Fosen Mekaniske Verksteder, Trondheim, Norway for *Stena RoRo*. After a short period with *Stena Line* on the Hook of Holland - Harwich service, she was chartered to *Sealink Stena Line* for their Southampton - Cherbourg route, initially for 28 weeks. At the end of the 1992 summer season she was chartered to *TT-Line* to operate between Travemünde and Trelleborg and was renamed the TT-TRAVELLER. In late 1995, she returned to *Stena Line*, resumed the name STENA TRAVELLER and inaugurated a new service between Holyhead and Dublin. In Autumn 1996 she was replaced by the STENA CHALLENGER (18523t, 1991). In early 1997 she was again chartered to *TT-Line* and renamed the TT-TRAVELLER. She operated on the Rostock - Trelleborg route. During Winter 1999/2000, her passenger capacity was increased to 250 and passenger facilities renovated. In early 2002 the charter ended and she was renamed the STENA TRAVELLER, chartered to *Stena Line* and placed on their Karlskrona - Gdynia service. Charter ended May 2003. Sold to *LISCO Baltic Service* and renamed the LISCO PATRIA. Placed on the Klaìpeda - Karlshamn service. In January 2006 transferred to the Klaìpeda - Kiel service to replace the *Scandlines* vessel SVEALAND following that company's withdrawal from the joint route. In Spring 2006 returned to the Klaìpeda – Karlshamn route.

MERMAID II Built by Oy Wärtsilä AB, Turku, Finland as the HANZ GUTZEIT and chartered to *Finncarriers* for Finland - Germany service. In 1982 she was sold to *EFFOA* of Finland and renamed the CAPELLA. She continued to be chartered to *Finncarriers* and this charter continued under a number of subsequent owners. In 1986 she was renamed the CAPELLA AV STOCKHOLM. In 1988 she was renamed the FINNMAID. In 1989 she was placed on the *FinnLink* service between Uusikaupunki (Finland) and Hargshamn (Sweden). In 1997 this service was transferred to the Kapellskär - Naantali route. In 1998 she was replaced by the FINNARROW and, after service on *Finncarriers'* Finland - Germany routes, was laid up. In 2000 she was chartered to *VV-Line* who operated between Västervik in Sweden and Ventspils in Latvia. Passenger capacity was raised from 48 to 69. She was then owned by *Rederi AB Gustaf Erikson* of Åland but in 2001 was purchased by *VV-Line* and renamed the MERMAID II. In 2003 chartered to *DFDS Tor Line* to operate between Kiel and Riga. In March the service transferred to Lübeck. In 2003 sold to *Skandia Liv Ab* of Panama. In 2004 chartered to *LISCO* and placed on the Klaìpeda - Karlshamn route. In 2005 operated once weekly between Lübeck and Riga and once weekly between Lübeck and Ventspils. This route now operates twice weekly to Riga.

TOR NERINGA Built by Ankerløkken Verft, Florø, Norway as the BALDUIN for *Fred. Olsen Lines*. In 1999 purchased by *DFDS Tor Line* and renamed the TOR NORVEGIA. Initially used on Norway - UK/The Netherlands services; in 2001 moved to the Fredericia - Copenhagen - Klaìpeda (Lithuania) service. In December 2001 sold to *LISCO Baltic Service* of Lithuania, renamed the TOR NERINGA and chartered back to *DFDS Tor Line*. In 2004 moved to the Gothenburg - Rotterdam/Harwich route. In January 2005 moved to the new Immingham - Zeebrugge route. In March 2005 chartered to *Cobelfret Ferries* to operate between Rotterdam and Purfleet. Later chartered to *ANEK* of Greece. Since 2006 has operated on a variety of *DFDS Tor Line* routes. In 2006 sold to Latvian interests and chartered back. In 2007 transferred to *DFDS LISCO* to operate on the Klaìpeda - Karlshamn route as extra vessel.

VILNIUS Train ferry as KAUNAS. Operated on the Klaìpeda – Kiel service until June 2003. Later chartered to *DFDS Tor Line* to operate between Lübeck and Riga. In Summer 2006 transferred to the Klaìpeda - Sassnitz route. In December 2006 service became Klaìpeda - Baltijsk - Sassnitz.

Under Construction

9	NEWBUILDING	24950t	09	23.0k	199.1m	600P	-	190t	A	LT	-

NEWBUILDING Under construction by Nuovi Canteri Apuani, Marina di Carrara, Italy. Fifth of an order of eight vessels for *Grimaldi Holdings* of Italy. Whilst under construction, sold to *DFDS*. To operate between Kiel and Klaìpeda.

DFDS SEAWAYS

THE COMPANY *DFDS Seaways* is the passenger division of *DFDS A/S*, a Danish private sector company.

MANAGEMENT CEO DFDS A/S Niels Smedegaard,

ADDRESS Sundkrogsgade 11, 2100 Copenhagen Ø, Denmark.

TELEPHONE Administration + 45 33 42 33 42, **Reservations** + 45 33 42 30 00.

FAX Administration & Reservations + 45 33 42 33 41.

INTERNET Website www.dfdsseaways.com (*Danish, Dutch, English, German, Norwegian, Swedish*)

ROUTE OPERATED Copenhagen - Oslo (Norway) (16 hrs; *1,2*; 1 per day). See Section 1 for services operating to Britain.

1	CROWN OF SCANDINAVIA	35498t	94	22.0k	169.4m	1940P	450C	50T	BA	DK	8917613
2	PEARL OF SCANDINAVIA	40039t	00	21.0k	178.1m	2000P	360C	70T	BA	DK	8701674

CROWN OF SCANDINAVIA Launched by Brodogradevna Industrija, Split, Croatia for *Euroway AB* for their Lübeck - Travemünde - Malmö service as the THOMAS MANN. However, political problems led to serious delays and, before delivery, the service had ceased. She was purchased by *DFDS*, renamed the CROWN OF SCANDINAVIA and introduced onto the Copenhagen - Oslo service.

PEARL OF SCANDINAVIA Built by Wärtsilä Marine, Turku, Finland as the ATHENA for *Rederi AB Slite* of Sweden (part of *Viking Line*) and used on 24-hour cruises from Stockholm to Mariehamn (Åland). In 1993 the company went into liquidation and she was sold to *Star Cruises* of Malaysia for cruises in the Far East. She was renamed the STAR AQUARIUS. Later that year she was renamed the LANGKAPURI STAR AQUARIUS. In February 2001 sold to *DFDS* and renamed the AQUARIUS. After rebuilding, she was renamed the PEARL OF SCANDINAVIA and introduced onto the Copenhagen - Oslo service.

REDERIJ DOEKSEN

THE COMPANY *Doeksen Transport Group BV* is a Dutch private sector company. Ferries are operated by subsidiary *Terschellinger Stoomboot Maatschappij*, trading as *Rederij Doeksen*.

MANAGEMENT Managing Director P Melles, **Marketing Manager** Irene Smit.

ADDRESS Waddenpromenade 5, 8861 NT Harlingen, The Netherlands.

TELEPHONE *In The Netherlands* 0900-DOEKSEN (3635736), *From abroad* +31 562 442 002

FAX +31 (0)517 413303.

INTERNET Email info@rederij-doeksen.nl **Website** www.rederij-doeksen.nl *(Dutch)*

ROUTES OPERATED Conventional Ferries Harlingen (The Netherlands) - Terschelling (Frisian Islands) (2 hrs; *1,3*) (up to 6 per day), Harlingen - Vlieland (Frisian Islands) (1 hr 45 mins; *7*; 3 per day), **Fast Passenger Ferries** Harlingen - Terschelling (45 mins; *2,4,6*; 2 to 3 per day), Harlingen - Vlieland (45 mins; *2,4,6*; 2 per day), Vlieland - Terschelling (30 mins; *2,4,6*; 2 per day), **Freight Ferry** Harlingen - Terschelling (1 hr 45 mins; *5*), Harlingen - Vlieland (1hr 45 mins; *5*).

1	FRIESLAND	3583t	89	14.0k	69.0m	1750P	122C	12L	BA	NL	8801058
2»p	KOEGELWIECK	439t	92	33.0k	36.7m	317P	0C	0L	-	NL	9035527
3	MIDSLAND	1812t	74	15.5k	77.9m	1200P	55C	6L	BA	NL	7393066
4»p	NAJADE	164t	99	32.0k	31.8m	184P	0C	0L	-	NL	9209489
5F	NOORD-NEDERLAND	361t	02	14.0k	48.0m	12P	-	9L	BA	NL	9269611
6»p	TIGER	660t	02	37.0k	50.0m	403P	0C	0L	BA	NL	9179191
7	VLIELAND	2726t	05	15.0k	64.0m	1300P	58C	-	BA	NL	9303716

FRIESLAND Built by Van der Giessen-de Noord, Krimpen aan den IJssel, Rotterdam, The Netherlands for *Rederij Doeksen*. Used on the Harlingen - Terschelling route.

KOEGELWIECK Harding 35m catamaran built at Rosendal, Norway for *Rederij Doeksen* to operate between Harlingen and Terschelling, Harlingen and Vlieland and Terschelling and Vlieland.

MIDSLAND Built by Werftunion GmbH & Co, Cassens-Werft, Emden, Germany as the RHEINLAND for *AG Ems* of Germany. In 1993 purchased by *Rederij Doeksen* and renamed the MIDSLAND. Used mainly on the Harlingen - Terschelling route but also used on the Harlingen - Vlieland service. She is now a reserve vessel.

NAJADE SBF Shipbuilders 31m monohull built at Henderson, Australia for *Rederij Doeksen* to operate between Harlingen and Terschelling, Harlingen and Vlieland and Terschelling and Vlieland.

NOORD-NEDERLAND Catamaran built by ASB, Harwood, New South Wales, Australia for *Rederij Doeksen*. Used on freight services from Harlingen to Terschelling and Vlieland.

TIGER Catamaran built by FBMA Babcock Marine, Cebu, Philippines as the SUPERCAT 2002 for *SuperCat* of the Philippines. In 2007 purchased by *Rederij Doeksen* and renamed the TIGER. Operates from Harlingen to Terschelling and Vlieland.

VLIELAND Catamaran built by FBMA Babcock Marine, Cebu, Philippines for *Rederij Doeksen* to operate between Harlingen and Vlieland.

Lisco Optima (FotoFlite)

Pearl of Scandinavia (Mike Louagie)

ECKERÖ LINE

THE COMPANY *Eckerö Line Ab Oy* is a Finnish company, 100% owned by *Rederi AB Eckerö* of Åland, Finland. Until January 1998, the company was called *Eestin-Linjat*.

MANAGEMENT Managing Director David Lindström, **Marketing Director** Anna Sagath.

ADDRESS PL 307, 00181 Helsinki, Finland.

TELEPHONE Administration & Reservations + 358 (0)6000 4300.

FAX Administration & Reservations + 358 (0)9 22885333.

INTERNET Email info@eckeroline.fi **Website** www.eckeroline.fi *(Swedish, Finnish, English)*

ROUTE OPERATED Helsinki - Tallinn (Estonia) (3 hrs 30 mins; *1,2*; up to 4 per day).

1	NORDLANDIA	21473t	81	21.0k	153.4m	2000P	400C	40T	BA	FI	7928811
2	TRANSLANDIA	13867t	76	17.0k	135.8m	100P	280C	70T	A	FI	7429229

NORDLANDIA Built by AG Weser Seebeckwerft, Bremerhaven, Germany as the OLAU HOLLANDIA for *Olau Line* of Germany for the service between Vlissingen (The Netherlands) and Sheerness (England). In 1989 she was replaced by a new vessel of the same name and she was sold to *Nordström & Thulin*. She was renamed the NORD GOTLANDIA and introduced onto *Gotlandslinjen* services between Gotland and the Swedish mainland. In 1997 she was purchased by *Rederi Ab Eckerö* of Åland for delivery in early 1998, following the ending of *Nordström & Thulin's* concession to operate the Gotland services. She was renamed the NORDLANDIA and placed on the *Eckerö Line* Helsinki - Tallinn service, operating day trips.

TRANSLANDIA Built by J J Sietas Werft, Hamburg, Germany as the TRANSGERMANIA for *Poseidon Schiffahrt OHG* of Germany for *Finncarriers-Poseidon* services between Finland and West Germany. In 1991 chartered to *Norse Irish Ferries* and used on their freight service between Liverpool and Belfast. In 1992 she was returned to *Finncarriers* and in 1993 sold to Cypriot interests for use in the Mediterranean and renamed the ROSEBAY. In 1994 chartered to *Stena Line* to inaugurate a new service between Harwich and Rotterdam (Frisohaven). In 1995 the service was switched to Hook of Holland following the construction of a new linkspan. She also, during the summer, carried cars towing caravans, motor caravans and their passengers. In 1997 she was chartered to *Sally Freight* and renamed the EUROSTAR, operating between Ramsgate and Ostend. Later in 1997 she was renamed the EUROCRUISER. In 1998 she returned on charter to *Stena Line* and resumed the name ROSEBAY. In 1999 she was temporarily transferred to the Irish Sea. In Autumn 2000 she was transferred to the Killingholme - Hook of Holland service but was withdrawn in 2001 when the delivery of the new STENA HOLLANDICA enabled the STENA SEARIDER to replace her. She was then sold to *Rederi AB Engship* of Finland, renamed the TRANSPARADEN and chartered to *Botnia Link*. In 2002 chartered to *DFDS Tor Line* to operate between Kiel and Riga. In January 2003 transferred to the *Latlines* Lübeck – Riga route. Later in 2003 chartered to *SCF St Petersburg Line*. In January 2004 sold to *Eckerö Line*, renamed the TRANSLANDIA and operated between Helsinki and Tallinn from May.

ECKERÖ LINJEN

THE COMPANY *Eckerö Linjen* is an Åland Islands company 100% owned by *Rederi AB Eckerö*.

MANAGEMENT Managing Director Björn Blomquist, **Marketing Director** Maria Hellman.

ADDRESS Torggatan 2, Box 158, AX-22100 Mariehamn, Åland.

TELEPHONE Administration + 358 (0)18 28000, **Reservations** + 358 (0)18 28300.

FAX Administration & Reservations + 46(0)175 30820.

INTERNET Website www.eckerolinjen.fi *(Swedish, Finnish, English, German)*

ROUTE OPERATED Eckerö (Åland) - Grisslehamn (Sweden) (2 hrs; *1*; 3 per day).

1	ECKERÖ	12358t	79	19.5k	121.1m	1500P	265C	34T	BA	SE	7633155

ECKERÖ Built by Aalborg Værft A/S, Aalborg, Denmark as the JENS KOFOED for *Bornholmstrafikken*. Used on the Rønne - Copenhagen, Rønne - Ystad and (until December 2002) Rønne - Sassnitz services. Rønne - Copenhagen service became Rønne – Køge in September 2004. In October 2004 sold to *Eckerö Line* for delivery in May 2005. Renamed the ECKERÖ and substantially rebuilt before entering service in early 2006. In 2007 transferred to the Swedish flag.

AG EMS

THE COMPANY *AG Ems* is a German public sector company.

MANAGEMENT Managing Director & Chief Executive B W Brons, **Marine Superintendent** Knut Gerdes, **Operations Manager** Hans-Jörd Oltmanns.

ADDRESS Am Aussenhafen, Postfach 1154, 26691 Emden, Germany.

TELEPHONE Administration & Reservations + 49 (0)1805-180182.

FAX Administration & Reservations + 49 (0)4921 8907-405.

INTERNET Email info@ag-ems.de **Website** www.ag-ems.de *(German, Dutch)*

ROUTES OPERATED Conventional Ferries Emden (Germany) - Borkum (German Frisian Islands) (2 hrs; *3,5*; up to 4 per day), Eemshaven (The Netherlands) - Borkum (55 mins; *1*; up to 4 per day), Wilhelmshaven - Helgoland (3 hrs; *2*; 1 per day) (Operated by subsidiary *HelgolandLinie* - tourist cars not conveyed). **Fast Ferries** Emden - Borkum (1 hr; *4,6*; up to 4 per day), Eemshaven - Borkum (30 mins; *4,6*; 1 per week in summer).

1	GRONINGERLAND	1070t	91	12.0k	44.4m	621P	30C	-	BA	DE	9002465
2	HELGOLAND	1812t	72	15.5k	77.9m	1200P	65C	10L	BA	DE	7217004
3	MÜNSTERLAND	1859t	86	15.5k	78.7m	1200P	70C	10L	BA	DE	8601989
4p»	NORDLICHT	136t	89	33.0k	38.8m	272P	0C	0L	-	DE	8816015
5	OSTFRIESLAND	1859t	85	15.5k	78.7m	1200P	70C	10L	BA	DE	8324622
6p»	POLARSTERN	636t	00	40.0k	45.0m	405P	0C	0L	-	DE	9124433
7p	WAPPEN VON BORKUM	287t	76	11.5k	42.8m	358P	0C	0L	-	DE	7525918

HELGOLAND Built by C Cassens Schiffswerft, Emden, Germany for *AG Ems* as the WESTFALEN. Rebuilt in 1994. In 2006 renamed the HELGOLAND and inaugurated a new Wilhelmshaven - Helgoland service for subsidiary *HelgolandLinie*.

GRONINGERLAND Built by Husumer Schiffswerft, Husum, Germany as the HILLIGENLEI for *Wyker Dampfschiffs-Reederei Föhr-Amrum GmbH* of Germany. Operated Schlüttsiel - Halligen – Wittdün (North Frisian Islands). In 2004 laid up. In late 2005 sold to *AG Ems*. In 2006 renamed the GRONINGERLAND and placed on the Eemshaven – Borkum route.

MÜNSTERLAND, OSTFRIESLAND Built by Martin Jansen GmbH & Co KG Schiffswerft, Leer, Germany for *AG Ems*.

NORDLICHT Fjellstrand 38m passenger-only catamaran built at Mandal, Norway for *AG Ems*.

POLARSTERN Oceanfast Ferries (Australia) 45m passenger-only catamaran built at Henderson, Australia for another operator as the CARAIBE JET. This order was cancelled before delivery and she passed into the ownership of the ANZ Bank. After a period of lay-up, she was sold to *AG Ems* and renamed the POLARSTERN. She was delivered in 2001.

WAPPEN VON BORKUM Built by Schiffswerft Schlömer GmbH & Co KG, Oldersum, Germany as the HANNOVER for *Friesland Fahrlinie* of Germany. In 1979 sold to *AG Ems* and renamed the STADT BORKUM. In 1988 sold to *ST-Line* of Finland, operating day trips from Rauma and renamed the PRINCESS ISABELLA. In 1994 returned to *AG Ems* and renamed the WAPPEN VON BORKUM.

FINNLINES GROUP

THE COMPANIES *Finnlines plc* is a Finnish private sector company. The Italian company *Grimaldi Compagnia de Navigazione SpA* has a controlling interest. It operates three passenger brands: *Finnlines HansaLink*, *FinnLink* and *Finnlines NordöLink*.

FINNLINES HANSALINK

MANAGEMENT President and CEO Olav K Rakkenes, **Vice-President** Simo Airas.

ADDRESS PO Box 197, Salmisaarenkatu 1, 00180 Helsinki, Finland. *Sales and marketing of Finnlines Passenger Services* Nordic Ferry Center Oy, Lönnrotinkatu 21, 00120 Helsinki, Finland.

TELEPHONE Administration + 358 (0)10 34350. **Reservations (Nordic Ferry Center Oy)** + 358 (0)9-2510 200.

FAX Administration + 358 (0)10 3435200, **Reservations** + 358 (0)9-2510 2022.

INTERNET *Finnlines* **Email** info@finnlines.fi *Nordic Ferry Center* info@ferrycenter.fi

Website *Finnlines* www.finnlines.fi *(English, Finnish, German)*

Nordic Ferry Center www.ferrycenter.fi/finnlines/en/index.shtml *(English)*

ROUTE OPERATED Helsinki - Travemünde *Hansa Class* (36 hrs; *1,5*; 3 per week), *Finnlady Class* (27 hrs; *2,3,4*; 6 per week).

1	FINNHANSA	32531t	94	21.3k	183.0m	90P	-	236T	A2	FI	9010151
2	FINNLADY	45923t	07	25.0k	216.0m	500P	-	300T	BA2	FI	9336268
3	FINNMAID	45923t	06	25.0k	216.0m	500P	-	300T	BA2	FI	9319466
4	FINNSTAR	45923t	06	25.0k	216.0m	500P	-	300T	BA2	FI	9319442
5	TRANSEUROPA	32534t	95	21.3k	183.0m	90P	-	236T	A2	DE	9010175

FINNHANSA 'Ro-pax' vessels built by Stocznia Gdanska SA, Gdansk, Poland for *Finnlines Oy* of Finland to provide a daily service conveying both freight and a limited number of cars and passengers on a previously freight-only route. Currently remains on the Helsinki - Travemünde route.

FINNSTAR Built by Fincantieri-Cantieri Navali Italiani SpA, Castellamare, Italy to operate between Helsinki and Travemünde.

FINNLADY, FINNMAID Built by Fincantieri-Cantieri Navali Italiani SpA, Ancona, Italy to operate between Helsinki and Travemünde. The FINNLADY was launched as the EUROPALINK and the name changed before delivery.

TRANSEUROPA 'Ro-pax' vessel built by Stocznia Gdanska SA, Gdansk, Poland for *Poseidon Schiffahrt* of Germany to operate on a joint service between Lübeck and Helsinki. In 1997 *Poseidon Schiffahrt* was acquired by *Finnlines* and in 2001 renamed *Finnlines Deutschland AG*. Remains on the Helsinki - Travemünde route.

FINNLINES NORDÖLINK

THE COMPANY *Finnlines NordöLink* is the trading name of *Rederi AB Nordö-Link*, a Swedish private sector company which is a subsidiary of *Finnlines* of Finland.

MANAGEMENT Managing Director Eje Wilör.

ADDRESS PO Box 106, 201 21 Malmö, Sweden.

TELEPHONE Administration + 46 (0)40 72417, **Reservations** + 46 (0)40 79603.

FAX Administration & Reservations + 46 (0)40 6119849.

INTERNET Website www.nordoe-link.se *(Swedish, German, English)*

ROUTE OPERATED Malmö - Travemünde (9 hrs; *1,2,3,4*; up to 4 per day but passengers are not carried on all departures).

1	EUROPALINK	45923t	07	25.0k	216.0m	500P	-	300T	BA2	SE	9319454
2	FINNPARTNER	32534t	94	21.3k	183.0m	90P	-	236T	A2	FI	9010163
3	FINNTRADER	32534t	95	21.3k	183.0m	114P	-	220T	BA2	FI	9017769
4	NORDLINK	45923t	07	25.0k	216.0m	500P	-	300T	BA2	SE	9336256

EUROPALINK Built by Fincantieri-Cantieri Navali Italiani SpA, Castellamare, Italy for *Finnlines* to operate for *Finnlines NordöLink* between Travemünde and Malmö. Launched as the FINNLADY but name changed before delivery.

FINNPARTNER 'Ro-pax' vessels built by Stocznia Gdanska SA, Gdansk, Poland for *Finnlines Oy* of Finland to provide a daily service conveying both freight and a limited number of cars and passengers on a previously freight-only route. In February 2007 replaced by the FINNLADY and placed on the Turku - Travemünde freight service; in May sent to the Remontowa Shipyard in Gdansk for rebuilding to increase passenger capacity and allow for two-deck through loading. In Summer 2007 transferred to the *NordöLink* Malmö - Travemünde route.

FINNTRADER 'Ro-pax' vessel built by Stocznia Gdanska SA, Gdansk, Poland for *Finnlines Oy* of Finland to provide a daily service conveying both freight and a limited number of cars and passengers on a previously freight-only route. In 2006/07 rebuilt to increase passenger capacity and allow for two-deck through loading. In 2007 transferred to the Malmö - Travemünde route.

NORDLINK Built by Fincantieri-Cantieri Navali Italiani SpA, Castellamare, Italy for *Finnlines* to operate for *Finnlines NordöLink* between Travemünde and Malmö.

FINNLINK

THE COMPANY *FinnLink* is a subsidiary of *Finnlines*.

MANAGEMENT Managing Director Christer Backman.

ADDRESS Satamatie 11, 21100, Naantali, Finland.

TELEPHONE Administration & Reservations +358 (0)10 436 7620.

FAX Administration & Reservations +358 (0)10 436 7660.

INTERNET Email finnlink@finnlink.fi **Website** www.finnlink.fi (*English, Finnish, Swedish*)

ROUTE OPERATED Naantali (Finland) - Kapellskär (Sweden) (6 hrs; *1,2,3,4*; 4 per day).

1	FINNCLIPPER	29841t	99	22.0k	188.3m	440P	-	210T	BA2	SE	9137997
2	FINNEAGLE	29841t	99	22.0k	188.3m	440P	-	185T	BA2	SE	9138006
3	FINNFELLOW	33769t	00	22.0k	188.3m	452P	-	220T	BA	SE	9145164
4F	FINNSAILOR	20783t	87	20.3k	157.6m	119P	-	146T	A	SE	8401444

FINNCLIPPER 'Ro-pax' vessel built by Astilleros Españoles, Cadiz, Spain. Ordered by *Stena Ro-Ro* of Sweden and launched as the STENA SEAPACER 1. In 1998 sold, before delivery, to *Finnlines* and renamed the FINNCLIPPER. Entered service on the Helsinki - Travemünde route in 1999. During Winter 1999/2000 she was converted to double-deck loading. In 2003 transferred to *FinnLink*. In 2005 transferred to *NordöLink* but in January 2006 returned to *FinnLink*. In 2007 an additional freight deck was added.

FINNEAGLE 'Ro-pax' vessel built by Astilleros Españoles, Cadiz, Spain. Ordered by *Stena Ro-Ro* of Sweden and launched as the STENA SEAPACER 2. In 1998 sold, before delivery, to *Finnlines* and renamed the FINNEAGLE. Although expected to join her sister the FINNCLIPPER on the Helsinki - Travemünde route, on delivery in late 1999 she entered service with *FinnLink*. During Winter 1999/2000 she was modified for two-deck loading.

FINNFELLOW Ro-pax ferry built as the STENA BRITANNICA by Astilleros Españoles, Cadiz, Spain for *Stena RoRo* and chartered to *Stena Line BV* to operate between Hook of Holland and Harwich. In 2003 replaced by a new STENA BRITANNICA, sold to *Finnlines*, renamed the FINNFELLOW and placed on

Bergensfjord (*(FERRY information)*)

Mercandia VIII (*Miles Cowsill*)

the Helsinki – Travemünde route. In 2004 transferred to *FinnLink*.

FINNSAILOR Built by Gdansk Shipyard, Gdansk, Poland for *Finnlines* of Finland for freight service between Finland and Germany. In 1996 converted to ro-pax format to inaugurate a new passenger/freight service between Helsinki and Norrköping (Sweden) for subsidiary *FinnLink*. In 1997 this service was transferred to the Kapellskär - Naantali route and passengers (other than lorry drivers) ceased to be conveyed. Later in 1997 she was transferred to the Helsinki - Lübeck route. In 2000 she was chartered to *Nordö-Link* to operate between Travemünde and Malmö. In 2002 she returned to *FinnLink*. In 2004 transferred to *Nordö-Link*. In 2007 returned to *FinnLink* as fourth ship; now operates only for freight.

FJORD LINE

THE COMPANY *Fjord Line* is a Norwegian company. During 2007 most of the shares of the company were purchased by Frode and Ole Teigen. The company merged with *Master Ferries* during December 2007 and all operations are branded as *Fjord Line*.

MANAGEMENT Managing Director Ingvald Fardal, **Marketing Managers** Nina Kramer Fromreide (Bergen-Hanstholm) and Svein Olav Olsen (Kristiansand – Hanstholm).

ADDRESS Skoltegrunnskaien, PO Box 6020, 5020 Bergen, Norway.

TELEPHONE Administration + 47 55 54 87 00, **Reservations** + 47 55 54 88 00.

FAX Administration & Reservations + 47 55 54 86 01.

INTERNET Email fjordline@fjordline.com **Website** www.fjordline.com (*Norwegian, Danish, English*)

ROUTES OPERATED Conventional Ferry Bergen – Haugesund - Egersund (Norway) - Hanstholm (Denmark) (15 hrs 30 mins; *1*; 3 per week), Egersund - Hanstholm (6 hrs 45 mins; *1*; up to 7 per week in summer), Kristiansand - Hanstholm (2 hrs; *1*; 2 per week (winter only)). **Fast ferry** Kristiansand - Hanstholm (4 hrs, *2*; up to 3 per day (summer only)).

1	BERGENSFJORD	16794t	93	19.0k	134.4m	882P	350C	44T	BA	NO	9058995
2»	FJORD CAT	5619t	98	43.0k	91.3m	663P	220C	-	A	NO	9176060

BERGENSFJORD Built by Fosen Mekaniske Verksteder, Rissa, Norway for *Rutelaget Askøy-Bergen* as the BERGEN and used on the *Fjord Line* Bergen - Egersund - Hanstholm service. In 2003 chartered to *DFDS Seaways* and, in April 2003, renamed the DUCHESS OF SCANDINAVIA and, after modifications, introduced onto the Harwich - Cuxhaven service. In 2004 sold to *Bergensfjord KS* of Norway, and chartered to *DFDS Seaways*. In 2005 sub-chartered to *Fjord Line* for 5 months (with *DFDS* officers and deck-crew) and renamed the ATLANTIC TRAVELLER. In 2006 chartered to *Fjord Line*. In 2008 purchased by *Fjord Line* and renamed the BERGENSFJORD.

FJORD CAT Incat 91 metre catamaran, built speculatively at Hobart, Tasmania, Australia. In Spring 1998, following *Incat's* acquisition of a 50% share in *Scandlines Cat-Link A/S*, she was chartered by *Nordic Catamaran Ferries K/S* to that company, operating between Århus and Kalundborg and named the CAT-LINK V. She is the current holder of the Hales Trophy for fastest crossing of the Atlantic during her delivery voyage between the USA and Falmouth, UK. In 1999 the charter was transferred to *Mols-Linien*, she was renamed the MADS MOLS and operated between Århus and Odden. Charter ended in July 2005. Laid up and renamed the INCAT 049. In 2006 sold to *Gabriel Scott Rederi* (*Master Ferries*) and renamed the MASTER CAT. In 2008 purchased by *Fjord Line* renamed the FJORD CAT.

HH-FERRIES

THE COMPANY *HH-Ferries* is a Danish/Swedish private sector company. In 2002 it was acquired by *Steneo AB* of Sweden, part of the *Stena Group*.

MANAGEMENT Managing Director Lars Meijer, **Marketing Manager** Jon Cavalli-Björkman.

ADDRESS Atlantgatan 2, 252 25 Helsingborg, Sweden.

TELEPHONE Administration + 46 (0)42-26 80 00, **Reservations Denmark** +45 49 26 01 55,

Sweden + 46 (0)42-19 80 00.

FAX Administration & Reservations *Denmark* + 45 49 26 01 56, *Sweden* + 46 (0)42-26 80 28.

INTERNET Email info@hhferries.se **Websites** www.hhferries.dk *(Danish, English)* www.hhferries.se *(Swedish, English)*

ROUTE OPERATED Helsingør - Helsingborg (20 mins; *1,2,3*; every 30 minutes).

1	GITTE 3	4296t	87	12.7k	95.0m	300P	170C	20T	BA	DK	8611635
2	MERCANDIA IV	4296t	89	13.0k	95.0m	420P	170C	18L	BA	DK	8611685
3	MERCANDIA VIII	4296t	87	13.0k	95.0m	420P	170C	18L	BA	DK	8611623

GITTE 3 Built by North East Shipbuilders Ltd, Sunderland, UK as the SUPERFLEX DELTA for *Vognmandsruten* of Denmark. In 1990 this company was taken over by *DIFKO* and she was renamed the DIFKO STOREBÆLT. In 1998, following the opening of the Great Belt fixed link, the service ceased and she was laid up. In 1999 she was chartered to *Easy Line*, renamed the GITTE 3 and operated between Gedser and Rostock. Laid up after August 1999 except for brief periods on charter to *HH-Ferries*. In 2003 sold to *HH-Ferries*.

MERCANDIA IV Built by North East Shipbuilders Ltd, Sunderland, UK as the SUPERFLEX NOVEMBER for *Vognmandsruten* of Denmark. In 1989 sold to *Mercandia* and renamed the MERCANDIA IV. In 1990 she began operating on their *Kattegatbroen* Juelsminde - Kalundborg service. In 1996 she was transferred to their *Sundbroen* Helsingør - Helsingborg service. In 1997 the service and vessel were leased to *HH-Ferries*. In 1999 she was purchased by *HH-Ferries*. She has been equipped to carry dangerous cargo.

MERCANDIA VIII Built by North East Shipbuilders Ltd, Sunderland, UK as the SUPERFLEX BRAVO for *Vognmandsruten* of Denmark and used on their services between Nyborg and Korsør and Copenhagen (Tuborg Havn) and Landskrona (Sweden). In 1991 she was chartered to *Scarlett Line* to operate on the Copenhagen and Landskrona route. In 1993 she was renamed the SVEA SCARLETT but later in the year the service ceased and she was laid up. In 1996 she was purchased by *Mercandia*, renamed the MERCANDIA VIII and placed on their *Sundbroen* Helsingør - Helsingborg service. In 1997 the service and vessel were leased to *HH-Ferries*. In 1999 she was purchased by *HH-Ferries*.

HURTIGRUTEN

SERVICE The *'Hurtigruten'* is the *'Norwegian Coastal Express Service'*. It is part cruise, part passenger ferry, part cargo line and part car ferry (although this is a fairly minor part of the operation). In recent years the service has been operated by a consortium of two operators - *Ofotens og Vesteraalens Dampskibsselskab* and *Troms Fylkes Dampskibsselskap*. In February 2006 the two companies merged as *Hurtigruten Group ASA*.

MANAGEMENT Chairman Ole Lund, **Managing Director** Olav Fjell.

ADDRESS Postboks 43, 8501 Narvik, Norway.

TELEPHONE Administration + 47 76 96 76 00, **Reservations** *Norway* + 47 810 30 000, *UK* + 44 (0)20 8846 2666.

FAX Administration & Reservations + 47 76 96 76 11, *Reservations (UK)* + 44 (0)20 8846 2677.

INTERNET Email firmapost@hurtigruten.com **Websites** www.hurtigruten.no *(English, Norwegian, Swedish)* www.hurtigruten.de *(German)* www.hurtigruten.co.uk *(English)*

ROUTE OPERATED Bergen - Kirkenes with many intermediate calls. Daily departures throughout the year. The round trip takes just under 11 days.

1	FINNMARKEN	15539t	02	18.0k	138.5m	1000P	50C	0L	SC	NO	9231951
2P	FRAM	11647t	07	18.0k	110.0m	500P	-	0L	-	NO	9370018
3	KONG HARALD	11204t	93	18.0k	121.8m	691P	50C	0L	SC	NO	9039119
4	LOFOTEN	2621t	64	16.0k	87.4m	410P	4C	0L	C	NO	5424562
5	MIDNATSOL	16151t	03	18.0k	135.7m	1000P	50C	0L	SC	NO	9247728

6	NORDKAPP	11386t	96	18.0k	123.3m	691P	50C	OL	SC	NO	9107772
7	NORDLYS	11204t	94	18.0k	121.8m	691P	50C	OL	SC	NO	9048914
8	NORDNORGE	11384t	97	18.0k	123.3m	691P	50C	OL	SC	NO	9107784
9P	NORDSTJERNEN	2191t	56	15.5k	88.8m	400P	0C	OL	-	NO	5255777
10	POLARLYS	11341t	96	18.0k	123.0m	737P	50C	OL	SC	NO	9107796
11	RICHARD WITH	11205t	93	18.0k	121.8m	691P	50C	OL	SC	NO	9040429
12	TROLLFJORD	16140t	02	18.0k	135.7m	822P	50C	OL	SC	NO	9233258
13	VESTERÅLEN	6262t	83	18.0k	108.6m	560P	40C	OL	SC	NO	8019368

FINNMARKEN Built by Kværner Kleven Skeppsvarv, Ulsteinvik, Norway for *Ofotens og Vesteraalens D/S* to replace the LOFOTEN.

FRAM Built by Fincantieri-Cantieri Navali Italiani SpA at Trieste for *Hurtigruten Group ASA* (ordered by *OVDS*). In 2008 she will operate cruises in Greenland during the summer period and in South America during the winter. It was originally stated that she would operate on the Hurtigruten during the winter and this may happen in future years.

KONG HARALD Built by Volkswerft, Stralsund, Germany for *Troms Fylkes D/S*.

LOFOTEN Built by A/S Aker Mekaniske Verksted, Oslo, Norway for *Vesteraalens D/S*. In 1988 she was sold to *Finnmark Fylkesrederi og Ruteselskap*. In 1996 she was sold to *Ofotens og Vesteraalens D/S*. In 2002 she was replaced by the FINNMARKEN but she then operated summer cruises and in the winter months substituted for the NORDNORGE when that vessel was sailing in the Chilean Fjords and Antarctica. For 2008 she has returned to the Hurtigruten roster.

MIDNATSOL Built by Fosen Mekaniske Verksteder, Rissa, Norway for *Troms Fylkes D/S*.

NORDKAPP Built by Kværner Kleven Skeppsvarv, Ulsteinvik, Norway for *Ofotens og Vesteraalens D/S*. During the Winters of 2005/06 and 2006/07 she operated cruises in South America but following the delivery of the FRAM she now remains on the Hurtigruten throughout the year.

NORDLYS Built by Volkswerft, Stralsund, Germany for *Troms Fylkes D/S*.

NORDNORGE Built by Kværner Kleven, Ulsteinvik, Norway for *Ofotens og Vesteraalens D/S*. During winter since 2002/03 has operated cruises in South America.

NORDSTJERNEN Built by Blohm & Voss AG, Hamburg, Germany for *Det Bergenske Damskipsselskab A/S* of Norway and placed into Hurtigruten service. In 1979 sold to *Troms Fylkes D/S*. In 1994 placed on the Tromsø - Svalbard route. Returned to Hurtigruten in 1995 and then back to the Tromsø - Svalbard route in 1996. During Winter 2005/06 chartered to *Ofotens og Vesteraalens D/S* to operate on the Hurtigruten. This was repeated during Winter 2007/08 (charterer now *Hurtigruten Group ASA*) and will occur again during Winter 2008/09.

POLARLYS Built by Ulstein Verft A/S, Ulsteinvik, Norway for *Troms Fylkes D/S*.

RICHARD WITH Built by Volkswerft, Stralsund, Norway for *Ofotens og Vesteraalens D/S*. In 2002 sold to Norwegian interests and chartered back.

TROLLFJORD Built by Fosen Mekaniske Verksteder, Rissa, Norway for *Troms Fylkes D/S*.

VESTERÅLEN Built by Kaarbös Mekaniske Verksted A/S, Harstad, Norway for *Vesteraalens D/S*. Since 1987 owned by *Ofotens og Vesteraalens D/S*.

KYSTLINK

THE COMPANY *Nye KystLink AS* is a Norwegian private sector company owned by *Taubåtkompaniet* of Trondheim. All assets of the previous company, *KystLink AS*, were purchased by this company in early 2006.

MANAGEMENT Managing Director Unn Ståland, **Marketing Director** Lone Midtgaard Jensen.

ADDRESS Kongshavn 8, 3970 Langesund, Norway.

TELEPHONE Administration & Reservations + 47 35 96 68 00, **Reservations** + 47 81 55 67 15.

FAX Administration & Reservations + 47 35 96 68 01.

INTERNET Email post@kystlink.no **Website** www.kystlink.com *(Norwegian, English)* www.kystlink.de *(German)*

ROUTES OPERATED Langesund (Norway) – Hirtshals (Denmark) (5 hours; *1*; 1 per day), Langesund - Strömstad (Sweden) (3 hrs 15 mins; *1 or 2*; 1 per day).

1	**FANTAASIA**	16405t	79	21.3k	136.1m	1700P	549C	46T	BA	EE	7807744
2	**PRIDE OF TELEMARK**	28569t	83	19.0k	154.9m	2036P	550C	85L	BA2	NO	7907257

FANTAASIA Built by Oy Wärtsilä Ab, Turku, Finland as the TURELLA for *SF Line* of Finland for the *Viking Line* Stockholm - Mariehamn - Turku service and later moved to the Kapellskär - Mariehamn - Naantali service. In 1988 she was sold to *Stena Line*, renamed the STENA NORDICA and placed onto the Frederikshavn - Moss (night) and Frederikshavn - Gothenburg (day) services. In 1996 the Frederikshavn - Moss service ceased and she was transferred to subsidiary *Lion Ferry* and renamed the LION KING. She operated between Halmstad and Grenaa. In December 1997 she was sold to *Tallink Line Ltd* of Cyprus and renamed the FANTAASIA. In February 1998, after substantial modification, she was placed on the *Tallink* service between Helsinki and Tallinn. In June 2002 moved to the Tallinn - Stockholm route, enabling a daily service to be reinstated. In 2004 inaugurated a new Helsinki - Tallinn - St Petersburg - Helsinki service. In 2005 chartered to *Algérie Ferries* of Algeria, to operate between Algeria and France. Returned in October 2005. In Spring 2006 inaugurated a service between Stockholm and Riga (Latvia). In May 2006 chartered to *Compagnie Maroccaine de Navigation* to operate between Morocco and France. In May 2007 chartered to *ENTMV* of Algeria. In November 2007 chartered to *KystLink*; charter due to end May 2008. In April 2008 sold to *Kystlink*. May be chartered out when the PRIDE OF TELEMARK returns.

PRIDE OF TELEMARK Built at Dunkerque, France as the STENA JUTLANDICA for *Stena Line* for the Gothenburg - Frederikshavn service. In 1996 she was transferred to the Dover - Calais route and renamed the STENA EMPEREUR. In 1998 she was transferred to *P&O Stena Line*. Later in 1998 renamed the P&OSL PROVENCE. In 2002 renamed the PO PROVENCE and in 2003 the PRIDE OF PROVENCE. In 2004 sold to *GA Ferries* of Greece and renamed the ALKMINI A. She was expected to be used on services to Patmos, Leros, Kalymnos, Kos and Rhodes. However, in Spring 2005 she was chartered to *KystLink* and placed on the Langesund – Hirtshals route. In October she was renamed the PRIDE OF TELEMARK (a name she had used as a marketing name from the start) and transferred to Norwegian registry. In 2007 sold to *Boa Ro Ro AS*; *KystLink* charter continued. Damaged in an accident in September 2007; after hull repairs at Gothenburg she was given a major engine rebuild by Wärtsilä and was due to return to service in summer 2008.

MR SHOPPY

THE COMPANY *Mr Shoppy* is a Swedish Company, part of the *Orvelin Gruppen*, who own a large shopping complex in Strömstad.

**MANAGEMENT Managing Director (*Orvelin Gruppen)* Ulf Palm.

ADDRESS Box 97, SE-452 22 Strömstad, Sweden.

**TELEPHONE Administration (*Orvelin Gruppen)* + 46 (0) 526-188 00

**FAX Administration (*Orvelin Gruppen)* + 46 (0) 526-405 50

INTERNET Website www.mrshoppy.com

ROUTE OPERATED Kålvik (near Strömstad, Sweden) - Alvim (near Sarpsborg, Norway) (1 hr 45 min; *1*; 2 per day), Kålvik - Skagen (Denmark) (6 hrs; *1*; 1 per week- single direction), Skagen - Alvim (6 hrs; *1*; 1 per week- single direction).

1	**MR SHOPPY ONE**	1170t	01	17.0k	71.0m	400P	60C	3L	BA	SE	9212450

MR SHOPPY ONE Built by *Panagiotakis Bros* of Piraeus, Greece as the AGIOS ANDREAS II for *Okänk Rederi* of Greece and operated between Piraeus - Agina. Later in 2001 laid up. In 2004 chartered to *Iokala Intressen* of Greece and operated between Sami and Neapolis. In 2005 sold to *Atlas V Shipping* of Greece and operated between Neapolis and Kythira. Renamed the ANDREAS II. In 2007 chartered to *Orvelin Gruppen*, renamed the MR SHOPPY ONE and, in 2008, began operating for *Mister Shoppy*.

MOLS-LINIEN

THE COMPANY *Mols-Linien A/S* is a Danish private sector company; previously a subsidiary of *J Lauritzen A/S*, it was, in 1988 sold to *DIFKO No LXII (Dansk Investeringsfond)*. Since 1994 shares in the company have been traded on the Stock Exchange. In January 1999 a 40% share in the company was acquired by *Scandlines Danmark A/S*. Their *Scandlines Cat-Link* Århus - Kalundborg service became part of *Mols-Linien* in February 1999 and the service was switched from Kalundborg to Odden in April 1999. The Ebeltoft - Odden ro-pax vessels were transferred to the Århus - Kalundborg route in January 2000. The *Scandlines* share in the company was acquired by the *Clipper Group* in 2007.

MANAGEMENT Managing Director Preben Wolff, **Marketing Manager** Mikkel Hybel.

ADDRESS Færgehavnen, 8400 Ebeltoft, Denmark.

TELEPHONE Administration + 45 89 52 52 00, **Reservations** + 45 70 10 14 18 (press 8).

FAX Administration + 45 89 52 52 90, **Reservations** + 45 89 52 52 92.

INTERNET Email mols-linien@mols-linien.dk **Website** www.mols-linien.dk *(Danish)*

ROUTES OPERATED Ro-pax Ferries Århus (Jutland) - Kalundborg (Sealand) (2 hr 40 mins; *2,5*; 6 per day). **Fast Ferries** Århus - Odden (Sealand) (1 hr 5 mins; *1,3,4*; 10 per day), Ebeltoft (Jutland) - Odden (45 mins; *1,4*; two hourly with some extras).

1»	MAI MOLS	3971t	96	43.4k	76.1m	450P	120C	-	BA	DK	9112997
2	MAREN MOLS	14379t	96	19.0k	136.4m	600P	344C	82L	BA2	DK	9112765
3»	MAX MOLS	5617t	98	43.0k	91.3m	800P	220C	-	A	DK	9176058
4»	MIE MOLS	3971t	96	43.4k	76.1m	450P	120C	-	BA	DK	9113006
5	METTE MOLS	14221t	96	19.0k	136.4m	600P	344C	82L	BA2	DK	9112777

MAI MOLS Danyard SeaJet 250 catamaran built by Danyard-Aalborg A/S, Aalborg, Denmark for *Mols-Linien*.

MAREN MOLS, METTE MOLS Ro-pax vessels built by Ørskovs Christensens Staalskibsværft A/S, Frederikshavn, Denmark for *Mols-Linien*. Initially operated on the Ebeltoft - Odden route. In January 2000 switched to the Århus - Kalundborg route.

MAX MOLS Incat 91 metre catamaran, built speculatively at Hobart, Tasmania, Australia. In Spring 1998, following *Incat's* acquisition of a 50% share in *Scandlines Cat-Link A/S*, she was sold to that company and named the CAT-LINK IV. In 1999 purchased by *Mols-Linien* and renamed the MAX MOLS. In 2000 chartered to *Marine Atlantic* of Canada to operate between Port aux Basques (Newfoundland) and North Sydney (Nova Scotia). Returned to *Mols-Linien* in Autumn 2000. In Summer 2002 chartered to *Riga Sea Lines* to operate between Riga and Nynäshamn. Returned to *Mols-Linien* in Autumn 2002. In 2004 chartered to *P&O Ferries* to operate between Portsmouth and Caen. Operated under the marketing name 'Caen Express'. In November 2004 returned to *Mols-Linien* and placed on the Århus – Odden route to enhance the service as second vessel.

MIE MOLS Danyard SeaJet 250 catamaran built at Danyard-Aalborg A/S, Aalborg, Denmark for *Mols-Linien*.

REEDEREI NORDEN-FRISIA

THE COMPANY *Aktiengesellschaft Reederei Norden-Frisia* is a German public sector company.

MANAGEMENT President/CEO C U Stegmann, **Managing Director/CFO** Prok. Graw, **Technical Manager** Prok. H Stolle.

ADDRESS Postfach 1262, 26534 Norderney, Germany.

TELEPHONE Administration + 49 (0)4932 9130.

FAX Administration + 49 (0)4932 9131310.

INTERNET Email info@reederei-frisia.de **Website** www.reederei-frisia.de *(German)*

ROUTES OPERATED *Car Ferries & Passenger Ferries* Norddeich (Germany) - Norderney (German Frisian Islands) (1 hr; *1,3*; up to 15 per day), Norddeich - Juist (German Frisian Islands) (1 hr 20 mins; *2,4,6*; up to 15 per day), *Excursion vessels (8,9*; varies).

1	FRISIA I	1020t	70	12.3k	63.7m	1500P	53C	-	BA	DE	7018604
2	FRISIA II	1125t	78	12.0k	63.3m	1340P	53C	-	BA	DE	7723974
3	FRISIA IV	1574t	02	12.0k	71.7m	1342P	60C	-	BA	DE	9246839
4	FRISIA V	1007t	65	11.0k	63.8m	1442P	53C	-	BA	DE	8827181
5	FRISIA VI	768t	68	12.0k	54.9m	1096P	35C	-	BA	DE	8827179
6F	FRISIA VII	363t	84	12.0k	53.0m	12P	30C	-	BA	DE	8891807
7p	FRISIA IX	571t	80	11.0k	57.0m	785P	0C	-	-	DE	7924310
8p	FRISIA X	187t	72	12.0k	36.3m	290P	0C	-	-	DE	7222308
9p	WAPPEN VON NORDENEY	154t	67	14.0k	31.1m	200P	0C	-	-	DE	7935395

FRISIA I, FRISIA II, FRISIA V, FRISIA VI Built by Jos L Meyer Werft, Papenburg, Germany for *Reederei Norden-Frisia*. Passenger capacities relate to the summer season. Capacity is reduced during the winter.

FRISIA IV Built by Schiffswerft und Maschinenfabrik Cassens GmbH, Emden, Germany for *Reederei Norden-Frisia* to replace the FRISIA VIII.

FRISIA VII Built by Schlömer Werft, Oldersum, Germany for *Reederei Norden-Frisia*. Conveys ro-ro freight to Norderney and Juist.

FRISIA IX, FRISIA X Built by Schiffswerft Julius Diedrich GmbH & Co. KG, Oldersum, Germany for *Reederei Norden-Frisia*. The FRISIA IX was built to convey 9 cars at the bow end but is now used in passenger-only mode. These ships are generally used for excursions.

WAPPEN VON NORDENEY Built by Cassens-Werft, Emden, Germany for *Reederei Norden-Frisia*. Used for excursions.

NORDIC JET LINE

THE COMPANY *Nordic Jet Line* is an international company, registered in Estonia. Main shareholders are *Förde Reederei Seetouristik* of Germany, *Finnmark Fylkesrederi og Ruteselskap* of Norway and *Kværner Investments* of Norway.

MANAGEMENT Managing Director Mikael Granrot.

ADDRESS *Estonia* Sadama 25-4, 10111 Tallinn, Estonia, **Finland** Kanavaterminaali K5, 00160 Helsinki, Finland.

TELEPHONE Administration *Estonia* + 372 (0)6 137200, **Finland** + 358 (0)9 68177150, **Reservations** *Estonia & Finland* + 358 (0)600 01 655

FAX Administration & Reservations *Estonia* + 372 (0)6 137222, **Finland** + 358 (0)9 6817111.

INTERNET Email marketing@njl.fi **Website** www.njl.info www.njl.fi *(English, Estonian, Finnish)*

ROUTE OPERATED Helsinki (Finland) - Tallinn (Estonia) (1 hr 40 mins; *1,2*; up to 6 per day (all year except during winter ice period)).

1»	BALTIC JET	2273t	99	36.0k	60.0m	430P	52C	-	A	NO	9198551
2»	NORDIC JET	2273t	98	36.0k	60.0m	430P	52C	-	A	NO	9174323

BALTIC JET, NORDIC JET Kværner Fjellstrand JumboCat 60m catamarans built at Omastrand, Norway for *Nordic Jet Line*. Alternative traffic mix is 38 cars and 2 buses.

POLFERRIES

THE COMPANY *Polferries* is the trading name of *Polska Zegluga Baltycka SA (Polish Baltic Shipping Company)*, a Polish state-owned company.

MANAGEMENT General Director & President of the Board Jan Warchol, **Shipping Policy Director and Board Member** Grazyna Bak, **Financial Director** Piotr Redmerski, **Technical Director** Wlodzimierz Miadowicz.

ADDRESS ul Portowa 41, PL 78-100 Kolobrzeg, Poland.

TELEPHONE Administration +48 (0)94 35 52 103, +48 (0)94 35 52 102, **Passenger Reservations** *Swinoujscie* +48 (0)91 32 26 140, *Gdansk* +48 (0)58 34 31 887, *Ystad* +46 (0)40 97 61 80, **Freight Reservations** *Swinoujscie* +48 (0)91 32 26 104, *Gdansk* +48 (0)58 34 30 212.

FAX Administration +48 (0)94 35 52 208, **Passenger Reservations** *Swinoujscie* +48 (0)91 32 26 168, *Gdansk* +48 (0)58 34 36 574, **Freight Reservations** *Swinoujscie* +48 (0)91 32 26 169, *Gdansk* +48 (0)58 34 30 975.

INTERNET Email info@polferries.pl **Passenger Reservations** *Swinoujscie* boas.pax@polferries.pl *Gdansk* pax.gdansk@polferries.pl **Freight Reservations** *Swinoujscie* boas.cargo@polferries.pl, *Gdansk* cargo.gdansk@polferries.pl **Website** www.polferries.pl (*Polish, English, Danish, Swedish*)

ROUTES OPERATED Swinoujscie - Ystad (7 hrs; *4*; 1 per day), Swinoujscie - Copenhagen (9 hrs 45 mins; *2*; 4 per week), Swinoujscie - Rønne (6 hrs; *2*; 1 per week (seasonal)), Gdansk - Nynäshamn (Sweden) (18 hrs; *1,3*; 6 per week (winter), daily (summer)).

1	BALTIVIA	17790t	81	19.0k	146.9m	250P	-	140T	BA	BS	7931997
2	POMERANIA	12087t	78	17.5k	127.4m	1000P	273C	26L	BA	BS	7516761
3	SCANDINAVIA	23842t	80	20.0k	146.1m	1800P	510C	38L	BA2	BS	7826788
4	WAWEL	25318t	80	19.0k	163.9m	900P	550C	75L	BA2	BS	7814462

BALTIVIA Built by Fartygsentreprenader AB, Kalmar, Sweden as the SAGA STAR for *TT-Saga-Line* and, from 1982, used on freight services between Travemünde and Trelleborg/Malmö. (Originally ordered by *Rederi AB Svea* as the SAGALAND). In 1989 sold to *Cie Meridionale* of France, renamed the GIROLATA and used on *SNCM* (later *CMR*) services in the Mediterranean. In 1993 she was chartered back to *TT-Line*, resumed her original name and was used on the Travemünde - Trelleborg service. Following delivery of the ROBIN HOOD and the NILS DACKE in 1995, she was transferred to the Rostock - Trelleborg route. In July 1997 she was purchased by *TT-Line* and in 1998 passenger facilities were completely renovated to full ro-pax format; following the delivery of the TOM SAWYER she was transferred back to the Travemünde - Trelleborg route, operating additional freight sailings. Briefly transferred back to Rostock - Trelleborg when the charter of the TT-TRAVELLER ended. Withdrawn in 2002, sold to Transmanche Ferries and renamed the DIEPPE. In 2006 replaced by the SEVEN SISTERS, sold to *Polferries*, renamed the BALTIVIA and, in 2007, placed on the Gdansk - Nynäshamn route.

POMERANIA Built by Stocznia Szczecinska im A Warskiego, Szczecin, Poland for *Polferries*. In 1978 and 1979 she briefly operated between Felixstowe and Swinoujscie via Copenhagen. In recent years she was the regular vessel on the Gdansk - Helsinki service before that service was withdrawn. She was rebuilt in 1997. Currently used on the Swinoujscie - Copenhagen and Swinoujscie - Rønne routes.

SCANDINAVIA Built by Öresundsvarvet AB, Landskrona, Sweden as the VISBY for *Rederi AB Gotland* of Sweden for their services between the island of Gotland and the Swedish mainland. In 1987, the franchise to operate these services was lost by the company and awarded to *Nordström & Thulin* of Sweden. A subsidiary called *N&T Gotlandslinjen AB* was formed to operate the service. The VISBY was chartered to this company and managed by *Johnson Line*, remaining owned by *Rederi AB Gotland*. In early 1990 she was chartered to *Sealink* and renamed the FELICITY. After modifications at Tilbury, she was, in March 1990, introduced onto the Fishguard - Rosslare route. Later in 1990 she was renamed the STENA FELICITY. In Summer 1997 she was returned to *Rederi AB Gotland* for rebuilding, prior to her entering service with *Destination Gotland* in January 1998. She was renamed the VISBY.

In late 2002 she was renamed the VISBORG. In March 2003 replaced by the new VISBY and laid up for sale or charter. In July sold to *Polferries*, renamed the SCANDINAVIA and placed on the Gdansk - Nynäshamn route.

WAWEL Built by Kockums Varvet AB, Malmö, Sweden as the SCANDINAVIA for *Rederi AB Nordö* of Sweden. After service in the Mediterranean for *UMEF*, she was, in 1981, sold to *SOMAT* of Bulgaria, renamed the TZAREVETZ and used on *Medlink* services between Bulgaria and the Middle East, later on other routes. In 1986 she was chartered to *Callitzis* of Greece for a service between Italy and Greece. In 1988 she was sold to *Sealink*, re-registered in The Bahamas and renamed the FIESTA. She was then chartered to *OT Africa Line*. During Autumn 1989 she was rebuilt at Bremerhaven to convert her for passenger use and in March 1990 she was renamed the FANTASIA and placed on the Dover - Calais service. Later in 1990 she was renamed the STENA FANTASIA. In 1998 transferred to *P&O Stena Line*. In 1999 she was renamed the P&OSL CANTERBURY. In 2002 renamed the PO CANTERBURY. In Spring 2003 replaced by the PRIDE OF CANTERBURY and laid up at Dunkerque. Later in the year sold to *GA Ferries* and renamed the ALKMINI A. In 2004 moved to Greece and, after a partial rebuild, placed on the Igoumenitsa – Brindisi route. Later in 2004 sold to *Polferries* and renamed the WAWEL; rebuilt to increase the number of cabins. In 2005 placed on the Swinoujscie – Ystad service.

RG-LINE

THE COMPANY *RG-Line Oy/Ab* is a Finnish private sector company, named after its owner, Rabbe Grönblom.

MANAGEMENT Chief Executive Börje Lassfolk.

ADDRESS Satamaterminaali, 65170 Vaasa, Finland.

TELEPHONE Administration & Reservations + 358 (0)20-7716 810.

FAX Administration & Reservations + 358 (0)20-7716 820.

INTERNET Email marketing@rgline.com **Website** www.rgline.com *(Finnish, Swedish)*

ROUTE OPERATED Vaasa (Finland) - Umeå (Sweden) (4 hrs; *1*; 1/2 per day).

1	RG 1		10271t	83	14.5k	140.1m	300P	800C	45L	A	FI	8306577

RG 1 Built as the KAHLEBERG by VEB Mathias Thesen Werft, Wismar, Germany (DDR) for *DSR* of Germany (DDR). In 1991 chartered to *TR-Line* (joint venture between *TT-Line* and *DSR*) for service between Rostock and Trelleborg. In 1995 *DSR* pulled out of the venture and the service became *TT-Line*. In 1997 she returned to *DSR* to operate for *Euroseabridge* (later *Scandlines Euroseabridge*). She initially operated on the Travemünde - Klaìpeda service. In 1999 she was transferred to the formerly freight-only Rostock - Liepaja service. In 2000 transferred to the *Amber Line* Karlshamn - Liepaja route as a ro-pax vessel. In 2003 chartered to *Polferries* to operate between Swinoujscie and Ystad. In 2005 sold to *RG-Line*. Operated in original mode for a short while before being rebuilt to increase passenger capacity to 300. Introduced into service during summer 2005. Later renamed the RG 1.

RØMØ-SYLT LINIE

THE COMPANY *Römö-Sylt Linie GmbH* is a German company, a subsidiary of *FRS (Förde Reederei Seetouristik)* of Flensburg. (**Note:** Although, being a German company, the company's official name uses the German version of the umlaut (ö), the company trades in both Denmark and Germany using the Danish version (ø).

MANAGEMENT Managing Director P Rathke.

ADDRESS *Germany* Am Fähranleger, 25992 List, Germany, *Denmark* Kilebryggen, 6792 Rømø, Denmark.

TELEPHONE Administration *Germany* + 49 (0)4651 870475, **Reservations** *Denmark* + 45 73 75 53 03, *Germany* + 49 (0)180 310 30 30.

FAX Administration *Germany* + 49 (0)4651 871446, **Reservations** *Denmark* + 45 73 75 53 05.

INTERNET Email romo-sylt@post12.tele.dk **Website** www.romo-sylt.dk (*Danish, German*)

ROUTE OPERATED List (Sylt, Germany) - Havneby (Rømø, Denmark) (35 mins; *1*; variable - approx 2 hourly). **Note**:The island of Rømø is linked to the Danish mainland by a road causeway; the island of Sylt is linked to the German mainland by a rail-only causeway on which cars are conveyed on shuttle wagons.

| 1 | SYLT EXPRESS | 3650t | 05 | 16.0k | 88.2m | 600P | 80C | 10L | BA | DE | 9321823 |

SYLT EXPRESS Built by Fiskerstrand Verft A/S, Aalesund, Norway for *Rømø-Sylt Linie*.

ROSMORPORT ST PETERSBURG AUTHORITY

THE COMPANY *Rosmorport St Petersburg Authority* (formerly *Sea Administration of St Petersburg*) is an agency of the Russian Government.

ADDRESS St Petersburg (agents) Port Authority, Port of Saint Petersburg, Gapsalskaya str, 10, Saint Petersburg, 198035, Russian Federation. **Kaliningrad (agents)** DFDS LISCO, Suvorova str, 45, Kaliningrad, 236039, Russia.

TELEPHONE St Petersburg (agents) + 7 812 380 70 95, **Kaliningrad (agents)** + 7 4012 660 401 - agency dept (*English speaking*).

FAX St Petersburg (agents) + 7 812 380 70 95, **Kaliningrad (agents)** + 7 4012 660 402.

INTERNET Email *St Petersburg* Kovalev@rosmorport.spb.ru, gan@rosmorport.spb.ru *Kaliningrad* office@dfdslisco.ru **Website** www.dfdslisco.ru (*English*)

ROUTE OPERATED St Petersburg (Russia) - Baltijsk (Kaliningrad, Russia) (36 hrs; *1*; every 5 days).

| 1 | GEORG OTS | 12549t | 80 | 17.0k | 136.8m | 341P | 107C | 21T | BA | RU | 7625835 |

GEORG OTS Built by Stocznia Szczecinska im A Warskiego, Gdansk, Poland for *Estonian Shipping Company (ESCO)*, then of the USSR, to operate between Tallinn and Helsinki. Later chartered to *Tallink* (which was at the time partly owned by *ESCO*). Rebuilt in 1993 to increase car capacity from 14 to 110 and be brought up to modern standards. In 2000 charter ended and she was returned to *ESCO*. In 2002 sold to *Sea Administration of St Petersburg* and placed on the St Petersburg - Baltijsk service.

SAAREMAA LAEVAKOMPANII

THE COMPANY *Saaremaa Laevakompanii AS* is an Estonian company, founded in 1992.

MANAGEMENT General Director Tõnis Rihvk.

ADDRESS Kohtu 1, 93812 Kuressaare, Estonia.

TELEPHONE Administration + 372-45-24350, **Reservations** + 372-45-24444.

FAX Administration + 372-45-24355, **Reservations** + 372-45-24373.

INTERNET Email slk@laevakompanii.ee **Websites** www.laevakompanii.ee (*Estonian, English*) www.slkferries.ee (*English, Estonian, German, Latvian, Russian*) www.narvaline.com (*Estonian, English, Finnish, Russian*)

ROUTES OPERATED *Domestic Services- Vehicle Ferries* Kuivastu - Virtsu (30 mins; *4,7,9,11*; up to 12 per day), Heltermaa (Hiiumaa) – Rohuküla (1 hr 30 mins; *6,8*; 5 per day), Triigi – Sõru (1 hr 5 mins; *5*; up to 3 per day), *Passenger-only Ferries* Roomassaare (Saaremaa) - Ruhnu (3 hrs; *1*; 3 per week), Ruhnu - Pärnu (3 hrs; *1*; 3 per week. *International Service* Mõntu (Saaremaa) – Ventspils (Latvia) (4 hrs; *8*; up to 4 per week) (*service branded as SSC Ferries*).

1P	AEGNA	101t	79	18.0k	25.9 m	93P	0C	0L	-	EE	8874366
2	HARILAID	1028t	85	9.9k	49.9m	120P	35C	0L	BA	EE	8727367
3	HIIUMAA	1549t	66	10.0k	53.8m	175P	28C	0L	BA	EE	6609286

4	KOGUVA	1305t	79	10.6k	55.5m	204P	41C	0L	BA	EE	7830832
5	KÖRGELAID	1028t	87	9.9k	49.9m	200P	35C	0L	BA	EE	8725577
6	OFELIA	3638t	68	14.4k	74.4m	600P	110C	12L	BA	EE	6809771
7	REGULA	3774t	71	14.5k	71.2m	580P	105C	12L	BA	EE	7051058
8	SCANIA	3474t	72	14.5k	74.2m	400P	80C	12L	BA	EE	7215290
9	ST OLA	4833t	71	16.0k	85.9m	500P	140C	12L	BA	EE	7109609
10	VARDO	116t	62	9.0k	27.1m	47P	17C	0L	BA	EE	8956712
11	VIIRE	4101t	88	12.7k	95.8m	469P	140C	36L	BA	EE	8611518

AEGNA Built by Fjellstrand, Omastrand, Norway as the RÅSA for *Helgeland Trafikkselskap* of Norway. In 2003 sold to *Jan og Torleif Charter DA*. In 2005 sold to *Saaremaa Laevakompanii* and renamed the AEGNA. Inaugurated a passenger-only service between Saaremaa and Ruhnu and Pärnu.

HARILAID Built by Riga Shiprepair Yard, Riga, Latvia (USSR) for *ESCO* of Estonia. In 1994 transferred to *Saaremaa Laevakompanii*.

HIIUMAA Built by P Høivolds Mekaniska Verksted A/S, Kristiansand, Norway as the TAARS for *Sydfyenske Dampskibsselskab A/S* of Denmark. Initially used on the Spodsbjerg – Nakskov route. In 1975 transferred to the Spodsbjerg – Taars route. Withdrawn in 1984 and in 1985 sold to *ESCO* of Estonia and renamed the HIIUMAA; she was placed on the Heltermaa – Rohuküla route. In 1992 renamed the HIIUMAA 2. In 1994 transferred to *Saaremaa Laevakompanii*. In 1996 renamed the HIIUMAA.

KOGUVA, KÖRGELAID Built by Riga Shiprepair Yard, Riga, Latvia (USSR) for *ESCO* of Estonia. In 1994 transferred to *Saaremaa Laevakompanii*.

OFELIA Built by Krögerwerft GmbH, Rendsburg, Germany for *Svenska Rederi-AB Öresund* of Sweden and used on the Limhamn - Dragør service. In 1980 sold to *Scandinavian Ferry Lines*. In 1990 transferred to *SweFerry* and later to *Scandlines AB*. In 1997 sold to *Saaremaa Laevakompanii*.

REGULA Built by Jos L Meyer, Papenburg, Germany for *Stockholms Rederi AB Svea* of Sweden for the service between Helsingborg and Helsingør operated by *Linjebuss International AB* (a subsidiary company). In 1980 she was sold to *Scandinavian Ferry Lines*. During Winter 1984/85 she was rebuilt to increase vehicle and passenger capacity. In 1991 ownership was transferred to *SweFerry* and operations to *ScandLines* on the Helsingborg - Helsingør service. Ownership later transferred to *Scandlines AB*. In 1997 sold to *Saaremaa Laevakompanii*.

SCANIA Built by Aalborg Værft A/S, Aalborg, Denmark for *Svenska Rederi-AB Öresund* of Sweden and used on the Limhamn - Dragør service. In 1980 sold to *Scandinavian Ferry Lines*. In 1990 transferred to *SweFerry* and later to *Scandlines AB*. In 1999 sold to *Saaremaa Laevakompanii*.

ST OLA Built by Jos L Meyer, Papenburg, Germany as the SVEA SCARLETT for *Stockholms Rederi AB Svea* of Sweden and used on the SL (*Skandinavisk Linjetrafik*) service between Copenhagen (Tuborg Havn) and Landskrona (Sweden). In 1980 she was sold to *Scandinavian Ferry Lines* of Sweden and *Dampskibsselskabet Øresund A/S* of Denmark (jointly owned). Initially she continued to serve Landskrona but later that year the Swedish terminal became Malmö. In 1981 she operated on the Helsingborg - Helsingør service for a short while, after which she was withdrawn and laid up. In 1982 she was sold to *Eckerö Linjen* of Finland, renamed the ECKERÖ and used on services between Grisslehamn (Sweden) and Eckerö (Åland Islands). In 1991 she was sold to *P&O Scottish Ferries* and renamed the ST OLA. In March 1992 she replaced the previous ST OLA (1345t, 1974) on the Scrabster - Stromness service. In September 2002 withdrawn and sold to *Saaremaa Laevakompanii*.

VARDO Built by Rauma-Repola Oy, Rauma, Finland as the VÅRDÖ for *Ålands Landskapsstyrelse* of Åland, Finland. In 1997 sold to *Saaremaa Laevakompanii* and renamed the VARDO.

VIIRE Built as the SUPERFLEX CHARLIE by North East Shipbuilders Ltd, Sunderland, UK for *Vognmändsruten* of Denmark to establish a new service between Korsør (Fyn) and Nyborg (Sealand). In 1990 this company was taken over by *DIFKO* and she was renamed the DIFKO KORSØR. In 1998, following the opening of the Great Belt road fixed link, the service ceased and she was laid up. In 1999 chartered to *Saaremaa Laevakompanii* and renamed the VIIRE. In 2000, the charter ended and she returned to lay-up in Denmark. In 2001 she was again chartered to *Saaremaa Laevakompanii*.

St Ola *(Richard Seville)*

Skåne *(FotoFlite)*

Under Construction

12	NEWBUILDING		3650t	09	16.0k	88.2m	600P	80C	10L	BA	EE	-

NEWBUILDING Under construction by Fiskerstrand Verft A/S, Aalesund, Norway for *Saaremaa Laevakompanii*. She will operate on the Rohukula - Heltermaa service.

SCANDLINES (DENMARK & GERMANY)

THE COMPANY *Scandlines GmbH* (formerly *Scandlines AG*) is a German company owned by Allianz Capital Partners (Danish company) (40%), 3i Group (UK company) (40%) and Deutsche Seereederei (German company) (20%). Until 2007 it was 50% owned by *Deutsche Bahn AG* (*German Railways*) (which is owned by the Federal Government) and 50% owned by the Kingdom of Denmark. In 1998 it took over *DFO* (*Deutsche Fährgesellschaft Ostsee mbH*) of Germany (renamed *Scandlines Deutschland GmbH*) and *Scandlines A/S* of Denmark (renamed *Scandlines Danmark A/S*). A 50% share in *Euroseabridge GmbH* was acquired in 1998 (by *Scandlines A/S* of Denmark before the merger with *DFO*) and the remaining 50% in 1999; the name was changed to *Scandlines Euroseabridge GmbH*. This company was later merged with *Scandlines Deutschland GmbH*.

Scandlines A/S was formerly *DSB Rederi A/S* and before that the Ferries Division of *DSB* (*Danish State Railways*). *DFO* was formed in 1993 by the merging of the Ferries Divisions of *Deutsche Bundesbahn* (*German Federal Railways*) (which operated in the Federal Republic of Germany) and *Deutsche Reichsbahn* (*German State Railways*) (which operated in the former DDR).

Stena Line-owned *Scandlines AB* of Sweden also trades under this name but remains a separate company. *Scandlines Sydfyenske A/S* which operated Danish domestic routes was sold to the *Clipper Group* in 2007.

MANAGEMENT CEO Michael Hassing, **CFO** Andreas Lübs.

ADDRESS *Denmark* Dampfærgevej 10, 2100 Copenhagen Ø, Denmark. ***Germany*** Hochhaus am Fährhafen, 18119 Rostock-Warnemünde, Germany.

TELEPHONE Administration *Denmark* +45 33 15 15 15, ***Germany*** +49 (0)381 54350, **Reservations *Denmark*** +45 33 15 15 15, ***Germany*** +49 (0)1805 116688.

FAX Administration *Denmark*, +45 35 28 02 01, ***Germany*** +49 (0)381 5435 678.

INTERNET Email scandlines@scandlines.dk **Websites** www.scandlines.dk (*Danish, English*) www.scandlines.de (*German, English*)

ROUTES OPERATED Helsingør (Sealand, Denmark) - Helsingborg (Sweden) (25 mins; *5,18*; every 20 mins) (joint with *Scandlines AB* of Sweden), Rødby (Lolland, Denmark) - Puttgarden (Germany) (45 mins; *3,6,12,13,16* (*6 road freight-only*); half-hourly train/vehicle ferry + additional road freight-only sailings), Gedser (Falster, Denmark) - Rostock (Germany) (1 hr 45 mins; *7,11,14*; every 2 hours (less frequent Dec - Feb), Rostock (Germany) - Trelleborg (Sweden) (5 hrs 45 mins (7 hrs night); *8*; 3 per day) (joint with *Scandlines AB* of Sweden), Sassnitz (Germany) - Trelleborg (3 hrs 45 mins; *15*; 4-5 per day) (joint with *Scandlines AB* of Sweden), Rostock (Germany) - Ventspils (Latvia) (24 hrs; *1,4,19*; 6 per week).

Denmark - Lithuania freight route operated by *Scandlines Balticum Seaways Division* Århus (Denmark) - Aabenraa (Denmark) - Klaìpeda (Lithuania) (from 30 hrs; *17*; 2 per week from Aabenraa (1 westbound via Århus), 1 per week from Århus via Aabenraa).

Sweden - Latvia routes operated by *Scandlines Amber Line* Nynäshamn (Sweden) – Ventspils (Latvia) (12 hrs; *10*; 5 per week).

Germany - Finland freight route Rostock - Hanko (38 hrs; *2,9*; 4 per week).

1	ASK		13144t	82	18.0k	171.0m	186P	-	104T	AS	DK	7826867
2F	AURORA		20381t	82	18.5k	154.9m	12P	-	160T	A	DE	8020599
3	DEUTSCHLAND		15187t	97	18.5k	142.0m	1200P	364C	30Lr	BA2	DE	9151541
4	FELLOW		14297t	73	15.0k	137.3m	111P	170C	84T	AS	LV	7315143

5	HAMLET	10067t	97	13.5k	111.2m	1000P	244C	34L	BA	DK	9150030
6F	HOLGER DANSKE	2779t	76	14.9k	86.8m	12P	-	12L	BA	DK	7432202
7	KRONPRINS FREDERIK	16071t	81	20.5k	152.0m	1082P	210C	46T	BA	DK	7803205
8	MECKLENBURG-VORPOMMERN	36185t	96	22.0k	199.9m	600P	445C	230Tr	A2	DE	9131797
9F	MERCHANT	20594t	82	17.0k	154.9m	12P	-	160T	A	UK	8020604
10	PETERSBURG	25353t	86	16.4k	190.8m	140P	329C	110T	A2	LR	8311883
11	PRINS JOACHIM	16071t	80	21.0k	152.0m	922P	210c	46Lr	BA	DK	7803190
12	PRINS RICHARD	14822t	97	18.5k	142.0m	1100P	364C	36Lr	BA2	DK	9144419
13	PRINSESSE BENEDIKTE	14822t	97	18.5k	142.0m	1100P	364C	36Lr	BA2	DK	9144421
14	ROSTOCK	17053t	81	17.0k	140.8m	1100P	450C	84T	BAS2	DE	8000226
15	SASSNITZ	21154t	89	18.5k	171.5m	875P	314C	50Tr	BA2	DE	8705383
16	SCHLESWIG-HOLSTEIN	15187t	97	18.5k	142.0m	1200P	364C	30Lr	BA2	DE	9151539
17F	SEA CORONA	12110t	72	17.0k	134.0m	12P	-	106T	A	NO	7222762
18	TYCHO BRAHE	11148t	91	14.5k	111.2m	1250P	240C	35Lr	BA	DK	9007116
19	URD	13144t	81	17.5k	171.0m	186P	-	104T	AS	DK	7826855

ASK Built by Nouvi Cantieri Aquania SpA, Venice, Italy as the LUCKY RIDER, a ro-ro freight ferry, for *Delpa Maritime* of Greece. In 1985 she was acquired by *Stena Line* and renamed the STENA DRIVER. Later that year she was acquired by *Sealink British Ferries* and renamed the SEAFREIGHT FREEWAY to operate freight-only services between Dover and Dunkerque. In 1988 she was sold to *SOMAT* of Bulgaria for use on *Medlink* services in the Mediterranean and renamed the SERDICA. In 1990 she was sold and renamed the NORTHERN HUNTER. In 1991 she was sold to *Blæsbjerg* of Denmark, renamed the ARKA MARINE and chartered to *DSB*. She was then converted into a ro-pax vessel, renamed the ASK and introduced onto the Århus - Kalundborg service. Purchased by *Scandlines AS* of Denmark in 1997. In 1999 she was, after some modification, transferred to *Scandlines Euroseabridge* and placed on the Travemünde - Klaìpeda route. In 2000 she was transferred to the Rostock - Liepaja route. Lengthened by 20m in 2001 and, in late 2001, chartered to *Nordö Link* to operate between Travemünde and Malmö. In late 2002 replaced by the FINNARROW and returned to *Scandlines*. She was transferred to the Rostock - Trelleborg route whilst the MECKLENBURG-VORPOMMERN was being rebuilt. She was then transferred to the Kiel - Klaìpeda route. In 2003 chartered to *Scandlines AB* to operate on the Trelleborg - Travemünde route. In April 2005 the charter ended and she returned to *Scandlines AG*. Initially she was due to replace the FELLOW on the Nynäshamn– Ventspils route during her annual refit. In Autumn 2005 moved to the Rostock - Ventspils route.

AURORA Built at Rauma, Finland as the ARCTURUS for *EFFOA* of Finland and chartered to *Finncarriers*. In 1991 renamed the AURORA. In 2003 chartered to *Scandlines Estonia* to operate between Rostock and Helsinki. During 2004 purchased by *Scandlines Estonia*. In 2005 chartered to *DFDS Tor Line* to operate between Immingham and Zeebrugge. In 2006 chartered to *Transfennica*. In January 2008 returned to *Scandlines* and placed on the Rostock - Hanko route.

DEUTSCHLAND Train/vehicle ferry built by Van der Giessen-de Noord, Krimpen aan den IJssel, Rotterdam, The Netherlands for *DFO* for the Puttgarden - Rødby service. During Winter 2003/04 extra mezzanine deck added for cars.

FELLOW Built by Oy Wärtsilä Ab, Turku, Finland for *Finncarriers* as the FINNFELLOW. In 1989 transferred to *FinnLink*. In 2002 chartered to *VV-Line* and renamed the FELLOW. In 2003 *VV-Line* went into liquidation and she was chartered to *Scandlines*, who took over the Nynäshamn – Ventspils service. In 2005 moved to the Karlshamn – Ventspils route. In Autumn 2007 moved to the Rostock - Ventspils route.

HAMLET Road vehicle ferry built by Finnyards, Rauma, Finland for *Scandlines* (50% owned by *Scandlines AG* and 50% owned by *Scandlines AB* of Sweden) for the Helsingør - Helsingborg service. Sister vessel of the TYCHO BRAHE but without rail tracks.

HOLGER DANSKE Built by Aalborg Værft A/S, Aalborg, Denmark as a train/vehicle ferry for *DSB* for the Helsingør - Helsingborg service. In 1991 transferred to the Kalundborg - Samsø route (no rail facilities). In 1997 transferred to subsidiary *SFDS A/S*. Withdrawn at the end of November 1998 when the service passed to *Samsø Linien*. In 1999 began operating between Rødby and Puttgarden as a road-freight-only vessel, carrying, among others, loads which cannot be conveyed on passenger vessels.

KRONPRINS FREDERIK Train/vehicle ferry built by Nakskov Skibsværft A/S, Nakskov, Denmark for *DSB* for the Nyborg - Korsør service. Withdrawn in 1997. After conversion to a car/lorry ferry, she was transferred to the Gedser - Rostock route (no rail facilities).

MECKLENBURG-VORPOMMERN Train/vehicle ferry built by Schichau Seebeckwerft, Bremerhaven, Germany for *DFO* for the Rostock - Trelleborg service. During Winter 2002/03 modified to increase freight capacity and reduce passenger capacity.

MERCHANT Built by Rauma Repola Oy, Rauma, Finland as the FINNMERCHANT for *Finnlines*. In 2003 sold to subsidiary *Nordö-Link* and chartered back. Later sold to *Finn Ro Ro* of Norway and renamed the MERCHANT; charter continued and later acquired by *Antique Shipping* of the UK. In recent years, operated on the Helsinki - St Petersburg - Hamina - Helsinki - Zeebrugge - Felixstowe (from 2005 Tilbury) – Amsterdam - Antwerp - Baltijsk service. In 2007 transferred to *TransRussia Express*. Later in 2007 transferred to the Lübeck - Turku route. Purchased by *Scandlines* and, in January 2008, placed on the Rostock - Hanko route.

PETERSBURG Built by Mathias Thesen Werft, Wismar, Germany (DDR) as the MUKRAN for *DSR* of Germany (DDR). In 1995 she was rebuilt to introduce road vehicle and additional passenger capacity and was renamed the PETERSBURG. She inaugurated the Travemünde service in 1995 but was then used on the Sassnitz - Klaìpeda service. This service was operated jointly with the *LISCO* vessel KLAIPEDA, a sister vessel which had not been converted to ro-pax format. In 2001 she was transferred to the Kiel - Klaìpeda service, replacing the sister vessel GREIFSWALD whose charter was ended. In 2003 replaced by the SVEALAND and transferred to the *Amber Line* Karlshamn - Liepaja route. In 2005 moved to the Nynäshamn – Ventspils service.

PRINS JOACHIM Train/vehicle ferry, built by Nakskov Skibsværft A/S, Nakskov, Denmark for *DSB* for the Nyborg - Korsør service. Withdrawn in 1997 and laid up. During Winter 2000/2001 modified in the same way as KRONPRINS FREDERIK and transferred to the Gedser - Rostock route.

PRINS RICHARD, PRINSESSE BENEDIKTE Train/vehicle ferries, built by Ørskov Christensen Staalskibsværft A/S, Frederikshavn, Denmark for *Scandlines A/S* for the Rødby - Puttgarden service. During Winter 2003/04 extra mezzanine deck added for cars.

ROSTOCK Built by Oy Wärtsilä AB, Helsinki, Finland as the TRAVEMÜNDE for *Gedser-Travemünde Ruten* of Denmark for their service between Gedser (Denmark) and Travemünde (Germany). In 1986 the company's trading name was changed to *GT Linien* and in 1987, following the takeover by *Sea-Link AB* of Sweden, it was further changed to *GT Link*. The vessel's name was changed to the TRAVEMÜNDE LINK. In 1988 she was purchased by *Rederi AB Gotland* of Sweden, although remaining in service with *GT Link*. Later in 1988 she was chartered to *Sally Ferries* and entered service in December on the Ramsgate - Dunkerque service. She was renamed the SALLY STAR. In 1997 she was transferred to *Silja Line*, to operate between Vaasa and Umeå during the summer period, and operated under the marketing name WASA EXPRESS (although not renamed). She returned to *Rederi AB Gotland* in Autumn 1997, was renamed the THJELVAR and entered service with *Destination Gotland* in January 1998. Withdrawn and laid up in December 2003. In 2004 chartered to *Color Line* to inaugurate a new service between Larvik and Hirtshals. Renamed the COLOR TRAVELLER. Operated in reduced passenger mode on this service but in summer peak period operated between Frederikshavn and Larvik in full passenger mode. In December 2006 returned to *Rederi AB Gotland*. In 2007 renamed the THJELVAR, chartered to *Scandlines* and placed on the Gedser – Rostock route. Renamed the ROSTOCK.

SASSNITZ Train/vehicle ferry built by Danyard A/S, Frederikshavn, Denmark for *Deutsche Reichsbahn*. In 1993 ownership transferred to *DFO*. Used on the Sassnitz - Trelleborg service.

SCHLESWIG-HOLSTEIN Train/vehicle ferry built by Van der Giessen-de Noord, Krimpen aan den IJssel, Rotterdam, The Netherlands for *DFO* for the Puttgarden - Rødby service. During Winter 2003/04 extra mezzanine deck added for cars.

SEA CORONA Built by Rauma Repola Oy, Rauma, Finland as the ANTARES for *Finska Ångfartygs A/B*

Tycho Brahe (Miles Cowsill)

Stena Nautica (Miles Cowsill)

of Finland and used on services between Finland and Germany. In 1975 she was chartered to *DG Hansa* of Germany and renamed the RHEINFELS. In 1977 she was sold to *Nedlloyd* of The Netherlands and renamed the NEDLLOYD ROCKANJE. In 1977 she was chartered to *Constellation Line* of the USA for services between the USA and Europe. In 1983 she was sold to *Kotka Line* of Finland, renamed the KOTKA LILY and used on their services between Finland, UK and West Africa. In 1985 she was chartered to *Jahre Line* of Norway, renamed the JALINA and operated freight services between Oslo and Kiel. Two years later, she returned to Baltic waters, being chartered to *Finncarriers* and renamed the FINNROVER. In 1988 she was chartered to *Kent Line*, renamed the SEAHORSE and used on their Dartford - Zeebrugge service. In 1991 she was chartered to *DFDS* and in 1992 she was renamed the DANA CORONA. She was initially used on the service between Immingham and Cuxhaven (Germany) but in 1995 she was transferred to the Fredericia - Copenhagen - Klaìpeda (Lithuania) service. In 2001 the charter was ended and she returned to her owners, being renamed the SEA CORONA. She was chartered to *Scandlines AG* and placed on the *Scandlines Balticum Seaways* Århus - Aabenraa - Klaìpeda route. In 2007 sold to *Cs & Partners* of Denmark; *Scandlines* charter continued.

TYCHO BRAHE Train/vehicle ferry, built by Tangen Verft A/S, Tomrefjord, Norway for *DSB* for the Helsingør - Helsingborg service.

URD Built by Nouvi Cantieri Aquania SpA, Venice, Italy as the EASY RIDER, a ro-ro freight ferry, for *Delpa Maritime* of Greece and used on Mediterranean services. In 1985 she was acquired by *Sealink British Ferries* and renamed the SEAFREIGHT HIGHWAY to operate a freight-only service between Dover and Dunkerque. In 1988 she was sold to *SOMAT* of Bulgaria for use on *Medlink* services in the Mediterranean and renamed the BOYANA. In 1990 she was sold to *Blæsbjerg* of Denmark, renamed the AKTIV MARINE and chartered to *DSB*. In 1991 she was converted into a ro-pax vessel, renamed the URD and introduced onto the Århus - Kalundborg service. Purchased by *Scandlines* in 1997. Withdrawn at the end of May 1999 and, after modification, transferred to the *Balticum Seaways* (later *Scandlines Balticum Seaways*) Århus - Aabenraa - Klaìpeda route. In 2001 lengthened and moved to the Rostock - Liepaja route. In Autumn 2005 this route became Rostock - Ventspils.

SCANDLINES (SWEDEN)

THE COMPANY *Scandlines AB* (formerly *SweFerry*) is a Swedish company, a subsidiary of *Stena Line Scandinavia AB* of Sweden.

MANAGEMENT Managing Director Gunnar Blomdahl.

ADDRESS Knutpunkten 43, 252 78 Helsingborg, Sweden.

TELEPHONE Administration + 46 (0)42-18 60 00, **Reservations *Helsingborg*** + 46 (0)42-18 61 00, ***Trelleborg*** + 46 (0)410-65 000.

FAX Administration + 46 (0)42-18 60 49, **Reservations *Helsingborg*** + 46 (0)42-18 61 87, ***Trelleborg*** + 46 (0)410-65 001.

INTERNET Email kundservice@scandlines.se **Website** www.scandlines.se (*Swedish, English*)

ROUTES OPERATED Conventional Ferries Helsingborg (Sweden) - Helsingør (Denmark) (25 mins; *1*; every 20 mins), Trelleborg (Sweden) - Rostock (Germany) (6 hrs; *3*; 4 per day), Trelleborg - Sassnitz (Germany) (3 hrs 30 mins; *4*; 3 per day), Trelleborg (Sweden) - Travemünde (Germany) (8 hrs; *2*; 1 per day - freight-only). All routes are joint with *Scandlines GmbH* except Trelleborg - Travemünde.

1	AURORA AF HELSINGBORG	10918t	92	14.0k	111.2m	1250P	225C	25Lr	BA	SE	9007128
2	GÖTALAND	18060t	73	17.0k	183.1m	400P	230C	102Tr	AS2	SE	7229514
3	SKÅNE	42705t	98	21.0k	200.2m	600P	520C	240Tr	AS2	SE	9133915
4	TRELLEBORG	20028t	82	21.0k	170.2m	900P	200C	90Tr	A2	SE	7925297

AURORA AF HELSINGBORG Train/vehicle ferry built by Langsten Verft A/S, Tomrefjord, Norway for *SweFerry* for *ScandLines* joint *DSB/SweFerry* service between Helsingør and Helsingborg. Now owned by *Scandlines AB* (previously leased from finance company).

GÖTALAND Train/vehicle ferry built by A/S Nakskov Skibsværft, Nakskov, Denmark for *Statens Järnvägar (Swedish State Railways)* for freight services between Trelleborg and Sassnitz. In 1990 transferred to *SweFerry*. In 1992 modified to increase passenger capacity in order to run in passenger service. She was on the Trelleborg - Rostock service until Autumn 1998 when she was replaced by the SKÅNE. She then inaugurated a new freight-only Trelleborg - Travemünde service.

SKÅNE Train/vehicle ferry built by Astilleros Españoles, Cadiz, Spain for an American trust and chartered to *Scandlines*. She is used on the Trelleborg - Rostock service.

TRELLEBORG Train/vehicle ferry built by Öresundsvarvet AB, Landskrona, Sweden for *Svelast* of Sweden (an *SJ* subsidiary). In 1990 ownership transferred to *SweFerry*. She is used on the Trelleborg - Sassnitz service.

SCF DFDS LINE

THE COMPANY *SCF DFDS Line* (previously *SCF St Petersburg Line*) is a joint venture between *DFDS* and *Sovcomflot* of Russia. Although the ships used are basically freighters, they market themselves as a passenger as well as freight line. *DFDS Tor Line* market the service as 'Nevabridge'.

MANAGEMENT Managing Director Alexander I Dashkov.

ADDRESS 122. 63, Zhukovskogo Str, St Petersburg, 193036, Russian Federation.

TELEPHONE + 7 (812) 324-7260.

FAX + 7 (812) 324-7263.

INTERNET Email info@scflines.com **Website** www.scflines.com *(English, Russian, German)*

ROUTE OPERATED St Petersburg (Russia) - Kiel (Germany) (61 hours; *1,2*; 2 per week).

1	AEGEAN SKY	13436t	74	18.5k	136.8m	12P	-	92T	A	VC	7369039
2	TOR BALTICA	14374t	78	18.5k	163.6m	12P	-	184T	A	BZ	7528594

AEGEAN SKY Built by Framnæs Mekaniske Verksted, Sandefjord, Norway as the TOR FINLANDIA for *Tor Line* of Sweden and operated on North Sea Services. In 1977 she was lengthened by 26.7m. In 1980 she was sold to *Rederi AB Salénia* of Sweden and from 1981 onwards she undertook many charters including *Fred. Olsen Lines*, *Bore Line* and *Tor Line*. In 1984 she was sold to *Salen Dry Cargo AB*, of Sweden and renamed the BALTIC WASA. Later that year she was sold to *Romulus Ltd* of the Cayman Island, renamed the OCEAN LINK and chartered to *Grimaldi Line* of Italy. In 1987 chartered to *Transfennica*. In 1992 sold to *Sea-Link AB* of Sweden and in 1992 to *Oosterems BV* of the Netherlands and renamed the ASSI SCAN LINK. For several years she operated from Piteå in Sweden to Chatham (UK) and other European destinations for *Kappa Packaging*. In 2004 replaced on that service by the BALTICBORG (see Section 3) and sold to *Gorthon International Shipping* and renamed the ACACIA. In 2006 sold to Greek owned *Crystalline Oeanway SA* of St Vincent and the Grenadines. In 2007 renamed the AEGEAN SKY and chartered to *SCF DFDS Line*.

TOR BALTICA Built by Hyundai Heavy Industries, Ulsan, South Korea as the ELK for *Stena Rederi* of Sweden and chartered to *P&O Ferrymasters* for use on services from Middlesbrough to Gothenburg and Helsingborg. Purchased by *P&O* in 1981 and lengthened in 1986; she was managed by *P&O North Sea Ferries Ltd*. In 2001 she was sold to *DFDS Tor Line*, who took over management of the vessel. *P&O Ferrymasters'* services ceased in May 2001. She was renamed the TOR BALTICA and transferred to the *DFDS Tor Line* Gothenburg - Harwich route. In 2005 briefly transferred to the new Immingham – Zeebrugge route before moving to the Fredericia – Copenhagen - Klaìpeda service. In June 2005 moved to the Norway - Immingham service. Later moved to the joint *DFDS Tor Line/SCF St Petersburg Line* (now *SCF DFDS Line*) service between Kiel and St Petersburg.

Stena Jutlandica (*Miles Cowsill*)

Stena Carisma (*Miles Cowsill*)

STENA LINE

THE COMPANY *Stena Line Scandinavia AB* is a Swedish private sector company.

MANAGEMENT Managing Director & Chief Operational Officer Gunnar Blomdahl, **Ship Management Director** Robert Åuerlund, **Communication Director** Joakim Kenndal.

ADDRESS 405 19 Gothenburg, Sweden (*Visitors' address* Danmarksterminalen, Masthuggskajen).

TELEPHONE Administration + 46 (0)31-85 80 00, **Reservations** + 46 (0)31-704 00 00.

FAX Administration & Reservations + 46 (0)31-24 10 38.

INTERNET Email info@stenaline.com **Website** www.stenaline.com (*Danish, Dutch, English, French, German, Norwegian, Polish, Swedish*)

ROUTES OPERATED Conventional Ferries Gothenburg (Sweden) - Frederikshavn (Denmark) (3 hrs 15 mins; *5,8*; up to 6 per day), Gothenburg - Kiel (Germany) (14 hrs; *7,12*; 1 per day), Frederikshavn - Oslo (Norway) (8 hrs 45 mins; *11*; 1 per day), Varberg (Sweden) - Grenaa (Denmark) (4 hrs; *9*; 2 per day), Karlskrona (Sweden) - Gdynia (Poland) (10 hrs 30 mins; *1,2,10*; 3 per day). **Fast Ferry** Gothenburg - Frederikshavn (2 hrs; *3*; 4 per day). **Freight Ferries** Gothenburg - Frederikshavn (Train Ferry) (3 hrs 45 mins; *13*; 2 per day), Gothenburg - Travemünde (15 hrs; *4,6*; 1 per day).

1	FINNARROW	25996t	96	21.0k	168.0m	200P	800C	154T	BA2	SE	9010814
2	STENA BALTICA	31910t	86	20.0k	161.8m	1800P	500C	45T	BA2	BS	8416308
3»	STENA CARISMA	8631t	97	40.0k	88.0m	900P	210C	-	A	SE	9127760
4F	STENA CARRIER	21089t	04	22.0k	182.6m	12P	-	200T	A	SE	9138800
5	STENA DANICA	28727t	83	19.5k	154.9m	2274P	555C	120T	BAS2	SE	7907245
6F	STENA FREIGHTER	21104t	04	22.0k	182.6m	12P	-	200T	A	SE	9138795
7	STENA GERMANICA	39178t	87	20.0k	175.4m	2400P	550C	120T	BAS2	SE	7907659
8	STENA JUTLANDICA	29691t	96	21.5k	183.7m	1500P	550C	156T	BAS2	SE	9125944
9	STENA NAUTICA	19504t	86	19.4k	134.0m	700P	330C	70T	BA2	SE	8317954
10	STENA NORDICA	24206t	01	25.0k	169.8m	405P	375C	122T	BA2	SE	9215505
11	STENA SAGA	33750t	81	22.0k	166.1m	2000P	510C	76T	BA	SE	7911545
12	STENA SCANDINAVICA	39169t	88	20.0k	175.4m	2400P	550C	120T	BAS2	SE	7907661
13F	STENA SCANRAIL	7504t	73	16.5k	142.4m	65P	-	64Tr	A	SE	7305772

FINNARROW Built by Pt Dok Kodja Bahri, Kodja, Indonesia as the GOTLAND for *Rederi AB Gotland* for charter. In 1997 briefly chartered to *Tor Line* and then to *Nordic Trucker Line*, to operate between Oxelösund and St Petersburg (a ro-ro service). In June 1997 she was chartered to *SeaWind Line*, enabling a twice-daily passenger service to be operated. In late 1997 she was sold to *Finnlines* and renamed the FINNARROW. She started operating twice weekly between Helsinki and Travemünde. During Summer 1998 she was transferred to *FinnLink*; a bow door was fitted and she was modified to allow for two-level loading. In 2003 transferred to *Nordö Link*. In 2005 returned to *FinnLink*. In 2006 transferred to *Finnlines Nordö Link* again. In 2007 chartered to *Stena Line* to operate between Karlskrona and Gdynia as third vessel.

STENA BALTICA Built by Van der Giessen-de Noord, Krimpen aan den IJssel, Rotterdam, The Netherlands as the KONINGIN BEATRIX for *Stoomvaart Maatschappij Zeeland* of The Netherlands for their Hook of Holland - Harwich service (trading as *Crown Line*). In 1989 transferred to *Stena Line BV*. In June 1997 chartered by *Stena Line BV* to *Stena Line Ltd* and used on the Fishguard - Rosslare service. In August 1997 transferred to the British flag. In 2002 renamed the STENA BALTICA and transferred to the Karlskrona - Gdynia service. In Spring 2005 rebuilt to increase freight capacity. In 2006 replaced by the EUROPALINK and initially chartered to *Scandlines* for a few weeks. She was then chartered to *Stena Line* to operate between Karlskrona and Gdynia.

STENA CARISMA Westamarin HSS 900 craft built at Kristiansand, Norway for *Stena Line* for the Gothenburg - Frederikshavn service. Work on a sister vessel, approximately 30% completed, was ceased.

Stena Danica *(Miles Cowsill)*

Stena Freighter *(Miles Cowsill)*

STENA CARRIER Laid down in 1998 by Societa Esercizio Cantieri SpA, Viareggio, Italy for *Stena RoRo*. In 1999 the builders went bankrupt and work ceased. The hull was purchased by *Enrico Bugazzi Shipmanagement*, named the ARONTE and in 2003 she was towed to Marina di Carrara, Italy for work to be completed. In 2003 she was sold to *Stena RoRo*; in 2004 she was transferred to *Stena Line* and was renamed the STENA CARRIER II. After further work at Gothenburg she entered service on the Gothenburg - Travemünde route. She was later renamed the STENA CARRIER.

STENA DANICA Built by Chantiers du Nord et de la Méditerranée, Dunkerque, France for *Stena Line* for the Gothenburg - Frederikshavn service.

STENA FREIGHTER Laid down in 1998 by Societa Esercizio Cantieri SpA, Viareggio, Italy for *Stena RoRo*. Due to be called the SEA CHIEFTAIN for charter to the *British MoD*. In 1999 the builders went bankrupt and work ceased. In 2003 the incomplete vessel was purchased at auction by a *Stena* subsidiary, she was renamed the STENA SEAFREIGHTER and towed to Kraljevica, Croatia for work to be completed. In 2004 she was renamed the STENA FREIGHTER and entered service with *Stena Line* between Gothenburg and Travemünde.

STENA GERMANICA, STENA SCANDINAVICA Built by Stocznia i Komuni Paryski, Gdynia, Poland (STENA GERMANICA) and Stocznia im Lenina, Gdansk, Poland (STENA SCANDINAVICA) for *Stena Line* for the Gothenburg - Kiel service. Names were swapped during construction in order that the STENA GERMANICA should enter service first. There were originally intended to be four vessels. Only two were delivered to *Stena Line*. The third (due to be called the STENA POLONICA) was sold by the builders as an unfinished hull to *Fred. Olsen Lines* of Norway and then resold to *ANEK* of Greece who had her completed at Perama and delivered as EL VENIZELOS for service between Greece and Italy. The fourth hull (due to be called the STENA BALTICA) was sold to *A Lelakis* of Greece and was to be rebuilt as a cruise ship to be called REGENT SKY; however, the project was never completed. She was broken up in 2004. During the summer period on some days, the vessel arriving in Gothenburg overnight from Kiel operates a round trip to Frederikshavn before departing for Kiel the following evening. During Winter 1998/99 they were modified to increase freight capacity and reduce the number of cabins.

STENA JUTLANDICA Train/vehicle 'ro-pax' vessel built by Van der Giessen-de Noord, Krimpen aan den IJssel, Rotterdam, The Netherlands for *Stena Line* to operate between Gothenburg and Frederikshavn. She was launched as the STENA JUTLANDICA III and renamed on entry into service.

STENA NAUTICA Built by Nakskov Skibsværft A/S, Nakskov, Denmark as the NIELS KLIM for *DSB (Danish State Railways)* for their service between Århus (Jutland) and Kalundborg (Sealand). In 1990 she was purchased by *Stena Rederi* of Sweden and renamed the STENA NAUTICA. In 1992 she was chartered to *B&I Line*, renamed the ISLE OF INNISFREE and introduced onto the Rosslare - Pembroke Dock service, replacing the MUNSTER (8093t, 1970). In 1993 she was transferred to the Dublin - Holyhead service. In early 1995 she was chartered to *Lion Ferry*. She was renamed the LION KING. In 1996 she was replaced by a new LION KING and renamed the STENA NAUTICA. During Summer 1996 she was chartered to *Trasmediterranea* of Spain but returned to *Stena RoRo* in the autumn and remained laid up during 1997. In December 1997 she was chartered to *Stena Line* and placed on the Halmstad - Grenaa route. This route ended on 31st January 1999 and she was transferred to the Varberg - Grenaa route. During Winter 2001/02 rebuilt to heighten the upper vehicle deck and allow separate loading of load vehicle decks; passenger capacity reduced. On 16th February 2004 she was hit by the coaster JOANNA and holed. Returned to service at the end of May 2004 after repairs at Gothenburg and Gdansk.

STENA NORDICA Built by Mitsubishi Heavy Industries, Shimonoeki, Japan as the EUROPEAN AMBASSADOR for *P&O Irish Sea* for the Liverpool - Dublin service. Service transferred to Mostyn in November 2001. Also operated between Dublin and Cherbourg once a week. In 2004 the Mostyn route closed and she was sold to *Stena RoRo*. Chartered to *Stena Line* to operate between Karlskrona and Gdynia and renamed the STENA NORDICA.

STENA SAGA Built by Oy Wärtsilä Ab, Turku, Finland as the SILVIA REGINA for *Stockholms Rederi AB Svea* of Sweden. She was registered with subsidiary company *Svea Line* of Turku, Finland and was used on *Silja Line* services between Stockholm and Helsinki. In 1981 she was sold to *Johnson Line* and in 1984 sold to a Finnish Bank and chartered back. In 1990 she was purchased by *Stena RoRo* of

Sweden for delivery in 1991. In 1991 she was renamed the STENA BRITANNICA and took up service on the Hook of Holland - Harwich service for Dutch subsidiary *Stena Line bv*, operating with a British crew. In 1994 she was transferred to *Stena Line's* Oslo - Frederikshavn route and renamed the STENA SAGA. During Winter 2002/03 rebuilt to increase passenger capacity by 200.

STENA SCANRAIL Built by Van der Giessen-de Noord, Krimpen aan den IJssel, Rotterdam, The Netherlands. Launched as the STENA SEATRADER for *Stena AB* and entered service as the SEATRADER. In 1976 she was lengthened and then demise-chartered to *Bahjah Navigation* of Cyprus and renamed the BAHJAN. In 1981 the charter ended and she was renamed the STENA SEARIDER. In 1983 chartered to *Snowdrop Shipping* of Cyprus and renamed the SEARIDER. The charter ended the following year and she resumed the name STENA SEARIDER. Later in 1984 she was renamed the TRUCKER and in 1985 again reverted to the name STENA SEARIDER. In 1987 she was converted to a train ferry to operate between Gothenburg and Frederikshavn, chartered to *Stena Line* and renamed the STENA SCANRAIL.

STRANDFARASKIP LANDSINS

THE COMPANY *Strandfaraskip Landsins* is owned by the Faroe Islands Government.

ADDRESS Yviri við strond 4, Postboks 88 - FO-110, Tórshavn, Faroe Islands.

TELEPHONE Administration + 298 34 30 30, **Reservations** + 298 34 30 00.

FAX Administration & Reservations + 298 34 30 01.

INTERNET Email ssl@ssl.fo **Website** www.ssl.fo *(Faroese)*

ROUTES OPERATED *Passenger and Car Ferries* Tórshavn (Streymoy) - Tvøroyri (Suduroy) (1 hr 50 mins; *5*; up to 2 per day), Klaksvík - Syòradali (20 min; *3*; up to 6 per day), Leirvik - Syòradali (20 mins; *3*; up to 4 per day), Skopun – Gamlarætt (30 mins; *7*; up to 9 per day), *Passenger-only Ferries* Sørvágur - Mykines (1 hr 15 mins; *6*; up to 3 per day), Hvannasun - Svínoy (40 mins) - Kirkja (20 mins) - Hatlarvik (10 mins) - Svínoy (30 mins; *1*; up to 4 per day), Sandur - Skúvoy (35 mins; *4*; up to 5 per day), Tórshavn - Nólsoy (25 mins; *2*; up to 5 per day).

1p	MÁSIN	39t	59	-	15.9m	63P	0C	0L	-	FA	
2p	RITAN	81t	71	10.5k	22.1m	125P	0C	0L	-	FA	
3	SAM	217t	75	9.7k	30.2m	115P	17C	-	A	FA	7602168
4p	SILDBERIN	34t	79	7.5k	11.2m	30P	0C	0L	-	FA	
5	SMYRIL	12670t	05	21.0k	135.0m	975P	200C	32L	A	FA	9275218
6p	SÚLAN	11t	87	-	12.0m	40P	0C	0L	-	FA	
7	TEISTIN	1260t	01	11.0k	45.0m	288P	33C	2L	BA	FA	9226102
8	TERNAN	927t	80	12.0k	39.7m	319P	0C	0L	BA	FA	7947154

MÁSIN Built by Tórshavnar Skipasmidja P/f, Tórshavn. Used on the Hvannasun - Svínoy - Kirkja – Hatlarvik - Svínoy route.

RITAN Built by Monnickenda, Volendam, The Netherlands. Used on the Tórshavn - Nólsoy service.

SAM Built by Blaalid Slip & Mek Verksted, Raudeberg, Norway.

SILDBERIN Built at Tvøroyri, Faroe Islands. Used on the Sandur - Skúvoy route.

SMYRIL Built by IZAR, San Fernando, Spain for *Strandfaraskip Landsins*. Operates on the Tórshavn – Tvøroyri service.

SÚLAN Built by Faaborg Værft A/S, Faaborg, Denmark. Used on the Sørvágur - Mykines service.

TEISTIN Built by P/F Skipasmidjan a Skala, Skala, Faroe Islands for *Strandfaraskip Landsins*. Used on the Skopun – Gamlarætt service.

TERNAN Built by Tórshavnar Skipasmidja P/f, Tórshavn, Faroe Islands for *Strandfaraskip Landsins*. Now a spare vessel.

SUPERSEACAT

THE COMPANY *SuperSeaCat* is the trading name of *Sea Containers Finland Oy* of Finland. Until 2006 the company operated as part of *Silja Line* but was not included in the sale of *Silja Line* to *Tallink*. 50% of the company was purchased by *Eugenides Group* of Greece in 2008, the remaining 50% being owned by *Sea Containers*.

MANAGEMENT Managing Director Peter C Walker.

ADDRESS Sea Containers Finland Oy: Makasiiniterminaali M4, Eteläsatama, 00140 Helsinki, Finland.

TELEPHONE Administration + 358 (0)40 50555522 **Reservations** + 372 (0)610 0000.

FAX Administration & Reservations + 372 (0)610 0011.

INTERNET Email: booking.tallinn@superseacat.com **Website:** www.superseacat.com *(English, Finnish, Estonian)*

ROUTE OPERATED Helsinki - Tallinn (1 hr 40 mins; *1,2*; up to 8 per day).

1»	**SUPERSEACAT THREE**	4697t	99	38.0k	100.0m	800P	175C	-	A	IT	9141871
2»	**SUPERSEACAT FOUR**	4697t	99	38.0k	100.0m	752P	164C	-	A	IT	9141883

SUPERSEACAT THREE Fincantieri MDV1200 monohull vessel built at La Spézia, Italy. In 1999 sailed on the Liverpool - Dublin service, operated by *Sea Containers Ferries Scotland*, replacing the SUPERSEACAT TWO. In 2000 she also operated on the Liverpool - Douglas service. In Summer 2001 she operated between Dover and Calais and Dover and Ostend; in Summer 2002 she operated from Liverpool to Dublin and Douglas. In 2003 she was transferred to the Helsinki – Tallinn service under the *Silja Line* branding. She operates on the route during the ice-free season.

SUPERSEACAT FOUR Fincantieri MDV1200 monohull vessel built at Riva Trigoso, Italy. Laid-up following delivery. In 2000 transferred to an Estonian subsidiary of *Sea Containers* to operate between Helsinki and Tallinn under *Silja Line* branding. She operates on the route during the ice-free season.

SYDFYENSKE A/S

THE COMPANY *Sydfyenske A/S* (formerly *Scandlines Sydfyenske A/S)* is a Danish private sector company owned by the *Clipper Group*. It was purchased from *Scandlines Danmark A/S* in 2007. It is managed by *Bornholmstrafikken*.

MANAGEMENT Managing Director Mads Kofod (*Nordic Ferry Services A/S*).

ADDRESSES Dampskibskajen 3, DK - 3700 Rønne, Denmark.

TELEPHONE Administration and Bookings + 45 56 95 18 66.

FAX Administration and Bookings + 45 56 95 57 66.

INTERNET www.alstrafikken.dk   www.fanoetrafikken.dk   www.langelandstrafikken.dk *(Danish)*

ROUTES OPERATED *Alstrafikken* Fynshav (Als) - Bøjden (Fyn) (50 mins; *7*; 6-8 per day), *Fanøtrafikken* Esbjerg (Jutland) - Nordby (Fanø) (12 mins; *1,3,5*; every 20-40 mins), *Langelandstrafikken* Spodsbjerg (Langeland) - Tårs (Lolland) (45 mins; *2,4,6*; hourly).

1	**FENJA**	751t	98	11.5k	49.9m	396P	34C	4L	BA	DK	9189378
2	**FRIGG SYDFYEN**	1676t	84	13.5k	70.1m	338P	50C	8L	DA	DK	0222824
3	**MENJA**	751t	98	11.5k	49.9m	396P	34C	4L	BA	DK	9189380
4	**ODIN SYDFYEN**	1698t	82	12.5k	70.4m	338P	50C	8L	BA	DK	8027896
5p	**SØNDERHO**	93t	62	10.0k	26.3m	163P	0C	0L	-	DK	
6	**SPODSBJERG**	958t	72	12.0k	67.3m	225P	50C	9L	BA	DK	7204394
7	**THOR SYDFYEN**	1479t	78	12.0k	71.0m	292P	50C	9L	BA	DK	7707475

FENJA Vehicle ferry built by Morsø Værft A/S, Nykøbing Mors, Denmark for *Scandlines Sydfyenske A/S* for the Esbjerg - Nordby service.

FRIGG SYDFYEN Vehicle ferry built by Svendborg Skibsværft A/S, Svendborg, Denmark for *Sydfyenske Dampskibsselskab (SFDS)* of Denmark for the service between Spodsbjerg and Tårs.

MENJA Built by Morsø Værft A/S, Nykøbing Mors, Denmark for *Scandlines Sydfyenske A/S* for the Esbjerg - Nordby service.

ODIN SYDFYEN Vehicle ferry built by A/S, Svendborg Skibsværft, Svendborg, Denmark for *Sydfyenske Dampskibsselskab (SFDS)* of Denmark for the service between Spodsbjerg and Tårs.

SØNDERHO Passenger-only ferry built by Esbjerg Jernstøberi & Maskinfabrik A/S, Esbjerg, Denmark for *Post & Telegrafvæsenet* (Danish Post Office). In 1977 taken over by *DSB*. Used on extra peak sailings and late night and early morning sailings between Esbjerg and Nordby.

SPODSBJERG Vehicle ferry built by Husumer Schiffswerft AG, Husum, Denmark as the ÆRØ-PILEN for *Øernes D/S* of Denmark for services to the island of Ærø. In 1974 sold to *Sydfyenske Dampskibsselskab (SFDS)* for the service between Spodsbjerg and Tårs.

THOR SYDFYEN Vehicle ferry built by Dannebrog Værft A/S, Århus, Denmark for *Sydfyenske Dampskibsselskab (SFDS)* of Denmark for the service between Spodsbjerg and Tårs. In 1998 (under *Scandlines Sydfynske A/S* management) she was transferred to the Fynshav - Bøjden route.

TALLINK/SILJA LINE

THE COMPANY *AS Tallink Grupp* is an Estonian private sector company. *Tallink Silja Oy* is a Finnish subsidiary, *Tallink Silja AB* is a Swedish subsidiary.

MANAGEMENT AS Tallink Grupp: Chairman of Management Board Enn Pant, *Tallink Silja Oy:* **Managing Director** Keijo Mehtonen, *Tallink Silja AB:* **Managing Director** Kadri Land.

ADDRESSES AS Tallink Grupp: Tartu mnt 13, 10145 Tallinn, Estonia, *Tallink Silja Oy:* P.O. Box 43, 02151 Espoo, Finland, *Tallink Silja AB:* Box 27295, 10253 Stockholm, Sweden.

TELEPHONE AS Tallink Grupp: + 372 (0)640 9800, *Tallink Silja Oy:* **Administration** + 358 (0)9 18041, **Reservations** + 358 (0)600 174552 and + 358 (0)600 15700, *Tallink Silja AB:* **Administration** + 46 (0)8 6663330, **Reservations** + 46 (0)8 222140.

FAX AS Tallink Grupp: Administration + 372 (0)640 9810, *Tallink Silja Oy:* **Administration** + 358 (0)9 1804484, *Tallink Silja AB:* **Administration** + 46 (0) 8 7823982.

INTERNET www.tallinksilja.com (*English, Estonian, Finnish, German, Swedish, Latvian*), www.tallink.com (corporate site)

ROUTES OPERATED Tallink branded services Helsinki - Tallinn: **Shuttle** (2 hrs; *11,15*; 5 per day), *Day Cruise Ferries* (2 hrs 30 mins; *12,13,14*; 1 per day), *22-Hour Cruise Ferry* (3 hrs 30 mins; *1*; 1 per day), Stockholm - Långnäs (Åland) - Tallinn (14 hrs; *5,18*; daily), Stockholm - Riga (Latvia) (16 hrs; *4,17*; daily), Helsinki - Rostock (Germany) (24 hrs; *12,13,145*; 1 per day) (**Note:** timetable will change in October 2008 when the SUPERFAST IX leaves the fleet), *Freight-only Ferries* Kapellskär - Paldiski (9 hrs - 11 hrs; *2,3*; 1 per day).

Silja Line branded services Helsinki (Finland) - Mariehamn (Åland) - Stockholm (Sweden) (16 hrs; *9,10*; 1 per day), Turku (Finland) - Mariehamn (Åland) (day)/Långnäs (Åland) (night) - Stockholm (11 hrs; *7,8,*; 2 per day).

SeaWind Line branded service *Freight-only Ferry* Stockholm (Sweden) - Långnäs (Åland) - Turku (Finland) (10 hrs 45 mins; *6*; 1 per day).

1	GALAXY	48915t	06	22.0k	212.0m	2800P	300C	82T	BA	EE	9333694
2F	KAPELLA	7564t	74	14.5k	110.1m	50P	-	42T	A	EE	7369118
3F	REGAL STAR	15281t	00	17.5k	156.6m	100P	-	-	A	EE	9087116
4	REGINA BALTICA	18345t	80	21.3k	145.2m	1450P	500C	68T	BA	LV	7827225
5	ROMANTIKA	40803t	02	22.0k	193.8m	2178P	300C	82T	BA	EE	9237589

Victoria I *(Miles Cowsill)*

Silja Festival *(Miles Cowsill)*

6F	SEA WIND	15879t	72	17.5k	154.4m	260P	55C	88Tr	BAS	SE	7128332
7	SILJA EUROPA	59912t	93	21.5k	201.8m	3000P	400C	68T	BA	FI	8919805
8	SILJA FESTIVAL	34414t	85	22.0k	170.7m	2000P	400C	80T	BA	SE	8306498
9	SILJA SERENADE	58376t	90	21.0k	203.0m	2641P	450C	70T	BA	FI	8715259
10	SILJA SYMPHONY	58377t	91	21.0k	203.0m	2641P	450C	70T	BA	SE	8803769
11	STAR	36249t	07	27.5k	185.0m	1900P	450C	120L	BA	EE	9364722
12	SUPERFAST VII	30285t	01	27.9k	203.3m	717P	695C	110L	BA2	EE	9198941
13	SUPERFAST VIII	30285t	01	27.9k	203.3m	717P	695C	110L	BA2	EE	9198953
14	SUPERFAST IX	30285t	02	27.9k	203.3m	728P	695C	110L	BA2	EE	9211509
15	SUPERSTAR	36000t	08	29.0k	175.0m	1800P	600C	140T	BA	EE	9365398
16»	TALLINK AUTOEXPRESS	25419t	97	37.0k	82.3m	700P	175C	-	A	EE	9150286
17	VANA TALLINN	10002t	74	18.0k	153.7m	1500P	300C	44L	BAS	LV	7329522
18	VICTORIA I	40975t	04	22.0k	193.8m	2500P	300C	823T	BA	EE	9281281

GALAXY Built by Aker Yards, Rauma, Finland to operate as a cruise ferry on the Tallinn - Helsinki route. In Autumn 2008 to be transferred to the Stockholm - Turku route and rebranded as a *Silja Line* vessel.

KAPELLA Built by Kristiansands Mekaniske Verksted, Kristiansand, Norway for *A/S Larvik-Frederikshavnferjen* of Norway as DUKE OF YORKSHIRE. In 1978 she was chartered to (and later purchased by) *CN Marine* of Canada (from 1986 *Marine Atlantic*) and renamed the MARINE EVANGELINE. She was used on services between Canada, USA and Newfoundland. In 1992 she was chartered to *Opale Ferries* of France and inaugurated a new Boulogne - Folkestone freight service. In 1993 the company went into liquidation and the service and charter were taken over by *Meridian Ferries*, a British company. She was renamed the SPIRIT OF BOULOGNE. In Spring 1995, *Meridian Ferries* went into liquidation and she returned to her owners, resuming the name MARINE EVANGELINE. After a period of lay-up she was chartered to *Stena Sealink Line*. She spent the summer on the Newhaven - Dieppe service and was then transferred to the Stranraer - Larne (from November 1995 Stranraer - Belfast) route. She returned to Newhaven in Summer 1996 but was laid up during most of 1997. In late 1997 she was chartered to *Tallink* and inaugurated a new ro-pax service between Paldiski and Kapellskär. She was renamed the KAPELLA. In 2004 transferred to the Helsinki – Tallinn route. In 2006, she was temporarily back to the Paldiski – Kapellskär service, replacing the REGAL STAR. In 2007 she returned to the Helsinki – Tallinn route but later returned to the Paldiski route; now operates only night sailings.

REGAL STAR Initially built by Sudostroitelnyy Zavod Severnaya Verf, St Petersburg. Work started in 1993 (as a deep sea ro-ro) but was never completed. In 1999 the vessel was purchased, taken to Palumba SpA, Naples and completed as a short-sea ro-ro with accommodation for 80 drivers. In 2000 she was delivered to *MCL* of Italy and placed on a route between Savona and Catania. In September of that year she was chartered to *Grimaldi Ferries* and operated on a route Salerno – Palermo – Valencia. In late 2003 she was sold to *Hansatee Shipping* of Estonia and, in 2004, placed on the Kapellskär – Paldiski route, replacing the KAPELLA. From February 2006 she was transferred to the Helsinki – Tallinn service, replacing the KAPELLA due to the hard ice conditions. She continued in this service for the summer, but is now back in Paldiski – Kapellskär service.

REGINA BALTICA Built by Oy Wärtsilä Ab, Turku, Finland as the VIKING SONG for *Rederi AB Sally* of Finland and used on the *Viking Line* service between Stockholm and Helsinki. In 1985 replaced by the MARIELLA of *SF Line* and sold to *Fred. Olsen Lines*. She was named BRAEMAR and used on services between Norway and Britain as well as Norway and Denmark. Services to Britain ceased in June 1990 and she continued to operate between Norway and Denmark. She was withdrawn in 1991 and sold to *Rigorous Shipping* of Cyprus (a subsidiary of *Fred. Olsen Lines*). She was chartered to the *Baltic Shipping Company* of Russia, renamed the ANNA KARENINA and inaugurated a service between Kiel and St Petersburg. In 1992 a Nynäshamn call was introduced. In 1996 the service ceased and she was returned to her owners and renamed the ANNA K. Later in 1996 she was sold to *Empremare Shipping Co Ltd* of Cyprus (a company jointly owned by *Nordström & Thulin* and *Estonian Shipping Company*), chartered to *EstLine* and renamed the REGINA BALTICA. In 2000 the charter transferred to *Tallink*; she continued to operate between Stockholm and Tallinn. Purchased by *Tallink* in 2002. In

May 2006 replaced by the ROMANTIKA and succeeded the FANTAASIA on the Stockholm - Riga service.

ROMANTIKA Built by Aker Finnyards, Rauma, Finland for *Tallink Grupp* to operate for *Tallink* between Tallinn and Helsinki. In Spring 2006 moved to the Tallinn - Stockholm route.

SEA WIND Train/vehicle ferry built by Helsingørs Skipsværft, Helsingør, Denmark as the SVEALAND for *Stockholms Rederi AB Svea* and used on the *Trave Line* Helsingborg (Sweden) - Copenhagen (Tuborg Havn) - Travemünde freight service. In 1981 she was sold to *TT-Saga Line* and operated between Travemünde and Malmö. In 1984 she was rebuilt to increase capacity and renamed the SAGA WIND. In 1989 she was acquired by *SeaWind Line*, renamed the SEA WIND and inaugurated a combined rail freight, trailer and lower-priced passenger service between Stockholm and Turku.

SILJA EUROPA Built by Jos L Meyer, Papenburg, Germany. Ordered by *Rederi AB Slite* of Sweden for *Viking Line* service between Stockholm and Helsinki and due to be called EUROPA. In 1993, shortly before delivery was due, *Rederi AB Slite* went into liquidation and the order was cancelled. A charter agreement with her builders was then signed by *Silja Line* and she was introduced onto the Stockholm - Helsinki route as SILJA EUROPA. In early 1995 she was transferred to the Stockholm - Turku service.

SILJA FESTIVAL Built by Oy Wärtsilä Ab, Helsinki, Finland as the WELLAMO for *EFFOA* for the *Silja Line* Stockholm - Mariehamn - Turku service. In 1990, following the sale of the FINLANDIA to *DFDS*, she was transferred to the Stockholm - Helsinki service until the SILJA SERENADE was delivered later in the year. In 1991 she was renamed the SILJA FESTIVAL and during Winter 1991/92 she was extensively rebuilt and ownership was transferred to *Silja Line*. In 1993 she was transferred to the Malmö - Travemünde service of *Euroway*, which was at this time managed by *Silja Line*. This service ceased in 1994 and she was transferred to the Vaasa - Sundsvall service. In 1994 and 1995 she operated on this route during the peak summer period and on the Helsinki - Tallinn route during the rest of the year. The Vaasa - Sundsvall service did not operate in Summer 1996 and she continued to operate between Helsinki and Tallinn. In 1997 she was transferred to the Stockholm - Turku route replacing the SILJA SCANDINAVIA (see the GABRIELLA, *Viking Line*). In Autumn 2008 to be transferred to the Stockholm - Riga route.

SILJA SERENADE, SILJA SYMPHONY Built by Masa-Yards Oy, Turku, Finland for *Silja Line* for the Stockholm - Helsinki service. In 1993, SILJA SERENADE was transferred to the Stockholm - Turku service but in early 1995 she was transferred back to the Helsinki route.

STAR Built by Aker Yards, Helsinki, Finland for *Tallink* to operate as a normal ferry on the Tallinn - Helsinki route, reducing the crossing time to 2 hours.

SUPERFAST VII, SUPERFAST VIII Built by Howaldtswerke Deutsche Werft AG, Kiel, Germany for *Attica Enterprises* (now *Attica Group*) for use by *Superfast Ferries* between Rostock and Hanko. In 2006 sold to *Tallink*. They now operate to Helsinki rather than Hanko and between Helsinki and Tallinn during the day.

SUPERFAST IX Built by Howaldtswerke Deutsche Werft AG, Kiel, Germany for *Attica Enterprises* for use by *Superfast Ferries*. She operated between Rostock and Södertälje from January until April 2002. In May 2002 she began operating between Rosyth and Zeebrugge (with the SUPERFAST X). In 2004 fitted with additional cabins and conference/seating areas. In 2005 transferred to the Rostock – Hanko route. In 2006 sold to *Tallink*. She now operates to Helsinki rather than Hanko and between Helsinki and Tallinn during the day. In October 2008 to be chartered to *Marine Atlantic* of Canada to operate on the North Sydney-Port aux Basques service.

SUPERSTAR Built by Fincantieri Cantieri Navali Italiani SpA, Riva Trigoso, Italy to operate on the Tallinn - Helsinki route from May 2008.

TALLINK AUTOEXPRESS 2 Austal Ships Auto Express 82 catamaran built at Fremantle, Western Australia as the BOOMERANG for *Polferries* and used on the Swinoujscie - Malmö route. In Autumn 1999 she was withdrawn and it was anticipated that she would no longer operate for *Polferries*. However, in Summer 2000 she returned to the Swinoujscie - Malmö route. She was laid up again in the Autumn and in May 2001 was sold to *Tallink* and renamed the TALLINK AUTOEXPRESS 2. Operated between Tallinn and Helsinki. In Autumn 2007 chartered to *Consolidado de Ferrys CA* of

Venezuela.

VANA TALLINN Built by Aalborg Skipsværft A/S, Aalborg, Denmark as the DANA REGINA for *DFDS* and used on their Esbjerg - Harwich service until 1983 when she was moved to the Copenhagen - Oslo route. In 1990 she was sold to *Nordström & Thulin* of Sweden, renamed the NORD ESTONIA and used on the *EstLine* Stockholm - Tallinn service. In 1992 she was chartered to *Larvik Line* to operate as a second vessel between Larvik and Frederikshavn and renamed the THOR HEYERDAHL. In 1994 she was sold to *Inreko Ships Ltd*, chartered to *Tallink* and renamed the VANA TALLINN. In November 1996 she was withdrawn and in December 1996 she was chartered to a new company called *TH Ferries* and resumed sailings between Helsinki and Tallinn. In January 1998 she was sold to *Hansatee* subsidiary *Vana Tallinn Line Ltd* of Cyprus and placed on *Tallink* service between Helsinki and Tallinn. *TH Ferries* then ceased operations. In Autumn 2002 moved to the Paldiski - Kapellskär route, replacing the BALTIC KRISTINA. In 2007 temporarily transferred to the Tallinn - Helsinki route. In April re-registered in Latvia and placed on the Riga - Stockholm route as second ship. In Autumn 2008 to be replaced by the SILJA FESTIVAL.

VICTORIA I Built by Aker Finnyards, Rauma, Finland for *Tallink* to operate between Tallinn and Stockholm.

Under Construction

19	BALTIC PRINCESS	48300t	08	24.5k	212.0m	2800P	300C	82T	BA	EE	9354284
20	NEWBUILDING 1365	48300t	09	24.5k	212.0m	2800P	300C	82T	BA	EE	-

BALTIC PRINCESS Under construction by Aker Yards, Helsinki. A large part of the hull was built at St Nazaire, France. In Autumn 2008 due to replace the GALAXY on the Tallinn - Helsinki route.

NEWBUILDING 1365 On order from Aker Yards for delivery in Summer 2009. Use is currently uncertain; a decision will be taken at the end of 2008.

TESO

THE COMPANY *TESO* is a Dutch private company, with most shares owned by inhabitants of Texel. Its full name is *Texels Eigen Stoomboot Onderneming*.

MANAGEMENT Managing Director C H S de Waal.

ADDRESS Pontweg 1, 1797 SN Den Hoorn, Texel, The Netherlands.

TELEPHONE Administration +31 (0)222 369600, **Reservations** Not applicable.

FAX Administration +31 (0)222 369659.

INTERNET Email info@teso.nl **Website** www.teso.nl (*Dutch, English, German*)

ROUTE OPERATED Den Helder (The Netherlands) - Texel (Dutch Frisian Islands) (20 minutes; *1,2*; hourly).

1	DOKTER WAGEMAKER	13256t	05	15.6k	130.0m	1750P	320C	44L	BA2	NL	9294070
2	SCHULPENGAT	8311t	90	13.6k	110.4m	1750P	156C	25L	BA2	NL	8802313

DOKTER WAGEMAKER Built at Galatz, Romania (hull and superstructure) and Royal Schelde, Vlissingen (fitting out) for *TESO* to replace the MOLENGAT.

SCHULPENGAT Built by Verolme Scheepswerf Heusden BV, Heusden, The Netherlands for *TESO*.

TRANSRUSSIA EXPRESS

THE COMPANY *TransRussia Express* is jointly operated by *Finnlines Deutschland GmbH* of Germany (wholly owned by *Finnlines* of Finland) and *JSC Baltic Transport Systems* of Russia.

ADDRESS Einsiedelstrasse 43-45, 23554 Lübeck, Germany.

TELEPHONE Administration & Reservations + 49 (0) 451 15 070.

FAX Administration & Reservations + 49 (0) 451 15 07 139.

INTERNET Email info@finnlines.de **Website** www.tre.de (*German, English*)

ROUTE OPERATED Lübeck - Sassnitz - St Petersburg (57/60 hours; *1,2,3,4*; 4 per week). Normally only the TRANSLUBECA conveys ordinary passengers. The FINLANDIA also calls at Kotka on the southbound voyage to load traffic for *Finnlines*; this is not part of the *TransRussia Express* service.

1F	**BALTIC EAGER**	14738t	79	18.0k	137.5m	12P	-	116T	A	UK	7804065
2F	**FINLANDIA**	19524t	81	19.0k	157.5m	24P	-	164T	A	DE	8002640
3	**GLOBAL FREIGHTER**	13145t	77	18.0k	156.0m	12P	510C	124T	A	FI	7528568
4	**TRANSLUBECA**	24727t	90	20.5k	157.0m	84P	-	152T	A	GE	8706040

BALTIC EAGER Built by Rauma Repola Oy, Rauma, Finland at the BALTIC EAGLE for *United Baltic Corporation* and used on *Finanglia Ferries'* services between the UK and Finland (joint with *Finncarriers*). In 1999 chartered to *Crowley American Transport Inc* for Caribbean service. In 2002 sold to *Jay Management Corporation* of Greece and renamed the OLYMPIC STAR. Later in 2002 chartered to *Seawheel* to inaugurate a Killingholme – Rotterdam service and renamed the SEAWHEEL HUMBER. This service finished at the end of 2004. In 2005 chartered to *Finnlines*, renamed the BALTIC EAGER and placed on the *TransRussia Express* service. In 2006 chartered to *SeaRoad*. In 2007 chartered to *TransRussia Express*.

FINLANDIA Built by Flender Werft AG, Lübeck, Germany as the TRANSFINLANDIA for *Poseidon Schiffahrt OHG* of Germany (now *Finnlines Deutschland AG*) and used on *Poseidon-Finncarriers* (later *Finnlines*) service in the Baltic. In 2003 transferred to *TransRussia Express*. Later in 2003 sold to Norwegian interests and chartered back. Renamed the FINLANDIA.

GLOBAL FREIGHTER Built by Hyundai Shipbuilders & Heavy Industries, Ulsan, South Korea as the MERZARIO AUSONIA for *Stena AB*, chartered to *Merzario Line* of Italy and used on services between Italy and the Middle East. In 1981 she was renamed the STENA FREIGHTER. In 1982 she was chartered to *Ignazio Messina* of Italy and renamed the JOLLY GIALLO; later that year she was renamed the JOLLY TURCHESE. In 1983 this charter ended and she resumed the name STENA FREIGHTER. In 1988 she was transferred to *Stena Line* and placed on the Gothenburg - Travemünde service. In 2004 sold to *Lillbacka Powerco Oy* of Finland (trading as *Power Line*), renamed the GLOBAL FREIGHTER and placed on a new Turku - Travemünde service. In 2006 chartered to *Finnlines* to operate between Turku and Travemünde. In 2007 chartered to *P&O Irish Sea* for the Liverpool - Dublin service, but initially served on the Hull - Zeebrugge route. In 2008 chartered to *Finnlines* and placed on the *TransRussia Express* service.

TRANSLUBECA Built by Gdansk Shipyard, Gdansk, Poland for *Poseidon Schiffahrt OHG* of Germany and used on *Poseidon-Finncarriers* service in the Baltic. In 1999 chartered to *DFDS Tor Line* and operated between Harwich and Gothenburg. In 2001 transferred to *TransRussia Express*.

TT-LINE

THE COMPANY *TT Line GmbH & Co KG* is a German private sector company.

MANAGEMENT Managing Director Hanns Heinrich Conzen & Dr Arndt-Heinrich von Oertzen. **Sales Manager** Dirk Lifke.

ADDRESS Zum Hafenplatz 1, 23570, Travemünde, Germany.

TELEPHONE Administration *Travemünde* + 49 (0)4502 801 452, **Rostock** + 49 (0)381 6707911, **Reservations** *Travemünde* + 49 (0)4502 801 81, **Rostock** + 49 (0)381 670790.

FAX Administration & Reservations *Travemünde* + 49 (0)4502 801 407, **Rostock** + 49 (0)381 6707980.

Regina Baltica (*Miles Cowsill*)

Nils Holgersson (*FotoFlite*)

INTERNET Email info@TTLine.com **Website** www.TTLine.com (*Dutch, German, English, French, Swedish*)

ROUTES OPERATED Passenger Ferries Travemünde (Germany) - Trelleborg (Sweden) (7 hrs; *3,4*; 2 per day). **Ro-pax Ferries** Travemünde (Germany) - Trelleborg (Sweden) (7 hrs; *2,5*; 2 per day), Rostock (Germany) - Trelleborg (Sweden) (5 hrs 30 mins; *1,5*; 3 per day (*2* or *5* operate one round trip per week for freight)), Travemünde - Helsingborg (Sweden) (10 hrs; *1,5*; 1 per week). **Note:** The Travemünde - Helsingborg service is freight-only.

1	HUCKLEBERRY FINN	26391t	88	18.5k	177.2m	400P	280C	121T	BAS2	SE	8618358
2	NILS DACKE	26790t	95	21.0k	179.7m	317P	-	157T	BA	SE	9087477
3	NILS HOLGERSSON	36468t	01	22.0k	190.8m	744P	-	171T	BAS2	DE	9217230
4	PETER PAN	36468t	01	22.0k	190.8m	744P	-	171T	BAS2	SE	9217242
5	ROBIN HOOD	26796t	95	21.0k	179.7m	300P	-	157T	BA	DE	9087465
6	TOM SAWYER	26478t	89	18.5k	177.2m	400P	280C	121T	BAS2	DE	8703232

HUCKLEBERRY FINN Built by Schichau Seebeckwerft AG, Bremerhaven, Germany as the NILS DACKE, a ro-pax vessel. During Summer 1993 rebuilt to transform her into a passenger/car ferry and renamed the PETER PAN, replacing a similarly named vessel (31356t, 1986). On arrival of the new PETER PAN in Autumn 2001 she was renamed the PETER PAN IV. She was then converted back to ro-pax format, renamed the HUCKLEBERRY FINN and, in early 2002, transferred to the Rostock -Trelleborg route.

NILS DACKE, ROBIN HOOD Ro-pax vessels built by Finnyards, Rauma, Finland for *TT-Line*. Primarily freight vessels but accompanied cars - especially camper vans and cars towing caravans - are conveyed. They operate on the Travemünde - Trelleborg and Travemünde - Helsingborg routes.

NILS HOLGERSSON, PETER PAN Built by SSW Fähr und Spezialschiffbau GmbH, Bremerhaven, Germany for *TT-Line* for the Travemünde - Trelleborg route.

TOM SAWYER Built by Schichau Seebeckwerft AG, Bremerhaven, Germany as the ROBIN HOOD, a ro-pax vessel. During Winter 1992/93 rebuilt to transform her into a passenger/car ferry and renamed the NILS HOLGERSSON, replacing a similarly named vessel (31395t, 1987) which had been sold to *Brittany Ferries* and renamed the VAL DE LOIRE. In 2001 converted back to ro-pax format and renamed the TOM SAWYER. Transferred to the Rostock - Trelleborg route.

UNITY LINE

THE COMPANY *Unity Line* is a Polish company, jointly owned by *Polish Steamship Company (Polsteam)* and *Euroafrica Shipping*.

MANAGEMENT Chairman of the Board Piotr Waszczenko, **Managing Director** *vacant*.

ADDRESS 70-419 Szczecin, Plac Rodla 8, Poland.

TELEPHONE Administration + 48 (0)91 35 95 795, **Reservations** + 48 (0)91 35 95 692, (0)91 35 95 755.

FAX Administration + 48 (0)91 35 95 885, **Reservations** + 48 (0)91 35 95 673.

INTERNET Email unity@unityline.pl **Website** www.unityline.pl (*Polish, Swedish, English*)

ROUTES OPERATED Passenger Service Swinoujscie (Poland) - Ystad (Sweden) (6 hrs 30 mins (day), 9 hrs (night); *6,7*; 1 per day (2 per day from summer), **Freight Services** Swinoujscie (Poland) - Ystad (Sweden) (8 hrs (day), 9 hrs (night); *3,4*; 2 per day), Swinoujscie (Poland) - Trelleborg (Sweden) (6 hrs 30 mins (day), 9 hrs (night); *1,2,8*; 3 per day).

1F	GALILEUSZ	14398t	93	19.0k	150.4m	50P	-	130T	A	CY	9019070
2F	GRYF	18653t	91	17.0k	158.0m	120P	-	130T	BA	BS	8010300
3F	JAN SNIADECKI	14417t	88	17.0k	155.1m	12P	-	40Tr	A2	CY	8604711
4F	KOPERNIK	13788t	77	18.0k	158.6m	400P	100C	66Tr	A	PL	7527887
5F•	MIKOLAJ KOPERNIK	8734t	74	15.5k	125.6m	41P	-	20Tr	A2	PL	7336721
6	POLONIA	29875t	95	17.2k	169.9m	920P	860C	160Tr	BA	BS	9108350
7	SKANIA	23933t	95	21.9k	173.7m	1400P	830C	110L	BA	B3	9086580

8F	WOLIN	22874t	86	17.5k	188.9m	370P	-	130Tr	A	BS	8420842

GALILEUSZ Built as the VIA TIRRENO by Van der Giessen-de Nord, Krimpen aan den IJssel, The Netherlands for *Viamare di Navigazione SpA* of Italy. Initially operated between Voltri and Termini Imerese. In 1998 transferred to the Genoa - Termini Imerese route and in 2001 to the Genoa - Palermo route. In 2006 sold to *Euroafrica Shipping*, renamed the GALILEUSZ and in November introduced onto the *Unity Line* Swinoujscie - Ystad service. In February 2007 transferred to the new Swinoujscie - Trelleborg route.

GRYF Built by Fosen Mekaniske Verksteder, Fevag, Norway for *Turkish Cargo Lines* of Turkey as the KAPTAN BURHANETTIN ISIM to operate between Trieste (Italy) and Derince (Turkey). In 2002 chartered to *Latlines* to operate between Lübeck and Riga (Latvia). In 2003 chartered to *VentLines* to inaugurate a new service between Travemünde and Ventspils. In 2004 sold to *Polsteam*, chartered to *Unity Line* and renamed the GRYF. Entered service in 2005. In February 2007 transferred to the new Swinoujscie - Trelleborg route.

JAN SNIADECKI Built by Falkenbergs Varv AB, Falkenberg, Sweden for *Polish Ocean Lines* to operate between Swinoujscie and Ystad. Now operates for *Unity Line* on this route.

KOPERNIK Train/vehicle ferry built by Bergens Mekaniske Verksted A/S, Bergen, Norway as the ROSTOCK for *Deutsche Reichsbahn* of Germany (DDR). Used on freight services between Trelleborg and Sassnitz. In 1992 modified to increase passenger capacity in order to run in passenger service. In 1993 ownership transferred to *DFO* and in 1994 she opened a new service from Rostock to Trelleborg. In 1997 she was used when winds precluded the use of the new MECKLENBURG-VORPOMMERN. Following modifications to this vessel in late 1997, the ROSTOCK continued to operate to provide additional capacity until the delivery of the SKÅNE of *Scandlines AB*, after which she was laid up. In 1999 she was sold to *SeaWind Line*, renamed the STAR WIND and operated in freight-only mode between Stockholm and Turku. Initial plans to bring her passenger accommodation up to the standards required for Baltic night service were dropped. Later in 2002 replaced by the SKY WIND and transferred to the Helsinki - Tallinn route. She carried a limited number of ordinary passengers on some sailings. In May 2005 returned to the Stockholm - Turku service, no longer carrying ordinary passengers, but laid up after a few weeks. In October sold to *Euro Shipping OÜ* of Estonia, a company linked to *Saaremaa Laevakompanii* and renamed the VIRONIA. In 2006 inaugurated a new service between Sillamäe (Estonia) and Kotka (Finland). In 2007 sold to *Euroafrica Shipping*, renamed the KOPERNIK and, in 2008, placed on the Swinoujscie - Ystad route, replacing the MIKOLAJ KOPERNIK.

MIKOLAJ KOPERNIK Built by A/S Trosvik Mekaniske Verksteder, Brevik, Norway for *Polish Ocean Lines* to operate between Swinoujscie and Ystad. Later operated for *Unity Line* on this route. In 2008 replaced by the KOPERNIK and laid up.

POLONIA Train/vehicle ferry built by Langsten Slip & Båtbyggeri A/S, Tomrefjord, Norway for *Polonia Line Ltd* and chartered to *Unity Line*.

SKANIA Built by Schichau Seebeckwerft, Bremerhaven, Germany at the SUPERFAST I for *Superfast Ferries* of Greece. Operated between Patras and Ancona (Italy). In 1998 transferred to the Patras - Igoumenitsa (Greece) - Bari (Italy) route. In 2004 sold to a subsidiary of *Grimaldi Lines*, renamed the EUROSTAR ROMA and placed on the Civitavecchia (Italy) - Barcelona (Spain) service. In 2008 sold to *Polsteam* and renamed the SKANIA. After modifications, she will be placed on the *Unity Line* Swinoujscie - Ystad service as second passenger vessel.

WOLIN Train/vehicle ferry built by Moss Rosenberg Værft, Moss, Norway as the ÖRESUND for *Statens Järnvägar (Swedish State Railways)* for the 'DanLink' service between Helsingborg and Copenhagen. Has 817 metres of rail track. Service ceased in July 2000 and vessel laid up. In 2001 sold to *Sea Containers Ferries* and in 2002 converted at Gdansk, Poland to a passenger ferry. She was chartered to *SeaWind Line*, renamed the SKY WIND and in Autumn 2002 replaced the STAR WIND on the Stockholm - Turku service. In 2007 sold to *Polsteam*, renamed the WOLIN and placed on the *Unity Line* Swinoujscie - Trelleborg service.

Under Construction

9	NEWBUILDING 1	-	10	22.0k	207.0m	300P	-	210L	A	-

Gabriella (*Miles Cowsill*)

Ålandsfärjan (*Miles Cowsill*)

| 10 | NEWBUILDING 2 | - | 11 | 22.0k | 207.0m | 300P | - | 210L | A | - |

NEWBUILDING 1, NEWBUILDING 2 Under construction by New Szczecin Shipyard, Szczecin, Poland for *Polsteam*. To operate for *Unity Line*.

VIKING LINE

THE COMPANY *Viking Line Abp* is an Åland (Finland) company (previously *SF Line*, trading with *Rederi AB Slite* of Sweden as *Viking Line*).

MANAGEMENT Managing Director Nils-Erik Eklund, **Deputy Managing Director** Boris Ekman.

ADDRESS Norragatan 4, 22100 Mariehamn, Åland.

TELEPHONE Administration +358 (0)18 26011, **Reservations** +358 (0)9 1235300.

FAX Administration +358 (0)18 12099, **Reservations** +358 (0)9 1235292.

INTERNET Email incoming@vikingline.fi **Websites** www.vikingline.fi (*Finnish, Swedish, English*) www.vikingline.se (*Swedish*) www.vikingline.de (*German*) www.vikingline.ee (*Estonian*)

ROUTES OPERATED Stockholm (Sweden) - Mariehamn (Åland) - Helsinki (Finland) (14 hrs; **3,5**; 1 per day), Stockholm - Mariehamn (day)/Långnäs (Åland) (night) - Turku (Finland) (9 hrs 10 mins; **2,4**; 2 per day), Kapellskär (Sweden) - Mariehamn (Åland) (2 hrs 15 mins; **6**; up to 3 per day), Helsinki - Tallinn (2 hrs 30 mins; **8**; 2 per day), Cruises from Stockholm to Mariehamn (21 hrs - 24 hrs round trip (most 22 hrs 30 mins); **7**; 1 per day).

1•	ÅLANDSFÄRJAN	6172t	72	17.0k	105.2m	963P	180C	19T	BA	SE	7211074
2	AMORELLA	34384t	88	21.5k	169.4m	2450P	450C	53T	BA	FI	8601915
3	GABRIELLA	35492t	92	21.5k	171.2m	2420P	400C	50T	BA	FI	8917601
4	ISABELLA	35154t	89	21.5k	170.9m	2420P	364C	30T	BA	FI	8700723
5	MARIELLA	37799t	85	22.0k	176.9m	2500P	400C	60T	BA	FI	8320573
6	ROSELLA	16850t	80	21.3k	136.0m	1700P	340C	40T	BA	FI	7901265
7	VIKING CINDERELLA	46398t	89	21.5k	191.0m	2500P	100C	-	BA	SE	8719188
8	VIKING XPRS	34000t	08	25.0k	185.0m	2500P	250C	60L	BA	SE	9375654

ÅLANDSFÄRJAN Built by Helsingør Skips & Maskinbygg, Helsingør, Denmark as the KATTEGAT for *Jydsk Færgefart* of Denmark for the Grenaa - Hundested service. She was used on this route until 1978 when the service became a single-ship operation. She was then sold to *P&O Ferries*, renamed the N F TIGER and introduced as the second vessel on the Dover - Boulogne service. Sold to *European Ferries* in 1985 and withdrawn in June 1986. In November 1986 sold to *Finlandshammen AB*, Sweden, renamed the ÅLANDSFÄRJAN and used on the *Viking Line* summer service between Mariehamn and Kapellskär. This service now operates all year round. In May 2008 replaced by the ROSELLA and laid up.

AMORELLA Built by Brodogradevna Industrija, Split, Yugoslavia for *SF Line* for the Stockholm - Mariehamn - Turku service.

GABRIELLA Built by Brodogradiliste "Split", Split, Croatia as the FRANS SUELL for *Sea-Link AB* of Sweden to operate for subsidiary company *Euroway AB*, who established a service between Lübeck, Travemünde and Malmö. In 1994 this service ceased and she was chartered to *Silja Line*, renamed the SILJA SCANDINAVIA and transferred to the Stockholm - Turku service. In 1997 she was sold to *Viking Line* to operate between Stockholm and Helsinki. She was renamed the GABRIELLA.

ISABELLA Built by Brodogradevna Industrija, Split, Yugoslavia for *SF Line*. Used on the Stockholm - Naantali service until 1992 when she was switched to operating 24-hour cruises from Helsinki and in 1995 she was transferred to the Stockholm - Helsinki route. During 1996 she additionally operated day cruises to Muuga in Estonia during the 'layover' period in Helsinki. In 1997 she was transferred to the Stockholm - Turku route.

MARIELLA Built by Oy Wärtsilä Ab, Turku, Finland for *SF Line*. Used on the Stockholm - Helsinki service. During 1996 additionally operated short cruises to Muuga in Estonia during the 'layover' period in Helsinki.

ROSELLA Built by Oy Wärtsilä Ab, Turku, Finland for *SF Line*. Used mainly on the Stockholm - Turku and Kapellskär - Naantali services until 1997. From 1997 operated 21-to 24-hour cruises from

Stockholm to Mariehamn under the marketing name 'The Dancing Queen', except in the peak summer period when she operated between Kapellskär and Turku. In Autumn 2003 transferred to a new twice-daily Helsinki - Tallinn ferry service. In May 2008 placed on the Mariehamn - Kapellskär route.

VIKING CINDERELLA Built as the CINDERELLA by Wärtsilä Marine Ab, Turku, Finland for *SF Line*. Until 1993 provided additional capacity between Stockholm and Helsinki and undertook weekend cruises from Helsinki. In 1993 she replaced the OLYMPIA (a sister vessel of the MARIELLA) as the main Stockholm - Helsinki vessel after the OLYMPIA had been chartered to *P&O European Ferries* and renamed the PRIDE OF BILBAO. In 1995 switched to operating 20-hour cruises from Helsinki to Estonia in the off peak and the Stockholm - Mariehamn - Turku service during the peak summer period (end of May to end of August). From 1997 she remained cruising throughout the year. In Autumn 2003 transferred to the Swedish flag, renamed the VIKING CINDERELLA and transferred to Stockholm - Mariehamn cruises. She operates these cruises all year round.

VIKING XPRS Built by Aker Yards, Helsinki to operate between Helsinki and Tallinn.

Under Construction

9	VIKING ADCC	15600t	09	22k	133.0m	1500P	320C	-	BA	SE	-

VIKING ADCC Under construction by Astilleros de Sevilla SA, Seville, Spain. To operate between Kapellskär and Mariehamn. VIKING ADCC is a project name; she is likely to be renamed before entering service.

WAGENBORG PASSAGIERSDIENSTEN

THE COMPANY *Wagenborg Passagiersdiensten BV* is a Dutch private sector company.

MANAGEMENT Managing Director G van Langen.

ADDRESS Postbus 70, 9163 ZM Nes, Ameland, The Netherlands.

TELEPHONE Administration & Reservations +31 (0)519 546111.

FAX Administration & Reservations +31 (0)519 542905.

INTERNET Email info@wpd.nl **Website** www.wpd.nl (*Dutch, German, English*)

ROUTES OPERATED *Car Ferries* Holwerd (The Netherlands) - Ameland (Frisian Islands) (45 minutes; *3,5*; up to 14 per day), Lauwersoog (The Netherlands) - Schiermonnikoog (Frisian Islands) (45 minutes; *2,4*; up to 6 per day), *Passenger Ferries* Esonstad - Lauwersoog – Schiermonnikoog (1 hr; *1*; up to 5 per day).

1p	ESONBORG	-	99	20.0k	30.5m	130P	0C	0L	-	NL	-
2	MONNIK	1121t	85	12.2k	58.0m	1000P	46C	9L	BA	NL	8408961
3	OERD	2286t	03	11.2k	73.2m	1200P	72C	22L	BA	NL	9269673
4	ROTTUM	1121t	85	12.2k	58.0m	1140P	46C	9L	BA	NL	8408959
5	SIER	2286t	95	11.2k	73.2m	1200P	72C	22L	BA	NL	9075761

ESONBORG River Runner 150 catamaran built by Damen Shipyards, Gorinchem, The Netherlands (under licence to NQEA Australia Pty Ltd) for the *Doeksen Group* of The Netherlands. Chartered to *Aqualiner BV* of The Netherlands as the AQUA-RUNNER. Operated between Damen and Gorinchem. In 2007 chartered to *Wagenborg*, renamed the ESONBORG and placed on the summer-only Esonstad - Lauwersoog – Schiermonnikoog route.

MONNIK Built by Scheepswerf Hoogezand, Hoogezand, The Netherlands for *Wagenborg Passagiersdiensten BV* as the OERD. In 2003, on delivery of the new OERD, she was renamed the MONNIK. Used on the Lauwersoog - Schiermonnikoog route.

OERD Built by Scheepswerf Bijlsma Lemmer, Lemmer, The Netherlands for *Wagenborg Passagiersdiensten BV*. Used on the Ameland - Holwerd route.

ROTTUM Built by Scheepswerf Hoogezand, Hoogezand, The Netherlands for *Wagenborg Passagiersdiensten BV* as the SIER and used on the Holwerd - Ameland route. In 1995 renamed the ROTTUM and transferred to the Lauwersoog - Schiermonnikoog route.

SIER Built by Shipyard Bijlsma, Wartena, The Netherlands for *Wagenborg Passagiersdiensten BV*. Used on the Ameland - Holwerd route.

St Catherine and **St Clare** *(Miles Cowsill)*

Stena Discovery (*FotoFlite*)

Emeraude France (*Miles Cowsill*)

SECTION 7 - OTHER VESSELS

The following vessels are, at the time of going to print, not operating and are owned by companies which do not currently operate services. They are therefore available for possible re-deployment, either in the area covered by this book or elsewhere. Withdrawn vessels not yet disposed of and owned by operating companies are shown under the appropriate company and marked '?'.

Rederi AB Gotland

1	GUTE	7616t	79	15.0k	138.8m	88P	-	60T	BA	SE	7802794

GUTE Built by Falkenbergs Varv AB, Falkenburg, Sweden for *Rederi AB Gotland* of Sweden. Used on service between Gotland and the Swedish mainland. In 1988 chartered to *Brambles Shipping* of Australia and used between Port Melbourne (Victoria) and Burnie (Tasmania). In 1992 she was renamed the SALLY SUN and chartered to *Sally Ferries*, operating between Ramsgate and Dunkerque. In 1994 she inaugurated a Ramsgate - Vlissingen service, which was later changed to Dartford - Vlissingen. In 1995 she was chartered to *SeaWind Line*, renamed the SEAWIND II and operated between Stockholm and Turku. In 1997 she was chartered to *Nordic Trucker Line* for the Oxelösund - St Petersburg service and in 1998 she returned to *SeaWind Line*. In 1998, after *Rederi AB Gotland*-owned *Destination Gotland* regained the franchise to operate to Gotland, she was renamed the GUTE and resumed her summer role of providing summer freight back-up to the passenger vessels, but with a number of short charters during the winter. In Autumn 2002 chartered to *Amber Lines* for the Karlshamn - Liepaja service. In February 2003 chartered to *NATO* for the Iraq crisis. Returned to *Destination Gotland* in Summer 2003. In Autumn 2003 chartered to *Scandlines Amber Lines* to operate between Karlshamn and Liepaja. In 2004 lengthened by 20.3m by Nauta Shiprepair, Gdynia, Poland. In Autumn 2004 chartered to *Riga Sea Line* to inaugurate a freight service between Riga and Nynäshamn. In Autumn 2005 service ended and vessel laid up. In January 2006 chartered to *LISCO* and placed on the Klaìpeda - Karlshamn route, also undertaking two trips from Klaìpeda to Baltiysk. In May 2006 chartered to *SeaWind Line*. In March 2007 chartered to *Baltic Scandinavian Line*. Charter ended September 2007.

EURO 7 Fernseh & Marketing GmbH

1	RIGEL	12281t	73	19.0k	128.0m	512P	50C	30T	PA	PA	7224459

RIGEL Built by Oy Wärtsilä AB, Turku, Finland as the BORE 1 for *Ångfartygs AB Bore* of Finland for *Silja Line* services between Turku and Stockholm. In 1980 *Bore Line* left the *Silja Line* consortium and disposed of its passenger ships. She was acquired by *EFFOA* of Finland and continued to operate on *Silja Line* service, being renamed the SKANDIA. In 1983 she was sold to *Stena Line* and renamed the STENA BALTICA. She was then resold to *Latvia Shipping* of the USSR, substantially rebuilt, renamed the ILLICH and introduced onto a Stockholm - Leningrad (now St Petersburg) service trading as *ScanSov Line*. In 1986 operations were transferred to the *Baltic Shipping Company*. In 1992 she inaugurated a new service between Stockholm and Riga but continued to serve St Petersburg. In 1995 the Swedish terminal was changed to Nynäshamn. In late 1995 she was arrested and laid up in Stockholm. In 1997 services were planned to restart between Kiel and St Petersburg under the auspices of a German company called *Baltic Line*, with the vessel renamed the ANASTASIA V. However, this did not materialise and she was sold to *Windward Line* of Barbados and renamed the WINDWARD PRIDE. In 1997, she was chartered to *ESCO* and renamed the BALTIC KRISTINA. In late 1997 she sailed for *EstLine* between Stockholm and Tallinn in a freight-only role. Following a major refurbishment, she entered service with *EstLine* in May 1998, allowing a daily full passenger service to be operated. In 2000 the charter was transferred to *Tallink*. Placed on the Paldiski - Kapellskär service. In late 2002 chartered to *Riga Sea Lines* to inaugurate a service between Riga and Stockholm. In Autumn 2005 *Riga Sea Lines* went into liquidation and the service ceased. In December, she was purchased by the *Riga Freeport Authority*, for later sale. In 2007 sold to *EURO 7 Fernseh & Marketing GmbH* and renamed the RIGEL.

Maritime Charter Sales

1»	EMERAUDE FRANCE	3012t	90	35.0k	74.3m	350P	80C	-	BA	BB	8903703

EMERAUDE FRANCE Incat 74m catamaran built at Hobart, Tasmania as the SEACAT TASMANIA for *Sea Containers* subsidiary *Tasmanian Ferry Services* of Australia to operate between George Town (Tasmania) and Port Welshpool (Victoria). In 1992 chartered to *Hoverspeed* to operate Dover - Calais and Folkestone - Boulogne services. Returned to Australia after the 1992 summer season but returned to Britain in Summer 1993 to operate Dover - Calais and Folkestone - Boulogne services during that summer. She was repainted into *Hoverspeed* livery and renamed the SEACAT CALAIS. In 1994 chartered for five years (with a purchase option) to *Navegacion Atlantida* for *Ferry Linas Argentinas AS* of Uruguay's service between Montevideo (Uruguay) and Buenos Aires (Argentina) and renamed the ATLANTIC II. The purchase option was not taken up and in 1999 she was returned to *Sea Containers* and operated for *Hoverspeed* between Dover and Calais. In 2000 she was chartered to *SNAV Aliscafi* of Italy to operate between Ancona (Italy) and Split (Croatia) in a joint venture with *Sea Containers* and renamed the CROAZIA JET. This operation was repeated in 2001. In 2002 she was renamed the SEACAT FRANCE and transferred to operate between Dover and Calais. At the end of the 2002 summer period she was laid up for sale or charter in Birkenhead. Returned to Dover in Summer 2004 to operate the during peak summer period. In February 2005 chartered to *Emeraude Jersey Ferries* and renamed the EMERAUDE FRANCE. In early April charter ended (following the ending of the one-year agreement with *Sea Containers Ferries* to provide a fast ferry) and she returned to *Sea Containers Ferries*. Laid up for sale. In 2007 sold to *Maritime Charter Sales* of the Isle of Man and chartered to *IOMSP* to replace the damaged SEA EXPRESS 1. Returned to lay-up at Tilbury in September 2007.

Sea Containers Ferries

1»	THE PRINCESS ANNE	-	69	50.0k	56.4m	360P	55C	-	BA	UK	-
2»	THE PRINCESS MARGARET	-	68	50.0k	56.4m	360P	55C	-	BA	UK	-

THE PRINCESS ANNE, THE PRINCESS MARGARET British Hovercraft Corporation SRN4 type hovercraft built at Cowes, UK for *Seaspeed*. Built to Mark I specification. In 1978/1979 respectively lengthened to Mark III specification. They underwent complete refurbishment at the beginning of 1999. Withdrawn in 2000 and laid up at the Hovercraft Museum at Lee-on-Solent.

Stena RoRo (Sweden)

1»	STENA DISCOVERY	19638t	97	40.0k	126.6m	1500P	375C	50L	A	NL	9107590

STENA DISCOVERY Finnyards HSS1500 ('High-speed Sea Service') built at Rauma, Finland for *Stena RoRo* and chartered to *Stena Line* to replace two vessels on the Harwich - Hook of Holland service. In early 2007 withdrawn and laid up at Belfast.

SECTION 8

SISTERS – A LIST OF SISTER (OR NEAR SISTER) VESSELS IN THIS BOOK

The following vessels are sisters or near sisters. This refers to 'as built' condition; some ships will subsequently have been modified and become different from their sister vessels.

AMORELLA, ISABELLA (*Viking Line*).

ÁRAINN MHÓR (*Arranmore Island Ferries*), CANNA (*Caledonian MacBrayne*), COLL (*Arranmore Island Ferries*), EIGG (*Caledonian MacBrayne*), MORVERN (*Bere Island Ferries*), RAASAY (*Caledonian MacBrayne*), RHUM (*Arranmore Island Ferries*).

ARGYLE, BUTE (*Caledonian MacBrayne*).

ASK, URD (*Scandlines (Denmark and Germany)*).

AURORA AF HELSINGBORG (*Scandlines (Sweden)*), HAMLET, TYCHO BRAHE (*Scandlines (Denmark and Germany)*).

BALTIC JET, NORDIC JET (*Nordic Jet Lines*).

BASTØ I, BASTØ II (*Bastø Fosen*).

BEN-MY-CHREE (*Isle of Man Steam Packet Company*), COMMODORE CLIPPER (*Condor Ferries*), DUEODDE, HAMMERODDE (*Bornholmstrafikken*) (Near sisters).

CAEDMON, CENRED, CENWULF (*Wightlink*).

CARRIGALOE, GLENBROOK (*Cross River Ferries*).

CHRISTIAN IV (*Color Line*), NORDLANDIA (*Eckerö Line*).

COLOR FANTASY, COLOR MAGIC (*Color Line*).

COLOR VIKING (*Color Line*), STENA NAUTICA (*Stena Line*).

CÔTE D'ÂLBATRE, SEVEN SISTERS (*Transmanche Ferries*).

CROWN OF SCANDINAVIA (*DFDS Seaways*), GABRIELLA (*Viking Line*).

DAGALIEN, DAGGRI (*Shetland Islands Council*).

DANA SIRENA (*DFDS Seaways*), LISCO GLORIA (*DFDS LISCO*).

DEUTSCHLAND, SCHLESWIG-HOLSTEIN (*Scandlines (Denmark and Germany)*).

DUBLIN VIKING, LIVERPOOL VIKING (*Norfolkline*).

EARL SIGURD, EARL THORFINN (*Orkney Ferries*).

ECKERÖ (*Eckerö Linjen*), POVL ANKER (*Bornholmstrafikken*).

ENVOY(*DFDS LISCO*), NORCAPE (*P&O Ferries*), STENA LEADER, STENA PIONEER, STENA SEAFARER (*Stena Line*).

ERNEST BEVIN, JAMES NEWMAN, JOHN BURNS (*Woolwich Free Ferry*).

EUROPALINK (*Finnlines NordöLink*), FINNLADY, FINNMAID, FINNSTAR (*Finnlines*), NORDLINK (*Finnlines NordöLink*).

EUROPEAN CAUSEWAY, EUROPEAN HIGHLANDER (*P&O Irish Sea*).

EUROVOYAGER, PRIMROSE (*TransEuropa Ferries*).

FANTAASIA (*Tallink*), ROSELLA (*Viking Line*).

FENJA, MENJA (*Scandlines (Denmark and Germany)*).

FINNCLIPPER (*Finnlines NordöLink*), FINNEAGLE, FINNFELLOW (*FinnLink*), STENA HOLLANDICA (*Stena Line*).

FINNHANSA, FINNPARTNER, FINNTRADER, TRANSEUROPA (*Finnlines/Finnlines NordöLink*).

KING OF SCANDINAVIA, PRINCESS OF NORWAY (*DFDS Seaways*).

FRIGG SYDFYEN, ODIN SYDFYEN (*Sydfyenske*).

FRISIA I, FRISIA V (*Reederei Norden-Frisia*).

FYLGA, THORA (*Shetland Islands Council*).

GITTE 3, MERCANDIA IV, MERCANDIA VIII (*HH-Ferries*).

GOTLAND, VISBY (*Destination Gotland*).

HARILAID, KÖRGELAID (*Saaremaa Laevakompanii*).

HJALTLAND, HROSSEY (*NorthLink Ferries*).

HUCKLEBERRY FINN, TOM SAWYER (*TT-Line*).

JUNO, JUPITER, SATURN (*Caledonian MacBrayne*).

KAUNAS, KLAÌPEDA *(DFDS LISCO)*, PETERSBURG *(Scandlines (Denmark and Germany))*, VILNIUS *(DFDS LISCO)*.

KONG HARALD, NORDLYS, RICHARD WITH *(Hurtigruten)*.

KRONPRINS FREDERIK, PRINS JOACHIM *(Scandlines (Denmark and Germany))*.

LAGAN VIKING, MERSEY VIKING *(Norfolkline)*.

LOCH DUNVEGAN, LOCH FYNE *(Caledonian MacBrayne)*.

LOCH LINNHE, LOCH RANZA, LOCH RIDDON, LOCH STRIVEN *(Caledonian MacBrayne)*.

LYNHER II, PLYM II, TAMAR II *(Torpoint Ferries)*.

MAERSK DELFT, MAERSK DOVER, MAERSK DUNKERQUE *(Norfolkline)*.

MAI MOLS, MIE MOLS *(Mols-Linien)*.

MAREN MOLS, METTE MOLS *(Mols-Linien)*.

MARIELLA *(Viking Line)*, PRIDE OF BILBAO *(P&O Ferries)*.

MIDNATSOL, TROLLFJORD *(Hurtigruten)*.

MIDSLAND, WESTFALEN *(Rederij Doeksen)*.

MONNIK, ROTTUM *(Wagenborg)*.

MÜNSTERLAND, OSTFRIESLAND *(AG Ems)*.

NILS DACKE, ROBIN HOOD *(TT-Line)*.

NILS HOLGERSSON, PETER PAN *(TT-Line)*.

NORBANK, NORBAY *(P&O Irish Sea)*.

NORDKAPP, NORDNORGE, POLARLYS *(Hurtigruten)*.

OERD, SIER *(Wagenborg)*.

PRIDE OF BRUGES, PRIDE OF YORK *(P&O Ferries)*.

PRIDE OF CALAIS, PRIDE OF DOVER *(P&O Ferries)*.

PRIDE OF CANTERBURY, PRIDE OF KENT *(P&O Ferries)*.

PRIDE OF HULL, PRIDE OF ROTTERDAM *(P&O Ferries)*.

PRIDE OF TELEMARK *(KystLink)*, STENA DANICA *(Stena Line)*.

PRINS RICHARD, PRINSESSE BENEDIKTE *(Scandlines (Denmark and Germany))*.

QUEEN OF SCANDINAVIA *(DFDS Seaways)*, STENA SAGA *(Stena Line)*.

RED EAGLE, RED FALCON, RED OSPREY *(Red Funnel Ferries)*.

ROMANTIKA, VICTORIA I *(Tallink)*.

SEAFRANCE BERLIOZ, SEAFRANCE RODIN *(SeaFrance)*.

SEAFRANCE CEZANNE *(SeaFrance)*, WAWEL *(Polferries)*.

SEAFRANCE MOLIERE *(SeaFrance)*, SUPERFAST IX *(Tallink)*

SILJA SERENADE, SILJA SYMPHONY *(Silja Line)*.

SOUND OF SANDA, SOUND OF SCALPAY *(Western Ferries)*.

SOUND OF SCARBA, SOUND OF SHUNA *(Western Ferries)*.

ST CATHERINE, ST CECILIA, ST FAITH, ST HELEN *(Wightlink)*.

STENA ADVENTURER, STENA BRITANNICA (*Stena Line*).

STENA DISCOVERY (*Stena RoRo*), STENA EXPLORER, STENA VOYAGER (*Stena Line*).

STENA GERMANICA, STENA SCANDINAVICA (*Stena Line*).

SUPERFAST VII, SUPERFAST VIII (*Tallink*).

SUPERSPEED 1, SUPERSPEED 2 (*Color Line*).

Fast Ferries

CONDOR 10 (*Condor Ferries*), EMERAUDE FRANCE (*Maritime Charter Sales*), SNAEFELL (*Isle of Man Steam Packet Company*).

CONDOR EXPRESS, CONDOR VITESSE (*Condor Ferries*), SPEED ONE (*SpeedFerries*).

FASTCAT RYDE, FASTCAT SHANKLIN (*Wightlink*).

RED JET 1, RED JET 2 (*Red Funnel Ferries*).

VIKING (*Isle of Man Steam Packet Company*), SUPERSEACAT THREE, SUPERSEACAT FOUR (*SuperSeaCat*).

Freight Ferries

AMBER (*Sea-Cargo*), BIRKA EXPORTER, BIRKA SHIPPER, BIRKA TRANSPORTER (*Finnlines*).

ANGLIAN WAY, FLANDERS WAY (*Cobelfret Ferries*).

ANVIL POINT (*Foreland Shipping*), BEACHY HEAD (*Transfennica*), EDDYSTONE, HARTLAND POINT, HURST POINT (*Foreland Shipping*), LONGSTONE (*Transfennica*), MAERSK VLAARDINGEN, MAERSK VOYAGER (*Norfolkline*).

AQUILINE, SERPENTINE (*Cobelfret Ferries*), TOR BELLONA (*DFDS Tor Line*).

ARK FORWARDER (*DFDS Tor Line*), STENA CARRIER, STENA FREIGHTER (*Stena Line*).

ARROW (*Norfolkline*), CHALLENGE (*Seatruck Ferries*), SHIELD (*Norfolkline*), TRIUMPH (*Seatruck Ferries*).

AUTO BALTIC, AUTO BANK, AUTO BAY (*UECC*).

AUTOLINE, AUTOTRANSPORTER (*UECC*).

AUTOPREMIER, AUTOPRESTIGE, AUTOPRIDE, AUTOPROGRESS (*UECC*).

AUTOSKY, AUTOSTAR, AUTOSUN (*UECC*).

AUTORACER, AUTORUNNER (*UECC*).

AEGEAN BREEZE, ARABIAN BREEZE, ASIAN BREEZE, BALTIC BREEZE (*UECC*).

BIRKA CARRIER, BIRKA EXPRESS, BIRKA TRADER (*Finnlines*), TRANS BOTNIA (*Transfennica*).

CAROLINE RUSS, ELISABETH RUSS, FRIEDRICH RUSS, PAULINE RUSS, SEAGARD (*Transfennica*), MIRANDA, MISTRAL (*UPM-Kymmene Seaways*).

CELANDINE, CELESTINE, CLEMENTINE, MELUSINE, VALENTINE, VICTORINE (*Cobelfret Ferries*).

CERVINE (*Cobelfret Ferries*), CFF SEINE (*Norfolkline*), HOBURGEN (*P&O Ferries*, PHOCINE (*Cobelfret Ferries*).

CLIPPER PACE, CLIPPER POINT (*Seatruck Ferries*)

CYMBELINE, EGLANTINE, SYMPHORINE, UNDINE (*Cobelfret Ferries*).

DIPLOMAT (*Celtic Link Ferries*), FINNFOREST, GLOBAL CARRIER (*Finnlines*), GLOBAL FREIGHTER (*TransRussia Express*), STENA PARTNER, STENA TRANSFER, STENA TRANSPORTER (*Stena Line*), TOR BALTICA (*DFDS Tor Line*).

EQUINE (*P&O Irish Sea*), URSINE (*P&O Ferries*), VULPINE (*Cobelfret Ferries*).

SECTION 8 – SISTERS

EUROPEAN MARINER (*P&O Irish Sea*), MOONDANCE (*Seatruck Ferries*).

FINNHAWK, FINNKRAFT, FINNMASTER, FINNREEL (*Finnlines*).

FINNMILL, FINNPULP (*Finnlines*), TOR CORONA, TOR FINONIA, TOR HAFNIA, TOR JUTLANDIA (*DFDS Tor Line*).

GARDENIA (*TransEuropa Ferries*), VIA MARE (*Baltic Scandinavian Line*).

GENCA, KRAFTCA, PLYCA, PULPCA, STEELCA, TIMCA, TRICA, WOODCA (*Transfennica*).

AMALIAHAVEN, MAXIMAHAVEN (*van-Uden RoRo*).

IPSWICH WAY, OSTEND WAY (*Cobelfret Ferries*).

LE CASTELLET, MONTLHERY (*UECC*).

MAERSK ANGLIA, MAERSK EXPORTER, MAERSK FLANDERS, MAERSK IMPORTER (*Norfolkline*).

MAERSK VLAARDINGEN, MAERSK VOYAGER (*Norfolkline*).

NORKING, NORQUEEN (*P&O Ferries*).

NORSKY, NORSTREAM (*P&O Ferries*).

OBBOLA, ORTVIKEN, ÖSTRAND (*SCF Transforest*).

PAULINE, YASMINE (*Cobelfret Ferries*).

SCHIEBORG, SLINGEBORG, SPAARNEBORG (*Cobelfret Ferries*).

STENA FORERUNNER, STENA FORECASTER, (*Transfennica*).

STENA LEADER, STENA TRAVELLER (*Stena Line*).

TOR BEGONIA, TOR FICARIA, TOR FREESIA, TOR MAGNOLIA, TOR PETUNIA, TOR PRIMULA (*DFDS Tor Line*).

TOR BELGIA, TOR DANIA (*DFDS Tor Line*).

TOR BRITANNIA, TOR SELANDIA, TOR SUECIA (*DFDS Tor Line*).

SECTION 9 - CHANGES SINCE FERRIES 2008 - BRITISH ISLES AND NORTHERN EUROPE

DISPOSALS

The following vessels, listed in *Ferries 2008 - British Isles and Northern Europe* have been disposed of - either to other companies listed in this book or others. Company names are as used in that publication.

AMANDA (*Stena Line*) In 2007 charter ended.

AMBER (*Finnlines*) In 2007 charter ended. Chartered to *Sea-Cargo*.

ANGLIAN WAY (*Ferryways*) In 2007 transferred to *Cobelfret Ferries* and operated on *Dart Line*-branded services.

BALTIC EAGER (*SeaRoad*) In 2007 charter ended. Chartered to *Finnlines* to operate for *TransRussia Express*.

BORDEN (*UECC*) In 2007 charter ended. Chartered to *Mann Lines*.

BRAKZAND (*Wagenborg*) In 2007 scrapped.

CALIBUR (*Ferryways*) In 2007 charter ended. Chartered to *P&O Ferries*.

CASINO EXPRESS (*RG Line*) In 2007 sold for scrapping at Alang, India.

CELTIC MIST *(Celtic Link Ferries)* In 2007 the vessel arrived in Southampton but was barred from entering service by the Maritime & Coastguard Agency. She then returned to Greece. She is now called the SARONIC STAR.

CELTIC STAR *(Celtic Link Ferries)* In 2007 charter transferred to *Seatruck Ferries*.

CELTIC SUN *(Celtic Link Ferries)* In 2007 charter ended. Chartered to *Acciona Trasmediterranea* of Spain and renamed the HELLENIC SAILOR.

CFF SEINE *(Ferryways)* In 2007 charter ended. Chartered to *Norfolkline*. Later sold to *Express Shipping A/S* of Denmark and renamed the EAST EXPRESS.

CLIPPER PEAK *(Seatruck Ferries)* The order for this vessel was cancelled.

COLOR FESTIVAL *(Color Line)* In 2008 sold to *Corsica Sardinia Ferries* of Italy. Renamed the MEGA SMERALDA and placed on the Civitavecchia - Golfo Aranci route.

COLOR SUPERSPEED 1, COLOR SUPERSPEED 2 *(Color Line)* Delivered in 2008 as SUPERSPEED 1 and SUPERSPEED 2.

EDMUND D *(Passage East Ferry)* In 2007 scrapped.

EMERAUDE FRANCE *(Isle of Man Steam Packet Company)* Charter ended in September 2007; returned to lay-up at Tilbury. Now listed under *Maritime Charter Sales* (Section 7).

FANTAASIA *(Tallink/Silja Line)* In 2008 sold to *Kystlink*.

FENJA *(Scandlines (Denmark and Germany))* In 2007 transferred to *Sydfynske A/S*.

FINNARROW *(Finnlines)* In May 2007 chartered to *Stena Line* to operate between Karlskrona and Gdynia.

FINNJET *(Sea Containers Ferries)* In 2008 sold to *Sea Club* of The Netherlands and renamed the DA VINCI. Later sold to breakers.

FINNOAK *(Finnlines)* In 2008 charter ended. Renamed the AHTELA.

FLANDERS WAY *(Ferryways)* In 2007 transferred to *Cobelfret Ferries* and operated on *Dart Line*-branded services.

FORTE *(Finnlines)* In 2007 charter ended.

FRIGG SYDFYEN *(Scandlines (Denmark and Germany))* In 2007 transferred to *Sydfyenske A/S*.

GLOBAL CARRIER *(P&O Ferries)* In 2008 charter ended. Chartered to *Finnlines*.

GLOBAL FREIGHTER *(P&O Irish Sea)* In 2008 charter ended. Chartered to *Finnlines* to operate for *TransRussia Express*.

GUTE *(Baltic Scandinavian Line)* In Autumn 2007 charter ended; returned to owners *Rederi AB Gotland*.

HUMBER WAY *(Ferryways)* In 2007 acquired by *Cobelfret Ferries*. Later chartered to *RMR Shipping Agency* to operate between Antwerp and Lagos (Nigeria) via Harwich. In 2008 sold to *Gumel Shipping NV* of The Netherlands and renamed the GUMEL.

IPSWICH WAY *(Ferryways)* In 2007 transferred to *Cobelfret Ferries* and operated on *Dart Line*-branded services.

KRONPRINS HARALD *(Color Line)* In 2007 sold to *Irish Ferries* and renamed the OSCAR WILDE.

LÜBECK LINK *(Finnlines NordöLink)* In 2007 sold to *Channel Ferries* of the UK. Renamed the ROPAX 2. In 2008 chartered to *Acciona Trasmediterranea* of Spain.

LYNGEN *(Hurtigruten)* In 2007 sold to *Lindblad Expeditions* of the USA and renamed the NATIONAL GEOGRAPHIC EXPLORER.

LYNHER *(Torpoint Ferry)* In 2007 scrapped.

MALMÖ LINK *(Finnlines NordöLink)* In 2007 sold to *Channel Ferries* of the UK. Renamed the ROPAX 1.

In 2008 chartered to *CoTuNav* of Tunisia.

MELOODIA *(Tallink)* In 2007 sold to *Equinox Offshore Accommodation* of Singapore for conversion into an offshore accommodation and repair vessel (ARV). Renamed the ARV 1.

MENJA *(Scandlines (Denmark and Germany))* In 2007 transferred to *Sydfyenske A/S*.

MERCHANT *(TransRussia Express)* In 2007 sold to *Scandlines (Denmark and Germany)* and in 2008 placed on the Rostock - Helsinki route.

MERCHANT BRILLIANT *(Norfolkline)* In 2007 charter ended. In January 2008 chartered to *Seatruck Ferries*. In April 2008 chartered to sold to *Express Shipping A/S* of Denmark and renamed the WEST EXPRESS.

MIDAS, MIMER *(UPM-Kymmene Seaways)* Service no longer calls at a UK port.

MIRANDA, MISTRAL *(Finnlines)* In 2007 charter ended. Chartered to *UPM-Kymmene Seaways*.

MOLENGAT *(TESO)* In 2008 sold to *Halani International* of India and renamed the HALANI 1.

NEWBUILDING 1, NEWBUILDING 2 *(Stena RoRo (Section 7))* The order for these vessels has been cancelled. Replaced by an order of two vessels from Hyundai by *Stena Line*.

NORCAPE *(P&O Ferries)* In 2008 transferred to *P&O Irish Sea*.

NORMANDY *(Irish Ferries)* In 2008 sold to *Equinox Offshore Accommodation* of Singapore for conversion into an offshore accommodation and repair vessel (ARV). She is to be renamed the ARV 2. However, work will not start immediately and during Summer 2008 she will be chartered to *Ferrimaroc* operate between Almeria (Spain) and Nador (Morocco).

ODIN SYDFYEN *(Scandlines (Denmark and Germany))* In 2007 transferred to *Sydfyenske A/S*.

OPERA *(Sea Containers Ferries)* In 2007 sold to *Louis Cruise Lines* of Cyprus and renamed the CRISTAL.

OSTEND WAY *(Ferryways)* In 2007 transferred to *Cobelfret Ferries* and operated on *Dart Line*-branded services.

PETER WESSEL *(Color Line)* In 2007 sold to *SNAV* of Italy. Delivered in April 2008 and renamed the SNAV TOSCANA. She operates between Civitavecchia and Olbia.

POLARIS *(Transfennica)* In 2007 charter terminated. Chartered to *Stella Line and* operates between Hamburg, Bremerhaven and Kotka.

PLYM *(Torpoint Ferry)* In 2007 scrapped.

RIVERDANCE *(Seatruck Ferries)* On 21st January ran aground on sands near Blackpool following the development of a severe list. Eventually declared a constructive total loss.

ROSLAGEN *(Eckerö Linjen)* In 2007 sold to *Agoudimos Lines* of Greece and renamed the IONIAN SPIRIT.

SC NORRLAND *(Sea-Cargo)* In 2007 charter ended. Renamed the NORRLAND.

SEA WIND *(SeaWind Line)* Now listed under *Tallink/Silja Line*.

SILVIA ANA L *(Color Line)* In 2007 sold to *Buquebus* of Argentina to operate between Buenos Aires (Argentina) and Montevideo (Uruguay).

SKY WIND *(SeaWind Line)* In 2007 sold to *Euroafrica Shipping*, renamed the WOLIN and placed on the *Unity Line* Swinoujscie - Trelleborg route.

SØNDERHO *(Scandlines (Denmark and Germany))* In 2007 transferred to *Sydfyenske A/S*.

SPIRIT OF SKYE *(Loch Ness Express)* In 2007 sold to the *Government of Kazakhstan* for use as a private yacht by the President.

SPODSBJERG *(Scandlines (Denmark and Germany))* In 2007 transferred to *Sydfyenske A/S*.

STENA FORETELLER *(Cobelfret Ferries)* This vessel did not operate for *Cobelfret Ferries* as expected.

Normandy (*John Bryant*)

Snaefell (*Miles Cowsill*)

STENA SEARIDER (*Stena Line*) In 2007 sold to *Ustica Lines* of Italy to operate between Sicily and Tunisia. Renamed the CLAUDIA M.

TAMAR (*Torpoint Ferry*) In 2007 scrapped.

THJELVAR (*Rederi AB Gotland*) In 2007 chartered to *Scandlines (Denmark and Germany)*, renamed the ROSTOCK and placed on the Gedser - Rostock service.

THOR SYDFYEN (*Scandlines (Denmark and Germany)*) In 2007 transferred to *Sydfyenske A/S*.

TOR MAXIMA (*DFDS Tor Line*) In 2008 chartered to *P&O Irish Sea*.

TOLOSA (*SCF DFDS Line*) In 2007 charter terminated. Sold to *Aegean Cargo* of St Vincent and the Grenadines and renamed the AEGEAN GLORY. Operates in the Mediterranean.

TOR NERINGA (*DFDS Tor Line*) In 2008 transferred to *DFDS LISCO*.

TRANS BOTNIA (*Transfennica*) In 2007 charter ended. Renamed the PELICAN.

URSINE (*Cobelfret Ferries*) In 2007 chartered to *P&O Ferries*.

VASALAND (*Transfennica*) In 2007 charter ended. Chartered to *Finnlines*.

VICTORIA (*HJ Lines*) In 2007 charter ended following ending of the service. Subsequently renamed the VICTORIA VI and chartered to *Smyril Line*. In 2008 charter terminated.

VIKINGLAND (*Rømø-Sylt Linie*) In 2008 sold to *SAIPEM* of Italy for use in connection with its oil prospecting activities in the Caspian Sea.

VIRONIA (*Saaremaa Laevakompanii*) In 2007 sold to *Euroafrica Shipping*, renamed the KOPERNIK and, in 2008, placed on the *Unity Line* Swinoujscie - Ystad route.

WISTERIA (*TransEuropa Ferries*) No longer listed as operates in the Mediterranean and now unlikely to return to Ostend.

RENAMINGS

The following have been renamed without change of operator:

ATLANTIC TRAVELLER (*Fjord Line*) In 2008 renamed the BERGENSFJORD.

MASTER CAT (*Master Ferries*) In 2008 renamed the FJORD CAT following the merger between *Master Ferries* and *Fjord Line*.

RR ARROW (*Norfolkline*) In October 2007 sold to *Seatruck Ferries* but charter to *Norfolkline* continued. Renamed the ARROW.

RR CHALLENGE (*Seatruck Ferries*) . In October 2007 sold to *Attica Group* of Greece. In 2008 sold to *Seatruck Ferries* and renamed the CHALLENGE.

RR SHIELD (*Norfolkline*) In 2007 sold to *Attica Group* of Greece and renamed the SHIELD. In January 2008 sold to *Seatruck Ferries* but continued to be chartered to *Norfolkline*.

SEA EXPRESS I (*Isle of Man Steam Packet Company*) In 2007 renamed the SNAEFELL.

SUPERSEACAT TWO (*Isle of Man Steam Packet Company*) In 2008 renamed the VIKING.

COMPANY CHANGES

Ferryways. This operator has ceased trading. Most vessels and services transferred to *Cobelfret Ferries* and operated under *Dart Line* brand.

Glenelg - Kylerhea Ferry. Now listed as *Skye Ferry*.

HJ Lines. This operator has ceased trading.

Loch Ness Express. This operator has ceased trading.

Master Ferries. Merged with *Fjord Line* and all services operated as *Fjord Line*.

Sea Road. This operator has ceased trading.

SeaWind Line. Now listed under *Tallink/Silja Line*.

Swansea Cork Ferries. No resumption in 2008. Effectively this operator has ceased trading.

LATE NEWS

ISLE OF MAN STEAM PACKET COMPANY

The company have purchase a new vessel to replace the VIKING:

4	INCAT 050	6360t	98	42.0k	96.0m	600P	240C	-	A	UK 9176072

INCAT 050. Incat 96m catamaran built at Hobart, Tasmania. Initially chartered to *Transport Tasmania* of Australia and operated between Port Melbourne (Victoria) and Georgetown (Tasmania). In 1999 chartered to *Fast Cat Ferries* of New Zealand and operated between Wellington (North Island) and Picton (South Island) under the marketing name 'Top Cat'. In 2000 laid up. In 2001 charted to the *US Navy* and renamed the USS JOINT VENTURE (HSV-X1). In 2008 purchased by *IOMSP*. Following conversion back to civilian use she will be renamed and probably enter service in spring 2009.

SUPERFAST FERRIES

The Zeebrugge - Rosyth service will cease in September 2008 and the BLUE STAR 1 will return to the Mediterranean.

COLOR LINE/STELLA LINES

The CHRISTIAN IV has been sold to *Stella Lines* of Russia. She will be renamed the JULIA and operated between St Petersburg and Helsinki.

STELLA LINES

New Russian operator will start later in 2008 (see above).

VIKING LINE

ÅLANDSFÄRJAN has been sold to *GAP Shipping* of Barbados.

rella
SILJA FESTIVAL
STOCKHOLM
KAT

Viking Cinderella and **Silja Festival** (*Miles Cowsill*)

FERRIES ILLUSTRATED

Maersk Dover and **SeaFrance Rodin** *(John Hendy)*

INDEX